Baby
&Child
Your Questions Answered

Baby
& Child
Your Questions Answered

Dr. Carol Cooper

LONDON, NEW YORK, MUNICH, MELBOURNE, DELHI

To Julian, Oliver and Anthony.
Without them this book might have been written
sooner, but would have been a lot less practical.

Revised edition
US CONSULTANT Aviva Schein MD
US EDITOR Shannon Beatty
SENIOR EDITOR Salima Hirani
SENIOR ART EDITOR Glenda Fisher
PROJECT EDITOR Pip Morgan
PROJECT DESIGNER Edward Kinsey
MANAGING EDITOR Penny Warren
MANAGING ART EDITOR Marianne Markham
PRODUCTION CONTROLLER Maria Elia
PUBLISHING DIRECTOR Corinne Roberts

Original edition
SENIOR EDITOR Dawn Bates
SENIOR ART EDITOR Karen Ward
DTP DESIGNER Rajen Shah
PRODUCTION CONTROLLER Claire Kelly
SENIOR MANAGING EDITOR Corinne Roberts
SENIOR MANAGING ART EDITOR Lynne Brown

CONSULTANT EDITOR Jemima Dunne
INITIAL DESIGN AND EDIT SP Creative Design
PHOTOGRAPHER Ruth Jenkinson

First published in the United States in 2000 by
DK Publishing, Inc., 375 Hudson Street
New York, New York 10014
A Penguin Company
This edition published 2007

ISBN 978-0-7566-2609-9

Reproduced by in Singapore by Colourscan
Printed and bound in Singapore by Star Standard

see our complete catalog at
www.dk.com

CONTENTS

INTRODUCTION

Raising a child is one of the most exciting and pleasurable challenges life can bring. However, at times the reality of family life can fall short of our ideal. Parenting has changed in the last 20 years. The pace of life is faster, the number of choices is greater, and at the same time the extended family support group of grandparents, aunts, uncles and cousins is the exception rather than the rule. Everyone proffers "helpful" advice that is often conflicting. No wonder new parents feel bewildered.

How this book will help

I wrote this book to provide detailed information in an easy-to-find format, equipping parents with the knowledge they need to give their children the very best. The practical advice, background explanations and medical facts are those I give parents in my consulting room and they are all based on my practice as a family doctor, as well as my own hands-on experience of being a parent (I was a novice too). The simple question-and-answer style means that you can easily find the solution to your concerns. The many hundreds of questions range from the practical—"Which is the best type of diaper?" or "When should I start to give my baby solid food?"—to emotive issues such as "Is my child developing normally?" or "How can I make time for myself?".

How to use this book

This book is divided into nine themed, color-coded chapters: *Your New Baby, Feeding and Nutrition, Encouraging Sleep, Everyday Care, Crying and Comforting, Growth and Development, Discipline and Behavior, Family Life* and, finally, *Child Health.* The first chapter, *Your New Baby,* covers everything you need to know to care for your newborn baby, from equipping the nursery, to feeding and dressing her, right up to the six-week check-up. Subsequent chapters are sub-divided by age: Young Babies, 6 weeks–6 months; Older Babies, 6 months–1 year; Toddlers, 1–2½ years; Preschool Children, 2½ years onward. Each section features everything relevant to that age group, making essential information really accessible. The *Child Health* chapter contains up-to-date advice on keeping your child healthy, as well as guidance on what to do and when to call the doctor when your child is unwell. And, while I hope you never have to deal with emergencies, there is a first aid section at the back of the book.

Parenting is not always straightforward

Throughout the book, there are Parent's Survival Guides. These are short, self-contained features that deal with particular problem areas, such as sleeping problems or toddler tantrums—potential flash-points for many families. I hope the Parent's Survival Guides will help you to defuse difficult situations and encourage you to cope with some of parenting's greatest challenges. In addition, this book deals with topics that are not always covered in general childcare books, such as fathers who stay at home, single parenting, bereavement, and that all-important juggling act, combining work with child-rearing.

The joys and challenges of being a parent

This book is not just there to help in a crisis, but to help you fulfill your potential as a parent. Your child may be dependent on you, but she is an individual with her own particular characteristics. Your aim as her parent is to help your child make the most of herself. The precious moments that you have with your child won't come back, so enjoy them for both your sakes.

It's often said that parenting is a job for which there is neither formal training nor any recognized qualifications. Learning is done on the job and there is no pay, other than the reward of a job well done (and that often only comes when your child has grown up). As a parent you do, however, have one vital attribute—your instincts. I wrote this book to give you the confidence to trust your instincts so that you can enjoy helping your child to fulfill her potential.

Many parents have been kind enough to say how helpful they found the first edition of this book. This new edition has been updated with the medical and other advances that have taken place in the few short years since the book first appeared. I hope it will serve to guide and reassure both existing readers and new generations of parents and carers.

Dr Carol Cooper

YOUR
NEW BABY

Having a baby is an extraordinary and joyous life experience. But it's also a **steep learning curve** and, if this is your first baby, you will inevitably have questions about her **everyday care**. In this chapter, there's a wealth of advice on preparing for your baby's arrival, as well as caring for her in the **first six weeks**. Clear step-by-step instructions guide you through **feeding** (breast and bottle), bathing, diaper changing, and dressing your baby. You'll find invaluable advice on **comforting** a crying baby as well as fascinating coverage of your **baby's progress**. There's also a section that focuses on your own needs at this time.

1

GET EQUIPPED FOR YOUR BABY

Q WHAT SHOULD I BUY BEFORE MY BABY ARRIVES ?

A You only need the bare minimum of clothes, diapers, and equipment. Buy most of the baby clothes after the birth so that you get the right size. Even full-term babies can vary greatly in weight and length. However, you will need essential items such as a bassinet or cradle, a car seat, a baby carriage or stroller, and a baby bath (see below).

Q DO I NEED TO BUY A CRIB FOR MY BABY TO SLEEP IN ?

A New babies can sleep anywhere—even in a drawer removed from a chest of drawers. For the first few weeks a bassinet or cradle is adequate, but eventually you will need a crib. Choose a sturdy crib because she will be spending a lot of time in it. Most cribs have drop sides; check that the mechanism is easy to use.

WHAT EQUIPMENT DO I NEED ?

Even buying the essentials can be very expensive. You can choose to spend a lot of money or spend less and get basic versions of what is needed—but remember that your baby's safety and comfort come first. The best-looking equipment is not necessarily the safest, however. Some parents are superstitious about buying baby things before the birth, but many stores will accept a deposit, and will deliver after your baby arrives.

Other essential items
You will also need the following items:
■ diapers and diaper-changing equipment (see p. 24)
■ clothes (see p. 12) for your baby to wear and a blanket to wrap her in
■ baby bathing equipment (see p. 30)
■ if bottle-feeding: bottles and nipples, sterilizing equipment, and formula (see p. 42)
■ washable blanket and three to four crib sheets
■ a baby monitor that can operate on electricity or a battery (often rechargeable).

BABY CHAIR
This will support a young baby before she can sit. Always place the chair on the floor, not on a table.

Lining should be washable

BASSINET
This enables your baby to sleep wherever you are, but will only last a few weeks.

Check that the crib bar spaces conform to safety standards

CRIB AND BEDDING
A crib with an adjustable mattress height is safer, and easier for your back, too.

Look for adjustable mattress heights

Q WHAT SORT OF BEDDING AND MATTRESS WILL MY BABY NEED?

A You need a washable blanket (ideally two), and at least three to four crib sheets in cotton or flannel. Pillows, quilts, and comforters are not advisable for babies under a year old. Avoid sheepskins, baby nests/sleeping bags, electric blankets, and hot water bottles, since these can overheat your baby—as can crib bumpers (which your baby could also get caught in). The mattress can be made of foam, natural or hollow fibers, or have a sprung interior. It should fit the crib snugly to avoid spaces in which a baby could get trapped. The cover must be easy to clean; cotton is ideal.

Q IS IT NECESSARY FOR ME TO BUY A BABY ALARM?

A It is vital to have a baby monitor if your baby is sleeping in a different room from you. There are also sleep alarms (apnea alarms) available that alert you if your baby makes no breathing movements for 20 seconds. However, these alarms are not always completely accurate. They can sound because of a broken contact, and because sometimes sleeping babies pause naturally for 20–25 seconds when breathing without coming to any harm. Alarms can also fail to sound, so it is better for you to be vigilant than to rely totally on an alarm, and you should know how to resuscitate your baby.

CHANGING BAG
Keep diapers, a fold up changing mat, cotton balls, barrier cream, wipes, and lotion in a handy bag.

BABY BATH
A portable baby bath makes giving baths easier.
Sturdy plastic

CAR SEAT
This is essential for car travel. It is also necessary for your trip home from the hospital.

Bags with detachable changing mats are very convenient in the early weeks

SLING
This must always have a support for the head of a newborn baby.

Baby can be strapped in securely

BABY CARRIAGES AND STROLLERS
Baby carriages or strollers that can take a baby lying flat can be used from birth. The choice depends on the climate and your lifestyle. A carriage offers more protection from the elements, is easier to push, but is harder to get into a car. Strollers are better for a car-based existence.

Bassinet fits onto the frame of the stroller

Choose one in which the seat can face either way

Q WHAT NONESSENTIAL ITEMS ARE USEFUL FOR MY BABY ?

A Aside from the absolute essentials, at this stage you might also consider purchasing a changing table with a wipe-clean surface on which your baby can lie. Other handy extras to get prior to the birth are a thermometer for the bedroom (see p. 46), and a pack of cloth diapers (for spills and spitting up). Toys are also important—all babies will benefit from something colorful to look at, such as a mobile. These will help stimulate your baby. Make sure that any soft toys you buy are washable as well as safe for a newborn baby; rattles and music boxes are also traditional toys for this age, but try them first since very noisy ones may damage a young baby's hearing.

Q IS IT SAFE TO BUY SECONDHAND EQUIPMENT FOR MY BABY ?

A With secondhand goods you don't have the same warranties or safeguards as when buying new, and certain equipment, such as car seats, should never be secondhand. The same applies to equipment that is loaned to you. Inspect carefully before buying and ask the seller any questions that you might have. If you are not totally happy, then don't buy it. You could consider buying a second-hand baby carriage, but check the brakes and buy a new mattress. If buying a crib, check the stability and adjusting mechanisms, and buy a new mattress. Secondhand baby slings should be fine, while toys should be checked to ensure that they are safe. Avoid secondhand electrical items; secondhand cloth diapers may be too harsh for a new baby's skin.

WHAT CLOTHES SHOULD I BUY FOR MY BABY BEFORE SHE'S BORN ?

Start with the bare minimum and buy more later. Although you may know the sex of your baby, you won't know how big or small she is until she arrives, and you might get clothes as presents. Most babies grow out of newborn clothes extremely quickly, so it is useful to be given different-sized items.

STRETCHSUITS
The most basic item of clothing for the first few months is the all-in-one stretchsuit. Choose one that is baggy, and made of cotton.

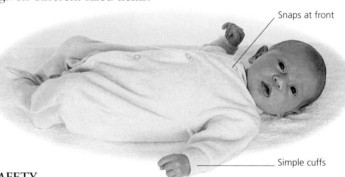

Snaps at front

Simple cuffs

COMFORT AND SAFETY

The key factors are comfort and safety for your baby, and practicality for you.
■ Natural fibers are usually more comfortable than synthetic fabrics.
■ Avoid clothes with drawstring necks, which can be dangerous. Buttons must be secure; snaps are easier to use.
■ Clothes should be washable and non-iron—time is too precious to waste on avoidable chores.
■ The best stretchsuits have snaps down the front as well as in the crotch and along the legs, so that your baby's legs can come fully out of the garment at diaper-changing time.

Summer baby:
■ 4 cotton undershirts
■ 4 stretchsuits (consider some without feet)
■ 1–2 sweaters or jackets
■ 2 hats with brims
■ baby blanket
■ dresses for girl babies
■ 2 nightgowns
■ fabric bibs
■ scratch mittens
■ socks.

Winter baby:
■ 4 undershirts (some thermal and long-sleeved)
■ 4 stretchsuits
■ 2–4 sweaters or jackets
■ warm hat
■ baby blanket
■ snowsuit with hood
■ 2 nightgowns
■ fabric bibs
■ scratch mittens
■ socks
■ bootees.

BECOMING A PARENT

Q WHAT HAPPENS TO MY BABY AFTER DELIVERY ?

A Immediately after the delivery, your baby will be checked by the doctor or midwife and will be given an Apgar score (see below). She will also be weighed and measured. If all is well, she will be handed to you to hold and put to the breast if you want to. Your baby will also be given a dose of vitamin K.

Q WHY IS MY BABY GIVEN VITAMIN K AT BIRTH ?

A Vitamin K is made in our bodies and is needed for blood clotting. Newborn babies lack vitamin K since they don't have the right bacteria in their gut to make it. So they can sometimes bleed, with serious results if this bleeding is into the brain. However, this so-called hemorrhagic disease of the newborn can be prevented by giving vitamin K. This is sometimes done at birth—one dose by injection. There's been some concern that vitamin K injections might be harmful to babies, but there seems to be no good medical evidence for this.

Q HOW SOON CAN MY BABY RECOGNIZE ME ?

A There's evidence that babies begin to recognize their parents by sight within a few days of birth. Your baby uses all her senses from early on. She already knows your voice—she heard it long before birth. Studies also suggest that babies learn distinct smells by the time they are three days old; even at this stage they prefer a pad soaked with a few drops of their own mother's milk to pads with someone else's milk. In general, new babies seem to like anything that vaguely resembles a human face.

Q I THINK MY NEWBORN BABY IS SMILING AT ME ALREADY. IS THIS POSSIBLE ?

A Real smiling is said to start at around six weeks. Those fleeting smiles that parents notice in the first few days were once thought to be due to gas or a random facial experiment by the baby. But now many doctors agree that very young babies can and do smile. This may be in response to your smiles. They can also imitate facial movements, such as sticking the tongue out, from an early age.

WHAT IS THE APGAR SCORE ?

Named after Dr. Virginia Apgar, this is a clinical assessment of your baby's short-term well-being at and soon after birth. The check is carried out by your doctor or midwife one minute after the birth and then usually again five minutes after birth (and more often if it's necessary).

BABY'S SCORE

SIGN	SCORE 0	SCORE 1	SCORE 2
Color of baby (A for appearance)	Blue body, pale limbs	Pink body, blue extremities	Pink all over
Heart rate (P for pulse)	Absent	Slow	More than 100 per minute
Response to stimulus (G for grimace or other response)	None	Grimace or some other response	Sneezing or coughing
Muscle tone (A for activity)	Limp	Some tone	Actively moving
Breathing (R for respiration)	Absent	Slow	Good or crying

A total score of 7 or over is normal; 10 is perfect, while 5 to 7 indicates that the baby may need observation or to have her airways cleared. A score of less than 5 usually suggests that the baby needs oxygen or other urgent treatment. The score should then rise.

YOUR NEWBORN BABY

Some babies are small while others are chubby. Many have very little hair, but a few have lots. The shape of their heads can vary, too, depending on the length of the mother's labor and the method of delivery.

WHAT WILL MY NEWBORN BABY LOOK LIKE?

In the first few days, a baby has some distinct physical features that can look alarming to a new parent. Don't panic. Some of what may seem to you to be peculiarities or even defects are really normal features that will change as your baby matures.

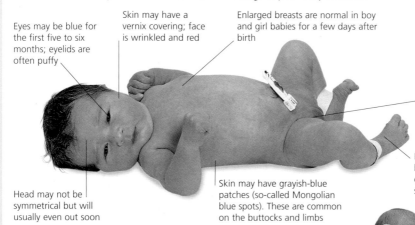

Eyes may be blue for the first five to six months; eyelids are often puffy

Skin may have a vernix covering; face is wrinkled and red

Enlarged breasts are normal in boy and girl babies for a few days after birth

A girl's vulva may appear red and inflamed and there may be a clear discharge and a little blood around the seventh day. (In boy babies, the scrotum may be red and swollen.)

Hands and feet are often bluish or mottled at first, or after sleeping. Peeling skin can occur later

Head may not be symmetrical but will usually even out soon

Skin may have grayish-blue patches (so-called Mongolian blue spots). These are common on the buttocks and limbs

WHAT CAN MY NEWBORN BABY DO?

She may be helpless without food and warmth from you, but she is equipped with some skills and reflexes.

■ She can see, especially in the range 8–10 in (20–25 cm). Her eye muscles lack coordination so she may be cross-eyed, but this does not mean she has a long-term problem. Her eyes don't adapt to distance vision as well as those of an older baby.

■ She can also hear well and has a sense of smell.

■ She has a sucking reflex: when your finger touches the roof of her mouth, she will respond with a strong sucking action.

STEPPING REFLEX
If you hold her upright, with her feet touching a firm surface, she will mimic a stepping action, even though she can't walk yet.

ROOTING REFLEX
If you stroke her cheek, she will turn toward your finger and open her mouth. This reflex helps her feed.

STARTLE (MORO) REFLEX
If you pull her arms to their extent and let go quickly, she will throw out her arms and legs.

Hands stretch out as if to grab something

GRASP REFLEX
Stroking her palm with one of your fingers will cause her to grip your finger tightly.

WHY DOES THE DOCTOR CHECK MY NEWBORN BABY?

In the hospital, a doctor examines your baby before you go home to ensure that she is well and to rule out physical abnormalities. At home births, the midwife or doctor examines her a few hours after birth.

What the doctor checks

- **Head:** The shape and size of your baby's head.
- **Heart and lungs:** A stethoscope is used to check that the lungs are clear and the heart sounds normal.
- **Mouth:** The doctor feels inside the mouth to check that the roof of her mouth has fully developed.
- **Abdomen:** The abdominal organs are felt to check that they are normal in size and the groin examined to rule out a hernia. You will be asked if your baby has moved her bowels. If she has not passed a stool in the first 24–48 hours, further tests may be performed.

WHAT IS THE HEEL PRICK TEST?

This is a small blood sample taken in the first 10 days by pricking your baby's heel. The blood is tested for thyroid deficiency and for phenylketonuria (a deficiency in body chemistry). If untreated, they can impair a baby's growth and mental development.

- **Genitals:** Your baby's external genitals are also examined by the doctor.
- **Hips:** Your baby's thighs are pressed downward and parted outward to see if the hip joints are stable.
- **Spine:** The pediatrician runs a finger along her back to ensure that the spine has formed normally.

COMMON CONCERNS

Why is my baby so blotchy?

A newborn baby's circulation is not fully developed. Because blood can "pool" in one part of the body, her upper half may look paler. Stork marks—red or purplish V-shaped marks on the back of the neck (occasionally elsewhere, especially the eyelids)—may be seen. Don't worry; they are harmless and will fade.

Why are my baby's eyes "sticky"?

Eyes can become sticky when infection of the lining of the eye causes a discharge or pus (conjunctivitis). This condition is very common in new babies because they can pick up germs on their way through the birth canal. The tear ducts of newborns aren't fully developed, so they can't get rid of bacteria as easily as older babies. Babies can get conjuncitivitis despite being given eyedrops at birth. Cases of conjunctivitis in newborns need a pediatrician's prescription for antibiotic eyedrops or ointment.

Is dry, flaky skin normal?

Many babies have dry skin, especially when they're a few days old. It is usually most obvious on the feet and ankles, but it can occur elsewhere—the diaper area, for instance. Babies born after their due date usually have drier skin, but it improves with the use of a mild lotion or oil after bath time. Avoid bath additives, since they can worsen dry skin.

What is jaundice and is it serious?

Mild jaundice (a yellowish tinge to the skin and/or the white of the eyes) is common in babies who are 2–3 days old. It occurs because your baby's liver is still too immature to cope fully with bilirubin—the yellow pigment produced by red blood cells as a normal waste product. Premature babies are more likely to be jaundiced because their livers are less mature. Jaundice usually subsides after a week or two. If the baby appears jaundiced the bilirubin level is checked before going home. If it is above normal the baby may stay at the hospital a few extra days.

I am considering getting my baby boy circumcised. Is this a good idea?

Circumcision is controversial but it has little or no medical benefit. There is no proof that it protects against urinary infections, or later against cervical cancer in the man's partner. The hygiene argument is even more doubtful. Circumcision is painful, so local anesthetic cream should be used if possible. Although serious complications are rare, they can lead to infection, gangrene, and death. Sometimes men who were circumcised as babies resent what they think of as an assault on their genitals without their consent. You have to weigh the advantages and disadvantages for your baby—if he is born into a faith or culture where circumcision is expected, he could later resent not having been circumcised.

BONDING WITH YOUR BABY

Q EVERYONE TALKS ABOUT BONDING. WHAT DOES IT REALLY MEAN?

A Bonding refers to the feeling parents have for their young baby—an emotional tug. It can start before birth when you see her on an ultrasound scan or feel her kick. It can also happen when you hear her heartbeat during a prenatal check. Many parents say they feel love for their baby as soon as she is born—but bonding doesn't always happen this quickly.

PARENT'S SURVIVAL GUIDE

I DON'T FEEL CLOSE TO MY BABY

If you don't feel an overwhelming surge of love for your new baby, you are not abnormal or inadequate. In one study, only two-thirds of mothers experienced a sudden rush of emotion for their baby (fewer in the case of mothers of twins, since it is hard to get acquainted with more than one new arrival at a time).

Is there something wrong with me?
If you don't feel an immediate emotional bond with your baby, it may be because you're tired, anemic, or ill—or that your baby may be very demanding or unwell. Hold your baby when you can, and get close to her whenever possible. If you feel very little for her now, just be gentle and try to smile. She needs you, and she will respond eventually.

Is it natural to feel this way?
If this is your first baby, then you may have mixed feelings about becoming a parent. Don't worry—this is perfectly natural. However, if you feel angry or depressed, you should talk it through with your doctor or midwife.

Can early separation prevent bonding?
Parents whose newborn baby goes to the Neonatal Care Unit (see p. 56), and mothers who have had a cesarean or a difficult delivery often worry about whether separation will ruin their bonding. It may delay it, and it is a shame to miss out on some of those early moments of contact, but there will still be time later.

Q DO I HAVE TO BREAST-FEED MY BABY FOR BONDING TO SUCCEED?

A No. Breast-feeding may bring a mother intense and pleasurable closeness with her baby, but it is not essential for bonding. The proof is that many fathers, bottle-feeding mothers, and adoptive parents bond well with their babies. It helps to hold your baby, establish eye contact, talk with her, and get to know her. This helps her to recognize your voice and face, too. These one-to-one conversations also play an important part in her development. You can do all these things without breast-feeding.

Q WILL I BOND MORE QUICKLY IF I KEEP MY BABY WITH ME ALL THE TIME?

A Although this is not essential, it can help with bonding. It is also usually safer if you keep your baby near you. In the hospital, many parents prefer the security of knowing at any time exactly where their baby is, and with whom. However, you don't need to feel that you must have her constant company all the time if you don't want to. If someone else watches your baby for a while, it does not mean that your parenting instincts are deficient, so there's no need for you to feel guilty.

Q IS IT IMPORTANT TO CUDDLE MY BABY FREQUENTLY?

A Yes. A new baby has only recently left the comfort of the womb and she still needs your touch, warmth, sight, and sound, so it is important to hug her a lot. She also needs the stimulation you can provide with eye contact and smiles. In some cultures it is normal for a mother to hold or carry her baby virtually all the time in the early months. You don't have to do this, nor does she need hugging all the time. She has to sleep sometimes—and so do you.

Q WHAT'S THE BEST WAY FOR ME TO COMMUNICATE WITH HER?

A Talking to your baby is very important from early on. The content of what you say may not be all that vital for now because the sounds alone play an active part in her development. Soon, however, she will be ready to socialize and to have "conversations" with you, so what you say will matter. Smile at her, too. Babies seem to be programmed to appreciate people's smiles. Smiling on your own may feel a little silly to begin with, but you will soon find that your baby will start smiling back at you.

COMING HOME FROM THE HOSPITAL

Q WHAT FOLLOW-UP SUPPORT WILL THERE BE AFTER I LEAVE THE HOSPITAL ?

A Your baby will have an appointment with the doctor or pediatrician within two weeks of discharge from the hospital. This appointment will be sooner if you are breast-feeding. You will have a postpartum office visit with your doctor or midwife between four and six weeks after you leave the hospital. Either healthcare provider can be telephoned for advice or to answer any questions you may have. If necessary, you can arrange an earlier appointment.

Q WILL I BE ABLE TO FOLLOW MY NORMAL ROUTINE WHEN I GO HOME ?

A You shouldn't struggle to continue your life exactly where you left off before the birth— sumptuous meals and an impeccably neat home will have to wait for the time being. It's important for you to adjust to the fact that you and your baby come first now and that you might need help with other household chores. You will probably feel very tired in the first few weeks after the baby's birth, and you should take life at the easiest pace possible. Your partner or a friend can organize some essentials for your baby, such as diapers, and instant meals for you.

Q HOW OFTEN SHOULD I SEE MY DOCTOR OR PEDIATRICIAN ?

A You should see them often. Your family doctor or midwife can help deal with any ailments, carry out your postpartum examination, and give you advice on contraception. You'll also see the doctor or pediatrician before leaving the hospital for your baby's developmental checks and for any health problems your baby may have.

Q I'M SO TIRED, EVEN IN THE HOSPITAL. HOW WILL I COPE WHEN I GET HOME ?

A It's completely normal to feel tired and anxious when you become a new parent. Having a baby is the biggest life change you can experience, and it will take time to adjust to your new lifestyle. Take care of yourself, and it will be easier to care for your baby, too.

Q I'M SURE I WON'T MANAGE. DO I NEED PRACTICAL HELP WHEN I GET HOME ?

A Yes. It is always a good idea to get some practical help with a new baby. Talk to friends, neighbors, and health professionals to help you get to grips with being a parent. Your partner may be able to take paternity leave to help you. Or maybe a grandparent or a good friend can help out.

WILL IT HARM MY BABY IF I SMOKE ?

Yes, it will. Since smoking poses so many dangers to a baby, it is hard not to make the health warnings sound like a lecture—so here comes my lecture! As a parent, you are responsible for protecting your baby from hazards. Becoming a parent can be the ideal opportunity for you to stop smoking, which will also benefit your whole family. Ultimately, the choice is yours. If you feel that you have to smoke, then please make sure that it is never in the same room with your baby.

- Cigarette smoke contains not only nicotine and tar, but also carbon monoxide, ammonia, cyanide, and a cocktail of other chemicals, some of which are cancer-causing.
- Up to a quarter of all crib deaths (SIDS/sudden infant death syndrome, see p. 46) are thought to be linked to passive smoking (exposure to cigarette smoke).
- Children who live in households of smokers tend to be shorter than those of nonsmokers.

- Young children who live in households with one or both parents who are smokers are more likely to suffer from asthma and chest infections.
- Allergies are around four times more common in the children of smokers.
- Chronic secretory otitis media (chronic ear infection), which can lead to intermittent deafness and poor speech, is linked with parents who smoke.
- About 10–15 percent of house fires are started by cigarettes, matches, and other smoking materials.

HOLDING AND HANDLING

Q WHAT IS THE BEST WAY TO HOLD MY BABY?

A The best way is the one that comes naturally to you, but always make sure you support her head. She has no head control yet and will feel insecure without support. A young baby likes to be able to see your face, which she can do if you hold her in one arm close to your side. Research suggests that babies prefer to be held on their parent's left arm. This may be because the baby can more easily feel and hear your heartbeat.

Q HOW CAN I FEEL MORE CONFIDENT ABOUT HANDLING MY BABY?

A Try to relax. Confidence will come as you grow more accustomed to handling your baby and settle into your new role as parent. Before you know it, you will feel at ease and develop your own way of handling her. When you hold her, smile at her and talk to her. This will help her feel secure. Hold her close as you pick her up and put her down.

Q WHAT'S THE SAFEST WAY TO CARRY HER WHEN I'M WALKING AROUND?

A Support her, and make sure you look where you're going. She's vulnerable if you fall, and some babies have been known to break a leg when their parent tripped. Don't carry your baby loosely in your arms if you are walking down the street, especially if it is dark or crowded—use a sling.

Q MY PARTNER IS AFRAID HE'LL HURT HER BY PICKING HER UP. IS HE RIGHT?

A Adults who aren't used to babies often worry that they might squash the new arrival with inexpert handling, but your partner is unlikely to hurt her as long as he remembers to support her head, and not to rush. If he cares for her, your baby will sense this. Let him handle her without too much interference from you. Now that you are a family, it's important from both the psychological and the practical angles that you should not be the only parent holding and hugging her.

Q DOES IT MATTER IF LOTS OF DIFFERENT PEOPLE HOLD HER?

A It doesn't really matter as long as they all know how to hold your baby and transfer her safely and lovingly. Remind people to support her head. Do not be shy of giving a demonstration—most grandparents have got out of the habit of holding babies. As her parent, you are (or soon will be) the expert on the subject of your baby. Explain how she likes to be held. Hand her over gently. Try not to dump her unceremoniously onto someone's lap or into their arms. Tactfully take your baby back when you think she's had enough. In the case of some children, this may be after only a minute or so. To avoid any unnecessary risks, it is better not to let anyone hold her if they have an infection, such as a cold sore, conjunctivitis, or impetigo.

PARENT'S SURVIVAL GUIDE

SHE WON'T LET ME PUT HER DOWN

I can't get anything done. What can I do?
Before the birth, some people think that their baby can go in a backpack to the office, or lie quietly in a bassinet for hours. However, face facts: you're not going to be able to do this. The reality is that your baby needs *you*, as well as food, warmth, and diaper changes. Even everyday activities—like brushing your teeth—might be different now. However, you will manage, albeit at a different pace. Even a long relaxing bath may have to wait until your baby has been fed, changed, and is fast asleep.

Can I carry my baby around with me?
You will learn to do many things with your baby balanced on your shoulder and stabilized with one arm. Not everything can be done like this, but a sling (see p. 20) can solve some of the problems.

How can I cope?
You will have to ditch some activities that aren't strictly necessary, and accept help. Don't be too ambitious—if you start a big task, your baby is guaranteed to wake up and howl for attention.

HOW SHOULD I HANDLE MY BABY ?

Many first-time parents are unsure about how to hold their new baby. The techniques below will help guide you, but holding and handling will soon come naturally.

PICKING YOUR BABY UP

Support her head at all times

1 Place one hand under your baby's head and neck, and the other under her bottom.

2 Lift her slowly, close to your body, continuing to support and cradle her with your hands.

3 Turn her toward your chest and shoulders as you straighten your back.

HOLDING YOUR BABY

You can hold your baby in several positions—the best being the one that is most comfortable and natural for you both. Your baby will need to feel secure, whether she's cradled in the crook of your elbow, held upright against your chest, or even held face down in your arms.

Hold her against your chest

Use your arm to support her head

ON YOUR SHOULDER
Put one hand under her bottom to take her weight and support her head with your other hand.

ON YOUR ARM, FACING YOU
Cradle your baby's head in the crook of your elbow, and support her bottom with your other hand.

ON YOUR ARM, FACING DOWN
Lay your baby along your forearm with one hand under her and the other supporting her body.

HOW DO I USE A SLING ?

A sling on your front can be used almost immediately, as long as it is not too big for your baby and her head is supported. Many slings have head supports built in. If you plan to use a sling later on, get your baby used to one in the first six weeks. If you have twins, a sling can still be useful for carrying one baby when the other one is asleep, or you and your partner can carry one baby each. Your baby will probably not want to be in a sling for too long. To begin with, half an hour might be her limit, but this will lengthen as she gets older.

HOW DO I PUT MY BABY IN A SLING ?

1 Securely fasten one side of the sling and hold your baby with her face toward you. With one hand, put a leg through the hole on the fastened side while you support her with the other hand.

Support her with an arm

You can support her with your hands

2 Supporting her with an arm, close the opposite side of the sling so that her hips and legs are securely in position. Close the top fasteners on both sides above her shoulders so her arms are free to move.

3 The strong back flap provides a young baby with the support she needs for her head and neck. You don't need to cradle her with your hands but you can if it makes you feel comfortable and protective. When she is a little older—at about three months—you can put her into the sling while she faces forward. A flap at the front of the sling folds down so she can see where she's going.

CAN I MAKE A SLING?

If necessary, you can make a sling from a crib sheet or a piece of strong fabric, measuring about 3 x 6 ft (1 x 2 m). Drape the fabric over one shoulder, ideally your left, and tie the ends together with a strong knot at the opposite hip.

Rotate the sling so that the knot is at your back. Then gently ease your baby into the pouch made at the front by the rest of the material. Make sure that she is held securely against your chest and cannot fall out.

DRESSING AND UNDRESSING

Q WHAT SHOULD MY BABY WEAR IN THE DAYTIME?

A She should wear an undershirt and stretchsuit and then a sweater or a jacket. This is usually enough if the temperature is around 64°F (18°C). In winter, she'll need a heavier sweater, but in summer she may not need one. If it's really hot, an undershirt and diaper may suffice—but keep her out of the sun. Her temperature control is quite rudimentary. In winter, take off her outdoor clothes when you bring her indoors, even if she's asleep.

Q HOW CAN I TELL WHETHER SHE'S TOO HOT OR TOO COLD?

A A baby's body should feel warm to your touch, but not damp or sweaty. If she's moist on the head, chest, or back of the neck, or she feels hot to the touch, then she has too many clothes on. You may have an inkling of this because hot babies can be fussy or may cry. If your baby's hands or feet feel cool to you, then she may be too cold. Her abdomen under her clothes may still feel warm even though she is cold. She may not cry from the cold because of the need to conserve energy to maintain her body temperature.

Q DOES SHE NEED A SWEATER OR A MATINEE JACKET?

A Your baby certainly needs one of these if it is cool, and it can be chilly indoors even in the summer. It's best to avoid jackets that have a tie or drawstring neck because these can cut into a baby's neck. Also, your baby could suck a loose end and even choke on it. Always check that any buttons on sweaters and jackets are sewn on securely.

Q WHEN SHOULD I PUT A HAT OR BONNET ON MY BABY?

A Always put a hat or bonnet on her if you're taking her outside in winter, because a baby loses a lot of heat from the head. Premature babies, in particular, have difficulty controlling their body temperature. If a bonnet has a string or ribbon under the neck, ensure that it can't cut or even strangle her—as with any other loose ties, she could choke by sucking the end. In summer, a hat with a brim is essential. The hat will help keep some light out of her eyes and off her face.

Q WHAT SHOULD MY BABY WEAR AT NIGHT?

A Your baby does not mind whether it's night or day, so—to make things easier for you— she may as well wear the same item of clothing at night as she has done in the day, minus the jacket. However, if you prefer, you can put her in a nightdress or nightgown, such as those with snaps at the hem. This will still keep her cosy but will make nighttime diaper changing much easier than with a stretchsuit. This can also help her become more aware of the difference between night and day.

DOES SHE NEED SHOES YET?

Your baby will need something to keep her feet warm. Socks and soft bootees are ideal for this age—bootees stay on better than socks. Shoes for young babies may look cute, but are too firm and restrict her movement. It is necessary for a baby to wiggle and even suck her toes.

SUITABLE SHOES
Woolen bootees can be a very good idea when it's cold. Alternatively, choose soft fabric shoes with elasticized ankles or even soft leather ones.

Soft cotton "boots" with elastic around the ankles keep her warm and stay on

Very soft leather shoes with elasticized ankles are easy to put on and keep on

How should I dress my baby ?

Dressing your baby should always be a pleasurable experience for you both if you are gentle, and talk and smile at her throughout. A young baby needs to be dressed and undressed frequently, and you will need to get several changes of clothes for her.

What clothes does my baby need ?

She will need a few practical, simple items, but buy only a few in small sizes at this stage because she is growing so fast that she will outgrow most of her clothes before they become worn out. Choose clothes that are machine-washable and easy to care for.

Sun hat and warm hat
A sun hat is essential for protecting your baby's head and face from the sun. A warm hat is needed in cold weather to conserve body heat.

Stretchsuit
You'll need several of these since you may have to change them frequently. Make sure that they are big enough for your baby.

Undershirt with snaps (body suit)
Choose one with a wide envelope neck that is easy to slip over your baby's head.

Scratch mittens
Some scratch mittens are cotton with ties around the wrists. Some newborn stretchsuits have cuffs that turn back to form mittens. These can be used to keep your baby from scratching her face with sharp nails.

Socks
Unless it's warm, your baby will need socks if she wears footless leggings or a stretchsuit. Otherwise, only put on socks if it is particularly cold.

Jacket or sweater
You will need these in cold weather, or even indoors if it is cool.

If your baby hates being dressed and undressed

■ Remember that all things pass—she will undoubtedly get over her hatred of a dressing or undressing session.
■ Keep changes of clothing to a minimum.
■ Keep the room warm and make sure that your hands are also warm.
■ Use simple clothes—sweatpants and a T-shirt, for example, would be good because less of her would be exposed at a time. This doesn't always make a difference, but it's worth a try.
■ Lay her on a warm but firm surface, like a bed (but kneel down to avoid straining your back).

■ If using a changing mat, cover the bare plastic surface with a soft towel or cloth diaper.
■ Get close to her when dressing and undressing so that your face is within her range of clearest vision (about 8–10 in/20–25 cm away).
■ Always be quick as well as gentle.
■ Stretch and pull the clothes to fit your baby, instead of stretching her to fit the clothes.
■ Keep her undershirt on as long as possible.
■ Make soothing noises as you take off or put on her clothes.
■ Reward her with a big hug afterward.

UNDERSHIRT

Avoid touching her eyes

1 Stretch open the neck of the undershirt before easing it over your baby's head.

2 Hold her fingers and thumb together and gently feed through sleeve.

3 Pull the undershirt over her tummy. Lift her legs and pull the back down. Fasten the snaps.

STRETCHSUIT

1 Pick up your baby while spreading the stretchsuit out flat on the changing mat. The snaps should be undone. Place your baby on her back on it, with her neck in line with that of the stretchsuit.

Wrap your fingers around her hand

Lay your baby over the stretchsuit

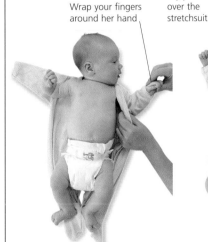

2 Guide your baby's hand and arm through the sleeve. Repeat for the other side.

3 Gently ease each foot in turn into the gathered-up legs of the stretchsuit.

4 Make sure that your baby's toes are fully pushed into the toe area of the stretchsuit.

5 Fasten all of the snaps. Work either from the crotch up or from the neck down.

DIAPERS

Q WHICH TYPES OF DIAPER ARE AVAILABLE FOR ME TO BUY?

A Diapers can be disposable or washable. The disposable type is convenient and time-saving, and comes in different shapes and sizes. Washable diapers are available in traditional cotton cloth squares, as well as other fabrics and shapes. Both diaper types have evolved in recent years and fabric diapers are no better at preventing diaper rash.

Q ARE THERE DIFFERENT DIAPERS FOR BOYS AND GIRLS?

A No, the distinction between boys' and girls' diapers was not important and, today, most major manufacturers make unisex diapers for infants and toddlers. They are all highly absorbent and are perfectly acceptable for either sex—just make sure that you purchase the appropriate diapers for your baby's age and weight.

WHICH DIAPERS SHOULD I USE?

Make your choice according to your circumstances and preferences. If you have very dry skin, for instance, you won't want to wash fabric diapers, and the disposable type will be more suitable.

Disposable diapers
■ Easier to use than fabric diapers because there's nothing to wash and sterilize.
■ No substantial capital outlay to begin with. However you do have to buy new packages every week and they therefore work out to be more expensive per use than fabric diapers which can be washed and then reused.
■ Highly absorbent, more so than non-disposables. It does not mean that you can change your baby less often, but it does mean that the diaper is less likely to leak and the baby's skin stays drier.
■ Not flushable. Since you can't dispose of them in the toilet, bags are needed to dispose of the used diapers in the garbage.

Non-disposable (fabric) diapers
■ Need diaper pins or Velcro tabs, and a one-way liner and waterproof pants.
■ Take time and effort to rinse, wash, and sterilize. If you use a laundry service, it can work out to be more expensive than disposables.
■ Although seemingly ecologically friendly, the detergents used for washing them may not be.
■ Can be cheaper than disposables though the initial outlay is high—you need about two dozen diapers (more for twins) and two diaper buckets for soaking and sterilizing.
■ You can't necessarily keep fabric diapers for your next baby, because they may feel harsh by then after being washed so many times.

WHAT ARE THE DIFFERENT TYPES OF DIAPERS?

There are several types of diaper, ranging from convenient disposable ones to washable fabric ones. If you choose to use fabric diapers, you will also need diaper pins, absorbent liners, and a supply of plastic pants.

Diaper liners

Disposable diaper

T-shaped fabric diaper

Velcro-fastened diaper

Cotton diaper

Plastic pants

Q WHEN SHOULD I CHANGE MY BABY'S DIAPER?

A "Often" is the best answer—there is no ideal time. To keep her comfortable, change a diaper as soon as it is dirty or when it feels full or heavy. It's hard to tell when modern disposable diapers are wet, so don't wait for a wet patch to appear on her clothes. She needs a diaper change about every two hours during the day, perhaps less often at night (never wake her to change it). On average, this is about 10 diapers in 24 hours to begin with. The best time to change your baby's diaper is usually just after you have fed her. This is because a reflex bowel action can follow, or even accompany, a feeding.

Q WHERE SHOULD I CHANGE MY BABY'S DIAPER?

A Always choose somewhere warm, on a firm but comfortable surface that is preferably at waist level to make it easier for you. A special changing table is ideal or a padded changing mat on a chest of drawers. Otherwise, put the changing mat on the floor, but this is not particularly good for your back because you will have to kneel down or bend over. If you live in a house with more than one story, it's a good idea to keep some extra diaper-changing gear on every floor. This will save you from running upstairs every time you need to change your baby's diaper.

HOW DO I CHANGE MY BABY'S DIAPER?

When changing a diaper, get everything ready beforehand. Keep all the essential equipment handy in a changing bag, either to use at home or to take with you when you go out. Use baby wipes if warm water and cotton balls are not an option.

CHANGING A DIAPER

WHAT EQUIPMENT DO I NEED?

- Changing mat
- Cotton balls
- Lukewarm water
- Towel (optional)
- Barrier cream
- Clean diaper

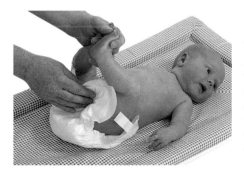

1 Undo the dirty diaper. Hold both your baby's legs up and gently wipe away any stools with the front of the diaper. Roll the diaper up from the front and put it to one side.

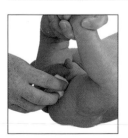 

2 Holding the legs up, clean your baby's bottom with a cotton ball dipped in lukewarm water or a baby wipe. If your baby is a boy (above left), pay particular attention to the fold between the scrotum and thigh. Wipe under the scrotum, too. There is no need to clean under the foreskin. For girls (above right), wipe from front to back.

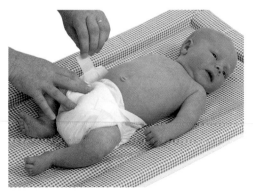

3 Dry the area with a towel or a cotton ball. Put a fresh diaper under the bottom. Apply a thin layer of barrier cream. Close the diaper.

Q WHAT SHOULD I DO IF MY BABY DEVELOPS DIAPER RASH?

A Always let the air get to your baby's bottom as much as possible. When you've cleaned and dried her, lay her on her changing mat to play without a diaper, preferably for at least 20 minutes several times a day. Before putting on a clean diaper, apply a thin layer of barrier cream (or barrier cream and antiseptic cream). If you see any little red spots, tell your pediatrician—they could be the result of a yeast infection, such as thrush, and she may need a prescription for some antiyeast cream (see p. 113).

Q CAN DISPOSABLE DIAPERS CAUSE DIAPER RASH?

A Yes they can—but only to the extent that any diaper can cause a rash if it is left on for too long. This is the reason why it is so important to change your baby's diaper regularly. Modern disposable diapers are probably superior to cloth ones in keeping a baby's bottom dry because they have a highly absorbent core that draws moisture away from the skin. In theory, the chemicals in disposable diapers could irritate a baby's skin, but in practice this doesn't seem to happen. If you suspect chemical irritation, change your brand of diaper and speak to your pediatrician.

Be affectionate with lots of smiles, talk and gentle touching.

Q ARE BABY WIPES USEFUL FOR CLEANING MY BABY'S BOTTOM?

A Baby wipes are very convenient when you're out and about. However, be aware that baby wipes can irritate a very young baby's skin, so it is best to use cotton balls dipped in warm water whenever possible.

Q DO I NEED TO CLEAN UNDER MY BABY BOY'S FORESKIN?

A There is no need to clean under a baby boy's foreskin and you should not even try to do so. You will actually do more harm than good because the average baby boy's foreskin is still adherent to the tip of his penis until he is about 12 months or more. Just use a small amount of cotton balls to gently clean the penis and then dry it thoroughly.

Q SHOULD I USE BARRIER CREAM OR LOTION WHEN CHANGING A DIAPER?

A Because stools are full of germs, and urine irritates the skin, your baby needs a cream as a waterproof barrier on the skin of her bottom and genital area. This, along with frequent diaper changes, is all you need do to prevent diaper rash. Zinc and lanolin and petroleum jelly are suitable barrier creams. All have to be applied to totally dry skin. A thin layer is enough; if you use too much, it can clog up a diaper lining and in particular, it can prevent a disposable diaper from absorbing urine. After applying the cream, put on your baby's clean diaper.

Q CAN I PUT TALCUM POWDER ON MY BABY'S SKIN?

A No. You should avoid using talcum powder: it has no benefits for a young baby's skin. The granules can irritate a young baby's skin, especially when they work their way into moist folds. It is also a potent irritant inside the body. There have even been suggestions that talcum powder may be positively harmful to girls—talc is believed to spread from the genital area right up into the peritoneum via the fallopian tubes and to set up chronic inflammation around the ovaries and possibly long-term pain and other symptoms.

TALK TO YOUR BABY
When you change your baby's diaper, talk to her and smile. This turns a routine task into a pleasant time for you both.

BOWEL AND BLADDER HABITS

Q **HOW OFTEN SHOULD MY BABY PASS URINE?**

A Although a baby has no control over her bladder, it still empties periodically rather than leaking continuously. Under six weeks, a baby usually passes urine 20 to 30 times every 24 hours, but you do not need to change her diaper this often. In a baby it is dry diapers that are a cause for concern.

Q **HOW CAN I TELL IF SHE'S PASSING ENOUGH URINE?**

A Although it's hard to feel moisture with many disposable diapers, as they lock urine away into highly absorbent padding, the weight of the diaper is a good clue. No urine for three hours or more may mean that your baby is dehydrated. If this is the case, you should always contact your pediatrician for advice.

Q **MY BABY'S DIAPERS ARE STAINED RED. IS THIS BLOOD IN THE URINE?**

A It is unlikely to be blood. The pink or even red tinge that's sometimes seen in a baby's urine is usually due to chemical salts called urates, which are a normal waste product. If you're not sure, then show the diaper to your pediatrician. Blood in the urine is unusual but it can be serious. In a boy, it may indicate a problem with the penis or foreskin. Around the seventh day, a girl baby may bleed from the vagina, which is nothing to worry about. This is just due to your hormones leaking into her circulation shortly before birth.

Q **WHAT DOES IT MEAN IF HER URINE IS SMELLY?**

A There are three main reasons for your baby's urine to smell unpleasant. Stale urine can smell, and the remedy is more frequent diaper changes. Urine can also be smelly if it's very concentrated, which may happen if your baby is short of fluids. Try offering an extra feeding if she's breast-fed, or cooled, boiled water between feeds if you're bottle-feeding. Dehydration can be serious, so if she's sick, or her diapers are dry, consult your pediatrician. A urinary tract infection can affect very young babies. If untreated, they are serious. Again, contact your pediatrician if your baby seems to be unwell.

Q **HOW OFTEN SHOULD SHE PASS A STOOL?**

A She'll probably move her bowels several times a day. In the first six weeks, the average is three or four bowel movements every 24 hours, but it can be more. Breast-fed babies can have very frequent, loose stools. As long as your baby seems well, it doesn't count as diarrhea. Some breast-fed babies can go for several days between each bowel movement, but your baby should have passed a stool at least once since birth.

Q **WHAT COLOR IS NORMAL FOR A NEWBORN BABY'S STOOLS?**

A In the first 24 hours of life, a baby produces meconium. This is a sticky, greenish black substance that is made up mostly of bile and mucus. Within another day or two, it changes to a stool, which is a light greenish brown— this is runny and less gluelike than meconium.

Q **WHY DO MY BABY'S STOOLS CHANGE COLOR?**

A Because she is now using her gut to absorb nutrients. Meconium was more of a pre-stool formed when she was sustained purely by blood flowing through the umbilical cord. When the color changes, the consistency may also change. If she seems well, you don't need to worry.

Q **WHAT SHOULD MY BABY'S STOOLS LOOK LIKE IF SHE'S BREAST-FED?**

A The stools of a breast-fed baby are usually ocher or orangey yellow, like mustard, and smell of sour milk or yogurt that has gone bad. They can be very frequent, with visible mucus or soapy-looking blobs. Breast milk stools can be bright green in color, which parents may mistake for diarrhea—but there is usually nothing wrong.

Q **WHAT SHOULD MY BABY'S STOOLS LOOK LIKE IF SHE'S BOTTLE-FED?**

A Formula milk tends to make the stools bulkier and more substantial. They are usually a light brown color and quite smelly, quite like an adult's excreta, because they contain a different mix of bacteria from that of a breast-fed baby. Green stools are more significant in a bottle-fed baby, especially if they're explosive or runny. They may mean she has gastroenteritis (infectious diarrhea) (see p. 218).

KEEPING YOUR BABY CLEAN

Q HOW OFTEN AND WHEN SHOULD I CLEAN MY BABY?

A You should clean her face, hands, and bottom every day (see opposite). A daily bath is unnecessary; bathing her once every two or three days will suffice. Choose a time when you won't be interrupted, because you can't leave her alone while you answer the phone or the door.

Q WHAT'S THE BEST WAY TO KEEP MY BABY CLEAN?

A You can either bathe your baby regularly, or simply clean her face, hands, and bottom daily (see opposite). The latter does not need to involve undressing your baby completely, and requires less effort, so it is ideal if neither of you particularly enjoys bath time yet.

HOW DO I TAKE CARE OF THE CORD STUMP?

Your newborn baby will have a cord stump ⅓–¾ in (1–2 cm) long, with a plastic clamp attached. Within 24 hours, the cord begins to shrivel up and turn dark. The clamp will be removed (or fall off) after about three days. You may see a demarcation line forming between the blackish part of the cord and the skin part of your baby's navel, before the shriveled part separates and drops off.

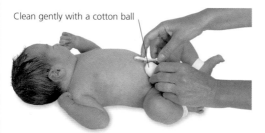

Clean gently with a cotton ball

CARING FOR THE CORD
Until it drops off, the cord should be kept as clean and dry as possible to avoid infection. Clean once a day with a cotton ball and cooled boiled water.

Should I clean the cord?
Yes. Use cotton balls and alcohol or alcohol wipes. You will be given instructions before you leave the hospital. When changing a diaper, fold the top below the cord.

Does touching the cord hurt my baby?
It doesn't hurt her unless there's an infection, so don't be afraid to touch the cord with cotton balls or antiseptic wipes.

When will the cord drop off?
Usually between the fifth and ninth day after delivery. It will happen sooner if the cord is kept dry, and will take longer if there is an infection.

Why is my baby's cord bleeding?
When the cord starts to separate, a few drops of old blood may seep out. Occasionally, the navel bleeds from a tiny area just after the cord drops off, but if you keep it clean this usually stops.

What should I do if it is weepy and red?
It is normal for the cord to weep slightly before it falls off. Ask your doctor or pediatrician for advice if this persists or the navel smells. A mild infection may need antiseptic. In a few cases, your baby may need a course of antibiotics by mouth.

Now that the cord has fallen off, there is a fleshy part left. What's happening?
This is granulation tissue, which will turn into ordinary scar tissue. A small fleshy-looking area is normal and usually settles down within a few days. Sometimes the granulation tissue is too angry or profuse. If so, see your doctor or pediatrician, who may dab it with a silver nitrate cauterizing stick, which temporarily turns the granulation tissue a silvery gray color.

Is swelling in the navel a hernia?
This may be an umbilical hernia. These are very common. Don't apply a dressing. It usually clears up within a few months. If it is prominent and persistent, a hernia can be fixed with surgery.

How do I clean my baby?

You should clean your baby once a day. Even if you are bathing her daily, you may need to clean her as well sometimes. If, for instance, she spits up (see p. 44) a lot, her neck, hands, and ears can easily get encrusted. Talk to your baby throughout the cleaning process. If she is not used to being cleaned, she will need reassurance. If she is, she will enjoy the social occasion.

What equipment do I need?

- Changing mat
- Cooled, warm boiled water for cleaning the eyes
- Ordinary warm water from the faucet
- Cotton balls for cleaning the eyes
- Two washcloths: use a separate washcloth for the diaper area
- Soft towel
- Baby bath liquid/lotion
- Clean diaper and barrier cream
- Change of clothes

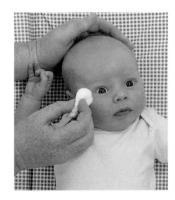

1 Lay your baby on his back on his changing mat or a towel, still clothed. Wipe his eyelids from the inner corner outward, using a new cotton ball, dipped in the warm, boiled water, for each eye.

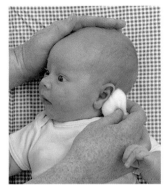

2 With a clean cotton ball dipped in warm water, clean his ears and the folds of his neck. Using a new cotton ball, wipe around your baby's mouth and nose. Then dry the area thoroughly.

3 Moisten a washcloth with warm water and clean his hands. Dry his face, neck, and hands with a towel. Take off his undershirt and then wash his armpits and dry thoroughly. If it's cold, or he doesn't like being undressed, put on a clean undershirt.

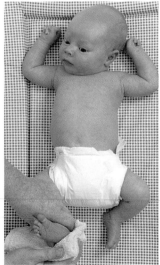

4 Leaving his diaper on, wipe his feet with another warm, damp washcloth.

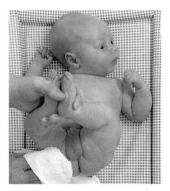

5 Finally, take your baby's diaper off and then wipe the diaper area with the washcloth. If he is dirty, use baby lotion as well, but make sure that you rinse the lotion off thoroughly. Dry your baby with the towel. Put a clean diaper on him and then dress him.

FIRST BATH

Q **WHERE SHOULD I BATHE MY BABY ?**

A Choose a warm room (preferably 68–75°F/ 20–24°C), such as the bathroom, living room, kitchen, or bedroom, with easy access to water. Because of her hormone changes, a new mother's back is very susceptible to injury, especially for the first three months, so don't carry heavy things, such as a baby bath full of water.

Q **WHAT IS THE BEST TIME OF DAY TO GIVE HER A BATH ?**

A It doesn't much matter what time it is—an hour or so before you expect to feed her is ideal, especially if you'd like her to nap after the next feeding. Midway between feedings is fine, too, but avoid bathing your baby when she's really hungry, or she may scream in protest. If you bathe her just after a feeding, she may throw up in the bath. Don't bathe her when either of you is very tired—you would probably both become even more upset and miserable, and you may even lose concentration and do something dangerous. Later on, as you get more used to bathing your baby, you can start bathing her in the evening as part of a developing nighttime routine.

Q **HOW OFTEN DOES SHE NEED TO HAVE HER HAIR WASHED ?**

A It's usual to wash a baby's hair at every bath. However, if you're giving your baby daily baths this is not strictly necessary, especially since most babies don't have much hair. You should wash it, however, whenever it looks greasy or stringy.

Q **MY BABY HAS A SCALY, GREASY SCALP. WHAT CAN I DO ?**

A This is cradle cap, caused by an accumulation of dead skin on her scalp. Even though it looks like crusty scales, it has nothing to do with dandruff, eczema, an infection, or poor hygiene. Many babies get cradle cap, and it will soon go away if you shampoo her hair regularly. If necessary, you can rub in a little olive oil to soften the scales and speed up the process. (Avoid using almond oil or other nut oils because of the risk of allergy.) There are also baby shampoos that you can buy that are formulated specially for treating cradle cap. They do dissolve some of the dead skin, but they don't work any better than olive oil.

HOW DO I BATHE MY BABY ?

You may already have been shown in the hospital how to give your baby a bath, but doing it on your own for the first time can be a different matter.

WHAT EQUIPMENT DO I NEED?

Get everything ready first before bathing your baby. You will need the following basic items:

Baby bathtub

Small bowl of cooled boiled water

Cotton balls

Baby bath liquid or soap and shampoo

Two soft towels

Apron

Other essential items
You will also need the following items:
- changing mat, diapers, and barrier cream
- clean clothes for your baby.

BATHING DRY SKIN

If your baby has dry skin, choose bath products carefully. If you are using soap, make sure that it is mild. You could add baby oil to the bath to soothe your baby's dry skin—but be careful, since this will make your baby extra-slippery, and he could slip out of your grasp.

GIVING YOUR BABY A BATH

The water temperature is very important—it should be around 96°F (35°C). If you are filling the bath from a faucet, always run the cold water first, and then add the hot water until the temperature feels just right (to a level of about 3 in/8 cm). You could half-fill some buckets with water and carry them to the baby bath. Never try to carry a full bathtub of water around. Throughout the bath, talk to your baby and smile to help make it an enjoyable experience for you both.

1 Fill the bath with water; dip in your elbow to test the temperature. It should feel just warm on your skin.

6 Put your baby in the bath, keeping one hand under his head and grasping his shoulders, and the other hand under his bottom. Hold on to your baby at all times because he will be very slippery when wet.

2 Wash your baby's face; use a separate cotton ball dipped in cooled boiled water for each eye, and a new piece for his ears and mouth.

3 Undress him but leave his diaper on. Wrap him in a towel, tucking his arms in to keep them out of the way.

4 Holding him firmly over the edge of the bath, wash his hair. Use bathwater with a little baby bath or a small amount of baby shampoo. Use a cupped hand to apply the water. Rinse hair.

Use a cupped hand to rinse his hair

7 Use the hand that was under the bottom to wet the baby and play with him. Use soap if he is dirty, but it must be mild—don't use if his skin is very dry.

8 Place one hand under his bottom and lift him out of the bath. Wrap him in a towel and dry thoroughly. Apply barrier cream on the diaper area, put on a clean diaper, then dress him.

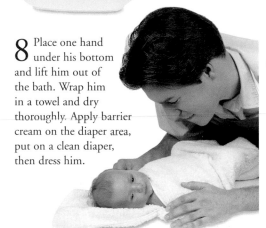

5 Lay your baby on a changing mat or your lap and dry his hair thoroughly with the second towel. Take off his diaper and clean the diaper area with water (as for cleaning; see p. 29). Add baby bath liquid to the water if you are using it.

FEEDING YOUR NEW BABY

WHICH IS BEST FOR MY BABY: BREAST OR BOTTLE ?

In general, breast-feeding is better, but, since it's your baby, you must decide which you want to do. Before you commit yourself, there are many points to consider.

CONCERN	BREAST-FEEDING	BOTTLE-FEEDING
Your baby's health	■ Breast milk is always the right consistency, with the correct amount of water and nutrients. ■ Cells and antibodies in breast milk protect her against infection in the first three months. ■ She is less likely to develop gastroenteritis because breast milk is sterile. ■ Gives some protection against eczema, asthma, and other allergic conditions. ■ Risk of childhood diabetes may be lowered. ■ She is unlikely to be overfed because breast milk is supplied according to her demands. ■ Breast milk adapts in quality to her needs; milk of mothers of preterm babies has higher fat and protein and lower lactose content. ■ More iron is absorbed from breast milk. ■ She will probably need less burping. ■ Her stools will be less smelly and the feedings she regurgitates will smell less rancid.	■ Your baby's supply of milk is not affected by your physical health, nutrition, or anxieties. ■ Any medicines you may have to take will not affect her milk. ■ You know exactly how much milk she is getting. ■ She is less likely to be underfed. ■ While breast milk is superior in most ways, formula milk is higher in iron, vitamin K (needed for normal blood clotting), and vitamin D. ■ If you are a vegetarian, your baby might be less likely to develop vitamin B12 deficiency.
Your health	■ Suckling helps your uterus contract. ■ You use up more calories, helping you return to your prepregnancy shape and size. ■ It stimulates your pituitary gland to produce prolactin, which inhibits ovulation. Breast-feeding can act as a contraceptive, although it's unlikely to be 100 percent effective and should not be depended on. ■ Your risk of developing breast cancer may be reduced by breast-feeding. ■ Breast-feeding can be a very satisfying experience.	■ It does not expose your breasts, which can be important in cold weather and in public places. ■ Milk will not leak from your breasts and stain your clothes. ■ Your nipples will not become sore or cracked. ■ Bottle-feeding requires less energy than breast-feeding. ■ Not every woman enjoys breast-feeding.
Convenience	■ No special equipment is needed and there are no time-consuming preparations. ■ Your milk is already sterile, at the right temperature, and ready wherever you are—which saves your baby from having to wait for a feeding, especially at night. ■ It is cheaper than bottle-feeding. ■ If you start breast-feeding, you can still decide to bottle-feed should you change your mind.	■ Someone else can prepare the bottles. ■ If you're going back to work or just want a night of uninterrupted sleep, someone else can feed your baby. ■ Breast-feeding is not always as simple and easy as one imagines it will be. ■ It is possible to start off bottle-feeding and then change to the breast, although this can be quite difficult.
Relationship and bonding	■ You and your baby will have more skin-to-skin contact. ■ It enhances the closeness you have with your baby and may improve bonding.	■ You can still cuddle your baby and hold her close to you. ■ You can still bond with your baby. ■ Other people can be benefit from being more closely involved in the baby's care. ■ An older sibling may be less jealous.

BREAST-FEEDING

Q DO I NEED TO DO ANYTHING TO PREPARE MYSELF FOR BREAST-FEEDING ?

A You will certainly need three well-fitting nursing bras that give your breasts proper support, have wide shoulder straps to ease the weight on your shoulders, and open in the front to allow you to feed your baby. You will also need some breast pads (disposable or washable) to put inside the bra cups to absorb any leakages.

Q WILL I PRODUCE MILK AS SOON AS MY BABY IS BORN ?

A No. For the first few days, you will produce only a yellowish fluid known as colostrum. Although it is watery, it is rich in protein and minerals, low in fat, and very important to a baby. Some of the proteins are antibodies that her immune system, being immature, cannot make. Colostrum also contains immune cells called lymphocytes that colonize the baby's gut and help to protect her against both infection and allergy. In many women, colostrum leaks out of the breasts in late pregnancy. Your body continues to make colostrum for a while after milk comes in (day three or four), although it is less noticeable once it is mixed in with milk.

Q CAN I BREAST-FEED IF I DON'T START IMMEDIATELY AFTER THE BIRTH ?

A You can delay breast-feeding for several days, but if you do, your baby will miss out on the benefits of colostrum. And the longer you wait, the more difficult it will be to breastfeed if you then choose to. If your baby is not with you, you may need to express milk (see p. 38). If you intend to breast-feed, tell the nursing staff so that she is not bottle-fed without your permission. It is possible to breast-feed a baby who has been started on bottles, but it's more difficult.

Q WHAT DOES BREAST MILK LOOK LIKE ?

A It is more watery than formula but is actually very rich. Breast milk varies in composition at different times. "Fore-milk" comes from the ducts just behind the nipple and is produced at the start of a feeding. It is low in fat and slightly watery to satisfy a baby's thirst. "Hind-milk" is richer in calories and higher in fat. It is produced in the later two-thirds of a feeding in response to sucking.

Q IS THERE ANY POINT IN BREAST-FEEDING IF I'M GOING BACK TO WORK SOON ?

A There is no reason not to start breast-feeding, but continuing when you're at work depends to a great extent on your job and your babycare arrangements. It's easier if your baby is cared for in a daycare center at your workplace. You'll feel very tired if you return to work as a breast-feeding mother, but you're going to be tired anyway, and breast-feeding after a day's work can be rewarding for you both. Even if you change to bottles after a few weeks, you will have given your baby a worthwhile start.

Q IF I HAVE LARGE BREASTS, COULD MY BABY SUFFOCATE ?

A It's possible for large breasts to block your baby's nostrils, making it difficult for her to feed and breathe at the same time. However, unless she's very small or premature, she's unlikely to suffocate, although she may stop feeding. Try to reposition yourself (see p. 34). You can also press the breast down just above the areola (the outer nipple area) to give her nostrils more space.

Q I HAVE SMALL BREASTS. WILL I PRODUCE ENOUGH MILK ?

A The size of a breast has nothing to do with how much milk the glands within it can make. Suggestions to the contrary are sometimes made, even by some health professionals, but they are incorrect and highly unproductive. Some small-breasted women do not succeed at breast-feeding, but—equally—some larger-breasted women fail also. The difference is that unhelpful and inaccurate comments can make a woman with small breasts feel inadequate, and her efforts may fail because of unfounded anxiety about the whole process.

Q IF I BREAST-FEED MY BABY, WILL MY BREASTS SAG LATER ?

A No. It is actually pregnancy rather than breast-feeding that causes the breasts to become less firm. Ligaments support the breast structure, and to keep these from getting overstretched, you should always wear a supportive nursing bra (see p. 37), especially if your breasts are large. You will need at least three front-opening bras, but they should not be bought before week 36 of pregnancy.

How do I breast-feed ?

Get yourself comfortable and into the correct position before you start to breast-feed your baby—you're likely to be there for a while. Sit on a chair, sofa, or bed and set aside 40 minutes or so. In the early stages, you will need time to get breast-feeding established. Concentrate on your baby and ignore any interruptions.

BASIC POSITIONS

SEATED IN A CHAIR
Sit down in a chair; support your back and arms with cushions. Hold your baby's head close to you, at the same level as your breast. Her whole body should face you, not just her head.

Support her weight with a pillow

LIE DOWN
Lie on your side on a sofa or bed with your legs up, supporting your head with your hand or lying on a pillow. Place your baby alongside you and facing you so that she can feed from the lower breast.

FEEDING TWINS

As breast milk is a matter of supply and demand, breast-feeding twins (or even triplets) is possible, but it is more tiring and takes longer to build up a supply of milk than with a single baby. Get comfortable first. A V-shaped or triangular pillow under the babies is a help, as is another adult who can help you get organized for each feeding.

In the early days, having someone with you is useful in case a baby comes off the nipple. Some mothers keep one breast for each baby but they risk becoming lopsided if one baby sucks harder than the other. You could try swapping the babies around at the next feeding, but this is more successful once breast-feeding is well established.

POSITIONING YOUR BABIES
It's often easier to feed your twins at the same time. The most convenient way is to use the "football hold" because you can hug both babies at the same time and they can't kick each other.

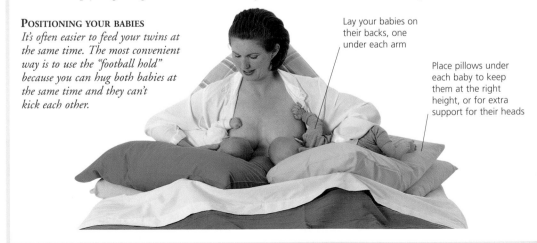

Lay your babies on their backs, one under each arm

Place pillows under each baby to keep them at the right height, or for extra support for their heads

LATCHING ON

This is the way that your baby's mouth grasps the nipple for feeding. She has to suck the nipple, massaging the area around it with her mouth to draw milk out. Just compressing the nipple itself will shut the ducts, and nothing will come out.

LATCHING ON PROPERLY
Your baby should latch on immediately. Ensure that the whole nipple and most of the areola are inside her mouth— the bottom part of the areola should be totally

covered. If she hasn't latched on properly, don't pull her off —this will make your nipple sore; use a finger on her gums to break the seal gently and then try again.

FEEDING AFTER A CESAREAN

Breast-feeding helps your uterus to contract, which is almost more important after a cesarean than after a vaginal delivery. With a recent incision that will take several weeks to heal, breast-feeding can be uncomfortable. Try the position below or use the "football hold" with your baby's body tucked under your arm rather than lying across your body (see opposite). Feeding while lying on your side is sometimes suggested, but rolling onto your side can be uncomfortable because of the wound.

GETTING COMFORTABLE
The most comfortable way to breast-feed your baby after a cesarean is to raise your baby up to breast height using lots of soft pillows or cushions. It keeps you from leaning forward and makes sure your baby's weight does not press on your abdominal wound.

EARLY DAYS

Q HOW OFTEN SHOULD I BREAST-FEED MY NEWBORN BABY ?

A You should put your new baby to the breast whenever she is hungry—"on demand." This will be very erratic to begin with, but stick with it. The benefit is that her sucking action increases your milk supply and, as you match her needs, feeding will settle into a more predictable pattern for you both. An average-sized baby under six weeks will settle for feeding at least eight times in 24 hours, with 1–2 feedings being during the night.

Q HOW LONG SHOULD I LET MY BABY FEED ?

A "As long as she wants" is the usual advice given, but this might not be entirely correct. Babies spend about 10–20 minutes per breast; some spend much longer, and not all of it in productive sucking. Leaving it to your baby is still the best policy, although this may be difficult or uncomfortable. Your breasts will need the stimulation of sucking to produce the right amount of milk for your baby. Ideally, offer both breasts every time you feed, but as babies normally take more from one side than the other, start with a different breast each time to keep your chest from feeling lopsided.

Q HOW CAN I TELL IF MY BABY'S GETTING ENOUGH MILK ?

A With breast-feeding it is difficult to tell. The proof is whether your baby is gaining weight, although it will take at least a week or two before this is reflected on the scale. If you're concerned, get your baby weighed more often. Some mothers weigh their babies before and after every feeding to estimate how much they have taken, but this isn't reliable. Breast milk varies in concentration, so the weight of the feeding isn't relevant. If your baby is wetting diapers throughout the day, she is taking enough milk.

Q WHAT SHOULD I DO IF MY BABY FALLS ASLEEP HALFWAY THROUGH A FEEDING ?

A Let her sleep, and you have a rest, too. It may not be that long until the next feeding. However, if you think she's taken very little, change her diaper. This may rouse her enough to resume her feeding. You can't force a baby to stay awake and take nourishment, and you shouldn't try—the only exception being if your baby is ill or very premature and finds it exhausting to suck.

Q SHOULD I FEED MY TWINS AT THE SAME TIME ?

A Feeding simultaneously saves time and makes use of any milk that leaks from your other breast, but your babies may not want to be fed at the same time. When one twin wakes for a feeding, many mothers rouse the other and put her on the breast, too. Feeding separately means each baby receives individual attention, but you will spend more time feeding, and have less time left for anything else.

Q DO I NEED TO BURP MY BABY AFTER BREAST-FEEDING ?

A Most babies need burping, but not all. Breast-fed babies need less burping than bottle-fed ones. You'll soon discover if your baby has a lot of gas. If she produces only a minimal amount of gas, she may need nothing more than a pause in the upright position after her feeding to give her the chance to bring it up (see p. 44).

Q SHOULD I EVER WAKE MY BABY FOR A FEEDING ?

A In general, babies respond to their own needs, so you shouldn't wake a baby for a feeding. However, very small or preterm babies may need more feedings than they request. If your baby is small or vulnerable for any reason, ask your doctor or pediatrician whether you should be putting her to the breast every two or three hours regardless of whether she wants a feeding or not.

Q DO I NEED TO GIVE MY BABY WATER TO DRINK AS WELL ?

A Unlike formula, breast milk is complete and adapts to her requirements. It is also lower in sodium, so she won't get dehydrated. You needn't give bottles of water unless the circumstances are exceptional—if you are ill, maybe, or in a heatwave. However, giving bottles of water to your baby can get her used to a bottle—making a later changeover from breast to bottle less traumatic.

PARENT'S SURVIVAL GUIDE

MY BABY SCREAMS AT THE BREAST

It's not unusual to have a frantically hungry baby who screams when placed on the breast instead of taking the nipple. Some possible causes are:
- your breasts are so engorged that your baby can't latch on properly
- your baby may have thrush in her mouth
- you may have eaten something that disagrees with her

- she may dislike some toiletries you are using
- your baby may be ill—for instance, with an ear infection (see p. 217)—or she may have a cold that blocks her nose
- if you have given your baby bottles at any time, she may dislike having to make the extra effort of getting milk from the breast
- she may be so hungry that she is unable to feed.

Possible solutions
- First, relax. Be patient and gentle. A feeding should not be a fight, and getting upset won't help, since your baby will pick up on your panic.
- If your breasts are over-full, lie in a warm bath with wet washcloths on your breasts. Alternatively, express some milk by hand or with a pump.
- Inspect your baby's mouth for thrush (*Candida albicans* infection). This looks like white spots or patches on the gums. The tongue can look red and glazed. If you find these signs, see your doctor.
- Feed her in a quiet place and tell people not to interrupt you while you are feeding.
- Try a different feeding position, such as the "football hold" (see p. 34).
- Let your baby suck your finger first.

- Try to tempt her to feed by expressing a few drops of your milk (or colostrum) onto her lips.
- Don't restrain your baby forcibly while trying to breast-feed her, but you could try wrapping her in a blanket (see p. 48).
- Make sure she's positioned properly and that her nose is not obstructed.
- If she still won't settle at the breast, give up and try again 30 minutes later.

When you find a solution, try to figure out why it worked and remember it for next time. If you don't know why your baby got so agitated, simply ensure that she's not kept waiting for a feeding in the future. If none of this works, you should consult your doctor in case your baby is unwell.

LOOKING AFTER YOURSELF

Q **WILL I NEED A SPECIAL BRA FOR BREAST-FEEDING MY BABY ?**

A Yes. Ordinary bras that fasten at the front are not practical when you are breast-feeding, and your normal bra will not be big enough. To make the process easier, you should buy nursing bras before your baby is born. These have cups that can be opened individually. Some bras have cups that unzip, while others unhook from the strap.

Q **WHY DOES MY OTHER BREAST LEAK DURING A FEEDING ?**

A Many women's breasts simply leak, whereas others spurt. Both are normal results of the letdown reflex, which makes milk gather toward the nipple. Letdown is also responsible for the drawing sensation that you may experience at the start of a feeding, and for the tightening you may feel in both breasts when you anticipate a feeding, or hear your baby cry from hunger. Wear an absorbent pad inside each bra cup to prevent your clothes from getting wet or stained.

Q **MY BREASTS ALWAYS LEAK AT NIGHT. IS THERE ANYTHING I CAN DO ?**

A To some extent, this is normal. Because you rest at night (and your baby may sleep), your breasts naturally produce more milk and therefore you may wake up soaking wet in the early hours. For comfort, put on a well-fitted nursing bra and some breast pads before going to bed.

Q **MY BREASTS FEEL TOO FULL. WHAT CAN I DO ?**

A It's common to feel over-full, especially on days two to four after the birth of your baby, when blood flow to the breasts increases and the milk comes in. This is called engorgement. Your breasts may throb and feel lumpy or painful. Your nipples can also be affected—engorgement may prevent them from standing out, and your baby may have trouble latching on. If this happens, soak in a warm bath or put wet washcloths on the breasts. If this isn't enough, express some milk manually or with a pump (see p. 38). Don't try to empty the breasts completely—just take off a little milk. Feed your baby often—every hour, if necessary. Massaging the breasts gently while feeding can help stimulate milk flow and relieve engorgement. Take one or two acetaminophen tablets, if needed.

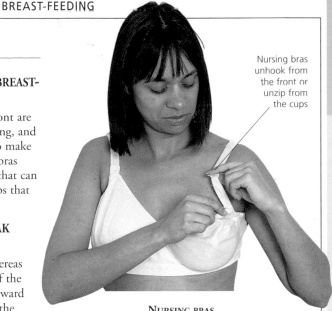

Nursing bras unhook from the front or unzip from the cups

NURSING BRAS
These are essential for breast-feeding. Ideally, you should buy two or three, 3–4 weeks before your baby is due. If possible, have them professionally fitted. You'll need a bigger cup and bra size than before. The cups may seem big at first, but won't be once your milk has come in.

Q **WHY DOES BREAST-FEEDING GIVE ME A STOMACHACHE LIKE A CONTRACTION ?**

A This can happen because your uterus really is contracting. The action of your baby sucking on your nipple stimulates the pituitary gland deep within your skull, causing it to secrete the hormone oxytocin. It is this hormone that makes your uterus contract, causing the lower abdominal pains you may be feeling when you breast-feed your baby. Don't worry. These are called "after-pains" and they will usually stop after a few days of breast-feeding. Oxytocin continues to be produced, but your uterus will have shrunk back to a more normal size by then, so you won't feel anything happening in your abdomen when you breast-feed your baby.

Q **WHERE CAN I GET HELP WITH BREAST-FEEDING ?**

A You can talk to your doctor who may be able to refer you to a lactation consultant. You will also find that there are local support groups consisting of other mothers who have had and overcome breast-feeding problems. Just because breast-feeding is a natural process, it doesn't necessarily make it easy to get started. Many women have trouble in the first few weeks, so talk to others before giving up completely.

Q WILL BREAST-FEEDING HELP ME GET MY FIGURE BACK ?

A Yes. Breast-feeding can help you regain your figure. This is because the breast-feeding process makes demands on your body's metabolism, so that you will use up more calories than if you were bottle-feeding your baby. Also, the hormones released encourage the uterus to shrink back to normal quite quickly. However, it is important to remember that this may take time—so don't get frustrated if it doesn't happen in the first few weeks after the birth. Also, there's no guarantee that you will go back to the same size and weight that you used to be before your baby was born.

Q WILL I NEED TO EAT MORE WHEN I'M BREAST-FEEDING MY BABY ?

A You need to eat more than before you were pregnant. On average, you will need an extra 500–600 calories a day to sustain milk production (more for twins or triplets). Your appetite will guide you but, to give you an idea, 500 calories is approximately one extra smallish meal a day. If you have twins (see p. 34), you will need at least an extra 1000 calories. Alternatively, you could just snack between meals on nutritious foods that contain plenty of protein, carbohydrate, and calcium rather than fats. Don't ever be tempted to skip any meals, even if you are overweight.

CAN I EXPRESS MY MILK ?

There may be times when you need to go out for the evening or be away from your baby for a while. You may also want to get your baby accustomed to taking feedings from a bottle, which is a useful skill if the unexpected occurs. If, for some reason, you're missing feedings because you're away from the baby (and she has a bottle of formula or expressed milk), expressing will help you keep up your supply. If you need to express milk regularly, you might consider using a breast pump—ask your lactation consultant for more information about breast pumps to find out which might be best for your needs.

EXPRESSING BY HAND

The most basic method is to express your milk by hand. It's a time-consuming process, but the advantage is that it needs no special equipment other than a sterile container for the milk. It's especially suitable for relieving engorged breasts or dealing with sore nipples.

How should I store expressed milk?

Keep breast milk in the refrigerator in a sterile bottle for up to 24 hours, or use a cooler bag and ice pack. Warm it by standing it in a bowl of warm water. To keep it longer, freeze it in plastic baby bottles and use within one month. Thaw at room temperature or in the refrigerator. Never refreeze or reheat expressed milk.

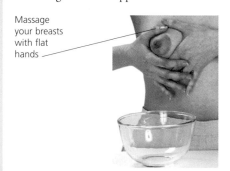

Massage your breasts with flat hands

1 Hold the breast supported with one hand, using the other hand to stroke toward the nipple. Massage the whole breast in this way.

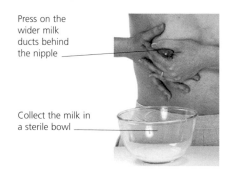

Press on the wider milk ducts behind the nipple

Collect the milk in a sterile bowl

2 Squeeze the junction between nipple and breast. Milk will spurt out. Continue massaging this part of the breast to make the milk flow.

Q WHAT IS THE BEST WAY OF BUILDING UP AND MAINTAINING MY SUPPLY OF MILK?

A You should let your baby feed whenever she's hungry—milk production works on the basis of supply and demand. Because big babies need more sustenance, a heavy baby may want to feed more often than a lighter one. It is also important to relax when feeding—tension can inhibit the let-down reflex. Since your own health will affect your milk supply, take care of yourself. Try to get enough rest; lying down in the afternoon is a great idea, as this will boost your milk supply in the early evening when it can be quite low. Postpone or delegate heavy physical work. Very vigorous exercise is not recommended either, even if you're usually quite athletic—it will use up calories and is said to increase the lactic acid content of the breast milk. Drink lots of water and eat a balanced, healthy diet. You need to have regular meals throughout the day. You may want to shed a few extra pounds, but don't go on a diet. Now is not the time to restrict your food intake.

Q CAN I BOOST MY MILK SUPPLY IF I'M NOT MAKING ENOUGH?

A Yes. The best advice is to get plenty of rest and to give yourself a chance of making more milk. You could try staying in bed for most of the day, taking your baby with you. Abandon all the usual household chores and ask your partner, family, or friends to do them instead. Do make sure that you eat well, drink plenty of fluids, and breast-feed your baby as often as possible. Within 48 hours you should have boosted your supply and made a lot more milk. If you are worried about this, ask your doctor for advice.

Q WHICH FOODS AND DRINKS SHOULD I AVOID WHEN BREAST-FEEDING?

A In general, there's nothing you should avoid as long as you eat wholesome food, but if there are allergies in your family, then it's best to avoid peanuts and peanut oil in any form. This may help prevent your baby from becoming allergic to peanuts later. Some women find that eating very spicy food, citrus fruit, cabbage, Brussels sprouts, or beans upsets their baby's digestion, causing crying, excess gas, or looser stools. Citrus fruit juice can also cause problems. If so, you should try cutting these foods out of your diet and seeing if it makes a difference to your baby. A few mothers believe that onions and garlic put babies off breast milk, but this is unlikely if they're cooked.

Q HOW MUCH FLUID SHOULD I DRINK WHEN BREAST-FEEDING?

A Drink as much fluid as you feel like. Many women get intensely thirsty at the beginning of a feeding, so you may find that it's a good idea to keep a drink within easy reach before you sit down to breast-feed your baby. However, there's no point in forcing down fluids if you don't want them. Forcing yourself to drink too much doesn't produce more breast milk.

Q SHOULD I AVOID DRINKING ALCOHOL IF I'M BREAST-FEEDING?

A No, but it can pass into the baby via your breast milk so you should always stick to only small quantities, such as one alcoholic beverage a day. Thousands of lactating women enjoy the occasional drink without their baby coming to any obvious harm. Alcohol can help to relax you, which is no bad thing.

IS IT SAFE TO TAKE MEDICATION?

Can I take painkillers?
Aspirin can get into breast milk and make a baby bleed excessively, with dangerous results. This probably happens at high doses only, but it's safer to avoid aspirin. For minor aches and pains, acetaminophen is a good alternative. Although it crosses into breast milk, the amounts are too small to matter.

What about other medicines?
A breast-feeding mother sometimes needs drugs which do potentially affect her baby. As with any medication, the balance between risk and benefit has to be carefully evaluated. Usually, though, another drug can be chosen, or you can bottle-feed while taking the drugs. Drugs that find their way into breast milk are:
- anticoagulants, such as warfarin
- certain antibiotics, such as tetracycline
- some antidepressants like fluoxetine
- many drugs for high blood pressure.
There can be other considerations, too. The combined estrogen–progestogen contraceptive pill depresses milk production, but you could take the daily progestogen-only pill instead. If you're prescribed something, or are buying medicine over the counter, check with your doctor or pharmacist.

BREAST-FEEDING PROBLEMS

Q IS IT NORMAL TO HAVE SORE NIPPLES WHEN BREAST-FEEDING ?

A Some soreness is usual at first, perhaps for up to two to three weeks as the nipples become toughened up by your baby's sucking. However, if it's more than just mild discomfort, then your baby may not be latched on correctly—clamping the tip of the nipple makes it sore (see p. 35). But you can get sore nipples even if your baby's positioning is perfect.

Q WHAT CAN I DO ABOUT MY SORE NIPPLES ?

A Make sure your baby is latched on correctly. Never pull her off the breast without first using your finger to break her hold on the nipple. If sore, inspect your nipples; if they are red, raw, and dotted with a white deposit, you may have thrush and should see your doctor for treatment. Always keep your nipples clean and dry between feedings—don't leave damp pads or tissues in your bra. Use a hairdryer on a low setting to dry your nipples, and forgo a bra altogether when you can. Don't use creams unless they are advised by your doctor or midwife. If you're not in acute pain, continue breast-feeding. You should feed just as often, but you may have to limit the time your baby spends at the breast. Most of the milk comes out during the first five to ten minutes, so she will almost certainly get enough nourishment even though she will get less of the hind-milk.

Q I HAVE A PAINFUL CRACK ON MY NIPPLE. DO I HAVE TO STOP FEEDING ?

A No. A crack can result from a sore nipple, or it may appear without warning. It may bleed a little, but you must never assume that blood in your milk is due to a crack in your nipple. If you can't see and feel a crack, check with your doctor. You may still be able to breast-feed your baby by using a nipple shield, which is available from pharmacies and some other stores. If you still have too much pain, stop breast-feeding from that side for 24 hours, give your baby bottles instead, and express your milk to prevent engorgement (see p. 38). When it gets better, put your baby back on the breast, limiting the length of each feeding but not the frequency of feeding. If the crack fails to heal quickly, then consult your doctor because you may need an antibiotic.

Q I HAVE DEVELOPED BLOOD BLISTERS ON MY NIPPLES. WHAT'S WRONG ?

A As long as you do not feel any pain, tiny blood blisters are nothing for you to worry about. They occur because of the force of your baby's sucking and are more common in the early weeks. See your midwife or doctor if the blood blisters are large or painful.

Q MY BREASTS HURT BUT MY NIPPLES LOOK NORMAL. WHAT'S WRONG ?

A Many women experience a shooting pain as they start to breast-feed their baby. This could be due to the sudden filling of the milk ducts. However, there's no need to worry. This pain is quite normal and it will subside as the feeding continues. If it does persist, you should check whether your breast looks red and inflamed. If so, talk to your doctor or midwife.

Q WHAT SHOULD I DO IF ONE BREAST FEELS SORE AND TENDER ?

A In the early weeks, a tender area in one breast is likely to be a blocked milk duct, and the skin over the area may look inflamed. If this does happen, drink plenty of fluids and stop wearing a bra for the time being, or otherwise put a fresh cabbage leaf inside your bra—this seems to help. Feed your baby often, starting with the sore breast, and, while feeding, gently massage just above the tender area, stroking toward the nipple. You should see your doctor or midwife if you develop a fever, generalized aches and pains, or shivering—they could be due to mastitis, which may need a course of antibiotics.

Q WHY DOES MY ARMPIT FEEL SWOLLEN NOW THAT I AM BREAST-FEEDING ?

A Part of the breast lies in the armpit—it's called the axillary tail. You may feel very full there just before a feeding, but this feeling should soon subside. If you have pain or persistent swelling in your armpit, see your doctor.

Q I HAVE DEVELOPED A BREAST LUMP. IS THIS CANCER ?

A A breast lump is not usually cancer. A lump that develops during lactation is often just a blocked duct or maybe even a small cyst filling with milk. This is quite common while breast-feeding is getting established. However, to be on the safe side, you should check with your doctor if your lump does not disappear within a few days.

MIXING BREAST- AND BOTTLE-FEEDING

Q CAN I CHANGE MY MIND AND BREAST-FEED IF I STARTED WITH BOTTLES ?

A Yes, although changing from bottle to breast is much more difficult than changing from breast to bottle. The earlier you put your baby back on the breast, the better, and this is best done before she has become accustomed to getting milk from a bottle—because the milk comes out faster, a rubber nipple is usually a lot easier to suck than a real nipple. Whenever you change from bottle to breast, you will have to work very hard at stimulating your milk supply. To increase your supply, you should make sure that you get plenty of rest, eat a healthy, nutritious diet, and drink lots of fluids throughout the day (see p. 39).

Q CAN I MIX BREAST-FEEDING AND BOTTLE-FEEDING SUCCESSFULLY ?

A Yes, but it is an effort. For successful mixed feeding, try to give your baby a regular breast-feeding when your milk supply is at its greatest. Early morning is the most obvious time, but there will be other good times, too, depending on your personal routine and lifestyle. When it works well, a combination of mixed breast- and bottle-feeding can seem like having the best of both worlds. This can be a nuisance for you, however, combining the commitment of breast-feeding with the trouble of sterilizing and preparing bottles. You might need or want time away from your breast-fed baby, so it is a good idea to introduce bottles between two and four weeks after the birth. Earlier than this, the baby gets confused between nipples and teats; too late, and she will refuse the teat, even if the bottle contains breast milk.

Q IS IT A GOOD IDEA TO GIVE A BOTTLE OF FORMULA AS WELL AS BREAST MILK ?

A It can be if you want to supplement your breast-feedings—for instance, because your baby is not gaining weight. If you are going to continue breast-feeding, the bottles should merely complement and not totally replace your breast milk. For this reason, many mothers offer a bottle in the early evening when the supply of breast milk is likely to be low. Or, if you are at work, you can give bottles during the day and the breast at night. If you want to continue with breast-feeding, it is best to leave introducing bottles until breast-feeding is well established at, say, three weeks or so.

Q WILL I HAVE TROUBLE GETTING MY BABY INTERESTED IN BOTTLES ?

A You may. A bottle and nipple do not smell as good as you do, so your baby may refuse it initially. Try letting someone else give her a bottle, so she doesn't get confused by having you so near. You could try using a different kind of nipple (see p. 42) if she still refuses. If your baby doesn't seem to like formula, then try expressed breast milk. Patience will usually reward you. However, if all else fails, she may take milk from a cup or off a spoon. Even very young babies can do this sometimes, although you must always be sure to sterilize the equipment (see p. 42).

Q DO I GIVE THE BOTTLE BEFORE OR AFTER A BREAST-FEEDING—OR INSTEAD ?

A If you want to continue breast-feeding, give your baby a bottle after she has had all she wants from both breasts. If you offer the bottle first, she may take all the milk she needs from it and hardly suck the breast, particularly since your nipple is generally harder to suck than a rubber nipple. If unstimulated, after a few days your breast milk supply will tail off. Offering the bottle instead of a breast-feeding has the same result.

Q WON'T BREAST-FEEDING JUST TAIL OFF ANYWAY IF I GIVE HER BOTTLES ?

A It probably will if you are not breast-feeding frequently. However, as long as you are meticulous about stimulating milk production, you should be able to combine breast-feeding and bottle-feeding successfully.

Q CAN I DO ANYTHING ELSE TO STIMULATE MY MILK SUPPLY ?

A If you have delayed breast-feeding your baby for more than about a week after the birth, you may find that you need to use a relactation (supplementation) device. This has a reservoir of formula that hangs from your neck. Your baby is fed through a thin tube (the outlet of which rests against your nipple) when she sucks at the breast. The device mimics breast-feeding but it provides your baby with formula milk. The action of your baby feeding in this way will help stimulate your own supply of breast milk. Adoptive mothers who want to breast-feed their baby can also use a device such as this with success.

BOTTLE-FEEDING

Q WHICH EQUIPMENT DO I NEED TO BOTTLE-FEED MY BABY ?

A You will need the following items: eight bottles (standard size) with caps; over eight nipples (since they tear and wear out); a sterilizing unit; formula (with scoop and a straight-edged knife for powdered formula); a measuring cup (optional); a bottle-brush for cleaning; and a funnel (made of plastic).

Q WHAT'S THE BEST KIND OF NIPPLE TO USE ?

A The one that suits your baby! A plain rubber nipple is the cheapest. Choose one with a medium hole unless your pediatrician advises otherwise. If the hole is too big, the milk could choke your baby, while one that's too small is frustrating for her. Rubber nipples wear out easily—discard them when they crack or feel sticky.

Q DOES FORMULA MILK VARY ? WHICH TYPE IS BEST ?

A Formulas differ slightly in their content and in taste. You should stick to one milk-based formula. These are more suitable for a newborn baby's digestion and kidneys. Some vegetarian formulas are on the market—ask your pediatrician what she suggests.

Q CAN I CHANGE MY BABY'S FORMULA TO ANOTHER BRAND ?

A This isn't usually recommended because a baby's digestion is still immature and it is believed that she needs to get accustomed to dealing with just one type of formula. She may also dislike the change in taste. However, talk to your pediatrician if you are worried that your baby is not gaining weight.

Q SHOULD I EVER ADD ANYTHING TO THE FORMULA ?

A The answer is almost always "No." However, if your baby is constipated, despite giving her extra formula and offering her water, and it's established that nothing is wrong, your pediatrician may suggest that you add a 1/2 teaspoon of prune juice to the formula. This softens the stool and makes it easier to pass, but it can get your baby used to sweet things. However, on rare occasions, adding sugar can be useful.

Q CAN BOTTLES BE HEATED UP IN A MICROWAVE OVEN ?

A No. Microwave radiation heats up fats faster than other substances, so it can create hot spots in the milk that can burn or scald your baby. The delicate tissues of her mouth and throat can swell up as a result, obstructing the flow of air. This could result in asphyxiation.

Q IS IT SAFE TO CARRY BOTTLES ALL DAY IN A CHANGING BAG ?

A It's safe as long as the bottles are kept cool. You'll need a picnic or cooler bag, preferably with a plastic ice pack. there are specially insulated bags that are designed to hold a baby bottle.

HOW DO I KEEP BOTTLES CLEAN ?

How do I clean bottles and nipples?
Wash the equipment in warm, soapy water and scrub out bottles and caps, and their rims, with the bottle brush. If you are using rubber nipples, turn them inside out, hold them under running water, and rub them with your fingers to remove milk residue. Rinse off any soap residue thoroughly.

Do I need to sterilize?
Yes. Because of the risk of gastroenteritis, you need to sterilize everything involved in bottle-feeding, including the knife for leveling off the powder in the scoop. There are two main methods of sterilizing:
■ steam sterilizers—made for baby bottles, either the plug-in units or the type you put in a domestic microwave
■ you can also sterilize bottles by boiling them in a pan of water for 10 minutes (nipples need four minutes). This method tends to leave a residue, but it is handy for emergencies.

What's the best way of sterilizing?
The one that suits you. Steam is probably the easiest method although the equipment is the most expensive. Whichever method you opt for, the bottles and nipples need to be washed in soapy water first to remove all traces of milk.

HOW DO I MAKE UP FEEDINGS ?

If you can, make up each feeding as it is needed. This is because bacteria multiply quickly in warm milk, posing a risk of infection for your baby. If you make up bottles in advance, store them in the refrigerator below 5°C (40°F).

BOTTLE METHOD

Always wash your hands first. Clean the surface where you prepare the bottle. Remove the bottle, nipple, cap, and knife from the sterilizer. Do not rinse them. Boil fresh water for the bottle each time. Bottles should be made up with water that is 158°F (70°C) or higher. If you use a full kettle, don't leave it more than half an hour or the water will be too cool to kill any bacteria. Don't use softened water as some domestic water softeners add sodium to the water.

1 Pour the correct amount of water into the sterilized bottle (or bottles). Add the correct number of scoops of formula, using the knife to level off each scoop. If you lose count, empty the bottle and start again.

Screw the cap on firmly

Shake the bottle to disperse any lumps

2 Place the nipple on the bottle and screw on the cap to create a seal. Then shake the bottle to disperse any lumps

3 Cool the bottle to the right temperature for your baby by holding the bottle under the running cold tap. Test the temperature of the formula carefully, by shaking the bottle first, then squirting or dripping some milk onto the inside of your wrist. It should be around 98°F (37°C), "blood heat," and will feel neither hot nor cold on your skin. If it isn't warm enough, put the top cap over the nipple and replace the bottle in warm water (see panel below). If it's too hot, add some cold water to the bowl to cool it down. Always shake the bottle again before testing the temperature.

BATCH METHOD

Wash your hands first. Remove the cup, scoop, knife, and funnel from the sterilizer. Do not rinse them. Boil fresh water for each batch of bottles.

1 Pour the correct amount of boiled water into a cup; let it cool slightly. Take the bottles and nipples out of the sterilizer. Add the correct number of scoops of formula to the water; if you lose count, start again. Stir milk to disperse lumps.

2 Pour the correct amount of milk into each bottle. Place the inverted nipple on the bottle, making sure that it doesn't touch the milk. Screw the cap on firmly.

3 Cool the bottles quickly by holding them under cold running water, then store in the refrigerator at no more than 40°F (5°C) for up to 24 hours.

HEATING UP MILK

If the milk is cold, stand the unopened bottle in a jug or a basin of hot water. The hotter the water, the quicker the milk heats up. You can use recently boiled water. Don't heat bottles in a microwave as the fats heat up faster than other substances, creating hot spots in the milk that can burn or scald the delicate tissues of your baby's mouth and throat.

HOW SHOULD I GIVE MY BABY A BOTTLE ?

Get everything ready before you start and sit down with your baby somewhere comfortable and quiet. Set aside some time for a feeding; don't hurry your baby. Try to ignore any interruptions while you feed her a bottle.

FEEDING YOUR BABY

1 Bring the warmed bottle (see p. 43) to your baby's mouth. Gently touch her lip or the corner of her mouth with the tip of the nipple. She will immediately turn toward the bottle (this is called "rooting") and then start sucking on the nipple.

2 Hold the bottle at an angle so that the milk always covers the inside of the nipple; this helps prevent her from swallowing any air. Remember to watch the level of formula to keep the angle right and also the nipple, which shouldn't flatten totally. If it does, pull it out of her mouth slightly to break the vacuum and then give it back to her.

BURPING YOUR BABY

What's the best way of burping my baby?
Hold a very small or young baby upright on your lap and gently rub her back, making sure that you support her neck and head. When she is about four weeks old, she can be burped by holding her against you with her head over your shoulder. When a baby brings up gas, she may bring up some of the feeding as well.

What if she falls asleep?
If your baby falls asleep during a feeding and you can't burp her without waking her up, don't worry. If your baby is generally full of gas, hold her upright for a while since she may bring up burp in her sleep. You could even hold her against your shoulder. As long as you stop her head from lolling about, you can still burp her even though she is asleep.

HOLD YOUR BABY OVER YOUR SHOULDER
After about four weeks, your baby can be burped over your shoulder. Some milk may come up too, so it is best to protect your clothes.

Gently pat or rub her back to relieve gas

BOTTLE-FEEDING CONCERNS

Q HOW WILL I KNOW WHEN MY BABY HAS HAD ENOUGH MILK?

A Your baby will stop feeding when she feels full. Her mouth may or may not still be on the nipple, and she may or may not have dozed off, but she'll have stopped sucking. Remove the bottle gently and put it down. If there's any milk left, throw it away and clean the bottle, or empty it out and clean it properly later. If she has emptied the bottle you won't know how much more she would have taken, so make up more formula than she needs (see p. 43).

Q SHOULD I GIVE MY BABY WATER TO DRINK AS WELL AS FORMULA?

A Yes. Although formula is usually sufficient, she may be more thirsty if she's hot or feverish, or if the weather is warm. Giving her extra formula in these situations will not satisfy this need or prevent dehydration because it contains salt, protein, carbohydrate, and other nutrients as well as water. Offer some cooled, boiled water in a bottle if she has had her milk but still wants more. For young infants, limit water to 2 fl oz (80 ml) per day, since she needs the calories in the formula to grow.

PARENT'S SURVIVAL GUIDE

I FEEL GUILTY ABOUT BOTTLE-FEEDING

Health professionals and other parents can be very negative about bottle-feeding. They may seem disapproving and you may feel that there's little support or even information for you if you deliberately choose not to breast-feed your baby. Remember that:

- formula milk is almost as good nutritionally as breast milk
- bottle-feeding does not in any way suggest your relationship with your baby is deficient
- you can still enjoy every feeding
- your baby can still be cuddled
- you will not be happy if you're coerced into breast-feeding when at heart you don't want to do it. If you decide to bottle-feed, it's best not to think about it as failing to breast-feed. Just be honest and be yourself. Get close to your baby and enjoy her.

Q CAN I PROP MY BABY UP WITH A BOTTLE?

A No. This is unsafe because your baby could choke. She will also miss out on the closeness from being held in your arms while you feed her. If, after the first few weeks, you need to keep one arm free, you could try using some cushions to support her while you hold the bottle at the right angle. However, even if you use this method of bottle-feeding, she will still lose out on some of the important physical contact with you. I believe it's much better to give your baby both your arms, as well as your undivided attention, while you give her a bottle feeding.

Q WHY DOES MY BABY BRING UP SO MUCH OF HER FEEDING?

A For unknown reasons, some babies bring up more than others. Those who guzzle the fastest tend to spit up more. A baby who brings up a lot of milk may simply have drunk more milk than she needed. The amount she brings up almost always looks like a lot more than it actually is. In fact, you can test this out for yourself by deliberately spilling, say, 1/4 fl oz (10 ml) of surplus formula on a cloth or a towel. You will be amazed at the amount of mess even a small volume can create. You should always make sure that you speak to your pediatrician if your baby is vomiting violently, bringing up large quantities of milk, or appears to be unwell.

Q WHY IS MY BABY CONSTIPATED?

A Bottle-fed babies usually have firmer stools than breast-fed babies, and they can become quite constipated, with hard stools that may be painful for them to pass. Constipation can also result from underfeeding (for instance, if you're not feeding your baby enough or not letting her take all the milk she wants); dehydration (usually in hot weather or when she's feverish); and disorders such as an underactive thyroid gland and megacolon (an abnormally dilated gut). Both diseases are rare, and your baby's heel-prick test (see p. 15) should have ruled out thyroid disease. Constipation usually clears up if you give more formula and also offer your baby drinks of cooled boiled water. Your pediatrician may advise you to add extra water to the formula. If your baby is over four weeks old, you can also give baby fruit juices, diluted first with cooled, boiled water. Talk to your pediatrician if constipation persists.

SLEEPING

CAN I PREVENT CRIB DEATH ?

Crib death, or sudden infant death syndrome (SIDS), is not understood fully, but some factors are becoming clear. Although one can never be 100 percent sure of preventing crib death, the risk can be greatly reduced.

■ Don't smoke or take your baby into smoky atmospheres. Tobacco smoke can rob a baby of oxygen; it also lowers the ability of her lungs and bronchial tubes to resist infection.
■ Put your baby to sleep on her back. If she is on her side there is a danger she may roll onto her tummy on her own.
■ Don't let your baby get too hot. Never use electric blankets, sheepskin, or hot-water bottles, or put her crib next to a radiator or heater. Avoid crib bumpers, and don't clutter her crib or carriage with a large collection of soft toys.
■ Contact your doctor or pediatrician if you think your baby might be ill. Most illnesses are minor, but some are not and can overwhelm a young baby's immune system.

SLEEPING SAFELY
To prevent her from wriggling under the bedding, lay her so that her feet touch the foot of the crib.

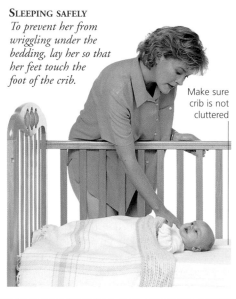

Make sure crib is not cluttered

Q WHERE SHOULD MY BABY SLEEP IN THE FIRST SIX WEEKS ?

A For the first four to six weeks, keep your baby near you—in your own room at night and near where you are in the daytime. During these weeks, she will be getting accustomed to the world outside the womb, just as you will be getting used to caring for her. You need to know if she vomits in the night, and she will be reassured by having you near. If she has to sleep alone in her own room, make sure you use a baby monitor so that you can hear her; go to her if she wakes.

Q WHICH TYPE OF BEDDING DOES SHE NEED ?

A She needs a sheet to cover the mattress; a sheet over her, tucked in to prevent it from covering her head; one or two washable blankets (not tucked in), depending on the temperature and time of year. Don't use a sheepskin, comforter, or sleeping bag for a very young baby—she could overheat, and fluffy bedding increases the incidence of SIDS.

Q WHAT'S THE IDEAL ROOM TEMPERATURE FOR BABIES TO SLEEP IN ?

A The room temperature should be at 65°F (18°C). It's very important not to overheat your baby's room.

Q SHOULD MY BABY'S ROOM ALWAYS BE KEPT QUIET ?

A Not necessarily. Babies can sleep in quite noisy environments and almost anywhere. It should never be necessary to tiptoe around when she is put down to sleep. However, a sudden noise can wake a baby, so don't put on the radio or begin to vacuum in a room where she is sleeping soundly.

Q WHAT'S THE BEST SLEEPING POSITION FOR MY BABY ?

A Newborn babies should sleep on their backs unless your doctor tells you otherwise. Your baby will not choke in this position, and it will also help to reduce the risk of crib death (see left). Her crib or bassinet should also be made up so that her feet are in contact with the end of it to stop her from wriggling down the bed, getting her head under the bedlinen, and suffocating or overheating.

Q HOW MUCH SLEEP DOES MY BABY NEED IN THE FIRST SIX WEEKS?

A Parents who expect their new baby to do nothing but sleep and feed are in for a rude awakening. Under the age of six weeks, the average baby may be awake for 4–10 hours in every 24. Your baby won't take all her sleep in one, single stretch; her waking time will be based around her feedings.

Q WHAT CAN I DO TO GET MY BABY TO SLEEP?

A Initially your baby will nod off whenever she needs to. You will not be able to get her to sleep whenever it suits you, any more than you can keep her awake on purpose. Many babies tend to doze off toward the end of a feeding, while others will still be awake but relaxed and will drift off eventually. If your baby can't relax and stays wide awake, you could try walking around with her in your arms or on your shoulder. This invariably seems to do the trick. If she cries when you put her down, pick her up and cuddle her until she starts to become drowsy, and then try again.

PARENT'S SURVIVAL GUIDE

SHE IS DEPENDENT ON A PACIFIER

Don't worry if your baby seems dependent on a pacifier—she won't need to have one forever. Pacifiers aren't as harmful as some people make out. They do not deform a baby's teeth or prevent speech development, unless they are used all the time. Recent research suggests sucking a pacifier may actually be better for a baby's teeth than sucking a thumb.

When should my baby use a pacifier?
Try to give your baby a pacifier only when she sleeps. Avoid giving her one when she doesn't need it. Her mouth should not be a permanent parking space for a pacifier.

Do I need to clean the pacifier regularly?
Pacifiers must always be sterilized (see p. 42) before they can be put in a baby's mouth. They should be resterilized every time they fall on the floor. It's unhygienic to lick a pacifier clean and then return it to your baby.

Q WHY DO SOME BABIES SEEM TO NEED LESS SLEEP THAN OTHERS?

A All babies differ. It is sometimes said, with some justification, that babies who are very active in the womb need less sleep than average after they are born. Because the amount of sleep needed depends partly on the maturity of the baby's brain, some people believe that very intelligent babies need less sleep. However, there's no hard evidence to support this view.

Q HOW CAN I GET MY BABY TO STAY ASLEEP FOR LONGER?

A You cannot prevent a baby from waking if she is hungry or no longer tired. However, you can prevent her from waking due to discomfort by making sure her clothes fit comfortably. Avoid tight stretchsuits—these can quickly become too small for a growing baby. Make sure that the room is at the correct temperature (65°F/18°C) and put a clean diaper on her shortly before she nods off.

Q WHAT'S THE BEST WAY TO HELP MY BABY SLEEP LONGER AT NIGHT?

A Attend to her swiftly at night. You'll still have night feedings for at least six weeks, but if you're lucky you may get six hours of uninterrupted rest. It helps to give her a last feeding before you go to bed. At night, put her in a crib rather than a bassinet or carriage, and give her a clean diaper. As the weeks pass, a darkened (not totally dark) room will help her distinguish day from night. From around one month, put on her nightclothes at bedtime.

Q WILL MY BABY SLEEP LONGER IF THE ROOM IS DARK?

A It's unlikely. A young baby can sleep when it's light, so you don't have to draw the curtains. However, she should not lie or sleep in direct sunlight because she could get too hot (or even burned, if the window is open). But it's a good idea to make a distinction between day and night so that by the time your baby is six weeks old, she develops a sense of when she's expected to sleep.

Q HOW CAN I HELP MY BABY SLEEP WHEN SHE HAS A COLD?

A You can raise the head of the bed slightly, if you can arrange to do this safely. Steam in your baby's room will help to decongest her air passages, as will a bath just before she goes to bed. If your baby coughs a lot or finds breathing difficult, ask your doctor for advice.

IS IT SAFE TO SWADDLE MY BABY?

Swaddling is a method of wrapping a baby in a way that mimics the security of the womb. The close wrapping will hold her arms in a comfortable position that feels secure for her. It may also help her sleep longer; if her limbs move or twitch while she's asleep, she is less likely to wake if she is swaddled. Some babies don't like it, and if yours doesn't, don't bother with it. Swaddling is safe in cold weather, but it is important that you always check her temperature by touching her skin. Be prepared to unwrap her immediately if she feels or looks hot rather than just being contentedly warm.

Use a baby blanket or a stretchy fabric crib sheet, folded diagonally

TAKING YOUR BABY TO BED

Q IS IT SAFE TO TAKE MY BABY TO BED WITH ME?

A The scientific jury is still out. There's no harm in taking her to bed with you for a cuddle and a feeding as long as you don't fall asleep. The AAP advises against sleeping with your baby since it can increase the risk of SIDS. The covers may get pulled up over your baby's head and she may suffocate or overheat, or she may fall out of bed.

Q HOW DO I KNOW IF MY BABY WILL GET TOO HOT IN MY BED?

A You can't know for sure, but minimize the risk by using a blanket instead of a quilt or comforter. Use a small pillow for yourself, and make sure your baby isn't overdressed. Stay awake while she is with you, which in practice means not taking your baby into bed for the whole night.

Q WILL I SQUASH MY BABY IF SHE SLEEPS WITH ME?

A You may if you sleep deeply, so don't take her to bed with you if you have taken alcohol or any sedative drugs, especially illegal drugs. Nor should you take her to bed if you smoke (even if it's not in the same room as her). If there's not much space in the bed, don't attempt to sleep with her. Don't put her on the outside edge, unless the mattress is on the floor—she could fall out of bed.

Q CAN I TAKE MY TWINS TO BED WITH ME?

A You will need a big bed for you all to have enough room. Even then, one twin will probably be near the edge because you'll have one baby on each side. There is a risk of dropping a baby over the side, so either have the mattress on the floor, or otherwise only take your twins to bed with you when you are taking an afternoon nap.

Q WHEN SHOULD I STOP TAKING MY BABY TO BED WITH ME?

A Many parents co-sleep for a year or more, but I think you should stop by the time she's six months old at the latest. The risk of overheating your baby decreases, but she will be bigger and also more able to stay awake at will. She could even be less tired than you and, since she will be increasingly mobile, accidents could happen after you have gone to sleep. By this age you could also disturb and wake each other throughout the night.

Q SHOULD I TAKE MY BABY TO BED WITH ME IF SHE'S ILL?

A Although there is no research to prove it, I think this could be risky. Overheating is the main hazard of taking your baby to bed with you. If she's feverish, she is even more likely to get too warm—perhaps dangerously so. Many parents prefer to take their sick baby to bed because they want to keep her close, but there are better ways. You could put her bassinet next to your bed, or move her crib into your bedroom.

PARENT'S SURVIVAL GUIDE
I'M STRUGGLING TO MANAGE WITH SO LITTLE SLEEP

When will my baby start sleeping through the night?
Some babies start sleeping through the night at three months; others are later, and some, mercifully, much earlier. However, it's rare to find a baby under six weeks who sleeps more than six hours at a stretch at night. For now, it may feel like one of life's darkest moments, but very few children "never" sleep through the night.

I'm so tired. How can I get some rest?
If you're not getting a full night's sleep, then you should acquire the habit of taking naps during the day. Unwind as soon as your baby dozes off— don't use this precious time for catching up on work or household chores. Learn to relax without sleep. A relaxation technique can help, or just listen to your favorite music.

I don't even have the energy to get dressed. How can I cope?
In the daytime, wear clothes rather than slopping around the house in night attire. A bathrobe may feel comfortable, but it blurs the distinction between your waking and sleeping hours and can perpetuate the nightmarish feel of this tiring time. If you're really at the end of your tether, ask a close friend or relative to take the baby for one night.

How can I catch up on my sleep?
When you put your baby to bed at night, turn in yourself—don't stay up late watching television. Ask your partner to get up in the night on a regular basis if possible. If you are breast-feeding, having your baby brought to you without getting up can be a little luxury every so often.

Do other parents feel the same as me?
Other new parents have the same problems with sleepless nights, but some people cope better than others. Adult sleep needs vary as much as a baby's. Some of us are crabby after anything less than eight hours a night, while some people can manage on as little as three hours. Appearances can be deceptive—other mothers who look as if they're flourishing may simply not be admitting how awful they feel. A little makeup can disguise the fact that they feel just as wretched as you do.

Can I take my baby to bed with me?
It may save you the hassle of getting up a lot to see to your baby. However, if you are exhausted you may sleep very deeply, which could be dangerous (see opposite).

Is my baby waking on purpose?
A baby's lack of sleep may indeed be torture for the parents, but it's not premeditated or deliberate. At this age her sleep–wake cycle is not under her control—nor under yours, unfortunately.

Can I do anything to make her sleep longer?
Not really. If your baby sleeps six hours at night, you may be able to gradually juggle these by advancing her feedings so that you reap maximum benefit from the hours of sleep she lets you have. You could try swaddling her to settle her down (see opposite), but don't let her become too warm. Beyond that, it's a matter of staying sane until she sleeps through the night. Half the battle is accepting that this is how she is. A parent who has coped successfully with a high-flying career can find this very tough, but, unlike employees, babies don't respond to orders! Once you learn to accept the situation, it will help you stay calm. This in turn will help you unwind more easily when you get the chance, enabling you to be more positive and less likely to become aggressive.

How can I get more done while she's awake?
This may seem like an impossible dream, but you'll get the hang of it. With a little practice, you'll be able to do most things while she's either on your arm or lying contentedly in a baby seat.

How can I cope with sleepless twins?
Although the situation will improve, for now it can be very hard. Try to involve your partner or a relative in helping at night. If you can afford paid help, get some—unfortunately, live-in help isn't always the boon one hopes for because a crying baby is more likely to wake the parent than someone else. However, you would at least have help around the house, and it may be a worthwhile expense. Try to get your babies' feedings synchronized as soon as you can. A routine is especially helpful to parents of multiples.

CRYING AND COMFORTING

Q WHAT ARE THE MAIN REASONS WHY
BABIES CRY ?

A Crying is the only way in which babies can
communicate. Parents often say they wish that
their baby didn't cry. However, without crying you
would never know what your baby needs, whether
it be food or relief from gas. Look at the chart
below, which lists the reasons for crying, as far as
they are known. The most common cause in a very
young baby is hunger, but other reasons include
being thirsty, too hot or too cold, having colic, or
feeling uncomfortable, bored, fearful, or tired. A
loud noise may also trigger a bout of crying, as can
overstimulation or lack of physical contact with a
parent. Cuddling your baby often stops the crying.

Q WHAT'S THE BEST WAY TO COMFORT
MY BABY ?

A Apart from attending to her basic needs, give
her contact with yourself. Many babies enjoy
skin-to-skin contact. Spend some unhurried time
smiling at her and talking to her. Hold her close to
you where she can hear your heartbeat; it may be
no coincidence that most mothers (rather than
fathers) hold their babies in their left arm, whether
they're right- or left-handed. Rocking your baby
gently while holding her is almost infallible—the
most soothing speed seems to be around once a
second. If you want to keep your hands free, use a
sling (see p. 20). You might consider a pacifier for
when she's really distressed.

REASONS FOR CRYING

CAUSES	COMMENTS
Hunger	The most common cause and the one you should try to deal with first. In these unsettled early days, even a feeding an hour ago does not preclude your baby from crying from hunger.
Thirst	This is very unusual in breast-fed babies, but more common in bottle-fed babies, especially in hot weather.
Heat	Your baby may look red in the face, or be sweating on the back of the neck.
Cold	Cold babies may cry, but they don't always. Feel the back of her neck, or her hands—if they're cold or look pale (even blue), she may be cold. If so, hold her to warm her up.
Discomfort	Because she can't turn over, a baby can get uncomfortable in the position in which she finds herself. Bear in mind also that her clothing—especially mittens and the feet of stretchsuits—may be too tight for her.
Pain	Colic is the most likely cause in a baby under six weeks, but there are other possibilities, such as diaper rash. If you're not sure what's wrong, contact your doctor or pediatrician.
Bowel movement	Some babies cry briefly when passing a stool, even if they're not constipated.
Shock or fear	Babies are sensitive creatures, and a sudden movement or a loud noise can often trigger crying.
Lack of contact	This is a common cause of crying in young babies, and the reason why picking a baby up and cuddling her will usually stop her from crying.
Boredom	This can happen at any time, but it is especially common from four weeks of age, when your baby may need a little action as well as human contact.
Fatigue	Babies cry when tired or overstimulated. They may be ready for sleep, not more fun.

Q COULD MY BABY BE CRYING FROM THE TRAUMA OF BIRTH ?

A It's possible. New babies (even unborn babies) can feel pain, and labor is a tremendous physical ordeal for the baby as well as the mother; it can even change the shape of a baby's skull temporarily. Birth is also an enormous emotional and environmental change, bringing a baby from a small confined space into a light world without 24-hour contact with her mother. No scientific research has entirely proven it, but it would be wrong to rule out birth trauma as a cause of crying in the first few days of life at least. However, as most parents find out, babies usually cry more after this period of time.

Q CAN I TELL WHAT'S WRONG FROM THE SOUND OF HER CRY ?

A You can't always tell, but there are distinctive types of cry, and you'll soon get more adept at knowing what she wants. You'll recognize the cry of hunger, which varies in pitch within each cry uttered. A grumbly cry may mean that she's tired. A loud, piercing or persistent cry that goes right through you may mean she's in pain; it could be colic (see p. 52), especially if she pulls her legs up.

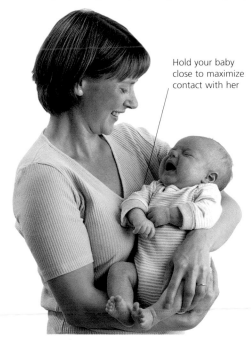

Hold your baby close to maximize contact with her

COMFORT YOUR BABY
Picking up your baby and holding her close may often calm her down when she cries. Smile at her and talk or sing to her softly to reassure her.

PARENT'S SURVIVAL GUIDE

MY BABY CAN'T BE CONSOLED

How do I figure out what she needs?
Go through all the possibilities in the chart (see opposite) and try to find the reason why your baby is crying. You may need to remove all her clothes to make sure that her diaper isn't too tight, or that a loose thread isn't cutting into one of her toes.

How do I know if she's in pain?
In the first two weeks, colic (see p. 52) is the most common cause of crying in newborn babies. However, other painful conditions include ear infection, strangulated hernia, and gastroenteritis. If you're concerned about your baby and think that she might be crying from pain, speak to your doctor without delay, especially if she is refusing feedings.

I've tried everything. Why does she still cry?
If your baby is overstimulated, she will go on crying unless you give her a chance to do nothing and go to sleep. Babies often do this more easily in someone else's arms.

Is it true that my moods will affect my baby?
It's thought that babies can pick up on other people's emotions at a very young age. They may be tuned in to their parents' moods or just responding to increased tension in the arms of the person who is holding them. So always try to stay calm, however much your baby cries.

Do I just have a baby who cries a lot?
Possibly—but remember that she will eventually grow out of it. If all else fails, take your baby out for a walk in her carriage or go for a drive in the car. When she nods off, you could park, turn off the engine, and relax for a while with a book before going back home. However, only do this as a last resort or your baby may come to depend on it.

Should I seek help?
Some parents have been known to lose their temper and harm their baby without meaning to. If you ever feel that you might injure your baby, call your doctor or contact a friend immediately. You must get help for your own sake as well as your baby's.

Q DO WOMB TAPES HELP TO STOP A BABY FROM CRYING ?

A Yes, they can help comfort a crying baby. These tapes mimic the sounds a baby hears before birth, but to be effective a baby usually has to start hearing womb tapes within a week or two of birth. Babies also sometimes enjoy the sound of a vacuum cleaner or untuned radio—although this is obviously less restful for you.

Q SHE CRIES LESS WITH OTHER ADULTS THAN WITH ME. IS IT MY FAULT ?

A No. Babies have a natural preference for their parent, but sometimes a friend or grandparent does not have the same pressures and therefore is more detached. If you often have to cope with her crying, or are worn down by the general demands of parenting, you may be stressed. Your baby may pick this up and cry more because she is in tune with your moods. Babies can also sense if a parent is ill or depressed. However, sometimes there's a simpler reason for her crying less with other people: she may just be enjoying a change of scenery.

Your baby may cry less with other adults

CALMING YOUR BABY
Babies can often sense their mother's mood and anxieties, and can cry because of this. You might find that the baby's father, or a friend or grandparent, can calm her when you are unable to.

WHAT IS COLIC ?

Colic is a pain from the gut (or colon) that some babies seem to experience within the first three months. Although one cannot tell for sure whether a baby has a stomachache, a diagnosis of colic is often made.

Does colic really exist?
Some people do not believe that colic exists but, like many other doctors and parents, I have seen enough babies with this type of crying to be convinced that it does.

What is the cause of colic?
Nobody knows for sure, but there are several theories. The most plausible one is that a young baby's intestines are still undeveloped and therefore oversensitive to the movement of food and air through the gut. The pain causes her to cry.

What are the symptoms of colic?
The most commonly recognized symptoms of colic are:
■ crying sessions that can last anything from 15 minutes to several hours, during which time it is very difficult to console your baby
■ your baby pulling her legs up while she cries
■ your baby crying excessively, regularly, especially in the evenings (so-called "evening colic")
■ the pattern of crying starting at around two weeks of age.

Could colic be my fault?
Almost certainly not. Some people blame parental anxiety, and some studies show that babies of professional middle-class parents have more colic. However, this is more likely to be because such parents are quicker in seeking help. Colic seems to be more common in boys than in girls, but medical research shows no convincing link between colic and bottle-feeding, birth weight, weight gain (or lack of it), or birth order.

When will it stop?
Colic usually stops within 10–12 weeks of starting. A few pediatricians call it three-month colic because it often stops by the time a baby is three months old. However, it can last until your baby is around four months old.

How can I relieve colic?

Burping your baby correctly (see p. 44) may help alleviate any air that is trapped in the gut and thereby reduce colic, although it's unlikely to prevent the symptoms altogether. If you're bottle-feeding your baby, watch the position of the bottle to be sure that she does not suck in any air. Some nipples that you can buy are labeled as being anticolic, with an inner ridge that acts as a valve. A few parents find them invaluable, but there is no real proof that they work. It is probably more important to make sure that the holes in the nipples aren't too small. Tiny holes are extremely frustrating for a baby because she has to suck harder and for longer. This in turn can increase the amount of air she swallows during feeding.

Are there any medicines that can help relieve my baby's colic?

There are several medicines that may help relieve colic. For instance, some baby colic drops contain dimethicone, which has an anti-foaming action on the stomach contents. It may be worth trying one of these medicines, although, of course, there is no guarantee that it will cure your baby's colic. However, you should never give a baby any medicine that is designed for older children or adults without checking with your doctor or a pharmacist first.

Should I give my baby a drop of wine or brandy?

No, definitely not. Her liver is too immature to deal with alcohol at this age (this would also be illegal in many countries). If you drink alcohol while breast-feeding, be aware that some alcohol can pass through your milk into your baby, and may harm her. I would recommend limiting yourself to one alcoholic drink per day.

My baby cries all the time. Could it be due to something that I'm eating?

It's possible, but babies who are prone to colic tend to have symptoms on most days, and your diet can obviously vary from day to day. However, eating citrus fruits or drinking the juices may worsen, or even perhaps trigger, colic in breast-fed babies. Another possible trigger is cow's milk, so try to eliminate milk and dairy products from your diet, but give up if this doesn't work within a few days—in the long term, this diet is too low in calcium for you to sustain for long.

If my baby is bottle-fed, should I change the formula?

Bottle-fed babies with colic may benefit from changing to a dairy-free formula, but there are many issues to consider. These include a possible allergy to soy, genetically modified ingredients in nondairy formula, and the cost of using a dairy-free formula, which can be more expensive. Talk to your doctor before deciding to change the formula because of colic.

Will holding my baby in a particular position help relieve colic?

Yes. Holding a colicky baby face down seems to relieve crying. According to guidelines on SIDS prevention, you shouldn't let your baby sleep on her stomach. But you can hold her face down over your arm and rub her back at the same time. You can walk around while you do this, but watch out for vomiting down your leg and onto your shoes.

COMPLEMENTARY THERAPIES

A baby massage (with baby oil) is usually soothing and well worth a try (see p. 122). However, you should avoid this if she is unwell or has a skin infection.

Homeopathy

There are some homeopathic remedies that may help to comfort a crying baby.

■ If a baby is bringing her legs up and likes pressure on her tummy, Colocynth (bitter cucumber) may help.

■ If a baby vomits and burps a lot and dislikes tummy pressure, Carbo vegetalis (vegetable charcoal) can be used instead.

■ An alternative, especially for very angry, screaming babies who strain while passing a stool, might be Nux vomica (poison nut).

Administering a homeopathic remedy

These homeopathic remedies are available from homeopathic practitioners and specialty stores. They come in tablet or granular form. Tablets need to be dissolved in a little cooled boiled water. The usual dose is half a teaspoon before feedings. If the colic improves, stop the treatment, but if it worsens, seek advice from your doctor.

WHEN YOUR BABY IS UNWELL

Q I THINK MY BABY MIGHT BE ILL. HOW CAN I BE SURE ?

A A baby who is ill can be subdued and lose her appetite. She may vomit or have loose, frequent stools. In babies, illnesses completely unrelated to the abdomen can cause diarrhea or vomiting. If she is feverish, she may feel hot when you touch her. Her diapers may be drier than normal because of dehydration. When she is ill, your baby may not be her usual self in a way that's hard to define. Many parents seem to develop a "sixth sense" to tell them when their baby is ill, and you, too, will soon learn to trust your instincts.

Q WHAT SHOULD I DO IF MY BABY IS UNWELL ?

A You need to find out why she's unwell, which will involve talking to, or visiting, your doctor or pediatrician. The younger the baby is, the more important it is not to delay. You'll also get appropriate advice on what to do: whether to change her feedings, give more water, or perhaps use a prescription medicine. Don't give a baby under six months acetaminophen or other over-the-counter medicines except on your doctor's advice. Avoid aspirin altogether until the age of 16 years—it is linked with a small but definite risk of a serious liver complication called Reye syndrome.

Q I'M NOT SURE THAT MY BABY IS ILL. WILL I BE WASTING MY DOCTOR'S TIME ?

A It isn't always easy for a new parent to know for sure when a baby is actually ill—occasionally, it's hard even for experienced parents. Doctors are human, and many of them are parents as well. They may be very busy, but they should take time to listen to you and understand your concern.

Q HOW CAN I GET MY DOCTOR TO UNDERSTAND MY WORRIES ?

A Describe any symptoms you've noticed. If you're worried about a specific disorder, such as eczema or meningitis, mention it explicitly. Your doctor may be able to put your mind at rest right away, in which case you can stop worrying. If you don't speak up, you'll never know if you and your doctor are on the same wavelength.

Q WILL SHE GET WORSE IF I TAKE HER TO THE DOCTOR'S OFFICE ?

A No. Contrary to what many people think, going to the doctor's office with a cough or fever does not instantly trigger double pneumonia. As long as your baby is protected from the elements, taking her to the doctor's office is safe. You should call the doctor's office first and tell the receptionist that you're bringing a young baby. Doctors should try to fit babies in so that you needn't wait once you get there. As for the risk of catching things from other patients, a good medical office will have a policy of keeping patients with rashes and infectious diseases away from the waiting room.

Q SOMETIMES I FEEL "FOBBED-OFF" BY MY DOCTOR. WHAT CAN I DO ?

A Some doctors can get irritated and impatient, especially if they are constantly having to deal with consultations that are apparently trivial. However, it is very difficult to respect a professional who fails to take you and your worries seriously, especially if you are a first-time parent and have many concerns about your baby's well-being. As a new parent, you and your family are embarking on a long-term relationship with health professionals, and it is therefore important that there should be a rapport between you. The relationship may never be "chummy"; however, it should allow you to say what you feel, and to respect your doctor's views. If you don't get along well, you should consider finding a different doctor.

Q WHICH CLOTHES ARE BEST FOR MY BABY TO WEAR WHEN SHE'S ILL ?

A It doesn't actually matter what clothes she wears; the most important thing is that she doesn't get too hot. Babies are not good at controlling their body temperature, especially when they have a fever, however slight it may be. It is very important not to overdress your baby when she's unwell. Always make sure that anyone looking after your baby keeps her lightly dressed when she's ill, regardless of any advice that you may get to the contrary—possibly from well-meaning older relatives.

WHEN SHOULD I CALL THE DOCTOR ?

If your baby seems unwell but you are uncertain whether you should contact your doctor, remember that it is always best to do so. Your doctor will agree that a false alarm every so often is much better than waiting until it's too late.

Symptoms to look for

If your baby has any of the symptoms listed here, you should see your doctor as soon as possible. Look for the following:

- a sunken fontanelle (can be a sign of dehydration)
- a bulging or swollen fontanelle
- diarrhea, especially if combined with vomiting. (taking a dirty diaper to the doctor can be helpful)

- screaming in pain
- a cough or rapid breathing
- refusing more than one feeding
- dry diapers when they should be wet
- vomiting on several occasions (more than just the usual regurgitating). If vomiting lasts for more than 12 hours, call the doctor
- a fever (or sweating despite being lightly clothed).

WHEN TO SEEK URGENT HELP

Seek urgent medical attention if your baby:

- has had a burn or other accident
- is blue or mottled, especially around the lips
- has had a seizure (convulsion)
- is unconscious, drowsy, or listless
- is floppy or lethargic
- vomits bile or blood.

Important

If you cannot contact your doctor immediately, you should go straight to the nearest hospital that has an emergency department. If your baby has potentially serious symptoms, you always need to act fast, so never delay in seeking medical help.

Q **HOW CAN I KEEP MY BABY FROM CATCHING COUGHS AND COLDS ?**

A In the first few years, your baby will catch almost everything that is going around. You can't entirely prevent this, but when she's very young, especially if she was premature, protect her the best you can. Breast-feed to give her valuable antibodies; avoid cigarette smoke; stay away from crowded places; and don't let people with infectious diseases handle her.

Q **IS THERE ANYTHING I CAN DO FOR MY BABY WHEN SHE HAS A COLD ?**

A Her nose will be blocked or runny, so your baby will have some trouble feeding and breathing at the same time. Be patient with her feedings. Wipe her nose with a cotton ball—tissues are usually too rough. Some doctors advise using saline nose drops and a nasal bulb syringe to remove mucus, but there is a small risk that they will drip down into the baby's chest and make her worse. Raise the head of the crib at night—if you can do so safely—with a firm pillow or a wedge under the mattress.

Q **WILL MY BABY NEED ANTIBIOTICS IF SHE HAS A COLD ?**

A Colds are caused by viruses and therefore there is no cure for them. Because of this, antibiotics will not help—so do not expect your doctor to prescribe them for a cold. However, you will need to visit your doctor if your baby is feverish, if she seems to be unwell, or if she will not take her feedings and fails to improve within a few days.

Q **ARE COMPLEMENTARY THERAPIES SAFE FOR MY BABY ?**

A Most homeopathic remedies are safe to use, but are not recommened for very young babies. For a stuffed-up nose, Kali bichromium (potassium bichromate) or Pulsatilla (wind anemone) is sometimes used. There is probably no harm in trying these as long as your baby has had a medical diagnosis and is otherwise well. But remember that it is vital to seek medical advice if a condition is potentially serious, and this is especially true with babies under six weeks old.

SPECIAL CARE BABIES

WHAT IS THE EQUIPMENT FOR ?

You may be alarmed to find that your baby is in the Neonatal Intensive Care Unit (NICU), not least because of the impressive technology on display.

The main items of equipment
- **Incubator** This controls temperature and humidity, creating, in effect, an artificial womb. Portholes allow access for nursing and medical care—and for you to touch your baby.
- **Monitors** These monitor your baby's pulse, respiration, and blood pressure, usually by continuous readout, and also her temperature and the amount of oxygen in her blood.
- **Ventilator** Helps pump air into your baby's lungs—there are several types.
- **Scanners** These may be ultrasound or CT (computerized tomography). They are sometimes used to see inside the baby's skull—this helps to diagnose the bleeding that premature babies can sometimes develop, and also helps to predict any future longer-term problems.

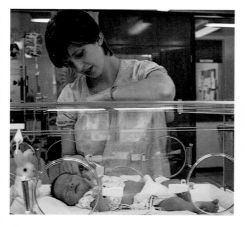

CARING FOR YOUR BABY
You can care for your baby while she's in Neonatal Intensive Care. You can talk to her and touch and stroke her through the portholes of the incubator.

Q WHAT EXTRA CARE DOES MY PREMATURE BABY NEED ?

A Because premature babies have missed out on some of the maturation time in the womb, they often need nourishment, warmth, and protection. Your baby's sucking may be underdeveloped and she may therefore need to be fed via a feeding tube or into a vein. She will also be more prone to low blood glucose levels than a baby who was full-term because her liver is immature. Her fat stores are fewer, so she gets cold easily. Her immune system isn't fully functional yet, but an incubator can shield her from some infections and provide warmth, too. She may also need other help—for instance, with her breathing. This is because a baby's premature lungs may be deficient in a chemical called surfactant, which is needed so that air can enter the lungs easily. She may therefore be on a ventilator.

Q WHAT IS THE NEONATAL INTENSIVE CARE UNIT ?

A Newborn babies who are premature or sick are admitted to the Neonatal Intensive Care Unit (NICU) where they are evaluated. This unit is staffed by specially trained nurses and pediatricians. Often, there is one nurse to every one to four babies, as well as sophisticated equipment (see left). When the babies are stable and no longer need NICU care, they are moved to the Intensive Care Unit (sometimes called the "Stepdown Unit"). Sometimes a baby has to be transferred to an NICU in a larger center, so do not be alarmed if this happens.

Q IS SHE IN PAIN WHEN THINGS ARE DONE TO HER ?

A It is not always possible to give painkilling drugs to a baby, so she may feel pain sometimes, just as she would if she had a heel-prick blood test (see p. 15)—but the pain is often short-lived. If your baby wriggles and writhes, it does not necessarily mean that she is in pain; this can be a natural reflex. However, if you are concerned, then ask the nurse or doctor who is caring for your baby whether she might be in pain and what measures can be taken to relieve it if she is.

Q WILL MY BABY ALWAYS BE WEAK BECAUSE SHE WAS PREMATURE ?

A Usually the answer is "No." The pediatrician will tell you if your baby is likely to get recurrent infections and what you should do about this. Ask if you are unsure.

Q WILL MY BABY'S DEVELOPMENT BE DELAYED BECAUSE SHE WAS PREMATURE ?

A Her rate of development won't necessarily be delayed at all, but leaving the womb earlier means she started off at a different point. If she was born eight weeks premature, then at, say, six months she'll be more like a four-month-old baby. Any discrepancy becomes less obvious with time.

Q CAN I STILL BREAST-FEED IF MY BABY IS IN INTENSIVE CARE ?

A Yes. However, sucking reflexes don't develop until around 30 weeks or so of pregnancy, so a baby born before this may not be able to suck. Even babies born later than this sometimes don't manage well with a real or rubber nipple, so you may have to express milk for her to have via a tube leading from her nose into her stomach. Breast milk is still the most suitable food for a premature or vulnerable baby, but vitamin D and phosphate may be added. If she is unable to digest food yet, she may be fed intravenously (with a drip running into a vein).

Q HOW WILL I COPE WHEN SHE LEAVES SPECIAL CARE ?

A Make sure you understand what to do, how often to feed her, what medicines to give her, and when to return for a follow-up appointment. You should get clear instructions on who to contact if you run into problems. Normally this is your doctor, but you may be told to bring your baby back to the hospital if she's not well. After leaving the Intensive Care Unit, your baby may go to a unit offering intermediate care in the hospital, giving you the chance to care for her yourself under some guidance before taking her home. Don't feel guilty about being concerned or nervous: parents whose babies haven't been to an Intensive Care Unit can also feel uncertain about their parenting abilities.

Q I'M AFRAID MY BABY MIGHT DIE. IS IT RISKY TO GET TOO ATTACHED ?

A It is natural for every parent of a special care baby to fear death; if possible, try not to worry, since you probably won't lose her. However, parents who have been bereaved certainly seem to treasure the time they spent with their baby. It is easier to mourn if you have some memories. Get as close as you can and create special memories, whether these are photos of your baby or footprints. It is even possible that contact with you can help your baby survive.

PARENT'S SURVIVAL GUIDE

I'M VERY WORRIED ABOUT MY SPECIAL CARE BABY

Is it normal to worry about my baby?
When your baby is in a Neonatal Intensive Care Unit, it's normal to worry and it's normal for both mothers and fathers to show their emotions. This is a sign that you care, so don't be afraid of letting it show—the staff are used to it. The Neonatal Intensive Care Unit will have a counselor with whom you can talk over your concerns.

Will my baby survive?
Obviously, the answer to this depends on the exact circumstances of your baby. Overall, about seven percent of babies are born premature—that is, before 37 weeks of pregnancy. A very premature baby who is born at, say, 28 weeks, faces more of a struggle than one who arrives only a week or so before her due date.

How can I keep my hopes up?
It is worth remembering that the level of neonatal care help is now better than it has ever been. More and more babies are surviving, and fewer have long-term problems. Every unit has a collection of photographs and letters from parents whose little one is now thriving. So try to keep your hopes up, and let your baby feel your optimism.

Should I ask about my baby's progress?
Yes. When you have any questions about your baby's progress, ask the nurse or the doctor in charge of the unit. Don't make comparisons with other babies. You'll probably get to know other parents who have babies in Neonatal Intensive Care, and these bonds are important at times of crisis.

HELP FOR PARENTS

Q I FEEL EXHAUSTED LOOKING AFTER MY BABY. IS THIS NORMAL?

A Yes. Few new parents are wholly prepared for the reality of having a baby, whatever they may have read in books or heard from other more experienced parents. The fact is that looking after a young baby is usually exhausting, especially for a mother who has recently given birth (more so if she has had a cesarean or a general anesthetic). To get through this tiring time, something has to give. Make sure that it's not you!

PARENT'S SURVIVAL GUIDE

I FEEL VERY NEGATIVE

Is there something wrong with me?
No. Many mothers-to-be think that a new baby should bring pure, unalloyed happiness. After the birth, if they're not brimming with joy as a new parent, they think there is something wrong with them. Well, there isn't. The reality may involve sleepless nights, sore, leaking breasts, a sagging belly, and no sex drive. You may feel ambivalent, especially if you were unwell in pregnancy, the birth was difficult (or unplanned), finances are tight, or the baby was not the sex you had hoped for. It's normal to feel less than ecstatic and to doubt your capabilities. Things will improve, however, and parenting will become more rewarding once your baby responds to you.

Is it my fault that I feel so low?
No. Try not to blame yourself for how you feel; society often has unrealistic expectations of how you should feel and behave as parents. Not everyone can be the perfect parent. Talk to other parents. They will soon admit that they have negative feelings at least some of the time. Try to get out every day—sitting at home can make things worse. Discuss your concerns with your partner. He may have similar worries and might welcome the chance to talk them over. Talk to your doctor or midwife if things don't improve—you could be sliding into depression.

Q I FEEL SO TEARFUL ALL THE TIME. IS IT JUST ME?

A It's not just you. Emotional ups and downs are normal after having a baby. The "downs" often coincide with the third or fourth day after the birth. Even though you may cry for no apparent reason, there's no need to feel silly—"baby blues" are probably due to hormonal fluctuations. If your mood doesn't improve within a few days, you may be suffering from postpartum depression.

Q I FEEL VERY LOW. IS IT POSTPARTUM DEPRESSION?

A Probably not—you may just have "baby blues." Postpartum depression is more severe and lasts longer. Apart from tearfulness, there's usually low self-esteem and also a feeling of hopelessness. Everything seems an effort and there is little to enjoy. To some extent, these feelings are normal in new mothers, so the diagnosis of postpartum depression can sometimes be missed when it's mild.

Q I HAVE HEARD THE PHRASE "PUERPERAL PSYCHOSIS." WHAT EXACTLY IS IT?

A Puerperal psychosis is more severe and less common than postpartum depression (it follows only one birth in every 1,000 or so). It tends to start abruptly within a few days or a week of having the baby. Without your realizing it, your behavior may become irrational and erratic, and your logical thought nonexistent. Speech may be chaotic and hard to follow. Hallucinations can occur, as in schizophrenia. Puerperal psychosis always needs expert psychiatric treatment, often in the hospital in a Special Mother and Baby Unit, but the outlook is usually good.

Q WHAT CAN I DO TO HELP MYSELF COPE WITH LOOKING AFTER MY BABY?

A Reassess your priorities so that you conserve your energy for what really matters—your baby. If you were a workaholic before the birth, you will simply have to be more relaxed now. Your home does not have to be perfect (but it should be hygienic). When your baby sleeps, try not to rush around cleaning—put your feet up and spend the time unwinding. Eat well and try to do your postpartum exercises.

WHAT CAN I DO ABOUT POSTPARTUM DEPRESSION?

How long will I have postpartum depression?
If untreated, postpartum depression can linger, perhaps even for years. However, with treatment it usually improves within a matter of weeks.

Could I have prevented it somehow?
Probably not. Women who are unprepared for birth or have little social support are more likely to develop postpartum depression. However, nobody knows for sure the cause (or causes) of postpartum depression, so it's difficult to see how it could be prevented in any one case.

Will it affect my relationship with my baby?
It could if you don't get treatment. Feeling low can sap your energy, impair your ability to cope, and color all your relationships, including the relationship with your baby. Postpartum depression can also be a factor in child abuse. So if you think you have it, you must get medical help as soon as possible, for your sake as well as your family's. Approach your doctor and explain how you feel.

Will I need medication?
You might. Some mothers improve with good solid support from their doctor or with counseling on a more formal basis. However, other women need treatment with antidepressant drugs. Unlike tranquilizers, these aren't addictive, even over several months, and they can make a world of difference to your well-being.

Can I breast-feed if I am taking medication?
Yes. It's usually possible even if you're on anti-depressants. However, some of these pass into the milk, so tell your doctor you're breast-feeding—it will affect the choice of antidepressant prescribed.

Will I get postpartum depression again when I have my next baby?
Not necessarily. However, the more severe your depression is this time, the more likely you are to develop it with future births. However, awareness of the condition may mean that in subsequent pregnancies you'll have more support and help, which could prevent depression from recurring.

Q HOW CAN I GET MY PARTNER MORE INVOLVED?

A Both parents need to adjust to having a baby, and some find it hard. Don't just delegate the less appealing chores, such as diaper-changing and bottle-washing—get him involved in every aspect of her care. Encourage him to hold the baby; don't wait until she is bigger before letting him bond with her. He can carry her in a sling or give her a bath. Show him what to do; try not to criticize.

Q HOW CAN I MAKE TIME FOR MY PARTNER AS WELL AS MY BABY?

A There will be times when you wonder if you'll ever return to the relationship that you and your partner had before the birth. You will, but it'll probably be on a different footing. A lot of men feel sidelined or even rejected when a baby arrives, which is understandable, since the mother has a new and very time-consuming role. Maybe you won't get around to doing things together for a while, but try. Rent a movie, talk to each other, and plan for later. Let your partner know that you still care even if you have no time or energy for sex right now. Whatever you do, don't ignore him.

Q I'M OVERWHELMED BY MY TWINS. HOW CAN I POSSIBLY MANAGE?

A The first six weeks is probably the most difficult period that you will have with your twins. But don't despair—you can manage. Get into a routine that cuts out any nonessential tasks, and accept any reasonable offers of help from friends and family. Someone may be able to shop for you or perhaps take care of one or both babies. Make time to enjoy your babies and get to know them. They will soon grow up. Don't be too influenced by advice from parents of single children. They are not in your position, and can't really comprehend what it is like for you.

Q WHAT'S THE BEST WAY OF DEALING WITH ALL THE ADVICE I'M GIVEN?

A It's amazing how everyone, including people you hardly know, suddenly become experts on baby care. You certainly can't put all of the advice into practice because some of it will conflict with what someone else said five minutes ago. Just take on board what seems sensible. Always use solid information, not hearsay, to help you develop your own style of parenting.

GROWTH AND DEVELOPMENT

Q DO I NEED TO TAKE MY BABY FOR CHECKUPS?

A Yes. She needs to be weighed regularly during the first six weeks, and she also needs to be examined by your pediatrician at six to eight weeks.

Q HOW OFTEN SHOULD MY BABY BE WEIGHED?

A On average, every two weeks or so, but it depends on her circumstances. A very small baby may need weighing more often, as will a baby who fails to put on weight at the expected rate.

WEIGHING TWINS

How often should my twins be weighed?
You may be tempted not to visit the pediatrician because it can be very stressful taking two babies along at the same time to be weighed. However, twins need weighing just as often as single babies, and sometimes more often, because they are generally smaller and lighter even if they weren't born prematurely.

How can I make visiting the doctor easier?
■ Ask if you can bring the carriage or stroller into the room where the weighing of the babies takes place. It is easier than carrying both babies in your arms.
■ Take a friend along to help you.
■ Ask someone at the doctor's office to hold one baby while you deal with the other one.
■ Weigh the babies fully clothed, having taken an identical outfit to weigh, then subtract that from each baby's clothed weight.

Should I worry if their weights are very different?
Not usually. Parents often tend to worry about this because any difference in the size of their twins is very obvious at a glance, and they feel that their babies should be the same weight. However, twins are often different in weight and this is quite normal. As long as each baby seems happy and is growing well in her own right, you needn't be concerned.

Q HOW QUICKLY SHOULD MY BABY GAIN WEIGHT?

A For the first three months or so, she should gain approximately 6 oz a week (around 150–200 g). This, as generations of doctors have learned, is an ounce every day except Sundays.

Q MY BABY'S WEIGHT DROPPED AT FIRST. SHOULD I WORRY?

A New babies, whether breast- or bottle-fed, do not take much food in the first few days of life. It's therefore normal to lose a little weight during this time. She may lose 7 oz (200 g) or more. Don't worry as long as she regains her birth weight by the time she is 10 days old.

Q MY BABY IS CHUBBIER THAN OTHERS. WILL SHE BE FAT?

A Not necessarily. She may have a chubby look, simply because that's how she's built—or the other babies with whom you've compared her may be underfed or born premature. In general, a baby will take the feedings she needs. She may, however, grow too fat if she is fed whether she's hungry or not. But even if you think she is fat, you should never try to make her lose weight.

Q WHAT SHOULD MY BABY WEAR WHEN SHE IS WEIGHED?

A It's usual to weigh a baby in an undershirt and diaper, to prevent her from getting distressed by lying naked on the scale, but for a more accurate reading, you may have to undress her completely. An alternative is to take along another identical diaper and undershirt and weigh these, then subtract their weight from the total weight of your baby clothed in her diaper and undershirt.

Q WHAT DOES IT MEAN IF MY BABY IS VERY LONG?

A It may mean that she's destined to be tall but, generally, a baby's length is not a very useful predictor of adult height. And, often, the length measurements can be wrong. Babies of this age lie curled up, and measuring length depends on how far the baby's legs can be stretched. I have often seen wildly inaccurate length measurements, even when they have been taken in the hospital.

Q DOCTOR'S APPOINTMENTS ARE AN ENDURANCE TEST. WHAT CAN I DO ?

A Try to undress your baby as little as possible and talk softly to her throughout. Although the doctor's office is unfamiliar, she'll get used to it. Right after weighing, offer her a feeding. Keep your appointments but try not to worry too much about the process of visiting the doctor's office, and do not place too much importance on her weight compared to that of other babies.

Q HOW IMPORTANT IS MY BABY'S HEAD CIRCUMFERENCE ?

A Head circumference is very important. It is an indication of your baby's growing potential. The rate of growth in head circumference also matters—a rapidly increasing measurement can be unhealthy and may even indicate hydrocephalus (water on the brain). If there's any cause for concern, your baby will be measured and weighed more often.

WHY WILL MY BABY BE MEASURED ?

To ensure that you and your pediatrician can assess your baby's progress, her weight, length, and head circumference will be plotted on growth charts.

What is a growth chart?

This is a graph that shows "percentile curves" based on measuring large numbers of babies. If your baby's weight is on the 25th percentile curve, for example, it means that 75 percent of all babies weighed would be heavier and 25 percent would be lighter. Or if your baby's weight is on the 9th percentile curve, it means that 9 percent of babies will be lighter and 91 percent heavier. The same goes for the other two important measurements— length and head circumference. Boys are slightly bigger and heavier than girls, even as babies, so there are different charts for each sex. Breast-fed babies tend to weigh a little less than formula-fed babies. Isolated results don't matter much; steady growth is much more important at this stage.

YOUR BABY'S PROGRESS

A rough guide to your baby's development.

AGE	MEASUREMENTS
At birth	Weight: anything between 3–10¾ lbs (2.3– 4.9 kg) Head circumference: between 12–15¼ in (31–39 cm) Length: between 17½–22½ in (45–57 cm)
At four weeks	Weight: between 6½–13 lbs (3–6 kg) Head circumference: between 13–15¾ in (33–40 cm) Length: between 19–23½ in (48–60 cm)
At six weeks	Weight: between 7–14 lbs (3.2–6.5 kg) Head circumference: between 13¼–16½ in (34–42 cm) Length: between 20–24¼ in (51–62 cm)

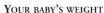

YOUR BABY'S WEIGHT
Your pediatrician or doctor will weigh your baby regularly to make sure that her weight is steady and she is develping normally. If you're concerned about your baby's progress or growth, talk to your pediatrician or doctor.

THE FIRST DEVELOPMENT CHECKUP

At about four to six weeks your baby will have her first development checkup since birth. This will be carried out by your doctor or pediatrician. In some places, this checkup might be done at eight weeks instead, together with her first immunization.

What do I need to take to the first checkup?
Take a spare diaper and the changing bag and a bottle if you're bottle-feeding. Dress your baby in something easy to put on and take off—not to make things quicker for the doctor but to spare your baby unnecessary handling. You want her to be in a cooperative frame of mind so the doctor can assess her social skills and development.

My baby was premature. When should she have her first check up?
Six to eight weeks after birth, but the doctor will make allowances for her prematurity.

I missed the first checkup. What should I do?
Have the examination as soon as you can. It is still better to have it late than not at all.

Will my baby need immunizations?
Yes. Without them, she is at risk of serious diseases such as hepatitis B, polio, diphtheria, tetanus, pertussis, and types of meningitis. Immunization means giving vaccines—by mouth or injection. A vaccine stimulates the body's immunity against a specific infection (see p. 213). She'll be given her first immunizations at birth. Not all vaccines are 100 percent effective, but they are all worth having.

WHAT CAN MY BABY DO AT SIX WEEKS OLD?

A newborn baby is floppy and has little control over her body, but has many primitive reflexes (see p. 14). By six weeks, things have changed: she is losing some of the early reflexes and, at the same time, learning to control her body voluntarily. The stepping reflex is gone and, though she may still have a grasp reflex, it is now much weaker. She will have better limb control and may be able to lift her head slightly when lying down. She will generally be more responsive and may cry less than before. Subtly but noticeably, she is also becoming better at communicating.

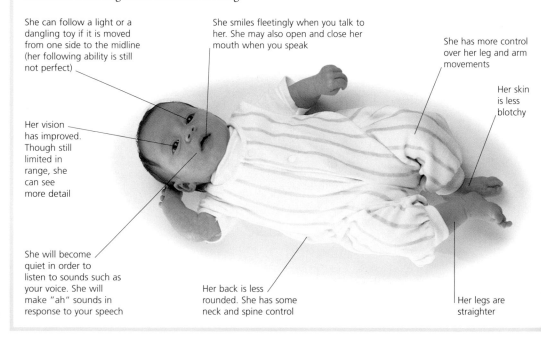

She can follow a light or a dangling toy if it is moved from one side to the midline (her following ability is still not perfect)

She smiles fleetingly when you talk to her. She may also open and close her mouth when you speak

She has more control over her leg and arm movements

Her skin is less blotchy

Her vision has improved. Though still limited in range, she can see more detail

She will become quiet in order to listen to sounds such as your voice. She will make "ah" sounds in response to your speech

Her back is less rounded. She has some neck and spine control

Her legs are straighter

WHAT'S THE DOCTOR LOOKING FOR?

The doctor will be checking your baby's weight, length, and head circumference. She will also examine your baby for:

- congenital heart disease
- hip dysplasia (dislocation)
- crossed eyes, cataracts, and other eye disorders
- hearing problems
- undescended testes (in boys)
- development so far, especially behavior and social response, muscle tone, and head control. Although you should mention any concerns to your doctor as they arise, the first checkup is also an opportunity to talk through any concerns together.

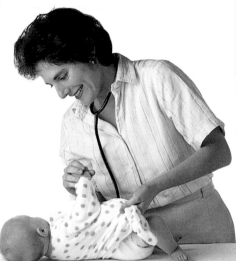

HIP CHECK
Your doctor will feel her hips to check for possible dislocation.

LIMBS AND MUSCLE TONE
The doctor will undress your baby to check muscle tone and how she moves her limbs.

HEAD CONTROL
The doctor will hold your baby in the air to see if she holds her head in line with her body.

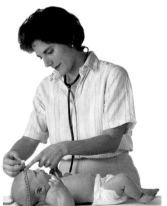

HEAD CIRCUMFERENCE
Your baby's head circumference will be measured to check for normal growth.

MUSCLE CONTROL
The doctor will also check how much control your baby has over her posture.

YOUR POSTPARTUM CHECKUP

Do I need a checkup as well?
Yes. You need to be examined at about six weeks, too, to check that your uterus has returned to its normal size, that your perineum is recovering, and that you're coping with breast-feeding. You and your doctor can discuss contraception then.

I had a cesarean. Do I still need a checkup?
Yes. The size of the uterus is still important. In fact, it contracts less well after a cesarean than after a vaginal delivery. Your doctor will also check on how the incision is healing. You can also discuss contraception at this checkup.

FEEDING AND NUTRITION

Your baby needs the **right nutrition** in order to grow into a thriving, contented child and eventually into a healthy adult. For this reason, feeding and nutrition can become **emotional subjects** for both parent and child. This chapter is full of **down-to-earth advice** on feeding and nutrition that will be relevant from when your baby is six weeks old through to early childhood. Common concerns are addressed and **solutions** offered on everything from breast- and bottle-feeding, weaning, and preparing **healthy, balanced meals** to food safety, allergies, dealing with picky eaters, and helping your child learn how to feed himself.

FEEDING A YOUNG BABY

Q WHEN DO I NEED TO START GIVING MY BABY MORE THAN JUST MILK ?

A Ideally, breastfeeding should be complemented with solid foods from 6–12 months, but solids may be introduced at four months. Before then, your baby is not physically ready for solid foods.

Q MY BABY IS GETTING BIGGER. WHAT IS A GOOD BREAST-FEEDING POSITION ?

A You can use the same breast-feeding positions as before, but ensure that you have plenty of support for your arm and your baby's increasingly heavy body. The "football hold" (see p. 34) will become more difficult as his body lengthens, but breast-feeding should be easier by now, and you will find that you can even get up and do things while feeding him if necessary. If you have to move around, make sure you hold him securely.

Q IS IT POSSIBLE TO OVERFEED A BREAST-FED BABY ?

A The received wisdom for this question is "No" because babies only suck when they are hungry. However, my own view, and that of some pediatricians, is that it could happen, although it is so rare that you probably do not need to worry about it. You can, for instance, overfeed a breast-fed baby if you give him something else as well as your breast milk. This usually happens only if solids are introduced too early (see p. 68). A baby who sucks for comfort could take more breast milk than he needs because your breasts will be stimulated to produce more milk by his sucking. However, the majority of breast-fed babies are not overfed.

Q MY BABY IS TEETHING. WILL HE BITE ME WHEN I FEED HIM ?

A He may. His gums can be sore at around six months of age, just before a tooth erupts, but teething can happen earlier. He'll probably be gnawing everything within reach at this stage, and your nipple is no exception. Just react naturally: yelp with pain, take your baby off the breast for a few minutes, and say "No" to him. He'll soon stop biting. Offer a teething ring between feedings.

Q I'M GOING BACK TO WORK. HOW CAN I COMBINE BREAST AND BOTTLE ?

A If your milk supply is abundant, simply feed your baby at the times you want to, letting him suck as long as he wants. If you are concerned about the amount of milk you are producing (fatigue can reduce the supply once you return to work), express milk at work (see p. 38). Your employer should provide the time and the place for you to do this. Make sure you take all the equipment you need, and keep it clean.

Q WHEN SHOULD I STOP BREAST-FEEDING MY BABY ?

A It depends on you and your lifestyle—there is no precise time. Babies develop a strong immune system if they are breast-fed for a year, so from this point of view, the longer you can breast-feed him, the better. By 12 months he will be taking in plenty of nourishment from solids and will also be drinking from a baby cup. If you leave it up to your baby, he'll probably wean himself off the breast at one year or even later.

PARENT'S SURVIVAL GUIDE

MY BREAST-FED BABY IS REFUSING THE BOTTLE

This sometimes happens, especially if your baby gets to six weeks without ever having had a bottle. Never force a bottle on him. He will get upset and may even choke. Try one of the following:
■ ask someone else to offer your baby the bottle (leave the room yourself if necessary to avoid distracting him while he bottle-feeds)
■ offer the bottle while walking around the room with your baby, gently jiggling him as you walk
■ try putting some expressed milk in the bottle instead of formula
■ try a different nipple on the bottle—silicone nipples tend to taste better than rubber (latex)
■ if he's nearly six months, try a baby cup instead.

Q **I WANT TO STOP BREAST-FEEDING. HOW SHOULD I DO THIS?**

A You should do this gradually, allowing up to three weeks in which to stop. If you're still fully breast-feeding, offer a bottle of formula at the feeding at which you have least milk. This is usually in the early evening. A few days later, drop another feeding from the daily schedule. Don't rush the process. The last feeding of the day should be the last to go, as it is the most satisfying for you both.

Q **CAN MY BABY GO STRAIGHT FROM THE BREAST TO DRINKING FROM A CUP?**

A You may be able to transfer your baby straight to a cup. Babies as young as three months sometimes take feedings from a baby cup, which has a cover and a spout. Choose a spout with small holes to prevent choking, and hold the cup for your baby. At first most of the milk will dribble out of his mouth, so put a bib under his chin.

Q **MY BABY WANTS TO HOLD THE BOTTLE HIMSELF. SHOULD I LET HIM?**

A Not until he's at least five months old. Keep a close eye on him and a hand on the bottle. Until he is more adept, he could drop it on the floor and you'd have to change the nipple. Don't leave him alone with his bottle—he could choke.

HOW DO I FEED MY TWINS?

Your twins will get increasingly lively and your arms will get tired, whether you are bottle- or breast-feeding.

If you are bottle-feeding
Put one twin in your arm and the other leaning on your leg, the sofa, or cushions next to you. You could also put both in car seats, bouncing cradles, or on a sofa while you kneel or sit on the floor facing them. As they learn to sit up, bottles become easier, but make sure the babies are safe and cannot roll onto the floor.

If you are breast-feeding
Continue with the "football hold" position (see p. 34), making sure their heads are well supported. Look after yourself so that you get plenty of food, fluids, and much-needed rest. This helps maintain your milk supply.

NIGHT FEEDINGS

Q **MY BABY GAVE UP NIGHT FEEDINGS AT TWO MONTHS. WHY IS HE WAKING AGAIN?**

A There are spurts in appetite at around six weeks, three months, and again between 4–6 months. Waking up again in the night at 4–6 months may mean he's ready for solids. If he's a big baby, his nutritional needs may have outstripped what milk alone (formula or breast) can provide.

Q **WHEN WILL MY BABY STOP WANTING NIGHT FEEDINGS?**

A Many babies continue with night feedings until the age of six months or so, but some give up earlier and some later. However, this may not give you uninterrupted nights: your baby may wake in the night for reasons other than hunger— such as teething, or because he is ill.

Q **HOW CAN I ENCOURAGE HIM TO GIVE UP NIGHT FEEDINGS?**

A After four months, offer water at night or diluted milk (see p. 84) if you're sure he's getting enough milk during the day and gaining weight. If he's bottle-fed, he shouldn't be draining the bottle at any feeding. It helps if he can fall asleep by himself—put him in bed while he's awake. Help him distinguish night from day (see p. 82).

Q **IS IT A GOOD IDEA TO GIVE HIM A BIG FEEDING BEFORE HE GOES TO SLEEP?**

A No. You can make sure that he goes to bed fully satisfied by offering a feeding shortly before bedtime, but, because you can't slow down his digestive process, this may not stop him from waking in the night. Many parents try to cram a baby full of milk just before bed in the vain hope of obtaining a night of unbroken sleep, but you can't make your baby take more than he needs—if you do he's liable to bring it back up or get a tummy ache. Some parents add a little baby cereal to their unweaned baby's bottle but you should never do this; it is very bad for the baby's digestive system.

Q **WILL HE NURSE LONGER AT NIGHT BECAUSE HE'S BREAST-FED?**

A The official view is "No." However, breast-fed babies are slightly more likely to clamor for a night feeding because they get more comfort at the same time. Mothers are also more likely to offer the breast to a crying baby because it's easy.

WEANING YOUR BABY

Q **WHAT EXACTLY DOES THE TERM "WEANING" MEAN ?**

A Weaning means introducing solid foods to your baby. Some people also use the term to mean changing from breast to bottle, but this is very confusing unless it is made explicit by adding the words "from breast to bottle."

Q **SOME PEOPLE SAY SOLID FOOD SHOULD START AT SIX WEEKS. IS THIS CORRECT ?**

A No. Babies aren't developmentally ready to take solids at six weeks. Their kidneys and gut are still immature so solid foods are not right for them nutritionally either. There is also evidence that if solids are started too early they can lead to a higher risk of developing food allergies. This is certainly true of a wheat allergy called celiac disease (gluten enteropathy). Research also shows that babies weaned early may cough more and breathe noisily.

Q **WHEN SHOULD I BEGIN TO WEAN MY BABY ?**

A You can start introducing solid foods when he is between four and six months of age. (Breast-fed babies don't need to be weaned until six months of age.) At first, solids will be extras to his milk feedings; they won't make up an appreciable part of your baby's feeding until he is having three meals a day.

Q **CAN I LEAVE WEANING MY BABY UNTIL HE'S A YEAR OLD ?**

A I wouldn't leave weaning him longer than six months, even if he was premature, unless you are advised otherwise by your doctor. If you wean too late, your baby may become deficient in valuable nutrients, such as iron, zinc, and vitamins A and D, because both breast milk and formula are relatively poor in these nutrients. Weaning too late also means that you will miss a window of opportunity when your baby is developmentally ready to start experimenting with solids and new tastes. Finally, he needs to chew solid food in order to help his jaw and his speech to develop.

Q **HOW WILL I KNOW WHEN MY BABY IS READY FOR WEANING ?**

A Your baby is probably ready if, between the ages of four and six months, he is waking for night feedings again, still seems hungry after a feeding, or is gaining weight less quickly.

Q **MY BABY IS CHEWING EVERYTHING. IS HE READY FOR SOLIDS ?**

A Not necessarily. At three months of age, all babies start putting their hands into their mouths, and they also use their mouths for exploring things (see p. 147). Alternatively, your baby may be chewing a lot because his gums are sore from teething. Teething can also make babies drool a great deal (see p. 127).

Q **SHOULD I CUT DOWN ON HIS MILK WHEN HE STARTS EATING SOLID FOOD ?**

A No. His first tastes of solid food are just that: tastes. He won't be taking enough to count yet. Continue with the same amount of milk feedings.

Q **WHAT'S THE BEST TIME OF DAY TO START GIVING HIM SOLID FOOD ?**

A When it is convenient to wash him afterward! Try to pick a time when your baby is fully awake, yet not desperate for his milk. Avoid early evening in case he reacts badly to the food and wakes during the night. You can give solids either before his breast- or bottle-feeding, or let him have some milk first, then take a taste of solids before going back to the rest of his milk.

Q **WILL STARTING WEANING HELP HIM TO SLEEP THROUGH THE NIGHT ?**

A Opinions differ but I'd say not. The amounts of food that are eaten at this age are so small that solids can't really make your baby sleep more. I think it's a coincidence that babies start giving their parents a whole night's uninterrupted sleep around the time that they're weaned. It's probably just because a baby is more settled then.

Q **SHOULD I START GIVING HIM MORE FLUIDS AS WELL AS FOOD ?**

A When he's eating solid foods, your baby will be more thirsty, so he may need extra fluids. You can give him baby fruit juice diluted with cooled, boiled water, and preferably offered in a baby cup. Only offer it to him at mealtimes when the flow of saliva is greatest. Other baby drinks can be high in sugar and are unnecessary. You can give your baby plain cooled, boiled water from any age. Mineral water, either still or sparkling, usually contains too much sodium and other minerals, as well as numerous bacteria.

STARTING YOUR BABY ON SOLID FOOD

Your baby was born knowing how to suck but not how to eat from a spoon, so you will have to teach him. To begin with, he will hardly take anything. However, relax and be patient—he will soon start to enjoy the taste of different foods.

WHAT EQUIPMENT DO I NEED ?

You will need a bowl, spoon, and cup, which should always be sterilized before use unless they have been washed in the dishwasher. You will also need bibs, either velcro-fastened, disposable, or pelican bibs.

Plastic bowl   Spoons   Baby cups

Food blender

A velcro-fastened bib is handy because you can easily put it on and take it off

A disposable bib is useful when you are traveling

A pelican bib is made of soft plastic and has a drip catcher, which is good for collecting food that spills

HOW SHOULD I FEED MY BABY ?

Wash your hands before preparing his food. Your baby's food should be room temperature or lukewarm. Test the temperature by dipping in your finger.

1 Put a little food onto the tip of a weaning spoon. Be careful not to overload the spoon since this will cause your baby to splutter.

2 Offer the spoon up to your baby's bottom lip and let him suck off the food. If he spits it onto his chin, scrape it up and offer it to him again.

3 If this fails, try offering him a small amount of food on your fingertip. Using your finger makes the experience less strange for your baby.

OFFERING FOOD
Make sure that you are both comfortable. Supporting your baby's head and upper body will help him to swallow.

SUITABLE FIRST FOODS

Q WHICH FOODS SHOULD I START MY BABY ON ?

A Baby cereal made from rice is a good first solid food (see also below). It is bland but nourishing, and unlikely to cause allergies. Mix it with a little warm formula milk, breast milk, or cooled boiled water. Do not give cow's milk as a milk drink until your baby is a year old (see next question). He can have some dairy products before then, and you can use cow's milk in cooking once he is six months old.

Q WHICH FOODS SHOULD I AVOID GIVING TO MY BABY ?

A Avoid any nut products until he is two years old (whole nuts until five); hard-boiled eggs until he is one year old; egg yolks and wheat until he is six months old; and fruit with small seeds, such as raspberries, until he is five months. You can mix your baby's cereal with ordinary pasteurized cow's milk and give him some dairy products, but remember that cow's, goat's, and sheep's milk has too much protein and too little vitamin D and iron for a baby of this age. If any relatives suffer from allergies, such as severe asthma or eczema, delay feeding eggs, fish, wheat, and cow's milk in any form until your baby is a year old. Honey is unsuitable for babies under a year old because their gut is too immature to kill botulism spores.

Q WHY CAN'T I GIVE MY BABY WHEAT BEFORE SIX MONTHS OF AGE ?

A The gluten component of wheat can cause a permanent sensitivity to all wheat products. This condition is called celiac disease (gluten enteropathy). Delaying the introduction of gluten until the age of six months greatly reduces the risk of the disease developing in a baby. Remember that melba toasts and hard cookies contain wheat, so avoid them until your baby is six months old.

Q WHEN CAN I GIVE MY BABY THE SAME FOOD AS THE REST OF THE FAMILY ?

A Not yet. He can have home-cooked food, but the meals eaten by adults will usually have too much salt and possibly too much fiber for him. They are generally too complicated; at this stage, what your baby needs is to sample just one or two ingredients at a time. Always leave a few days in between introducing each new food.

Q SHOULD I GIVE MY BABY PREPARED BABY FOODS ?

A Yes, these are suitable for a baby of this age, but check the package to make sure that the sugar content is not too high. However, using prepared baby foods will be wasteful at this stage, since he will only take small tastes, so opening jars is best deferred until he's eating larger amounts of solid food. Some organic baby foods are now available in supermarkets and pharmacies.

WHICH FOODS CAN I GIVE AND WHEN ?

AGE	WHAT TO FEED YOUR CHILD	HOW TO GIVE IT
Four months	Single tastes. One meal a day is best. Try: baby rice cereal, fruit (cooked apple, cooked pear, uncooked banana, uncooked papaya), vegetables (broccoli, carrot, cauliflower, zucchini, parsnip, potato, turnip, sweet potato).	Bland and smooth. Food should be cooked (apart from banana or papaya) and then either sieved or blended, or put through a hand mill (such as a mouli grater) until it is about the same texture as ketchup or thick soup with no lumps. These are just tasters, so your baby will want only tiny amounts.
Five months	More complex combinations. Your baby can have two meals a day, although these will still be small. Try: baby rice cereal in the morning, then fruit or vegetables (see above) at lunchtime, or in the evening if you prefer.	Still bland, but the food can be rougher—for instance, pushed through the bigger holes of a sieve, or mashed thoroughly with a fork.
Six months	A greater variety, including: meat, poultry, fish, family food (avoid salt, spices, and garlic), wheat/gluten (such as pasta), baby yogurts, semolina, tapioca.	Start mashing the food with a fork instead of sieving it. Some babies still dislike lumps, so if this is the case, mash more thoroughly until he will eat it. Use a baby cup for drinks.

Q WHICH IS BETTER—POWDERED BABY FOOD OR FOOD IN JARS ?

A Both are satisfactory. In the early stages of weaning, powdered baby foods are more economical because you can make up the amount of food you want and the rest will keep as long as it's dry. Mix in the milk or cooled boiled water and get rid of any lumps of powder. Always read the preparation instructions carefully.

Q WHAT'S THE BEST WAY TO COOK FOOD FOR MY BABY ?

A Boil, steam, or bake his food. You can also prepare food in the microwave, but remember that there may be hot spots. To disperse the hot spots, let the food stand, mix it well, and leave it to cool before serving it to him. Do not fry food for him unless you use little or no oil.

Q HOW CAN I FREEZE SMALL PORTIONS FOR MY BABY ?

A Use a clean ice-cube tray or empty yogurt cartons or cottage cheese containers for freezing small portions of baby food—whichever is the most convenient for you and the size of your baby's appetite. Always make sure that you wash and dry the chosen containers thoroughly before using them as freezing containers for baby food.

Q HIS FOOD SEEMS TASTELESS. SHOULD I ADD SALT OR SUGAR ?

A Never add anything to his food. Your baby needs bland food—not salty food, or all the sodium in salt, either. Sugar is unnecessary, too, unless a little is needed to counteract the acid in some fruit. So don't be tempted to add any to his food even if it doesn't taste sweet enough to you.

USING A BABY CUP

Your baby may be thirsty because she's eating more solids, but refuse her bottle. If so, try a baby cup.

USING BABY CUP
Supervise your baby when using a baby cup to prevent her from choking. Be prepared to wipe up spills.

Cup should be sturdy

Q CAN I KEEP LEFTOVER FOOD SAFELY FOR ANOTHER MEAL ?

A No. You must not keep any cereals that have been mixed with milk or water. You should never keep any leftovers that have been in your baby's bowl (or that have been touched by his spoon, his mouth, or his fingers, or yours). You can keep the remains of a jar of food, unless they have already been decanted into his bowl or you have been feeding him straight from the jar.

PARENT'S SURVIVAL GUIDE

MY BABY WON'T EAT SOLIDS

Why won't my baby eat solids?
■ He could be very hungry, and want milk rather than tastes of solid food at that time.
■ He may not like that particular food.
■ You may not be offering it to him in the right way—make sure that the food is the correct temperature and check how you are offering the food to him (see p. 69).
■ He may need a lot less of it than you think.

What can I do?
■ Check that the food is not too hot for him.
■ Feed him some milk to take the edge off his hunger, then try giving him solids again before feeding him the rest of his milk.
■ Try a smaller spoon, putting it on the inside of the bottom lip only.
■ Don't worry if he refuses. Just try again later. Once he gets used to solids, he'll be eager to eat them.

NUTRITIONAL REQUIREMENTS

Q I'M A VEGETARIAN, BUT SHOULD MY BABY EAT MEAT ?

A Not necessarily. A vegetarian diet can be satisfactory and provide all the nutrients a baby needs, including iron, as long as you take a little extra care with his diet (see below). However, meat is beneficial for babies aged five months or over because it is rich in iron, zinc, and protein.

Q I'M A VEGAN. CAN I RAISE MY BABY AS A VEGAN TOO ?

A My view is that a strict vegan diet (no animal protein and no nutritional supplements) is not satisfactory nutritionally. The main problem is getting enough protein, calcium, vitamin D, and vitamin B12. You could compromise and raise your baby on a vegetarian diet.

Q WHAT VITAMIN SUPPLEMENTS DOES MY BABY NEED IN THE FIRST SIX MONTHS ?

A A balanced diet should provide your baby with the vitamins he needs, but you can make sure by giving him supplements of vitamins A, C, and D in drop form from four to six weeks of age until he is five years old. Many babies need vitamin D from the age of one month, especially those at risk of vitamin D deficiency. These are mainly children from the Indian subcontinent living in less sunny areas, but babies who breast-feed exclusively may also need vitamin D supplements. Vitamin D, like vitamin A, depends on the absorption of fat.

WHAT DOES MY BABY NEED ?

Babies need a diet that is relatively high in energy (calories), high in fat, low in fiber, and low in salt. It should contain enough protein for growth and carbohydrate for energy.

Approximate daily requirements

AGE	ENERGY	PROTEIN	FAT	IRON
Up to 3 months	530 Cals	13 g	4 g	2 mg
3–6 months	700 Cals	13 g	4 g	4 mg
6–9 months	800 Cals	14 g	4 g	8 mg
9–12 months and over	1,200 Cals	20 g	4 g	9 mg

Q WHAT IS THE BEST VITAMIN PREPARATION FOR A BABY ?

A You should consult your doctor or pediatrician if you think that your baby could benefit from taking vitamin supplements. The doctor will assess your baby, and if she agrees, she can advise you on which vitamin supplement is the most suitable one for your baby. Babies are not generally too fussy, so he won't have a preference for a particular brand.

WHAT FOODS SHOULD I GIVE MY VEGETARIAN BABY ?

If you feed your baby no meat, poultry, or fish, he must get adequate nutrients from other sources. Vitamin B12 comes mainly from animal sources, and milk and dairy products (and egg yolks from six months) will supply enough for your baby.

From four months:
- pureed vegetables (potatoes, carrots, spinach, zucchini, parsnips, sweet potatoes)
- pureed fruit (cooked apple, pear, raw banana, cooked and pureed dried apricots)
- baby rice, corn, millet, sago
- NO NUTS OR EGGS.

From five months, add:
- mashed or pureed lentils
- widen the range of vegetables and fruit—try avocado, mango, grapes (peeled, deseeded, and halved)
- some dairy foods, such as baby yogurt
- NO NUTS OR EGGS.

From six months, add:
- tofu, mashed lentils, baked beans (reduced salt and sugar)
- dairy foods (e.g., cheese)
- hard-boiled egg yolks (if no family history of allergy)
- wheat products (e.g., bread), oatmeal, and cereals
- NO NUTS.

Q CAN VITAMIN SUPPLEMENTS BE HARMFUL TO MY BABY?

A Approved supplements are safe, but don't exceed the recommended dose, even if your baby was premature, sickly, or weaned late. The body can get rid of excess vitamin C, but other supplements, especially vitamin A, are toxic in large doses. Iron is toxic in large doses, but most baby's and children's supplements don't contain iron.

Q WILL EXTRA VITAMINS OR MINERALS MAKE MY BABY A BRIGHTER CHILD?

A No. There has been a lot of publicity about vitamins and minerals increasing your child's intelligence, but they will only improve your child's brain power if he is vitamin- or mineral-deficient. A shortage of iron and other minerals can impair concentration, but it is more dangerous to give your child too many supplements.

How CAN I TELL IF MY BABY HAS A FOOD ALLERGY?

Nobody knows for sure, but food allergies could be quite common. The gut lining lets in more proteins in the first three months of life, and some foods can trigger a process that later causes allergic reactions. However, some people tend to blame all symptoms on food allergies, and some children (and adults) are fed very restricted diets when there is no real evidence of an allergy.

What are the most common food allergies?
In young children, the most common are:
■ allergy to peanuts and other nuts
■ celiac disease (wheat/gluten allergy)
■ cow's milk protein intolerance (this often clears up by the age of two).

What is the difference between food allergy and food intolerance?
Both terms mean that eating a food causes a reaction. Allergy means that the immune system is at fault. Intolerance means there's no hard evidence of the immune system being involved.

What symptoms can food allergies cause?
Symptoms range from mild to severe, and can include:
■ rashes (such as eczema and hives)
■ diarrhea or vomiting
■ failure to grow or put on weight
■ coughing or wheezing
■ anaphylactic shock (a rare but acute reaction that can kill—see p. 230).

Do food allergies run in families?
Allergies are more prevalent in some families than in others, so food allergies can be familial, but this is not necessarily always the case.

Is diarrhea always the result of a food allergy?
No. Although diarrhea can result from food allergy, it isn't a common cause. Diarrhea can also be the effect of the form or texture of a food item rather than the ingredient itself. This happens with many foods, especially corn and whole-wheat bread. Leave the suspect food out of your baby's diet for a few days; if the diarrhea resolves, you can always try again, but mash or sieve the food more finely next time.

FOOD RASHES
A rash around the mouth may be caused by an allergy or just by food irritating delicate skin. Wipe the face gently with cotton balls and water and see if the rash subsides. Next time your baby has this food, try wiping her face as soon as she is done eating.

FEEDING YOUR OLDER BABY

Q HOW MANY MEALS SHOULD I FEED MY BABY, AND SHOULD I REDUCE HIS MILK ?

A Three meals a day plus snacks. He will get to the point where he has solid food first, followed by milk. This usually happens at about six months of age, when he will start taking less milk.

Q WHAT IS ADVANCED FORMULA AND WHEN SHOULD I GIVE IT TO MY BABY ?

A This is formula milk that contains more iron, protein, and vitamin D than standard formula milk. Give it to your baby from the age of six months, until he is ready for cow's milk as a drink.

Q WHEN CAN I START GIVING MY BABY COW'S MILK ?

A From about six months onward, you can use cow's milk for mixing cereals, unless your family has a history of allergy. Don't give cow's milk as a main drink until your baby is a year old.

Q WHEN SHOULD MY BABY STOP USING A BOTTLE ?

A By the time he is a year old. He needs to drink from a cup for social reasons and for the sake of his teeth—cavities can be caused by drinking too much milk from a bottle. Let him hold a baby cup himself to encourage him to use it.

Q WHICH FOODS SHOULD MY BABY AVOID UNTIL HE'S A YEAR OLD ?

A Until he is a year old, you should avoid giving your baby honey, or cow's milk as a main drink (it has too much protein and too little iron). If any of your close relatives has an allergy to eggs, you should avoid these as well. Don't give your child any nut products until he is two years old or whole nuts until he is five years old.

Q WHICH MEATS AND POULTRY ARE SAFE TO GIVE TO MY BABY ?

A Many parents are concerned about the safety of giving meat to a baby, but it is safe if you take a few precautions. The most important thing is to make sure that you give your baby good cuts of meat because these are more tender and easier for him to swallow. Chicken and turkey are ideal meats to give a baby of this age because they have a mild taste that he may prefer, but you can give him lamb, pork, and beef as well. It is vital that you always cook meat thoroughly—beef can carry *E. coli*, and poultry can harbor salmonella and campylobacter. These germs are all destroyed by thorough cooking. Keep meat in the refrigerator below 41°F (5°C), and store raw meat at the bottom of the refrigerator so that the meat juices cannot contaminate other foods.

SHOULD I BUY A HIGHCHAIR ?

A highchair provides a secure place for your baby to eat from about seven months of age. At this stage you can give him small pieces of food that he can eat with his fingers. This will also allow him to start feeding himself, rather than depending on you to feed him. Stay with your baby while he eats and use the harness provided.

USING A HIGHCHAIR
Your baby will enjoy the independence of eating finger foods from a highchair. Chewing is soothing for a teething baby.

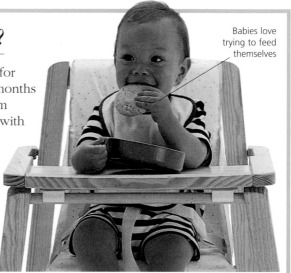

Babies love trying to feed themselves

WHICH FOODS CAN I GIVE DURING THE LATER STAGES OF WEANING?

AGE OF CHILD	WHAT TO GIVE	HOW TO GIVE IT
6–9 months	**Can use** cow's milk to mix cereals. **Offer:** vegetables, meat, fish, hard cheeses. Consider eggs (hard-boiled).	■ Two to three meals a day, snacks, and drinks. ■ The texture can be rougher. ■ Start offering finger foods, such as bread and toast.
9–12 months	**Offer:** legumes (peas and beans), eggs (hard-boiled), and moderate helpings of butter or margarine.	■ Finger foods become very important. ■ Move toward three meals a day, plus snacks and drinks as needed. ■ The texture of food can be more like adult food, but add little salt and sugar, if any.

Q HOW CAN I MAKE SURE MY BABY GETS ENOUGH IRON?

A Provide plenty of variety in his diet. Apart from meat, iron is naturally present in many vegetables and fruits—for example, prune juice, pureed apricots, lentils (mashed or sieved), and well-mashed beans. Vitamin C aids iron absorption, so a vegetarian baby will benefit from drinking diluted orange juice with his meals. Avoid bran because it can prevent iron absorption. Continue feeding him breast or formula milk.

Q WHEN CAN MY BABY USE A SPOON HIMSELF?

A Let him try to use a spoon as soon as he shows an interest in holding one, but competent use of the spoon means rotating it correctly, and he probably won't manage that until he's 12 months or older. But there's no reason why he can't hold a spoon earlier, while you use a second one to feed him. He may dip his into the food and, one way or another, nourishment will reach his mouth.

Q MEALTIMES ARE SO MESSY. WHAT CAN I DO ABOUT THIS?

A Wear old clothes and relax. Put newspapers around his highchair (this is better than plastic sheeting—you can throw paper away). A plastic bib with a trough is useful, but don't leave it on for too long—it can cut into his neck. A bib with sleeves is useful as well. Keep cloths and paper towels handy.

Q I'M WORRIED MY BABY MIGHT CHOKE. HOW CAN I PREVENT THIS?

A Sit with your baby all the time while he's eating. Don't give him whole or half hard nuts until he's about five years old. Wait until he can chew better before offering raw carrot.

Q WHEN CAN I STOP STERILIZING HIS BOWL, SPOON, AND CUP?

A You can stop sterilizing your baby's feeding implements from about six months onward, unless you have a dishwasher (see p. 69). However, everything still has to be as clean as possible, so always make sure that all his feeding equipment is washed thoroughly.

Q HOW CAN I MAKE EATING OUT WITH MY BABY LESS STRESSFUL?

A You should avoid formal restaurants, since you need to be very relaxed about eating out with your baby. Take his own harness and bib with you, and don't make meals too protracted. By the time the adults are choosing their desserts, your baby may be feeling tired or bored.

HOW CAN I MAKE MEALTIMES FUN?

Let him enjoy himself
He will enjoy trying to feed himself, so let him. Position him away from the walls and cover the floor to minimize the mess. Eating with your baby will help him to see mealtimes as a social occasion. Finger foods will keep your baby busy.

Don't force him to eat
Making your baby eat when he doesn't want to will only make the occasion more stressful for both of you. Let his appetite be your guide.

Keep your baby safe
Always make sure your baby is secure in his highchair and use the harness. Do not leave him unattended.

FEEDING YOUR TODDLER

Q MY CHILD'S VERY ACTIVE BUT DOESN'T EAT MUCH. SHOULD I WORRY ?

A No, as long as he's happy and growing. It's normal for a toddler's appetite to drop a little at around 15 months. Some toddlers actually eat very little considering their strenuous pace. Strangely enough, placid toddlers (there are a few!) seem to eat more than very active ones. Make sure that your toddler is not filling himself up with vast quantities of milk or juice instead of food.

WHAT SNACKS SHOULD I GIVE MY TODDLER ?

Fresh fruit, cheese (including cottage cheese), yogurt, milk, unsweetened cereals, sandwiches, chopped hard-boiled egg, breadsticks, and raw vegetables all make healthy snacks. Limit raisins and dried apricots, both of which are sweet and chewy and more damaging to your child's teeth.

SUITABLE HEALTHY SNACKS
Offer raw vegetables, low-sugar cookies, and breadsticks as snacks. Cutting them into fun shapes can make them appeal to your baby.

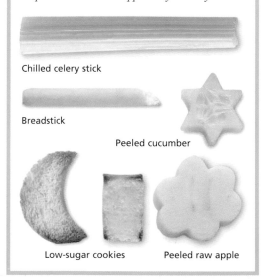

Chilled celery stick

Breadstick

Peeled cucumber

Low-sugar cookies

Peeled raw apple

Q HE NO LONGER LIKES A NUMBER OF FOODS. WHAT CAN I DO ?

A This, too, is fairly normal, especially if you often serve the same food. Try to provide a variety of different foods. He may be too thirsty to eat. If so, give him a glass of water or juice, but not too much or it will fill him up. If he always refuses a certain food, you could drop it from his diet. He may accept it at some time in the future, but forcing him to eat it now won't work—he may resort to dawdling over his meal, spitting it out, vomiting later, or throwing his bowl on the floor. He may even develop a life-long dislike for that food, so it's not worth persevering with it. He will not become malnourished if there is one item missing from his diet. Adults don't eat the foods they don't like, either.

Q CAN A TODDLER REALLY SURVIVE ON A VERY LIMITED RANGE OF FOODS ?

A Toddlers can live (and grow) on an amazingly restricted diet of their own choosing, often defying all the nutritional experts. However, it is obviously better for them to have a healthy, varied diet that contains all the required nutrients. Iron deficiency is the main problem at this age. Many toddlers are short of iron. Even if your child doesn't develop an iron deficiency on a limited diet, it's better for him socially if he eats a more varied range of food.

Q HE WON'T EAT MEALS. WHAT CAN I DO IF HE SNACKS FIVE OR SIX TIMES A DAY ?

A Presumably he likes his snacks, so try offering some of the same "snack" foods together as a meal. For instance, if your toddler wants a few crackers at 11 am and then yogurt at 1 pm, you could try combining the two at 11:30 am or noon and get him to sit down to eat them. Always make a point of eating with him if possible.

Q HOW CAN I STOP HIM FROM HELPING HIMSELF TO SNACKS ?

A Try to keep snacks out of reach if possible, since it's better if he doesn't help himself. However, give him something to eat when he's feeling hungry. Some toddlers have a huge appetite, and they need snacks as well as three meals a day.

Q WHY DOES HE ALWAYS LEAVE FOOD ON HIS PLATE?

A You may have served him too much, or he may want to get up and do something else. Don't give him alternatives like cookies if he won't eat a meal. Just let him get up and go. This is hard, but it's the only thing you can do. Next time, give him a smaller helping. It may upset you less if you don't spend too long cooking his food, although you must give him a reasonably varied diet.

Q LEFTOVER FOOD IS SUCH A WASTE. WHAT CAN I DO WITH IT?

A Throw it away. Your child's food can't be kept once it's been contaminated by his spoon, bowl, or fingers. Don't eat his meal unless you're prepared for the consequences—you may put on weight, and his eating habits won't improve.

Q MY CHILD EATS SO SLOWLY. IS THERE A WAY OF SPEEDING HIM UP?

A No, there isn't. Let him eat what he wants and then remove the plate when he has had enough. Toddlers can be uncooperative, so it's counterproductive to try to coax or bribe him.

Q HOW CAN I IMPROVE MY TODDLER'S TABLE MANNERS?

A Set a good example and try to eat together as a family and with friends as often as possible. Let him feed himself. He won't be adept with a spoon or fork yet, so be patient.

HAPPY FAMILY MEALS

- Ask your toddler to help set the table. He might enjoy this if he feels it's special.
- Provide at least one thing you know he likes to eat. Try not to get upset if that's all he eats.
- Relax. He's bigger than he once was but still far from adult, so be realistic. It also helps if everyone else, including grandparents and guests, has reasonable expectations of him, too.

Q CAN I GIVE MY CHILD COW'S MILK AS A MAIN DRINK?

A From the age of 12 months, he can start having pasteurized cow's milk as a main drink. To start with, you should give him whole milk. Unless you are advised to by a doctor, do not give your child reduced-fat milk until he is at least two years old. By this stage your child should have 10 fl oz (400ml) of milk each day in some form.

Q CAN I CONTINUE TO BREAST-FEED MY TODDLER?

A Yes, but he'll be having three meals a day, so this won't be his main source of nourishment. He will probably suck for only brief periods at a time. You may find it difficult mixing with other mothers who aren't breast-feeding their toddlers because of their disapproval, implicit or explicit.

PARENT'S SURVIVAL GUIDE

MY TODDLER REFUSES TO EAT

It is quite common for toddlers to exhibit uncooperative behavior at mealtimes. Many parents have trouble coaxing their toddler to eat; you haven't done anything wrong. Try to remain calm. The situation will improve eventually.

What can I do?
Congratulate him on what he does eat. You'd be surprised how many picky toddlers turn into older children (and adults) who love their food, so try not to worry or lose your patience. Be as relaxed as possible. Try other foods. He might also like to help in the kitchen. Even very young children enjoy making a sandwich—of sorts!

Isn't there any way of making him eat?
No. A toddler cannot be persuaded to eat if he doesn't want to. Threats of punishment will have no effect, other than to upset both of you. Nor will he be inclined to eat if you try to distract him with airplane impressions or ask him to eat something for you or someone else at the table, so you will just have to give up gracefully. Do nothing special other than provide the food. As long as he isn't actually ill, he will eat when he's feeling hungry. Remember that neither children nor adults can eat when they are feeling upset or angry, so try to avoid bringing highly charged emotions to mealtimes.

FEEDING PRESCHOOLERS

Q HOW CAN I MAKE FAMILY MEALS MORE ENJOYABLE FOR EVERYONE?

A Making the meal a bit more grown-up may appeal to your preschool child because he'll want to feel more adult. Let him have a napkin, grown-up utensils, and a real plate (not plastic). You'll still need to make family meals relatively simple and short. His attention span and his ability to sit still won't be equal to yours. Give him attention when he's good rather than naughty. Also ensure that your own manners are up to scratch— no talking with your mouth full, putting your elbows on the table, or getting up in the middle of a meal.

Q WHAT CAN I DO IF HE WON'T SIT DOWN OR GETS UP BEFORE WE'VE FINISHED?

A It depends on your attitude and what kind of discipline you want to enforce. A preschool child should be capable of sitting down for a whole meal as long as it's not too long. He can also learn that he has to ask before he leaves the table. Stick to this so that if he gets up without asking, he doesn't get any more food during that meal. You could make breakfast an exception because the whole family is likely to be in a rush and getting up and down from the table.

Q HE ALWAYS WANTS SNACKS. SHOULD I FORBID THIS?

A I don't think so. Growing children get genuinely hungry, and it is an unpleasant sensation. If it is nearly time for a meal, explain that the food will be served soon. A child of this age cannot always wait for food, so he may still need a small snack to stave off hunger pangs. Make the snack a healthy food (see opposite).

Q WHAT ARE THE BEST DRINKS TO GIVE MY CHILD?

A You should limit your child's intake of sugary drinks. Fruit-flavored drinks are high in calories, but have little other nutritional value. In large quantities they may make your child irritable, give him diarrhea, and even slow his growth. Carbonated drinks are high in phosphorus and impair absorption of calcium. Tea inhibits absorption of iron and coffee is also a diuretic. Both are stimulants and should be avoided.

HOW DO I COPE WITH FADS?

Children often go through phases of only eating certain foods. This can be very wearing, but try not to worry.

My child used to eat everything. Now she's really picky. What can I do?
Many food fads last only a few weeks, but they may be followed by another fad. It's hard to know whether this is intended as attention-seeking behavior, but it does get a lot of attention. Be patient and try the following:
- encourage her to eat what she will eat
- provide a variety of different foods
- don't coax her or make disparaging remarks— if she's growing, that's all that matters
- give her vitamin drops (see p. 72)
- praise her for what she does eat.

Will she ever eat normally?
For now she may eat only food that is of a certain color or shape. One day she will eat normally, so try not to worry too much.

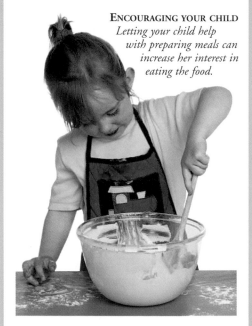

ENCOURAGING YOUR CHILD
Letting your child help with preparing meals can increase her interest in eating the food.

How do I maintain my child's weight?

Try to give your child a healthy, balanced diet and plenty of exercise. However, don't place too much emphasis on weight. A preschool child's weight will not necessarily indicate his weight later. It was thought that the number of fat cells formed in infancy affected obesity in adulthood, but this is no longer believed to be a factor.

An apple, a piece of cheese, or a glass of milk are ideal snacks

HEALTHY SNACKS
A growing child gets hungry frequently, so provide plenty of healthy snacks when she needs something to eat.

Overweight

How can I tell if my child is fat?
Many youngsters look round without actually being overweight. You could take him to the doctor to have his weight and height checked, and see where both measurements fall on the growth chart. Remember that even if your child's weight is on the 95th percentile, he isn't necessarily overweight—all it means is that 95 percent of children of the same age will weigh less. Also consider his height and build. If he is tall or well-built, he may weigh more. If you are concerned about your child being fat, make sure he has plenty of opportunities to be active. Inactivity is a common cause of obesity at this age, so make sure he walks and runs around every day.

Should I put my child on a diet?
No. He is still growing. However, you can offer healthier food so that he doesn't continue to gain weight too fast. At the preschool stage, you can reduce his fat intake, especially of fried foods. Reduce his milk intake to 10 fl oz (600 ml) a day, change to reduced fat milk, and cut down the amount of candy and desserts he eats.

How can I help my overweight child?
Avoid talking endlessly about your child's weight. A preoccupation with body weight may lead to eating disorders later, even in a very young child. Try to find out if anything is worrying him—some youngsters overeat for comfort.

Underweight

If you are really worried that your child might be underweight, then ask your doctor or pediatrician to monitor his height and weight.

My four-year-old is much thinner than his friends. What can I do?
Some preschool children are thin, and the odds are that your child is normal. Some illnesses, such as celiac disease and chronic infections, can sometimes cause poor weight gain, but if he is gaining weight regularly and he's full of energy, then you needn't worry about him.

One of my twins is a lot thinner than his brother. Does it matter?
It doesn't matter if he's well. Even so-called identical twins are often different in weight and stature. Any discrepancy tends to be very obvious when a parent has another child the same age who is available at all times for comparison. So stop drawing these comparisons. Above all, you should not force Adam to eat to "be more like Joe." Understandably, he probably wants to be himself, and being told to be more like his brother could be the beginning of real problems with food.

ENCOURAGING SLEEP

Sleep is as essential to your child's **well-being** as it is to your own. Parents often want to know exactly **how much sleep** babies and children need—the answer is that, like adults, every child is different. Only one thing is certain —without enough sleep, **alertness and mood** suffer. Many parents worry about safe sleeping positions, optimum room temperature, and appropriate nightwear for their baby. This chapter offers **reassuring guidance** on all these issues and more. There's practical advice on routines for helping a baby sleep through the night, tips for encouraging a child to sleep in her own bed, and **strategies for parents** existing on little sleep.

SLEEP FOR YOUNG BABIES

IS A ROUTINE A GOOD IDEA ?

Yes. Preparing your baby for bed with a calm and pleasant ritual winds down the day's activities and becomes a predictable and comforting part of her life, helping to promote sleep.

How can I establish a bedtime routine?
Change her from day clothes into night attire. Before you take her to her crib, you could say good night together to the rest of the family. Sing to her or say the same things every night when you put her down in her crib. However, don't make bedtime routines too complicated or she could go on expecting a lengthy performance every night when she is much older.

Can I make bathing part of her bedtime routine and if so, when should this start?
You can include this in her bedtime routine as soon as you like. If she is on solids, her stools will be smellier and bulkier so a daily bath is a good idea. If she enjoys a bath and finds it relaxing without being too stimulating, you can make it part of her usual early evening routine.

How can I get my baby used to going to bed in the early evening?
Take her for an outing in the afternoon, then give her a bath followed by a late afternoon feeding. However, a baby who sleeps in the early evening is a luxury—yours may not. It is unfair to expect her to sleep if there is a lot of evening excitement such as a parent returning from work.

Can I encourage her to sleep longer at night?
Make sure she is ready for sleep by giving her some fresh air and stimulation every day. As you become accustomed to her needs, you will find that her feedings and other activities begin to form a pattern and the daytime routine leads naturally up to bedtime. Start using her crib for nighttime sleep rather than a bassinet or carriage, and put her down while she is still awake so that she learns to fall asleep without you.

Q HOW MUCH SLEEP DOES MY BABY NEED IN 24 HOURS ?

A There are no hard and fast rules, although she may need less sleep than you think. Babies under six months old tend to sleep around 13–15 hours in every 24, distributed into three or four distinct sleep periods. For instance, she may have two to three daytime sleeps and one or two periods of sleep at night. At three months, nearly half of all babies start to sleep through the night.

Q HOW WILL I KNOW WHEN MY BABY IS READY FOR SLEEP ?

A You will learn to recognize her needs. However, use your common sense, too. If she wakes up from a two-hour nap at 5 pm, she won't be ready for a night's sleep at 6:30 pm. It may help to give her the last feeding of the day in her bedroom; dozing, relaxed babies have a disconcerting habit of perking up when carried upstairs to the bedroom.

Q HOW CAN I HELP HER DISTINGUISH BETWEEN NIGHT AND DAY ?

A Keep lighting subdued and have thick curtains to keep light out. If she wakes for a feeding, keep it low-key; deal with the feeding or diaper change quietly, without fuss, then put her back to bed. Keep social activities to a minimum at night, and talk in a soothing, not stimulating, way.

Q SHOULD I USE A NIGHT-LIGHT IN MY BABY'S ROOM ?

A A night-light can help you see your baby and keep you from tripping in the dark, but your baby may not need one during her first year. Some people believe that getting a baby used to a night-light from an early age will be useful when she is older and wants to find her way to the toilet in the night. A low-watt bulb is adequate.

Q HOW CAN I ENCOURAGE MY BABY TO GO TO SLEEP BY HERSELF ?

A Make sure she is relaxed, contented, and not hungry, then put her into her crib and give her time to settle. Stroke or pat her and say good night, but stay near her for a short while before leaving the room. Alternatively, just move a bit farther away and then leave.

Q MY BABY GOES TO SLEEP AT THE END OF A FEEDING. IS THIS A PROBLEM?

A There is nothing wrong with this when she is very young; some babies can't keep their eyes open when replete from a feeding. However, by the age of six months at the latest you should aim to finish the breast- or bottle-feeding and put your baby in the crib while she is still awake. This applies to both daytime and nighttime sleeps.

Q SHOULD I WAKE HER IF SHE FALLS ASLEEP DURING A FEEDING?

A If she falls asleep during a feeding, rouse her gently for a moment. You may not be able to wake a sleeping baby fully, but it is usually possible to get a baby awake enough to notice that she is being transferred to her crib. If you always put your baby to bed when she is already asleep, you will have problems getting her to bed when she is older.

Q I ALWAYS ROCK MY BABY TO SLEEP. IS THIS A GOOD IDEA?

A This is fine in the first couple of months if you both enjoy it, but she must get used to falling asleep on her own without being rocked. Evidence suggests that babies can learn to sleep unaided from an early age; acquiring this habit is a good idea so that she can go to sleep on her own.

Q HOW CAN I MAKE SURE SHE'S WARM ENOUGH DURING THE NIGHT?

A If she kicks off her cover repeatedly, either go in and cover her, or put her in thicker pajamas or a stretchsuit for bed. She can wear socks if it is really cold. A sweater may be needed, but buttons, ribbons, and loose-knitted cuffs can be a hazard. From four months, you could dress her in a sleeping sack that fastens at the hem, which will keep her warm and allow her to kick her legs freely.

HOW CAN I MAKE MY BABY COMFORTABLE AND SAFE?

Make sure she has the correct bedding; depending on the temperature, she needs one or two blankets. Add or take away layers as needed. Until she is a year old, avoid comforters, pillows, sheepskins, and soft mattresses—any of these may cause her to overheat.

POSITIONING YOUR BABY
Reduce the risk of Sudden Infant Death Syndrome (SIDS) by putting your baby down on her back with her feet at the base of the crib.

MAKING SURE SHE IS SAFE

It is important to put your baby to sleep with her feet at the base of the crib. This will prevent her from sliding down and getting her head covered by the bedlinen, which could cause her to overheat. Continue putting your baby down on her back to sleep until she is about six months old. By then, the main danger period of SIDS (see p. 46) will have passed, and she will be so active that she will probably turn over in her crib anyway and find her own position.

What other measures can I take?
Always keep the temperature in your baby's bedroom at about 65°F (18°C)—she must not get too hot or cold at night—and avoid smoking in any part of the house. If your baby is ill, contact your doctor or pediatrician. Most illnesses tend to be mild and are due to colds or similar viruses, but occasionally an infection can overwhelm a young baby's defenses, with serious results, so don't delay in seeking advice.

COMMON SLEEP PROBLEMS

Q SHE KEEPS WAKING AT NIGHT. SHOULD I CHECK HER EVERY TIME SHE WAKES?

A No. A whimper or a short "testing" cry can be ignored, especially after four months. Most babies wake at intervals, make a tentative noise, then nod off again. This is because a baby's sleep-waking cycle is shorter than yours. It takes a three-month-old baby 45 minutes to go from drowsiness to deep sleep to being awake, compared to 90 minutes for an adult. Your baby will therefore often wake up in the night, but she has to learn to fall asleep again on her own. This will happen if she isn't hungry, is dry, and the room is dark. However, go to her if you hear a piercing scream or she is sick.

CAN I HELP MY TWINS TO SLEEP?

Twins can sleep badly, especially if born small or premature and in need of frequent feedings.

My twins wake at different times. Is there anything I can do?
Don't expect them to have exactly the same sleep needs, even if they're identical. Marshal any resources to help you, such as domestic help by day, a few more weeks' maternity leave, or your partner doing some of the night shifts.

Should my twins share a crib?
Many twins share a crib at first, but between six weeks and six months, each twin will need her own crib. Parents worry about twins waking each other. This can happen, but it seems to be more common in the morning than during the night. If they do disturb each other, they may need separate rooms.

Should I put them to bed while awake?
Yes. It would be hard to get two babies to sleep and then put them down safely.

I'm finding it hard to cope. What can I do?
Tell yourself that you can cope and you will. Unnecessary tension won't help you or your babies, but trying to be more relaxed and cheerful may help you to cope.

Q MY BABY WAKES IN THE NIGHT AND WANTS A FEEDING. SHOULD I FEED HER?

A You should feed her if she is genuinely hungry. This should be a milk feeding (breast or bottle), not a meal consisting of solids, even after your baby has been weaned. However, toward the end of six months you can start giving her less milk at night. If you're breast-feeding, try limiting the time spent at the breast. If you're bottle-feeding, either give her a smaller volume of formula or dilute it more than usual. You can do this by putting in one less scoop of formula powder or, if you prefer, by adding more water to the same number of scoops. Either way, you can make the feeding progressively weaker. When it is more like water, she will not find it worth clamoring for.

Q WHY HAS MY THREE-MONTH-OLD BABY STARTED TO WAKE AGAIN AT NIGHT?

A Babies who previously slept through the night may start waking again. (To be accurate, they were probably always waking but not crying.) If your baby has become more clingy during the day and requires more attention than usual, her night waking may be a normal part of her development. This seems to happen at around six weeks, 12 weeks, and again at four months and six months. However, your baby might be hungry; although she is not ready for solids yet, she may need more milk than usual in the day. Alternatively, she may be very hot or sick (see pp. 214–19), or there may have been some change in her usual routine, perhaps due to a vacation or houseguests.

Q SHE WAKES VERY EARLY. WHAT CAN I DO TO MAKE HER SLEEP LONGER?

A Try to shift her routine so that you put her to bed later in the evenings. Eventually, she will wake later, as long as there is nothing disturbing her, like strong sunlight at the window. Even so, you may still have a baby who has an earlier start to the day than you're ready for. If she is not crying with hunger when she wakes, there is no harm in leaving her in her crib to babble happily to herself. This may allow you to doze off again, or at least to rest in bed without having to jump up to see to her. If she won't leave you in peace in the mornings, you have two options: give her a quick feeding and put her down again in the hope that she will be satisfied or, alternatively, start going to bed earlier yourself.

CAN THUMB-SUCKING OR A PACIFIER DAMAGE TEETH?

Although thumb-sucking and pacifiers help to comfort your baby when she is tired and won't sleep, some parents are concerned about possible damage to their baby's teeth.

Sucking her thumb

At about three months old, babies start playing with their hands and often begin to suck their thumb. In the long term, this can cause the top front teeth to overhang the lower ones. But, once she's "found" her thumb, there's not a lot you can do other than give her plenty of attention and help her to manage without it when she's older.

Sucking a pacifier

Introduce a pacifier at one month of age when putting your baby to sleep. Research suggests that this helps reduce the risk of SIDS, and pacifiers aren't bad for teeth. However, try to restrict her use of it when she is awake so that she doesn't rely on it all the time. When your baby reaches one year of age, try to wean her off the pacifier.

USING A PACIFIER
Never sweeten your baby's pacifier with honey or juice.

ENCOURAGING SLEEP   YOUNG BABIES 6 WEEKS–6 MONTHS

Q I STILL TAKE MY SIX-MONTH-OLD BABY TO BED WITH ME. SHOULD I DO THIS?

A In my opinion, you should stop taking your baby to bed with you on a regular basis by the time she is six months at the latest. Your baby is becoming increasingly mobile, and is therefore in greater danger of falling out of the bed. Also, she is bigger, takes up more space, and may disturb you more often in the night. She needs to learn to sleep independently at some point and, after the first few weeks, the longer you allow her to sleep with you, the more difficult this becomes. If she spends her first year in your bed, she could still be sleeping there by the time she starts preschool or even school. If you are a single parent, then co-sleeping may well be comforting and stave off loneliness for both of you, but at a price—your baby will lose out on her independent development and you may sacrifice potential new relationships.

Q CAN I LET MY BABY TAKE TOYS TO BED WITH HER?

A Yes, you can. Obviously, a toy must be safe in case she lies on top of it, so avoid any hard or sharp-edged objects. Soft toys are fine, but they should always be clean—make sure that your baby is not clutching the teddy bear that fell onto the sidewalk three times earlier that day. Don't overfill her crib with soft toys. Believe it or not, they can cause a young baby to overheat or even suffocate.

PARENT'S SURVIVAL GUIDE

I'VE HARDLY SLEPT ALL WEEK

How will losing sleep affect me?

After 24 hours of being awake, mood, alertness, and performance all drop. In the longer term, depression can result. However, your baby is not torturing you deliberately—at this age she can't stay awake on purpose.

Is there any way I can encourage her to sleep more during the night?

Make sure that conditions in her room are optimal for sleep (see p. 83) and stick to a consistent bedtime routine (see p. 82).

How can I cope with less sleep?

Reframe your expectations and accept that your baby may not sleep as much as other babies. To some extent, you can learn to rest without sleep. For example, you could learn a relaxation technique or start to meditate. Instead of feeling resentful, try to stay relaxed so that you can make the most of the opportunity to rest when your baby does sleep at night.

What can I do about the household chores?

If you are tired, cut corners where you can and don't waste time on chores.

SLEEP FOR OLDER BABIES

Q HOW MUCH SLEEP DOES MY BABY NEED FROM SIX MONTHS ONWARD ?

A On average, a baby between 6–12 months of age will need about 12 hours' sleep a night and also two naps of about an hour each during the day. By the end of the first year, she will probably be down to one daytime sleep, but this could last for as long as two hours.

Q SHE WON'T GO TO SLEEP AS READILY AS SHE USED TO. WHY ?

A At around eight months of age, your baby acquires the ability to stay awake on purpose even when she is tired. She will only rarely fall asleep at the breast or bottle and you will have to put her down in her crib at night while she is still wide awake. That is why it is such a good idea to get your baby into the habit of going to bed awake before she gets to this age. Furthermore, at some time between 6–10 months, most babies go through a period of not wanting to be without their mother and can become very clingy.

Q WHAT BEDCLOTHES AND BEDDING SHOULD I USE NOW SHE IS OLDER ?

A You can put your baby in a nightgown with a closed hem (a sleeping bag), which keeps her warm but allows her to move around her crib. You should start using one of these before she can stand up, otherwise she will find it limiting and dislike it. Until she is a year old, you should continue to avoid using comforters and pillows. Also, do not use crib bumpers at any time as a baby can climb up onto them and fall out of the crib.

Q SHE STILL USES A PACIFIER AT NIGHT. IS THIS A PROBLEM ?

A No, as long as the pacifier is just for sleep. But there are drawbacks—she may wake up crying because it has fallen out of her mouth, and you will have to locate it for her. First, try to limit her use of the pacifier during the daytime by giving her more attention and stimulation, and then try to wean her off the pacifier completely between 12 and 18 months of age.

IS IT NORMAL FOR HER TO HAVE A "COMFORT" TOY ?

This is quite normal behavior, but make sure that the toy is safe for a baby of her age, and preferably quiet too. It is common for an older baby to develop a dependence on a particular blanket, teddy bear, or toy.

COMFORT ITEMS

A few babies do become attached to a particular object. Consider investing in two identical ones, just in case the worst happens and the favorite item is lost or falls apart. Remove ribbons from the necks of soft toys or sew them in place securely as they can be a hazard for a baby.

TAKING TOYS TO BED
A favorite toy may be helpful in getting your baby to sleep, but avoid toys with hard or sharp edges.

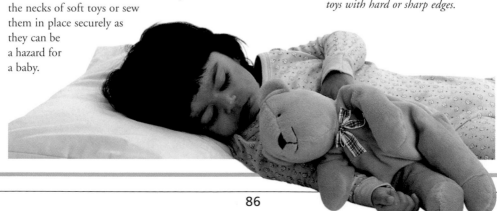

Q SHOULD I LEAVE A LIGHT ON FOR HER TO SLEEP?

A Leaving the light on may suggest to her that the dark is scary. Also, recent research suggests that leaving bright lights on at night may cause nearsightedness later. If you already leave a light on, think about substituting a dim night-light or install a dimmer switch in your baby's room.

Q MY BABY WON'T SLEEP IF MY PARTNER PUTS HER TO BED. WHAT CAN I DO?

A This is very common, especially if one parent spends more time with the baby. Be loving but firm: to stop her from being dependent on you putting her to bed, he could put her to bed for a week. You should both stick to her normal bedtime routines and act confidently as you put her down.

Q MY BABY STANDS UP IN HER CRIB. SHOULD I TRY TO STOP HER?

A No. She will lie down eventually, but you can't make her. Kiss her and say goodnight, as if she was lying down, then leave if she is happy. Don't leave a light on unless you keep it on every night, and don't linger. If she howls after you leave, wait a few moments before you go back, say goodnight again, then leave. She will soon sit down, if she isn't already sitting, and then will go to sleep. Later you can cover her up so that she doesn't get cold.

Q SHOULD I GO TO HER IF SHE CRIES DURING THE NIGHT?

A After six months, a short whimper or a cry is probably quite normal. If she continues to cry, just stay long enough to reassure her, then stroke her, say goodnight, and leave the room.

Q AFTER A WEEKEND AWAY SHE WON'T SLEEP. WHAT CAN I DO?

A Just get back into the daily routine as best you can, and the nighttime routine should follow. If it doesn't and she still won't sleep, institute "the checking method" described in the box below.

Q I'VE STARTED WORK AGAIN AND SHE WON'T SLEEP. WHAT CAN I DO?

A Quality time is an over-used phrase, but you do have to give her some. Do this earlier in the evening and make the later proceedings more mundane (and therefore more conducive to sleep). Don't wait for her to sleep before you have your meal. Putting your own activities on hold will make you feel more resentful. Start unwinding as soon as you return from work, for instance by changing your clothes and having a bath. Some parents find it helpful to have a bath with their baby in the early evening. Save time by keeping your life simple—meals should be easy to cook, and chores avoided wherever possible.

PARENT'S SURVIVAL GUIDE

MY BABY WON'T SETTLE WHEN I PUT HER IN HER CRIB

The best approach for a baby who won't settle, and one that is recommended by many pediatricians and childcare experts, is a method known as controlled crying or "checking." This is when the parent simply checks the child rather than picks her up or rocks her.

When she's ready for the checking method
Before using this method, the daily routine should be firmly established and your baby should be going through the night without a feeding. If she shows anxiety when she's apart from you in the day, she's not really ready for the checking method.

Make her aware of your presence
Let her know that you're in the house, it is safe for her to sleep now, and the day's activities are over.

The checking method
After putting your baby to bed, tuck her in, pat her, say goodnight, then leave. If she cries, return, pat her, and leave again. If she continues to cry, wait a few minutes. Agree with your partner how long this will be, for example, three minutes, and stick to it. Go back, check and pat her, and say goodnight again. Do not relent and cuddle her. Gradually lengthen the period between checks.

Be consistent
It may sound cruel, but there is nothing unkind about this technique. It can work within the space of a week, but you must both be consistent. Until it works, you must continue your normal routine and get up each morning at the usual time, no matter how little sleep you have had.

NIGHTTIME SLEEP PROBLEMS

Q IS IT A GOOD IDEA FOR OUR BABY TO SLEEP IN OUR BED?

A I would say not. She will probably disturb you when she wakes up and babbles at 2 am. If you or your partner snore or talk, she could wake up and find this more fascinating than sleep. Also, it could be habit-forming; if she still comes to bed with you after six months, this may continue throughout the toddler years or later.

Q SHE WAKES IN THE NIGHT. SHOULD SHE STILL BE HAVING A NIGHT FEEDING?

A She doesn't need a feeding during the night, so just give her water if she is thirsty. If this doesn't work, try diluting her formula progressively (see p. 84). If you're breast-feeding, are you doing this for your benefit rather than hers? You could breast-feed her in the evening and early morning, and offer water at night. Or ask your partner to give her water for the first few nights.

Q WHAT CAN I DO IF MY BABY KEEPS WAKING UP EARLY?

A Use same method as for a younger baby: try putting her to bed a little later than usual (see p. 84). Delaying her bedtime by five or 10 minutes each night will soon add up. This does not always work right away, however, so you should be prepared to go to bed earlier yourself. Make sure that sunlight isn't waking her in the early mornings. If all else fails, resign yourself to the fact that your baby is an early bird, and leave toys in her crib so that she can amuse herself without rousing you.

PARENT'S SURVIVAL GUIDE

I'M FINDING IT DIFFICULT TO COPE ON SO LITTLE SLEEP

Is my baby waking up on purpose?
No, she isn't, even if it feels like it. She may have become more clingy, which is common around six months, and babies who used to sleep through the night become more wakeful.

Should I talk to my doctor?
You may find your doctor very sympathetic, especially since many will have been through the same experience themselves as parents, so don't be too proud to ask for advice. If your sleepless baby makes you feel aggressive, you should go to the doctor for advice and support.

Would sedatives for my baby help?
Sedatives are rarely used, and don't really help except in an extreme situation (see p. 90).

How can I unwind?
Get your partner (or a friend) to help look after your baby; use ear-plugs when it is his turn to do the night shift. Try to maintain a calm atmosphere in the home. If you still can't sleep, try to unwind with some music or a book. As soon as your baby is ready, use the checking method (see p. 87).

MY TWINS WON'T SLEEP. HOW CAN I COPE?

If you are at the end of your tether, follow the guidelines below to help you cope physically and emotionally.

Practical solutions
■ Provide a crib for each baby.
■ Use the checking method (see p. 87).
■ Take turns with your partner on the night shift.
■ Try to provide plenty of daytime attention. This is for your benefit too; your nights may be hard, so it's important that you spend time enjoying your babies during the day.

Surviving emotionally
■ Remember that it is not your twins' fault or yours, and be assured that the first year is the worst, and it will soon be over. If you're depressed, talk to your doctor.
■ Snatch daytime siestas whenever you can so that you feel calmer and more able to cope.

Getting help
Doctors are experts, but they may have limited experience with twins. Seek advice from other parents of twins (see p. 235).

DAYTIME SLEEP PROBLEMS

Q HOW LONG SHOULD MY BABY SLEEP DURING THE DAY ?

A There is no "should." On average, a six-month-old baby sleeps about three hours, while a 12-month-old sleeps for two hours—but some babies sleep for only 20 minutes. It depends on your baby's personality and your family's lifestyle. Your baby will probably be down to one daytime nap by the time she is a year or 18 months old.

Q SHE SLEEPS IN THE DAYTIME BUT WON'T SLEEP AT NIGHT. WHAT CAN I DO ?

A Be realistic and appreciate that your baby's sleep needs are decreasing as she gets older. If you want to shorten her daytime nap, try waking her with a drink. You can also give her a small meal rather than a hefty one just before her main nap to keep her from sleeping for too long. Instead of putting her in her crib for a nap, try putting her on a blanket on the floor in the same room as you to discourage her from sleeping for quite as long.

Q IS IT BETTER FOR MY BABY TO NAP IN THE MORNING OR THE AFTERNOON ?

A It really depends on what you prefer. Late morning is probably better if you put your baby to bed early at night, but afternoons are preferable for the main nap if you intend to keep her up until 8 pm or later. If you don't want her to nap in the late morning, bring forward her lunch to help her sleep in the early afternoon. Give her a small snack soon after waking from her siesta and keep her awake until after her evening meal.

Q HOW WILL I KNOW WHEN MY BABY IS READY TO SLEEP LESS IN THE DAY ?

A She may nap less readily, or she may nap as usual but go to bed correspondingly later. There is often an interim period during which one nap isn't enough but two are too many, so you may have to wake her from her second nap of the day.

Q MY BABY NEVER SLEEPS IN THE DAYTIME. SHOULD I BE CONCERNED ?

A No, although it is unusual for babies under a year to go without a daytime sleep. A lively baby may not need a nap, which means you will have little time to yourself. If this is the case, you must get used to doing chores in the company of your wakeful and increasingly mobile baby.

HOW CAN I GET HER TO NAP ?

If your baby seems reluctant to take a nap during the daytime, try to encourage her by following some of the suggestions listed below.

Helping her to sleep during the day

■ Try to give her an outing and a variety of experiences every day. Do this in the morning, and follow it up with a hot meal when you get home; she may then be ready to sleep.

■ Provide a peaceful, quiet atmosphere.

■ Give her a warm drink, but do not leave the bottle with her.

■ Take her out in the car or her stroller.

■ When she looks tired, put her in a crib and say "sleep tight." She may find the familiar sound of a favorite music box lulls her to sleep. If all fails, don't worry. It may mean she doesn't need to sleep—even if you do! Half an hour spent cuddled up together on the sofa looking quietly at a book may be enough to rest her.

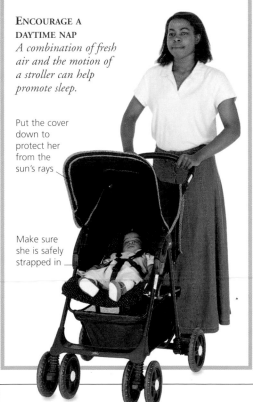

ENCOURAGE A DAYTIME NAP
A combination of fresh air and the motion of a stroller can help promote sleep.

Put the cover down to protect her from the sun's rays

Make sure she is safely strapped in

SLEEP ROUTINES FOR TODDLERS

Q HOW CAN I HELP MY TODDLER GO TO SLEEP BY HERSELF ?

A Make her bedroom warm and welcoming. It should be a place full of her favorite things, where she is comfortable. Once she is in her crib don't tiptoe around—continue with the usual domestic chores; it is helpful if there are kitchen or other noises to reassure her that everything is normal. Before she goes to bed, avoid arguments and punishments, as well as scary stories, television programs, or videos. As soon as you put her into her crib, ignore any small murmurs of protest. Many toddlers want to stay up longer, but remember, you're in charge.

Q MY TODDLER SCREAMS WHEN I PUT HER INTO HER CRIB. WHAT CAN I DO ?

A Give her lots of love and attention in the run-up to bedtime rather than after it. Institute a bedtime routine that is pleasant and calm—not a military march into her room. However, do not pander to her every whim. Demands for a glass of water or another bedtime story can grow in number and complexity until they become a completely unmanageable ritual, such as taking in a couple of hot drinks, extra stories, kissing pictures on the wall goodnight, and making sure that the bedroom door is positioned at a specific angle.

BOOKS AT BEDTIME

Reading your toddler a bedtime story can become a regular part of her evening routine and is also good preparation for sleep.

READING STORIES
Most toddlers enjoy cuddling up with their parents for a bedtime story.

PARENT'S SURVIVAL GUIDE

SHE DOESN'T SLEEP THROUGH THE NIGHT

Many youngsters at this age start waking in the night again after months of unbroken sleep. If your toddler does this, don't worry. Toddler sleep problems are very common, but preschool ones aren't, so you can take heart—things will improve. First, try using the checking method (see p. 87). It is not too late to put this into effect, even at this age, just as long as:

■ your toddler feels secure—if there is a new baby around, she may feel a little less secure, so it could pay to wait until things have settled

■ she sleeps in her own bedroom and likes being there, surrounded by her own things.

When you feel desperate
In extreme cases, for example, where a sleepless toddler drives a parent to physical or emotional abuse, doctors may suggest a sedative for the child. This should never be a long-term solution, but it can occasionally help short term, for a couple of nights. However, it is only an adjunct to managing a child's sleep problems with consistent loving handling and a good pre-bedtime regimen and is only acceptable when needed to preserve family sanity. Talk to your pediatrician or consider other options, such as support groups where you can talk to parents with similar problems (see p. 235).

Q **MY TODDLER WON'T GO TO BED UNTIL 10 PM. DOESN'T SHE NEED MORE SLEEP?**

A She probably does. If it is proving difficult to get her to bed at the appointed time, then try putting her to bed five minutes earlier each night until you reach your target bedtime. However, don't be unrealistic—if your toddler has just woken from a substantial daytime sleep, she is unlikely to be tired enough to go to bed for the night a mere two hours later. It is also possible that she now needs less sleep during the daytime (see below). If necessary, cut down or eliminate her daytime sleep.

Q **CAN SHE STILL HAVE A FEEDING OR WARM MILK BEFORE BED?**

A She can as long as she doesn't take the drink to bed with her to linger over. If she drinks anything before bed, make sure that she brushes her teeth afterward.

Q **CAN MY TODDLER HAVE A COMFORTER IN HER CRIB NOW?**

A Yes, once she is over a year old she can have a comforter if the bedroom temperature requires it. If she becomes too hot, she can always kick it off during the night. If you are concerned about the room temperature, check her yourself before you go to bed—pull the comforter down if you think that she feels too hot; or alternatively, pull the comforter up if you consider that she might get too cold during the night without it.

BEDTIME TOYS
Some children take a favorite toy to bed well into their school years (see p. 86) or cuddle it when they're ill or stressed.

Make sure toys conform to safety standards

Q **SHE WANTS TO TAKE ALL HER TOYS TO BED. HOW CAN I RESTRICT THIS?**

A Try choosing around three toys each night and make the process of choosing part of her bedtime routine. By doing this, you can successfully restrict the number of toys she takes to bed and at the same time avoid any conflict or tantrums. Your child will feel involved in the choosing process rather than deprived of her bedtime companions. However, if this is not successful, don't worry. Having lots of toys isn't as hazardous as when she was younger, but don't leave big toys in the crib that she could use to climb out.

ENCOURAGING SLEEP   TODDLERS 1–2½ YEARS

DOES MY TODDLER NEED A DAYTIME SLEEP?

There are no firm rules about daytime sleeps, but one nap in the afternoon is about average at the age of 2–2½. Avoid late afternoon naps, and don't expect them to be as long as they used to be— if they are, your toddler might not sleep so readily at night.

What can I do if he won't have a daytime nap?
You can't force your toddler to sleep in the day. If he won't sleep when you put him in his crib, then ensure that he has a quiet period during the day. Give him some toys and put him in his crib or on a blanket and allow him to play quietly by himself for an hour or so. This means that he will have a rest during the day and you can relax too.

When is the best time for his daytime nap?
This depends on what time you want him to go to bed. If you want him to go to sleep in the early evening, try to time his nap for before lunchtime. However, routines vary; if your toddler's routine is such that late bedtimes are accepted, he may continue napping in the afternoon.

He naps in the daytime, but won't sleep at night. What should I do?
If he is beginning to sleep badly, or it is becoming difficult to get him to bed, he may be sleeping too much in the daytime. If he only has one nap, try not letting him sleep every day. If he has more than one nap, reduce this to one and encourage morning rather than afternoon naps.

COMMON SLEEP PROBLEMS

Q WHAT CAN I DO IF MY TODDLER WAKES IN THE NIGHT ?

A First wait to see if she has a real need, in which case her noises will develop into a cry. She may, for instance, have teething pain. (But don't suggest this to her.) Just supply whatever she needs in a quiet and soothing way and put her back to bed. Only take her into your bed if you're prepared for the possible consequence of it becoming a habit that is hard to break.

Q SHOULD I GIVE HER A DRINK IN THE NIGHT IF SHE WANTS ONE ?

A Toddlers don't need a milk feeding in the night, so this should just be water. If she often wakes for a drink, you could let her keep a cup of water nearby.

Q SHE IS STARTING TO CLIMB OUT OF HER CRIB. WHAT SHOULD I DO ?

A You should move her to an adult bed soon, before she has an accident. In the meantime, as soon as you see signs of your toddler being able to climb out (for instance, your child putting one leg over the rail), then keep the crib sides down all the time. This won't stop her from falling out, but it is less far for her to fall. You could also put a chair next to her crib to help her climb out safely.

Q SHE WAKES VERY EARLY. CAN I ENCOURAGE HER TO SLEEP LONGER ?

A You can't make her sleep longer, but you can provide soft toys and books in her crib to occupy her, and make sure she is safe if she decides to get up. To get more sleep yourself, go to bed earlier and use ear-plugs if your partner is taking the night shift so you don't hear her babbling to herself at the crack of dawn.

Q SHE WON'T GO TO BED WITHOUT A NIGHT-LIGHT. IS THIS A PROBLEM ?

A No. She will probably grow out of this eventually (see opposite), but in the meantime, there is nothing wrong with it. Some toddlers like the reassuring glow provided by a dim night-light, and I don't think there is any harm in this. Even if the night-light becomes a permanent fixture throughout childhood, it is still very handy to keep your toddler from tripping in the dark once she has moved to a bed and is able to get up in the night. Equally, you may find it useful to stop you from tripping over furniture if you check on her in the night. Make sure the night-light is not too bright; the room should be dark enough to rest your toddler's eyes. You could also try to minimize early morning sunlight if you want your toddler to stay in bed longer in the mornings.

WHEN CAN SHE MAKE THE TRANSITION TO A BIG BED ?

There is no fixed time when this should happen, but for practical reasons it is usually around the age of two because this is when a toddler often starts wanting to scale the sides of the crib.

How should I make the change?

Talk to your toddler about being big and moving to a new bed; if possible, however, keep both the crib and the bed in the same room for a while. Make the bed appealing by putting her favorite toys in it and keep her bedtime routine the same as far as possible. Don't evict your toddler from the crib to make way for a new baby—it is better to put the baby in a bassinet, or borrow or buy another crib to tide you over this period.

My toddler wants to stay in her crib. How can I encourage her to move to a big bed?
Don't worry too much about this. Unless she is climbing out of her crib, there is no point in putting pressure on her to give it up. A child can sleep in a crib until the age of four—it is unusual, but I know some children who do, and who don't come to any harm unless they try to climb out. It is a safety issue rather than anything else.

Is a junior bed a good idea?

No. A junior bed (or child bed) is smaller than a regular adult bed, and I think that it is a waste of money because your toddler won't be using it for long—a few years at most. However, it might be worthwhile if the bedroom is too small for a normal-sized single bed.

SLEEP FOR PRESCHOOLERS

Q MY CHILD DRAGS OUT HER BEDTIME. WHAT CAN I DO?

A Youngsters often like to stay up past bedtime so as not to miss out on any action. Set an appropriate time and tell her that's when she's going to bed, then give her about half an hour's notice before bedtime. Involve your partner and be consistent and firm. It may be tiring at first, but it will work in the end. You will also have to decide between you whether "bedtime" means "lights out" or whether she can stay awake looking at a book and have the light turned out later. It is really a lifestyle choice that you need to make together with your partner.

Q AFTER DAYCARE SHE IS TIRED BUT WON'T SLEEP. WHAT CAN I DO?

A You may have to compress her quality time with you in the evening. Ask her about her day and show an interest in her activities, but don't overstimulate her. End the evening in a low-key way, so that she goes to bed in the knowledge that she is not missing out. To ensure that you both get much-needed rest, you could promise her an outing with you at the weekend on the condition that she goes to bed on time during the week. But the promise must be one you'll be able to deliver.

Q SHE ALWAYS WANTS A DRINK BEFORE BED. WHAT SHOULD I GIVE HER?

A I suggest either water or milk. For the sake of her teeth, avoid sweetened drinks unless she brushes her teeth again afterward. When you're trying to keep her dry at night, it's also wise to avoid carbonated drinks, fruit juice, and acidic drinks late in the day.

Q SHE WON'T SETTLE UNLESS I LEAVE THE DOOR OPEN. WHAT SHOULD I DO?

A It is perfectly reasonable to leave it open. In fact, there is no real reason for the door to remain shut, unless you need to keep a family pet out. Many people, adults included, like to have the bedroom door ajar and the reassurance of household noises as they fall asleep. There are other advantages for you as a parent—you will be able to see if, for instance, your child turns the light on again and starts playing after bedtime.

Q SHOULD MY CHILD STILL HAVE A NIGHT-LIGHT?

A I can't see anything wrong with using a night-light. It is the obvious answer when a child dislikes the dark. It is also useful when your child starts to get up during the night to use the potty or the toilet.

Q WILL SHE OUTGROW HAVING THE LIGHT ON DURING THE NIGHT?

A Eventually, but it can take time. One way of weaning her off having a light on is to move the lamp progressively farther from her bed, until it is outside her room, but make sure that she can't trip over the cord if she gets up. Alternatively, put a light (or night-light) in the hall near the door of her room.

Q MY CHILD SNEAKS INTO MY BED AT NIGHT. WHAT CAN I DO?

A This may be very endearing from time to time, but you really should stop it unless you are prepared for it to become a habit. Return her to her own bed every time you realize she is with you. This is hard work, but if you're consistent it will work eventually. You could also use a reward chart, with a star for every night she stays out of your bed. After two weeks or so, a series of stars can earn her a treat (see p. 176). Make your reward method realistic—if she gets into your bed every night, she will never get a star and will be disappointed. The aim should therefore be achievable, so to begin with, you might have to award a star if you only have to return her to her bed once during the night.

Q SHE WAKES VERY EARLY IN THE MORNING. HOW CAN I STOP THIS?

A You can't stop her from waking spontaneously, but you can let her have toys, books, a drink, or even a cookie to keep her occupied; she can play quietly on her own for a while in her room when she wakes up. If necessary, provide her with a light on a timer to make her aware of what time it is. An alarm clock is an alternative, but many youngsters cannot resist fiddling with it, so it can become an ordeal for you when it goes off at the wrong time. To supplement these measures, use reward systems (see previous question and p. 176).

DO HOMEOPATHIC REMEDIES WORK FOR SLEEPING PROBLEMS ?

Many parents use homeopathy for their children's sleeping problems, and there is anecdotal evidence that it does work. However, a homeopathic remedy should not replace other methods of dealing with a child's sleep problems, and giving your child any medicine, complementary or orthodox, is not an excuse for continuing with bad bedtime habits.

HOW HOMEOPATHY WORKS

Remedies are taken from animal, plant, and mineral extracts and are then diluted. The principle behind homeopathy is that the more diluted the remedy, the greater its potency. The doses prescribed are the same regardless of age—a child could be given the same dose as a 70-year-old. Homeopathy won't do any harm and it can be worth trying. If you have any doubts about which remedy to try, consult a qualified homeopath first (see p. 235).

CHOICE OF REMEDIES

The choice of remedy depends on the particular sleeping problem. All remedies can be bought in tablet form and some as sugarlike granules (see p. 227). Homeopathic remedies can be used for babies and older children, but you should check that a particular remedy is suitable for your child's age.

Chamomilla
If teething is affecting sleep, chamomilla (chamomile) is said to be very good.
Calcarea carbonica
For night terrors, calcarea carbonica (crushed oyster shells) can be useful.
Phosphorus
This can be an adjunct to a night-light if your child is sensitive and afraid of the dark.

Important note
Unlike orthodox medication, homeopathic remedies should be stopped when symptoms improve. It is believed that continuing these treatments when there are no longer symptoms for them to work against can be counter-productive and may even undo the good that has been done.

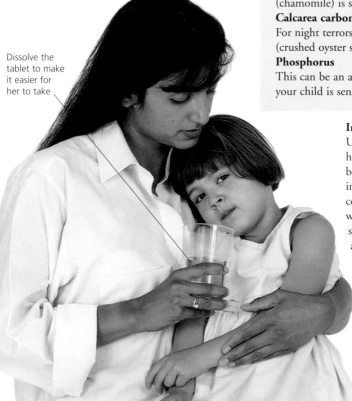

Dissolve the tablet to make it easier for her to take

ADMINISTERING A REMEDY
Crush the tablet between two spoons or with a mortar and pestle, then dissolve in a little water for your child to drink.

NIGHTMARES AND NIGHT TERRORS

Q HOW CAN I ENCOURAGE HER TO GO TO BED IF SHE IS AFRAID?

A Make her room as pleasant as possible, with good lighting and attractive bedlinen (even if she still wets the bed) and a bedside table with some of her favorite things. Help her keep her room neat by putting toys away with her, and make sure she associates her room with enjoyable activities—for example, read her a bedtime story in her room. Once she is in bed, tuck her in and leave.

Q MY CHILD HAS NIGHTMARES. IS THIS COMMON?

A Yes, minor nightmares or bad dreams are especially common between three and four years of age. A child who has a nightmare usually wakes screaming or crying. She may tell you what she dreamed, or simply say that she had a bad dream. Don't worry; nightmares do not mean that your child is disturbed, but they can reflect something that she has seen or heard, such as a scary story or video.

Q CAN I DO ANYTHING TO STOP HER FROM HAVING NIGHTMARES?

A You can help by making sure that she avoids exciting or overstimulating bedtime stories, television programs, or videos at bedtime, any of which may put the idea of monsters or aliens into her head. If she seems afraid before she goes to bed, reassure her that the house is safe and secure, that you are there for her, and that only friends or family can come into the house.

Q WHAT SHOULD I DO WHEN MY CHILD HAS A NIGHTMARE?

A Cuddle and reassure her, then tuck her back into bed when she is feeling more secure. If you make her feel safe, she will usually sleep soundly again after a nightmare.

Q WILL A NIGHT-LIGHT HELP IF SHE HAS NIGHTMARES?

A It won't necessarily prevent her from having nightmares, but it may help reassure her if she wakes up from one during the night. Conversely, the shadows that a night-light create in her room may have quite the opposite effect on your child and even cause a nightmare—children have vivid imaginations.

Q MY CHILD WAKES SCREAMING IN THE NIGHT. WHAT IS WRONG?

A This may be a night terror, characterized by a child who wakes up screaming with her eyes wide open but who is not actually awake. This is rarer than a nightmare and happens during a stage of deep sleep, which is why it doesn't wake her up. During a night terror, the child will sit bolt upright, scream, and sweat. Nothing you can say will get through to her and you may be very frightened by her appearance.

Q WHAT CAN I DO DURING A NIGHT TERROR?

A There is nothing much you can do except perhaps put on the lights, although this is mainly to reassure yourself. Don't try to wake her, argue, or cajole, since this could make things worse. Just wait for the terror to pass. When it has, settle her back in bed and try to go to sleep yourself.

Q IS THERE SOMETHING WRONG IF MY CHILD HAS NIGHT TERRORS?

A No, so try not to worry. Night terrors are alarming to witness, but there is usually nothing emotionally or physically wrong with your child. For some reason, night terrors are more common in boys over four years old, and they all grow out of them.

Q MY CHILD TALKS IN HER SLEEP. SHOULD I WORRY ABOUT THIS?

A This is rarely a sign of anything wrong. Many children talk, mumble, or shout in their sleep, and the only problem with this is that it can disturb the rest of the household.

Q MY CHILD SLEEPWALKS. SHOULD I BE CONCERNED ABOUT THIS?

A Sleepwalking isn't a sign of a serious problem, but it can be dangerous. It happens during deep sleep, so even if your child wakes you, you can't communicate with her. The main worry is your child's safety. Make sure windows and outside doors are securely shut and locked. Many parents worry about their sleepwalking child falling down the stairs, but this is rare. Barricades at the top of the stairs can make accidents more likely because your child does not expect the route to be blocked. But if you usually use a stair gate, lock it at night.

EVERYDAY
CARE

Looking after a young child is a demanding, but **rewarding job**. By arming yourself with practical knowledge and an understanding of your **child's needs**, you can turn mundane tasks into an opportunity for him to play and learn. Here you'll find everything you need to know about **routine tasks** such as bathing, hairwashing, choosing clothes for your child to wear, and dressing him. There is also a wealth of **reassuring advice** on topics such as toilet training, as well as strategies to help you avoid unnecessary conflict when your **increasingly independent child** insists on dressing himself or refuses to wear his shoes.

DRESSING YOUR CHILD

DRESSING YOUNG BABIES

Q WHAT ARE THE MOST SUITABLE CLOTHES FOR MY BABY NOW?

A The most convenient outfits are stretchsuits or sweatpants and tops. Overalls look cute and often have snaps in the crotch for easy diaper-changing. However, try to avoid metal clasps on the straps because they may rub your baby's neck. Also, some denim can be rough on a young baby's skin.

Q DOES HE NEED TO WEAR AN UNDERSHIRT?

A Yes. An all-in-one body undershirt with snaps in the crotch will keep him warm and help to hold his diaper in place. Undershirts also protect tender skin from being chafed by the inside seam of some clothes. Use thermal undershirts with sleeves during the winter; in the summer, a sleeveless undershirt may be all your baby needs.

Q WHAT SHOULD MY BABY WEAR OUT OF DOORS?

A This depends on the weather and the form of transportation. A young baby is not capable of controlling his body temperature as easily as an adult and can become overheated or too cold. Therefore, if he is exposed to the elements in a stroller during the winter he might need a snowsuit, but if he's in a baby carriage, then a blanket and a sweater may be ample. A hat or bonnet is essential in the cold, and bootees and mittens will help keep your baby warm. When it's warm, your baby is probably most comfortable with very little clothing (but make sure he is protected from the sun, see below); add layers if it becomes chillier.

Q DOES HE REALLY NEED A SUNHAT DURING THE SUMMER?

A Yes. Under six months of age, your baby's skin should be protected at all times from direct sunlight. A hat keeps the sun off his face and neck. The most effective hats are those with a wide brim that shade most of the face and neck. Some have a flap at the back to protect his tender neck. In addition to protective clothing, you may also need an umbrella or shade and sunblock (see p. 208).

Q CAN SOCKS AND STRETCHSUITS DAMAGE MY BABY'S FEET?

A Yes, if they are too tight, so move him up to the next size if necessary. If you do not have any stretchsuits in a bigger size, as an interim measure you can always cut the feet off his existing ones, or rip out the seams at the feet.

Q DOES MY BABY NEED TO WEAR SHOES?

A No, not until he is walking. If it is cold you can use bootees or socks. Avoid stiff shoes—they have no function and can be harmful because they restrict movement. His toes should be free to move around, point, and curl.

Q DOES HE NEED SEPARATE CLOTHES FOR NIGHTTIME?

A Yes, from about six weeks of age, since this will help him differentiate between night and day. You can change his stretchsuit or he can wear pajamas. From about four months old, he could sleep in a nightgown that closes up at the hem to form a sleeping sack. Most night clothes have snaps, which are more comfortable and less hazardous than buttons. Unless it is warm, he also needs to wear an undershirt at night.

PARENT'S SURVIVAL GUIDE

MY BABY SCREAMS WHEN HE IS DRESSED AND UNDRESSED

Many babies cry when being dressed or undressed. The following can minimize distress:
- make sure the room is warm enough
- keep clothing changes to a minimum
- make sure his clothes are large enough and buy clothes that are quick to get on and off; avoid stretchsuits with snaps up the back and in the crotch
- hold him gently but firmly during dressing
- smile at your baby and make reassuring noises as you dress or undress him.

HOW SHOULD I PUT A COAT OR JACKET ON MY BABY ?

If your baby is very young, he won't be able to sit up when you dress him. When putting on coats and jackets, lay him on his back and follow the steps below.

1 Lay him on his back on top of the open jacket and ease the sleeves over each arm in turn.

Make sure the neck opening isn't too tight

Guide the arm gently but firmly

Make sure his nails don't get caught

2 Put your fingers down the sleeve to hold his hand while drawing the sleeve over his arm.

3 Once both sleeves are on, fasten the snaps and pull up the hood if necessary.

WASHING BABY CLOTHES

Q WHAT IS THE BEST WAY TO WASH MY BABY'S CLOTHES ?

A For hygiene reasons, ideally you should wash baby clothes separately from the rest of the household laundry. If an adult or older child's clothes must be in the same load as the baby's, leave out the older person's socks and underwear. A washing machine gets clothes cleaner than hand-washing and is a lot more convenient, which may well dictate the clothes you choose for your baby. Avoid overloading the machine, since this will prevent it from washing the clothes thoroughly.

Q WHICH TYPE OF LAUNDRY DETERGENT SHOULD I USE ?

A Always use an enzyme-free laundry detergent, since other types can leave enzymes in the fabric that may irritate young, sensitive skin. Rinse clothes well to remove any traces of detergent, and then dry the clothes thoroughly.

Q CAN I USE FABRIC CONDITIONER ON MY BABY'S CLOTHES ?

A Yes. Conditioner is especially useful if the water is hard (full of calcium salts). Without conditioner, his clothes could feel very rough. However, conditioner can cause allergic reactions, so choose one that has been dermatologically tested and formulated for sensitive skin.

Q WHAT'S THE BEST WAY TO DRY MY BABY'S CLOTHES ?

A If you have a clothes dryer, this often gets clothes softer than drying them on the line and it is a lot quicker, too. Unfortunately, not all baby clothes can go in the dryer, since it will cause some of them to shrink—if in doubt, check the washing instructions. If you remove the labels from your baby's clothes for comfort, keep them somewhere that you can easily find them. Be careful about putting clothes straight from the dryer onto your baby—sometimes metal snaps and other fastenings may be dangerously hot for your baby's delicate skin.

DRESSING OLDER BABIES

WHICH CLOTHES ARE SUITABLE FOR MY BABY ?

When you are buying clothes for an older baby, you will find that the choice is much wider. Bear in mind that your baby is becoming more and more mobile, so even if it seems wise to buy clothes with lots of growing space, make sure they are not too large; clothes that are too big will hamper movement and will get worn out, stained, and drooled on before they are outgrown.

CHOOSING CLOTHES

Buy clothes that are easy to wash and dry, and that need no ironing. Avoid pale colors because they won't stay clean long: the knees collect dirt from the floor and tops get spattered with food.

STRETCHSUITS
These are still useful items of clothing, especially for nighttime. You can buy them with or without feet.

Mix and match separates to make her wardrobe more versatile

OVERALLS
These are ideal for this age group, especially if reinforced at the knees.

PANTS AND TOPS
Separate items are perfect for a baby who is crawling. The pants can be washed if dirty, or discarded if the knees are threadbare, while the top can be kept.

Choose dresses that are easy to get on over your baby's head

DRESSES
Dresses can be worn over thick leggings. Make sure dresses are not too long, since this could hamper crawling.

Make sure that her movements are not restricted

SNOWSUITS
An all-in-one snowsuit is ideal for cold weather when out in the stroller.

OLDER BABIES 6–12 MONTHS   EVERYDAY CARE

Q DOES MY BABY STILL NEED TO WEAR AN UNDERSHIRT ALL THE TIME ?

A Yes. An undershirt with snaps underneath is ideal to keep the diaper in place and to stop it from moving out of place as your baby wriggles.

Q WHICH ARE THE MOST SENSIBLE CLOTHES FOR MY BABY WHEN IT IS HOT ?

A In very hot weather, a baby can just wear an undershirt over his diaper, but put plenty of sunblock on him, too. Always make sure that he wears a sunhat—although this won't be enough to stop him from burning, it will help shade his face and neck. A legionnaire-style hat is particularly effective (see right). Both boys and girls can wear shorts and clothes in lighter fabrics. Girls can wear cotton dresses or skirts, but these should be short so that they do not get in the way when crawling; alternatively, reserve dresses for special occasions.

Q WHAT SHOULD MY BABY WEAR IN COLD WEATHER ?

A Practical options for cold weather include a snowsuit, a padded ski-type jacket with a hood, all-in-one leggings that will keep his feet and legs warm in the stroller without restricting his movements, and woolen or sheepskin bootees (although babies tend to kick off their footwear). Keep outfits as simple as possible, and don't opt for garments with complicated fastenings. The simpler the clothes, the easier it is to get your baby into them—and out again for diaper changes. Babies have a knack for passing a stool just when they are all dressed up and you are halfway out the door.

Q WHAT KIND OF HAT SHOULD HE WEAR IN COLD WEATHER ?

A Bonnets are preferable to hats, since they are less likely to come off, but make sure that the string on the bonnet does not cut into your baby's neck.

Q WHAT KIND OF SOCKS ARE BEST ?

A While he is crawling, it doesn't really matter what socks your baby wears as long as they fit him. I would suggest that you buy many pairs of cheap ones because, between you, your baby, and the washing machine, you will be losing a lot of socks. Once he starts to stand and move around between pieces of furniture, make sure that the socks have nonslip soles.

A hat with a flap gives added sun protection to the back of the neck

PROTECTIVE HEADGEAR
During the summer, it is important that you protect your baby from harmful UV rays. Put a sunhat on him to protect the tender skin on his face and neck.

Q DOES MY BABY NEED SHOES YET ?

A He will need shoes when he starts to walk. Until then, his feet are best left bare. If it is too cold for him to go barefoot, dress him in slipper-socks or bootees with nonslip soles. Avoid socks without nonslip soles unless the room is fully carpeted; if he slips, this may discourage him from trying to stand in the future.

Q WHAT SHOULD MY BABY WEAR AT NIGHT ?

A Any of the following are suitable: stretchsuits, pajamas (these can be short- or long-sleeved, depending on the temperature), pajama bottoms and an undershirt (for hotter weather); for girls, nightdresses (useful for diaper changing in the night). In hot weather, an undershirt may be all he needs; otherwise, undershirts are unnecessary at night now, unless you use a plain one without snaps.

Q HE THINKS THAT DRESSING IS A GAME AND RESISTS. HOW CAN I DRESS HIM ?

A You can put his clothes on more easily if you join in with the fun; if he crawls out of the room, sit in the doorway ready to put his T-shirt over his head as he passes. If all else fails, tickle his tummy. He will probably roll onto his back in a fit of giggles, and you will be able to dress him without resistance. Otherwise, you may find it easier to dress him while he is sitting on your lap—at this stage, babies prefer sitting to lying down. Keep dressing as simple as possible and avoid elaborate outfits. Two items of clothing are often easier to get on than an all-in-one. If he always struggles when you dress him, ask yourself whether everything you are putting on him is necessary.

EVERYDAY CARE

OLDER BABIES 6–12 MONTHS

DRESSING TODDLERS

Q WHAT ARE THE MOST SUITABLE CLOTHES FOR MY TODDLER ?

A Sweatpants or shorts are ideal for toddlers, but opt for elasticated waists rather than a zipper or button fly. He can wear sweatshirts or T-shirts on top. Jeans are more practical than overalls if he needs to go to the toilet in a hurry, but make sure they have an elasticated waist. Girls can wear similar clothes, or else leggings. Dresses and skirts can be dangerous when a toddler is climbing stairs because they may make her trip. Whatever you choose, it should allow a bit of room for growth, but not too much, since this can hamper movement and your toddler is likely to wear clothes out faster than he outgrows them.

Q DOES HE STILL NEED TO WEAR AN UNDERSHIRT EVERY DAY ?

A Only when the weather is cold. You can continue with snap undershirts for now, and then graduate to simple undershirts or T-shirts, which are easier for toilet training.

Q WHAT SHOULD MY TODDLER WEAR WHEN IT IS HOT ?

A Toddlers of either sex can wear shorts, a T-shirt, and a sunhat—the legionnaire-style hat protects the back of the neck (see p. 101). A girl can wear a short dress that doesn't trip her up.

Q WHICH CLOTHES ARE MOST SUITABLE FOR MY TODDLER IN COLD WEATHER ?

A Get him a warm, washable coat or padded rainproof jacket, preferably one that has a hood and that eventually he can learn to fasten himself. A good woolen winter coat may look charming, but it is hard to keep clean and is soon outgrown. Don't forget mittens and boots (with warm socks) for wet weather.

Q WHAT CAN MY TODDLER WEAR DURING THE NIGHT ?

A Pajamas are the most practical; he can wear short-sleeved ones in hot weather and long-sleeved ones in the winter. He is too old now for sleeping-sack nightgowns. It is best to avoid nighties because a young toddler can easily fall over by stepping on the hem. A bathrobe is optional, although it can encourage a reluctant toddler to get ready for bed and is nice and cozy.

KEEPING CLOTHES CLEAN

This is a time when your child's clothes can collect a wide variety of stains. Follow the guidelines below as well as the washing instructions inside the garment—if you remove labels for comfort, keep them somewhere safe. Always keep cleaning agents out of your child's reach.

STAIN	WHAT YOU CAN DO
Felt tips, ball point pens, and wax crayons	Dab lightly with rubbing alcohol before washing in the machine.
Blood	Sponge with hydrogen peroxide. Soak in cool, salty water, then wash in cool or lukewarm water.
Grass	Rub with rubbing alcohol. If it's still green, rub with a little glycerine and then wash in the machine.
Shoe polish	Rub with dishwashing liquid before machine washing.
Grease	This is difficult, but you may succeed in removing stains with either a blob of dishwashing liquid, or a little glycerine, before machine washing.
Chocolate	Sponge with warm, soapy water, then use a stain remover and machine wash as usual.
Milk	Soak in borax solution, then wash in the machine.
Jam, honey, marmalade	Fresh spills are easy, but dried ones may need soaking in borax or soap solution before machine washing.

Q MY TODDLER CONSTANTLY REMOVES HIS SHOES. SHOULD I WORRY ?

A Not unduly. As long as he wears them outside, he doesn't need to keep them on inside the house. When he is older and muddy from playing games, you will be pleased that he removes his shoes. Try to keep track of where he puts his shoes when he takes them off so that you don't have to spend hours looking for one tiny shoe.

Q MY TODDLER TAKES HIS CLOTHES OFF IN PUBLIC PLACES. WHAT CAN I DO?

A Try to explain that he should keep his clothes on in public, but don't let it worry you. Taking clothes off is easier than putting them on, and this is quite common in toddlers 12–18 months. Other parents will understand.

Q MY TODDLER HATES GETTING DRESSED. WHAT IS THE BEST APPROACH?

A Be organized. Get the clothes out the night before and keep your choice simple—lots of elaborate garments can be discouraging. Use stealth to dress him: distract him with a toy or book while you put an undershirt over him. Encourage him to put some items on himself. Imitation is useful, so let him see you or your partner get dressed.

Q MY TODDLER WANTS TO DRESS HIMSELF. HOW CAN I HELP HIM?

A Even if he isn't very good at it, help him as little as possible and be discreet when you have to assist. Put on one item of clothing in return for him putting on the next one. Don't rush him; if he needs more time, then let him have it, even if it means getting up earlier in the morning. You can encourage him by making things easy for him. For instance, avoid clothes with zippers—these will be frustrating—and provide elasticated sweatpants and other similar clothes instead. Buttons can also be difficult for toddlers to fasten, so choose clothes with elasticated waists or Velcro fastenings. Your patience will pay off; by the age of two and a half, he should be able to put on underpants and pants without help, and will feel proud of himself.

WHEN IS MY TODDLER READY FOR SHOES?

If he has been walking for about a month and is very sure on his feet, then he is ready for shoes. Go to a good shoe store to have his feet measured, and choose shoes that fit well. His shoes must be the same shape as his foot, but they needn't be supportive—the bones and muscles of his feet will do the supporting. Avoid shoes with very hard leather; they should be flexible enough for him to walk easily but have a secure fastening, such as a buckle or Velcro.

How many pairs of shoes does he need?
Apart from some waterproof boots for wet weather, your toddler only needs one pair of shoes at a time. He is growing so fast that he will very quickly outgrow his first pair.

How often should I have his feet measured?
Take him to have them checked approximately every six to eight weeks after he gets his first pair of shoes.

Does he need shoes in width fittings?
If his feet are of average width, he may not. However, you won't know this until you have his feet measured correctly, so it is important to go to a specialist children's shoe store or department for the first few years at least.

Should I buy him canvas shoes?
If they fit well, canvas shoes are perfectly adequate for most purposes, certainly for around the house and outdoors in warm weather. However, they don't give much protection against injury.

He hates trying on shoes. What can I do?
Be positive. If you expect him to be awkward, he will pick this up and will behave badly. If all else fails, secure his cooperation with a bribe such as the promise of a small treat afterward.

How can I make him wear his shoes?
If he is reluctant to wear them, they may be uncomfortable. You can check that his socks fit correctly and don't have a hard seam near the toes, or take the shoes back to the store and ask them to check the fitting. If he is still reluctant, compromise by getting him to wear shoes outdoors and go without indoors.

He keeps falling down. Are his shoes too small?
They may be, or the style may not suit him—the rim may be too chunky. If your toddler stumbles without shoes on, consult your doctor. Some children fall when they first start walking because their toes point inward. This can be due to a rotation of the thigh bone, which disappears on its own as the child develops.

DRESSING PRESCHOOL CHILDREN

Q SHOULD MY CHILD BE ABLE TO DRESS HIMSELF BY THE AGE OF FIVE ?

A Not necessarily, but if your child is due to start school at the age of five, it is very useful if he can dress himself. However, you shouldn't be too ambitious in your choice of clothes. Small buttons, pants with a fly that zips, and lace-up shoes are usually too difficult for a five-year-old child to master, so keep it simple for both your sakes. Continue buying pants and skirts with elasticated waists. Try to choose shoes that fasten with Velcro or buckles instead of ones that have laces.

Q HOW CAN I ENCOURAGE HIM IF HE HAS DIFFICULTY DRESSING HIMSELF ?

A Always praise his attempts at dressing and only adjust his clothing if there is something seriously amiss. If a T-shirt is inside out, it's no great disaster. However, if others are going to think he looks silly, you can tactfully point this out to him and suggest he has another try putting on that particular garment. If he resists your attempts to help, just let him be—he will eventually get the hang of dressing correctly.

Q SHOULD HE HAVE CLEAN CLOTHES EVERY DAY ?

A I think this is unnecessary. However, he should have clothes that *look* clean. I would suggest making each outfit last for two days, unless there are stains or mishaps, or, of course, it is a special occasion, such as a party.

Q WHAT SHOULD MY CHILD WEAR IN BED AT NIGHT ?

A A nightgown or pajamas are fine for your preschool child. Whatever he wears at night should keep him warm and allow him to make independent visits to the potty or toilet during the night without hampering him.

Q HOW MANY SPARE SETS OF NIGHT-CLOTHES DOES HE NEED ?

A It is worth having several sets because even when your child is reliably dry during the night, you should still be prepared for the odd accident. With this in mind, it is also advisable to keep the mattress covered with a protective sheet for several more years.

WHICH TYPE OF SHOE IS BEST FOR MY CHILD ?

Although your child may be becoming increasingly fashion-conscious, remember that shoes should be sensible and that comfort and convenience are the most important considerations when choosing shoes for your child.

Which style of shoe is best?
Choose shoes that are easy to put on—Velcro or buckle fastenings are easier than laces. Some styles can be slipped on, but can slip off just as easily while your child is playing. The choice also depends on your child's feet—sometimes only lace-ups fit well.

How often do I need to get his feet measured?
Every three or four months is about right. If you bought them with a little bit of growing room, he will probably be able to wear the same shoes for four months or so. Obviously, this may vary, since children's feet can go through growth spurts, often over the summer months, so inspect his shoes and feet yourself from time to time. If you watch the store sales clerk check the fit, you'll soon learn how to do this at home.

Can I let him choose his own shoes?
I think he should have a say in the choice of shoes. Comfort is very subjective, so give his opinion some weight. If you don't, you may end up buying something he won't wear. When shopping for shoes, you may find two pairs that fit well, so allow him to make the final choice between the two.

My child screams in shoe stores. What can I do?
He needs shoes and you need his cooperation, so bargain with him. You may have to resort to a bribe—he tries on shoes and you let him have or do something he likes. Some parents threaten a child with having to go barefoot unless he behaves in the shoe store, but this doesn't work because the threat is not carried out. To minimize the potential for outbursts, shop when it is not too crowded.

Q SHOULD I LET HIM CHOOSE HIS OWN CLOTHES NOW?

A If he shows an interest, don't discourage him—making choices of all kinds is an important part of growing up. Some preschool children will not show an interest, while others as young as three will want a say in what they wear. Of course, there will be considerations such as price, washing instructions, and color matching that a child can't be expected to handle. Take his views into account, but be the final judge of what is suitable.

Q HOW CAN I ENCOURAGE MY CHILD TO BE NEAT WITH HIS CLOTHES?

A It takes a lot of patience and you will need to put away his clothes with him at first. Explain why clothes need to be folded away, and why some should go into a basket for washing. However, getting a young child to put these instructions into practice isn't always easy. Apart from anything else, youngsters are easily distracted. Sometimes your child will cooperate, while on other occasions he might leave his clothes strewn all over the floor. Keep repeating the message in a neutral way, and, of course, be sure to set a good example yourself.

Q MY FRIENDS' CHILDREN ARE BETTER AT DRESSING. SHOULD I WORRY?

A Don't worry unless he gets to the age of three or four without any interest in dressing himself, in which case mention it to your doctor or pediatrician. Children learn to dress at different ages, depending on the complexity of the clothing, whether their parents allow them to learn by trial and error, and their own personality. It is worth giving your child plenty of time to get dressed each morning without distractions.

MAKE DRESSING EASY

Your child will find it easier to dress himself if you give him plenty of time and encouragement. Don't criticize him if he is slow or occasionally puts things on the wrong way around.

Keep his clothes simple and avoid complicated outfits

FASTENERS
When choosing clothes for your child, take into account the type of fastenings. Velcro fasteners make it easier for your child to put on and take off shoes, while hooks and snaps are much easier for a child to handle than buttons.

PARENT'S SURVIVAL GUIDE

HE WON'T WEAR WHAT I WANT HIM TO WEAR

Try to look at it from your child's point of view to see if there is a reason why he doesn't want to wear a particular item of clothing—for example, it may be too tight or too hot. Alternatively, he may just be being uncooperative. Instead of a head-on confrontation, try compromise. He could, for instance, choose his own socks while you choose the rest of his outfit. You're not entirely capitulating by doing this—instead, you're teaching him valuable negotiating skills for use in later life. Similarly, if you nag him, you are just teaching him how to nag. While there are some issues that are not negotiable, such as when to cross the road, I don't believe there is any point in standing firm on issues such as a jacket or winter hat. If he doesn't want to wear these, he can go out without them. You can take the garments with you, in case he gets cold later and changes his mind.

BATHING AND HYGIENE

BABIES

HOW DO I WASH HIS HAIR ?

Shampoo your baby's hair with mild soap or baby shampoo. A young baby can be wrapped up in a towel and held over the bath (see p. 31).

1 If your baby can sit up, lay him back, supported by one of your hands, and use a pitcher or cup of water to wet his hair.

Take care not to wet his face

2 Sit him up and rub a small amount of shampoo into his wet hair. Create a lather.

Support his back

3 After rubbing his hair, lean him back to rinse the shampoo off with clean water.

Remove all traces of shampoo

Q HOW OFTEN SHOULD MY BABY HAVE A BATH ?

A Many parents give their baby a daily bath, which is fine as long as you and your baby enjoy this. However, until four months or so, it doesn't matter if you only give him a bath once every three days, as long as you wash his face, hands, feet, and bottom every day (see p. 29). When he starts solids, he may need a daily bath, although if he has dry skin, baths can make this worse, so twice weekly would be enough.

Q DO I STILL NEED TO WASH HIM IN THE BABY BATH ?

A You will probably need to use this until he is around six months old, although some babies graduate to a regular bath earlier than this. By six months he will be splashing more, so the baby bath will be too small.

Q HOW CAN I MAKE SURE HE IS REALLY CLEAN ?

A Use a mild soap and wash his face, then the back and front of his neck. Clean behind the ears, but don't allow any water or soap to get into the ear canal itself. Wash under his armpits and clean his hands. Gently wash his navel—it can become red if cleaned too energetically. Finally, wash his feet, heels, and ankles, and his knees if they are grubby.

Q WHAT IS THE BEST WAY TO WASH MY LITTLE BOY ?

A Wash around the scrotum and between the buttocks with a washcloth or sponge. Rinse well. There's no need to wash under his foreskin— you'll do more harm than good if you try to pull it back to keep it clean.

Q HOW SHOULD I CLEAN MY LITTLE GIRL'S VULVA ?

A With a wet washcloth or sponge, wipe her gently from front to back—never the other way around. This is to avoid getting germs from around the anus into her urethra or vagina. There's no need to do anything more than this.

MY BABY HATES BATHS. HOW CAN I CLEAN HIM?

You needn't give your baby a daily bath if he really dislikes it. If he is scared of baths, just clean the dirtiest parts as best you can with some warm water and a washcloth or cotton ball. If you wish, you can do this in his bedroom on a changing mat (a mobile above his head can make a useful distraction while he is being washed), or on your lap with a soft towel on it. Make sure that his room is warm, dry him thoroughly, and give him a hug afterward. This will suffice to keep him clean.

How can I help him enjoy bath time?

Seize any opportunity that arises to get your baby used to water play so that he starts to associate water with having fun. For example, you could put a dishpan filled with water on the bathroom floor and then sit down and play with the water together. Blowing bubbles is also fun; although he is still too young to blow them himself, he may enjoy watching you do so. If he is still unhappy about having a bath, don't worry, eventually he will be ready for one. By the time they are eight or nine months old, most babies delight in having baths.

SPONGE BATHS
If your baby doesn't like water, give him a daily sponge bath on your lap. Partially undress him, wash him with a wet sponge, then dry with a soft towel.

Q SHOULD I PUT BATH OILS IN MY BABY'S BATH?

A If your baby has dry skin, this can be useful. Use baby oil or, if your baby has eczema, your doctor may prescribe an emollient oil. Be careful if you use oil in the bath because it will make the bath more slippery, and your already slithery baby can easily slide from your grasp.

Q IS THERE ANY HARM IN USING BUBBLE BATH?

A I don't think that bubble baths, even those made for infants, have much to recommend them, since they tend to be very drying. However, they can entice a reluctant bather to take a bath.

Q MY BABY SUCKS HIS BATH SPONGE. WILL IT HARM HIM?

A It could harm him. Pieces of sponge can break off and your baby could swallow them or choke on them. It is preferable either to use a more robust sponge, or to change to a washcloth.

Q HE CRIES WHENEVER I WASH HIS HAIR. WHAT CAN I DO?

A Try using less water when washing his hair. Wet his hair with a sponge or washcloth, making sure not to get his face wet, and use just a small amount of shampoo so that you can rinse it easily. If this fails to pacify him, give up and just use a sponge or a cloth for a couple of weeks to remove any lint from his hair, and comb it daily with a damp comb. Don't despair—this is just a phase, and he will accept hair-washing one day.

Q HOW SHOULD I DRY MY BABY AFTER HIS BATH?

A Use a soft, clean towel that is kept for his use only. Carefully dry the front and back of his neck, behind his ears, and between his fingers and toes. His hair can be dried with a towel, too—most babies have fine hair, so they don't need a hairdryer. If you like, you can buy a special baby towel with a built-in hood, but this is not essential—any large, soft towel is perfectly adequate.

Transferring to a Big Bath

Q HOW CAN I GET HIM USED TO A BIG BATHTUB ?

A Some babies move happily to a big bath, but others are intimidated. If your baby is not happy, put the baby bath inside the big bath for a week or two to get him used to the high sides. An alternative is for him to have a bath with you. This is for his benefit alone as you won't be able to wash yourself effectively while keeping hold of him.

Q HOW MUCH WATER SHOULD I RUN INTO THE BIG BATH ?

A He will need about the same 3 in (8 cm) of water as he had in the baby bath. For the time being, this is ample for both washing and playing.

Q CAN I MAKE THE BATH WATER HOTTER NOW THAT HE IS OLDER ?

A Not really. The water must not be too hot for his tender skin, so test it with your elbow as before. You may have to use more hot water to achieve the same temperature in a bigger bath.

Q WHEN WILL MY BABY BE ABLE TO SIT UP BY HIMSELF IN THE BATH ?

A Once he is proficient at sitting up on dry land and is happy having baths, you may be able to take your hand off him. Until then you should continue to support him.

Q CAN I LEAVE HIM ALONE IN THE BATH ONCE HE CAN SIT UP ?

A No. Baths are very slippery, hazardous places so you should *never* leave the room while he is having a bath. Put the answering machine on and ignore the doorbell if it rings. For safety's sake, you should supervise his bath until about the age of four—even longer if there are two children in the bath, as they can be more dangerous together.

Q ARE THERE ANY AIDS TO HELP HIM SIT UP IN THE BATH ?

A There are various seats and rings for use in the bath, some with suction pads to grip the bottom of the bath. They can be fun for some babies because it is easier to play in the bath from a seated position. However, never rely totally on such a gadget. You still need a hand to steady your baby all the time until he is older—probably over a year and possibly 18 months.

Q HOW CAN I MAKE SURE HE IS SAFE IN THE BATH ?

A Gather all you need before you start and put it within easy reach so that you don't have to leave him even for a split second. Before he can sit up alone, support him at all times with an arm behind his head and neck, and the fingers of that hand around one of his arms. Put a nonslip rubber mat into the bath and run all the water before you put him in the bath. If he is in the big bath, consider covering the hot tap with a cold, wet washcloth so that he can't burn himself if he reaches out without warning.

Q HOW CAN I MAKE BATH TIME MORE ENJOYABLE FOR MY BABY ?

A There are lots of bath toys and water games to make bath time enjoyable. Ducks, wind-up toys, water wheels, and plastic bath books are all fun. When he is a bit older he may enjoy pouring water from one cup to another; in the meantime he will probably be fascinated if you do this for him.

BATH-TIME FUN
Make bath time more interesting for your baby with colorful toys and water games.

TEETH AND NAILS

Q WHEN SHOULD I START TO CLEAN MY BABY'S TEETH?

A He doesn't need to have his teeth cleaned until his first tooth appears, which usually happens at around six months. However, it's useful to get him accustomed to putting a toothbrush in his mouth before then. You could give him a dry toothbrush to play with from the age of about four months, which is when he will be starting to put lots of things into his mouth.

Q WHAT KIND OF TOOTHBRUSH SHOULD HE HAVE?

A A baby toothbrush is ideal. If you have given him one to experiment with, use a different but identical one for real toothbrushing.

Q HOW OFTEN SHOULD I BRUSH HIS TEETH?

A Brush them twice a day, morning and night. To protect his teeth even further, restrict sugary foods and drinks to mealtimes, if possible, when the flow of saliva is greatest.

Q WHAT IS THE BEST BRUSHING TECHNIQUE?

A Brush up and down, not from side to side and use a circular motion on the gums. Demonstrate by brushing your own teeth in front of your baby. Toothpaste manufacturers suggest using a blob the size of a small pea, but I think that just a small smear of toothpaste is plenty.

Q DO I REALLY NEED TO USE A SPECIAL TOOTHPASTE FOR CHILDREN?

A Yes, you do, for two reasons. The first is that there is still some debate about how much fluoride a youngster should have. Although fluoride strengthens teeth and is proven to protect them from decay, an excess amount can accumulate in bones and cause blotching of the teeth. As it is difficult to prevent a baby or child swallowing some toothpaste before and after brushing, toothpastes for babies are specially formulated so that they contain less fluoride than adult toothpastes. The other reason you should choose children's toothpastes is that adult toothpastes contain peppermint oil which can irritate a young stomach. Most baby toothpastes do not contain any peppermint oil.

CARING FOR HIS NAILS

Your baby's nails should be kept short and clean. To keep them clean, wash his hands frequently with soap and water, especially once he starts to crawl around. When he is this young, there is no need for you to wash his hands with a nailbrush. If you keep his fingernails short, this will help to keep them clean.

My baby's nails grow very fast. Is this normal?

Nail growth is variable. Some babies' nails do seem to grow very fast, especially during the summer months, and this is fine. You must, however, keep them short. This will help to keep them clean and will prevent your baby from scratching himself (and you!). If he dislikes having his nails trimmed, try cutting them while he is asleep.

How should I cut his nails?

Use baby nail scissors or clippers. Sit your baby, facing forward, on your lap. Cut each nail, holding one finger at a time and following the shape of the fingertips.

Can I bite my baby's nails?

This is no longer recommended. Nail biting is not something you want to encourage in your child. Also, once he starts to crawl, it is unlikely that you will want to put his fingers in your mouth.

CUTTING YOUR BABY'S NAILS
Hold his hand gently but firmly in yours and, as you cut his nails, carefully follow the shape of your baby's fingertips.

TODDLERS AND PRESCHOOL CHILDREN

Q HOW CAN I TEACH MY TODDLER GOOD HYGIENE HABITS ?

A You can help him get into a routine of washing his hands (or rather, having them washed) by letting him know when it is important for him to wash them—for example, after playing in the backyard, going to the toilet, or before eating. From the age of two or three years, you should explain to him why he needs to wash his hands. But make sure that you set a good example by practicing what you preach.

Q HE IS RELUCTANT TO WASH HIS HANDS. DOES IT MATTER ?

A Yes, but it can take time to change his habits. Your toddler won't have the same attitude to dirt, mud, stools, and urine as you. He will also be easily distracted as well as in a constant hurry, so, understandably, hand-washing won't always be at the forefront of his mind.

Q WHAT CAN I DO TO ENCOURAGE MY CHILD TO TAKE A DAILY BATH ?

A Entice him by making bathtime more fun. Provide toys for the bath, let him blow bubbles, and use bubble bath, too, if necessary. Although bubble bath is drying to sensitive skins, it does get the dirt off him with minimal effort on your part, and usually leaves the tub fairly clean, too. If he still hates baths, consider making a deal; you read him a favorite story, for example, as long as he takes his bath without too much protest.

Q WHAT GAMES CAN HE PLAY IN THE BATHTUB ?

A There are some ingenious toys for this age group that attach to the side of the tub. Shapes that can be stuck onto bathroom tiles (and lifted off again safely when he's finished) are fun. Your child may also enjoy wind-up toys, boats, other floating toys, and water wheels.

Q IS IT A GOOD IDEA FOR HIM TO SHARE A BATH WITH ANOTHER CHILD ?

A This is a mixed blessing. Your toddler might enjoy bathing more with a sibling or a friend, and it can save you time and water. However, two children in the bath at the same time is twice as dangerous and more than twice as wet, so they need constant supervision from an alert adult.

MY CHILD IS STILL AFRAID OF WATER. WHAT CAN I DO ?

Some toddlers still dislike bathing, and many more hate having their hair washed. If your child is afraid of water, you could try the following:

- Encourage him to shampoo himself, under your close supervision.
- Let him hold the shower attachment himself.
- If it's the size of the bath that worries him, run less water into it.
- Some children become happier with bathing after a few outings to the swimming pool, so take him swimming.

Whatever you do, don't force your child to take a bath. Toddlers and young children can be very negative, so pressure usually achieves the opposite of what you intended.

Q MY CHILD LOVES BATHS. HOW CAN I GET HIM OUT ?

A There is no easy way to get a child out of the bathtub, but you can encourage him to get out, for example, by promising to read a favorite story or to let him do something he enjoys.

Q SHOULD I LET HIM TAKE A SHOWER INSTEAD OF A BATH ?

A He can take showers from around three years of age, provided that the showerhead is at an appropriate height for him (one with an adjustable height is best). However, he will need a nonslip mat as well as close supervision from an adult, so you will probably get wet, too, whether you need a shower or not.

Q MY CHILD HATES HIS NAILS BEING CUT. CAN I LET THEM GROW ?

A This is not advisable—fingernails should be kept short for reasons of hygiene and safety. If he makes a fuss when you suggest cutting them, it may be easier to cut them when he is watching television, engrossed in a book, or even asleep. An emery board is sometimes helpful if he struggles too much to let you use scissors or nail clippers.

Q HOW OFTEN DOES MY CHILD NEED A HAIRCUT?

A Whenever you think he needs one. The first haircut is often an exciting occasion, at least for the parent, but your toddler may howl in protest. Keep haircutting simple and avoid high-maintenance styles. There is no need to visit the barber or hairdresser if your child really hates going there—you can often find someone who doesn't mind coming to your house and who may even do your hair at the same time. Although shorter styles are easier to keep clean and presentable, there is little point in subjecting your youngster to frequent haircuts if he finds it traumatic.

Q SHOULD I CUT MY CHILD'S HAIR MYSELF?

A You could. It is much easier than you may think, especially if your child has slightly wavy hair (very straight hair is harder). Your child may appreciate having his hair cut in familiar surroundings. You also have the flexibility to do it at a time that is convenient for you both. However, you do have to be very careful not to cut yourself or him. I have cut my three sons' hair for many years with the help of an electrical hair trimmer. It saves a lot of time and money, and they have fun telling me how they want it done and checking the result in a hand mirror.

HOW CAN I ENCOURAGE MY CHILD TO BRUSH HER TEETH?

To begin with, you will probably have to brush her teeth for her, but there is no reason why she can't try it herself. Young children are great mimics, so you could brush your teeth together. She might like a mirror positioned lower down so she can see herself. As an added incentive, let her choose her own toothbrush.

IMPROVING HER BRUSHING

When she is ready to brush her teeth herself, encourage her to make "lots of suds" with the toothpaste. Some parents warn their child that they will get painful cavities if they don't brush well, but I think this is a bit brutal. From the age of four, plaque-disclosing tablets can also help show any areas she's missed.

Show her how to hold her brush to reach all her teeth

BRUSHING TOGETHER
Encourage her to brush her teeth by setting a good example. If she sees you enjoying this activity, she will want to join in the fun.

BOWEL AND BLADDER

BABIES

Q WHAT ARE THE MAIN CAUSES OF DIAPER RASH ?

A Prolonged contact with stools or urine causes diaper rash. Some babies are more prone to diaper rash because their skin is drier or more sensitive, but one basic rule applies—the less time spent with a diaper on, the better. So let your baby play and kick around sometimes without a diaper.

Q WHAT CAN I DO TO KEEP MY BABY FROM GETTING DIAPER RASH ?

A Change his diaper frequently. He may need ten changes a day—more if he has loose, frequent stools. Don't use baby wipes or lotions—these can cause diaper rash. Always wipe the area gently and apply a thin layer of barrier cream (for instance, zinc and lanolin cream) to clean, dry skin.

BOWEL AND BLADDER PROBLEMS

SYMPTOM	WHAT IS WRONG ?	WHAT CAN I DO ?
My breast-fed baby is constipated	Breast-fed babies over six weeks old often have phases of passing infrequent stools—for example, this may be perhaps only once every 5–10 days. Your baby may look as if he is straining when he does pass a stool, but the stools are usually soft and do not cause pain.	If your baby is otherwise well, continue as usual. If he seems unwell or passes any blood or mucus, consult your doctor or pediatrician.
My bottle-fed baby is constipated	He may be either dehydrated or underfed.	If it is hot, give him plain, cooled boiled water in between feedings. If he is hungry, feed him. Consult your doctor if your baby is unwell or passes blood or mucus in his diaper. Apart from water, don't add anything to his bottle without checking with your doctor. Never give him a laxative, enema, or suppository because these could harm him.
My baby's stools are very smelly	This is quite normal in bottle-fed babies, and in all babies after starting solids.	If he is on solids, he may be unable to digest a particular food yet. If he is well, no action is needed. If he is unwell, consult your doctor.
My baby's stools are runny and frequent	He may have gastroenteritis (infectious diarrhea). Alternatively, this may be quite normal, since bowel action varies with diet.	See your doctor if your baby is vomiting, seems unwell or his loose frequent bowel actions persist. If your baby is on solids, stop the most recently introduced food for a week or two before trying it again—or sieve it more finely next time you offer it.
My baby's urine is very smelly	He might be dehydrated, or he could have a urinary tract infection.	If he is unwell, consult your doctor. Otherwise, offer more fluids and change his diaper more often. If it is still smelly, consult your doctor.
My baby's diapers are dry	He is probably dehydrated, or you have changed to a new type of disposable diaper that does not feel wet even when it is saturated.	Offer him more fluids. If your baby seems unwell or his diapers remain drier than expected, see your doctor.
My baby's stools are green	This can be normal, or it may be due to infection or underfeeding.	If he is well, assume it is normal. If he is vomiting or seems ill or miserable, see your doctor.

Q IS HE LESS LIKELY TO GET DIAPER RASH WITH FABRIC DIAPERS ?

A No. Non-disposables are not any better. What matters is how often you change your baby and your diaper-changing technique (see below).

Q WILL MY BABY NEED PRESCRIBED MEDICATION IF HE HAS DIAPER RASH ?

A This is unlikely. Diaper rash hardly ever needs antibiotics since it is rarely due to a bacterium. However, it can be due to thrush (*Candida albicans*), which is common in babies. Sometimes called a fungus, thrush is actually a yeast that also causes vaginal thrush in adult women. The rash responds to an antiyeast cream prescribed by your doctor.

Q HOW CAN I TELL IF MY BABY HAS THRUSH IN THE DIAPER AREA ?

A You may notice single red spots outside the main area of the rash, or the rash could have a raw, glazed appearance. Alternatively, the rash may fail to improve after a few days, even after letting the air get to it and using an antiseptic cream.

Q IF THE RASH IS DUE TO THRUSH, DOES HE HAVE THIS INFECTION ELSEWHERE ?

A Some babies with a diaper rash caused by thrush also have it in the mouth. The gums may look red and raw, or there may be a creamy deposit. A baby with oral thrush can find it painful to feed and may refuse the breast or bottle.

HOW DO I TREAT DIAPER RASH ?

The best way to treat diaper rash is to leave your baby's diaper and clothes off as much as possible. Ideally, he should have several sessions of diaper-free play every day. If he is crawling, then spread out some towels, shut the door, and let him move around freely without his diaper.

CHANGING HIS DIAPER

If your baby has diaper rash, at least twice a day leave his diaper off for half an hour, or even longer, when changing him. Within a day or two, his rash will fade to a less angry red and should heal. Sometimes a mild antiseptic cream helps.

1 Remove his diaper, clean and dry the area, and leave him naked for a while.

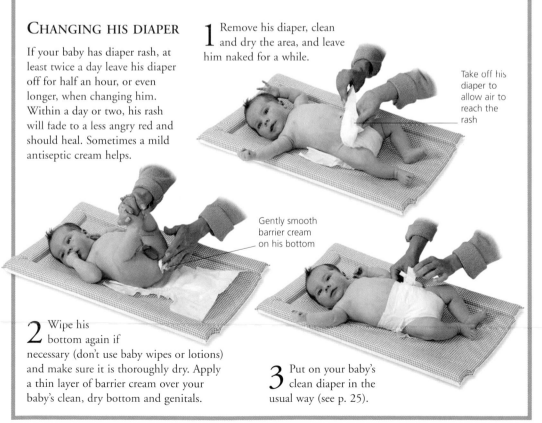

Take off his diaper to allow air to reach the rash

Gently smooth barrier cream on his bottom

2 Wipe his bottom again if necessary (don't use baby wipes or lotions) and make sure it is thoroughly dry. Apply a thin layer of barrier cream over your baby's clean, dry bottom and genitals.

3 Put on your baby's clean diaper in the usual way (see p. 25).

POTTY TRAINING

Q WHEN CAN I START POTTY TRAINING MY TODDLER?

A Even if your child has regular bowel movements, there's no point in potty training until he's at least 18 months old. Until then, he won't have voluntary bowel and bladder control.

Q WHEN CAN I EXPECT HIM TO BE CLEAN AND DRY IN THE DAYTIME?

A This varies, but as a rough guide many children are clean and dry between the ages of two and two and a half. Boys are often later, so your son may be nearly three before he is clean and dry.

Q WHEN WILL MY TODDLER BE ABLE TO GIVE UP DIAPERS AT NIGHT?

A Probably not before he is three years old. Even then, there will be the occasional lapse due to upset or illness, but these are only minor setbacks.

Q MY TODDLER REFUSES TO USE HIS POTTY. WHAT SHOULD I DO?

A There is really nothing you can do about this. He might not be physically or emotionally ready to sit on the potty, in which case you shouldn't force him. There should be no pressure or anxiety, since the time when a toddler is likely to be most uncooperative coincides with toilet training. If he passes a stool nowhere near the potty, try not to get annoyed; some accidents are inevitable.

Q CAN I TRAIN MY TODDLER TO USE THE TOILET INSTEAD OF A POTTY?

A You may be able to, but there are drawbacks: a toilet seat is more intimidating to a small child than a potty and you will need a special seat to make the toilet seat small enough for his bottom. Also, even with a special step, the toilet will still be higher and more difficult to reach.

BOWEL AND BLADDER PROBLEMS

Toilet habits vary widely from one child to the next and parents can easily worry. The bowels and bladder can assume huge importance during the toddler years, with the family's whole routine appearing to revolve around the potty or toilet, but there is usually no real cause for concern.

My toddler is clean and dry at home, but not when we go out. What can I do?
A toddler is often unable to empty his bladder unless it is full, so the concept of using the toilet before outings is alien to him. If you are worried, take a potty with you or keep your eyes open for public restrooms—when he needs the toilet, he's unlikely to be able to wait. Until he is consistently dry, he may prefer to wear a diaper when he is out. If not, take a change of clothes and put old towels on the car seat or in the stroller.

He was dry, but has now regressed. Why?
Possible causes include a new baby in the family (wetting is a common symptom of sibling rivalry); a vacation (toddlers often regress when away from home); and cold weather (he may not want to bare his bottom). Teething and illness are other causes. If you think your toddler might be ill, or he fails to regain bladder control within a week or two, talk to your doctor or pediatrician.

My toddler is dry but continues to soil his pants. Is there a problem?
This is common in toddlers who are toilet training and is nothing to worry about. He may move his bowels in his pants when hidden from view. In time, this will resolve itself, so ignore it and deal with the dirty pants tactfully.

He often has loose stools. Is something wrong?
Diarrhea is common in toddlers. If your child is well and his growth is good, give him more fluids to drink; otherwise see your doctor because your child may have a gut infection (see p. 218). Another possible cause is a condition known as "toddler diarrhea," in which there are episodes of intermittent diarrhea. The stools can be explosive and sometimes contain visible pieces of undigested food. The cause is not certain, but it may be related to factors such as drinking continually or not chewing food thoroughly. It is common in children under two, especially boys.

HOW SHOULD I POTTY TRAIN MY TODDLER ?

Around the age of two, she will probably start to become aware of her bowel movements. Explain what a potty is for and put one in a convenient place so that she can reach it quickly. In the summer you can leave the diaper and bottom half of her clothing off. You will know when a bowel action is imminent because she will screw up her face and crouch down. When this happens, remind her where the potty is. You can also try sitting her on the potty for a short while after meals.

What type of potty should I use?
Any type of potty is fine. For boys, you will need one with a higher front to avoid accidents. Don't expect him to be as amused as you are by a novelty potty—for example, one that plays tunes.

What is the best way to encourage her?
Tell her you're pleased when she sits on the potty, but don't go overboard. The potty shouldn't become the focal point of the entire household. If your toddler thinks using the potty is good, she will assume she is naughty when she makes a mess. Producing stools is neither good nor clever—it is just a normal bodily function that she is learning to control.

Are trainer pants useful when potty training?
They can be. Pull-up diapers are convenient, especially when you are out, because they're disposable. Ordinary cotton cloth pants are very comfortable and relatively cheap.

How should I clean her potty?
Empty the contents down the toilet, wipe the inside of the potty with toilet paper, then rinse it out with water, if necessary using dishwashing liquid as well. Leave it to dry, or dry it with toilet paper or a paper towel, not a cloth. It doesn't need sterilizing.

GETTING HER USED TO A POTTY
Start by sitting her on a potty for a minute or so during diaper changes, maybe while you sit on the toilet. However, don't force her if she is reluctant.

Q DOES INTELLIGENCE AFFECT TOILET TRAINING ?

A Control over bowels or bladder is not a sign of intelligence. A bright child is not necessarily out of diapers any sooner than less bright child. However, if there is intellectual delay, this can make toilet training late, but this would not be the only symptom—there would be delay in other areas, too.

Q MY PARENTS SAY I WAS POTTY-TRAINED AT ONE YEAR. HOW IS THIS POSSIBLE ?

A This isn't potty training. It is holding a baby over the potty at the appropriate moment. Some parents put quite young babies on a potty and then, if a stool is produced, call it potty training. It has no bearing on how quickly a baby acquires bowel and bladder control.

Q WHEN WILL MY LITTLE BOY LEARN TO URINATE STANDING UP ?

A Only when he is tall enough to reach the toilet (with the help of a step if needed). It is pointless to stand him in front of the potty, since there will be a lot of misses, but don't stop him if he wants to urinate standing up. Don't worry if there is no male at home to imitate—boys usually learn from friends. Girls, too, sometimes want to urinate standing up but soon realize this is not effective.

Q SHOULD I WIPE MY CHILD'S BOTTOM ?

A You can after a bowel movement. Wipe a girl from front to back, to stop bacteria from the anus from entering the vagina and urethra. After urinating, your child can usually clean himself, although urine may dribble down his leg.

PRESCHOOL CHILDREN

Q WHEN CAN MY CHILD GO TO THE TOILET ON HIS OWN ?

A Although your child may physically be able to manage going to the toilet on his own from around two and a half to three years of age, he will probably still depend on you for wiping and handwashing till he is about four years old. From about four years of age, he will probably be able to wash his hands on his own most of the time.

Q PUBLIC RESTROOMS ARE OFTEN DIRTY. SHOULD I LET HIM USE THEM ?

A Sometimes you may have no choice. You can, however, make sure you are well equipped when out and about. Take wet wipes to wipe his bottom and his hands (and yours). If you really don't want him to use public toilets, take a potty (or travel potty that fits over the toilet seat) with you on outings. Empty the potty into the toilet before slipping the potty back into a plastic bag.

Q HE STILL HAS "ACCIDENTS" IN THE DAYTIME. SHOULD I WORRY ?

A No. Youngsters can only concentrate on one thing at a time, and there is often something more interesting to do than go to the toilet. If you see your child begin to jiggle around, hop from one foot to the other, crouch down, or clutch his pants, his bladder may be full. When this happens, remind him gently that he may need the toilet.

Q MY CHILD IS DRY BUT WILL ONLY PASS STOOLS IN A DIAPER. WHAT CAN I DO ?

A This is quite common. You can modify his behavior gradually over several weeks. When he asks for a diaper, put it on in the bathroom, so that he passes stools in that room. The next step is to encourage him to sit on the toilet with the diaper on. Later still, he can sit on the toilet with the diaper on but undone, and finally, sit him on the toilet with the diaper stretched over the seat.

Q HE IS STILL NOT DRY AT NIGHT. IS THIS NORMAL ?

A Yes. He might not be dry until age three or later. Boys tend to be later than girls in acquiring bladder control at night. Sometimes the age at which a child is dry by night runs in a family, so if you or your partner wet the bed until the age of four, then your child might, too.

Q IS THERE ANY WAY I CAN ENCOURAGE MY CHILD TO STAY DRY AT NIGHT ?

A Wait until he has reasonable bladder control during the day—say, for about four hours—and a dry diaper every so often when he wakes in the morning. Then suggest that he might like to do without a nighttime diaper. If he agrees, cover the mattress with a protective sheet (if you don't have one on already) and make sure that all his bedding is easily washable. You should both be relaxed about the proceedings. Anxiety will make him more likely to wet the bed, and make you more likely to get upset about it.

Q CAN REWARD CHARTS HELP MY CHILD HAVE DRY NIGHTS ?

A If your child is approaching the age of five, you could try a reward chart to encourage him to stay dry during the night (see p. 176), but make the objective realistic. For example, don't offer a star for a dry night if your child still wets his bed every night, because he will become despondent and will fail to learn anything. Reward what he is capable of achieving. Initially, for instance, you may give him a star for still having a dry bed at midnight (or whatever time you go to bed yourself), or for remembering to urinate just before he goes to sleep.

Q SHOULD I RESTRICT THE NUMBER OF DRINKS HE HAS IN THE EVENING ?

A No. If the only reason your child has a dry bed is because his bladder has hardly any urine in it, then he hasn't really learned anything and has no genuine bladder control. You should, however, reduce or cut out drinks that stimulate the bladder, such as fruit juices, carbonated drinks, soft drinks containing caffeine, and tea and coffee, which children under five shouldn't have anyway.

Q IS IT A GOOD IDEA TO PUT HIM ON THE POTTY BEFORE I GO TO BED ?

A I think so. This will certainly help to avoid some of the wet beds. For maximum effect, he needs to be alert enough to appreciate the sensation of emptying his bladder, so wake your child rather than lift him onto the potty while he is asleep. Otherwise, he is still passing urine in his sleep, albeit not in bed. He will be fast asleep again within moments of your putting him back to bed.

Q WHAT SHOULD I DO IF HE WETS THE BED?

A Change the bedding with minimum fuss as soon as you notice it is wet. Waking in a cold, wet bed is bad enough for a child without being confronted by an angry parent. I know from experience that it is very hard to deal with wet beds, especially when you are tired or ill, but you must. The more you lose your temper, the longer it will take your child to achieve bladder control.

Q HE WON'T WEAR A DIAPER EVEN THOUGH HE WETS THE BED. WHAT CAN I DO?

A Be patient. You can't force him to wear a diaper, although you might be able to persuade him to wear pull-down diapers that are halfway between pants and diapers. Otherwise, try to wake him once in the night or the early morning to use the potty. To protect the bed and give you less laundry, put a protective covering and a fitted sheet on the bed.

Q MY CHILD STILL WANTS TO WEAR A DIAPER AT NIGHT. SHOULD I LET HIM?

A Yes. He will only get anxious or wet (or both) if you make him sleep without a diaper before he is ready, which could set back both his sleeping habits and his toilet training. The decision to give up diapers should be a joint one. Don't pressure him by telling him diapers are too expensive, or that they're only for babies or don't come in his size (in fact, they do come in child sizes).

Q WOULD DIFFERENT BEDDING HELP IF HE STILL WETS THE BED?

A No, different bedding will not help your child to stay dry during the night; the only possible benefit is if it can be more easily washed.

Q I KNOW YOU CAN BUY ALARMS. ARE THEY WORTH TRYING?

A They are not necessary at this age. These are called enuresis alarms and there are two main types: some work with a sensor pad or mat under the child, while others are worn on the child's body. Both give off a loud buzz when the child passes urine in his bed. The child learns to beat the buzzer by getting up quickly. Wet patches become smaller and the child eventually becomes dry during the night. Although alarms can work well, they are usually only used for children age six and over. You cannot condition a younger child to avoid what he can't help doing.

Q HE IS NEARLY FIVE YEARS OLD AND STILL WETS THE BED. IS SOMETHING WRONG?

A Almost certainly not. At the age of five, at least one child in 10 still wets the bed on a regular basis, and this is usually nothing to worry about. However, you should always consult your doctor if your child soils his bed or has been dry during the night for a while and then loses bladder control. In these cases, there is occasionally something amiss. For example, there may be stress in the family, such as a new baby, moving, or a bereavement, or there may be a urinary tract infection or other illness.

Q ARE THERE ANY MEDICATIONS THAT COULD HELP?

A Yes, there are medications, but I think the use of drugs to control bladder and bowel function in young children is best avoided. Establishing better bedtime habits, such as using the potty before bedtime, is a much safer bet.

HOMEOPATHIC REMEDIES

Homeopathic treatments, where remedies are taken from natural extracts and diluted (see p. 227), can be quite successful in treating bladder and bowel problems.

■ **Equisetum** (Scouring Rush)
This helps a child who wets the bed early on in the night, before you have a chance to lift him.

■ **Lycopodium** (Club Moss)
This can be suitable for a child who is anxious or who wets the bed later in the night.

Can I buy these in a pharmacy?
Homeopathic remedies are available from homeopathic practitioners and specialty stores. However, you should really consult a qualified homeopath before using these remedies.

Do other complementary therapies work?
A few parents resort to other complementary therapies, but I seriously doubt whether these have anything to offer for this problem. A therapy such as acupuncture can be painful for a young child, and using this as a form of treatment for bedwetting is somewhat extreme.

CRYING AND COMFORTING

Crying is your child's way of **securing attention** from you, but what you should do in response isn't always obvious. It can be hard to know whether your baby is **hungry or tired**, or simply in need of a hug. Guiding you through the reasons why babies and children cry, this chapter explains the key causes of crying and offers helpful strategies for **soothing and calming** your child. With these strategies at your fingertips, **your confidence** will increase, as will your ability to deal with a potentially distressing experience. This chapter also offers **invaluable advice** on where to get help on those occasions when you feel unable to comfort your child.

5

COMFORTING YOUR BABY

WHY BABIES CRY

CAUSES	WHAT YOU CAN DO
Hunger	This is the most basic need of all. Try giving a feeding if you have not fed your baby for 2–3 hours (depending on her age and size), or if she drained her last bottle.
Thirst	Offer her cooled boiled water, especially if the weather is hot, she has been feverish recently, or her diaper seems to be drier than usual.
Heat/cold	Does the back of her neck feel hot or damp? She may have a fever or the room might be too hot. If so, take off a layer or two of her clothing. If your baby's hands or feet feel cool, she might be cold. Add a layer of clothing if necessary.
Dirty diaper	Change her diaper if she is dirty or wet. This is especially important if she is prone to rashes.
Boredom	Try holding your baby or talking to her, or move her to a place where she can see what is going on and can watch you working.
Pain	If she pulls her legs up, her cries are piercing, or you cannot console her for long, she may be in pain. This could be due to colic (see p. 52), teething (common from 4–6 months), or illness.
Fear or other emotions	Crying can be triggered by a loud noise, a strange adult, or even a toy falling out of reach. Offer her comfort with a hug and some words of reassurance.
Fatigue	A baby may become too tired to sleep. She needs to be helped to calm down, perhaps with a hug somewhere quiet.
Over-stimulation	Constant sound and action can be too exciting for a young baby, and it may cause her to cry. Try to find a quiet place to put her so that she can calm down and eventually go to sleep.

Q WHAT IS THE BEST WAY OF COMFORTING MY BABY ?

A The best thing that you can give a crying baby is yourself. In some societies, mothers are in virtually constant contact with their babies, but this is rare in the West. Assuming that you have attended to her basic needs (see left), try cradling her or holding her close. This may work best if she can also hear your heartbeat. Put her in a sling on your front if she is not too heavy, or sit with her in a rocking chair. Rock her gently but *never* shake her. Babies like rhythmic sounds, so sing or hum to her. You could try playing classical music, since it has a very calming effect on some babies.

Q WHAT ARE THE MOST COMMON REASONS FOR CRYING ?

A Babies cry to get attention. It's the only way they can communicate their needs. As shown in the chart (left), there are a number of causes of crying in young babies, but they always cry for a reason. As a parent, you are programmed to respond to your baby's cry. This is a good thing, although a crying baby can be very stressful.

Q WHY DOES MY BABY CRY SO MUCH OF THE TIME ?

A By six weeks, your baby should be more settled than at birth. Babies vary in personality and outlook; some are placid and easy to handle, and others more restless—and thus more vocal. Do not feel bad if your baby cries a lot—one theory is that more lively and intelligent babies cry more. However, constant crying is extremely draining.

Q COULD SHE BE CRYING BECAUSE SHE IS LONELY OR BORED ?

A Yes. Babies can and do get bored during the first six months. Until they can sit up or crawl around unaided, there's not much they can do. Your baby may be happier if you put her in a bouncing cradle or her car seat and let her watch you. You can sit her up supported by cushions, making sure that she is safe, and put different things within her reach—a small empty box can be more exciting than a familiar toy. Show her a board book or read to her—she can enjoy picture books even if she is too young to understand the story.

Q I NEVER LET HER CRY. WILL I SPOIL HER IF I ALWAYS GO TO HER?

A You can't spoil her by picking her up because a young baby doesn't cry on purpose. Your baby is still quite immature physically and she needs your help most of the time. However, toward the end of the first six months, you need not jump up and attend to every little whimper. Wait and see whether the noises she makes escalate from a tentative sound into a really heartfelt cry. Some of the sounds that she makes at this age are actually early forms of speech rather than true crying.

Q SHOULD I EVER GIVE UP AND LET MY BABY CRY?

A If she continues to cry despite all your efforts to comfort her, she may be overstimulated, so leaving her alone in a quiet place could be the only solution. Make sure that she is comfortable and safe in her crib or carriage, and then leave the room.

Q HOW LONG SHOULD I LEAVE HER TO CRY IF SHE DOESN'T STOP?

A Five minutes is usually long enough to leave your baby to cry at this age. It will seem much longer to you, so check your watch. During this time, you should move out of earshot and take a short break. Walk around the backyard or sit down in another room with a cup of tea before returning to her. Playing soothing music in your baby's room may help to quieten her. If she is still crying after five minutes, go back to her, settle her down, and then leave the room again for about another five minutes.

SEEING TO YOUR BABY'S NEEDS
You, as a parent, are the main source of comfort for your baby. Holding her will help reassure her.

I CAN'T COPE WITH THE CRYING

All parents are programmed to respond to the cry of their baby, but constant crying can be very stressful and draining for tired parents. There may be times when it seems that nothing will stop your baby from crying. Feelings of anger and resentment toward a demanding baby are normal, so do not worry about feeling bad. The situation is only dangerous if these emotions become actions.

Calm down
When you are feeling under pressure, put your baby down safely in her crib or carriage before things get out of control, and then leave the room. Take a deep breath and try to unwind. See if you can find someone to help you; if your partner is not available, ask a friend, relative, or neighbor to spend some time with you. Better still, if possible, ask them to take your baby out for half an hour (or even longer) just to give you a break. Alternatively, take your baby out in her carriage yourself; her crying will not seem as loud when you are outside.

Make time for yourself
It is important that you look after yourself as well as your baby. Make sure you find time for the things that you enjoy doing. Postpone the housework and other chores in order to leave more time for yourself. Recharging your batteries will leave you feeling happier and more refreshed. This is not selfish; you need to be at your best to care for a baby properly.

Pamper yourself
If you have had a really bad day, ask your partner to take the baby for a while when he comes home so that you can pamper yourself—have a long, warm bath, watch television undisturbed, or read the newspaper. Do whatever will help you to relax.

Keep your perspective
Do not let things deteriorate so much that you are at the end of your tether. Try talking to a friend who has the same problem, or who has been through it in the past. Your baby will not cry forever, even if it seems like it now.

Is massage good for my baby ?

Yes. Massage or touch is a very old method of healing and soothing. You may already massage your baby to some extent when stroking her head, neck, chest, or limbs, but you can also use massage in a more organized way to benefit both you and your baby. To find out more about baby massage, you should ask your pediatrician if there are any classes available in your area.

How can massage help my baby ?

Massage can soothe unsettled babies, relieve crying, and may even ease colic (see p. 52). Premature babies and those with cerebral palsy or other special needs respond especially well. Baby massage enhances the bond between you and your baby and it can help parents with postpartum depression cope with a demanding baby. It certainly alleviates some parental anxiety and may ease the baby's anxiety. Some people claim that it can boost the immune system, deep-cleanse the skin, get rid of toxins, improve suppleness, or increase muscle tone—nothing has been proved, but massage can be very enjoyable for you both.

Is massage safe ?

As long as it is done properly there are few dangers. Adults in many Western countries are often unused to touching other bodies, so the concept of baby massage may seem alien. Sometimes we have to rediscover our more primitive or emotional instincts that are normally repressed in polite society, in order to benefit. However, there are some precautions you should take. You should avoid massage entirely if:
- your baby has had an immunization during the last 72 hours
- she has a skin infection or other infection
- she is feverish or unwell
- your hands or the room are cold
- your baby is asleep
- she gets upset. Neither of you will enjoy the experience if you massage your baby against her will. Some babies dislike being undressed for a massage, but they enjoy having their feet massaged. If so, try this first to get her used to the idea of massage.

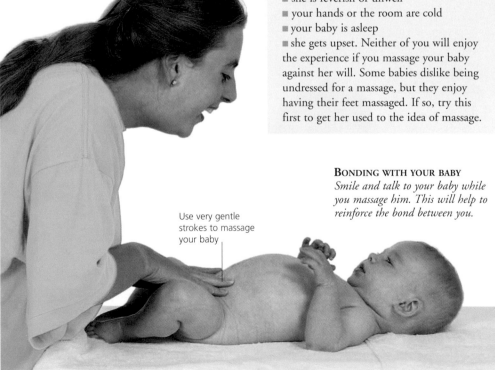

Use very gentle strokes to massage your baby

BONDING WITH YOUR BABY
Smile and talk to your baby while you massage him. This will help to reinforce the bond between you.

How do I massage my baby?

Always wash and warm your hands before you begin. You should also test the oil you intend to use on a small patch of your baby's skin. Wait 30 minutes to see if there is any adverse reaction to the oil before starting to massage him. Make sure your baby is warm, contented, and comfortable. Smile and talk calmly to your baby throughout the massage to reassure him.

What oils can I use?

You can use baby oil or one of several organic oils. Of these, grapeseed oil and coconut oil are probably the safest to use. Note: Avoid using sweet almond nut oil because of the risk of nut allergy. Check suitability of oil for a baby before using.

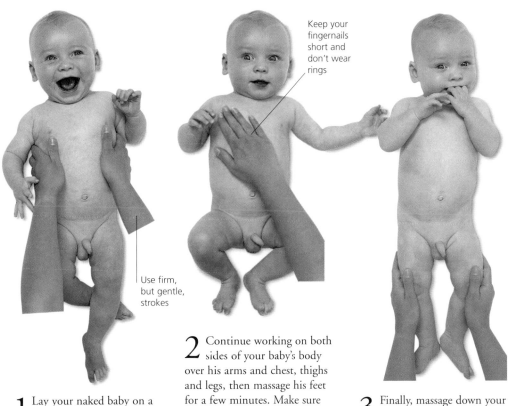

Keep your fingernails short and don't wear rings

Use firm, but gentle, strokes

1 Lay your naked baby on a soft towel on his back or front (there's no risk of SIDS from him lying on his front for a massage since you are with him all the time and he is awake). Begin the massage by first stroking down both sides of your baby's body, using a gentle action and working from the shoulders down.

2 Continue working on both sides of your baby's body over his arms and chest, thighs and legs, then massage his feet for a few minutes. Make sure that you are relaxed, don't rush the strokes, and keep talking to your baby throughout. Add more oil to your hands if necessary. Then, using a clockwise action, gently stroke your baby's chest (or his back if he is lying on his tummy). Continue these strokes for approximately one minute.

3 Finally, massage down your baby's legs and feet again. If he is lying on his front, massage down the back of his hips and the base of his spine. At this point, if your baby is contented and still enjoying the massage, you can turn him over and repeat the whole of the massage on the other side of his body.

COMMON CONCERNS

Q IS IT MY FAULT THAT MY BABY CRIES SO MUCH ?

A No. Although your emotions and the way you handle your baby can affect her, it is unkind and inaccurate to blame a parent for a baby's crying. Many people suggest that a calm parent results in a calm baby. I believed it until I had twins—from the start, one of them was placid while the other was high-strung, despite having received the same handling.

Q WHY DOES MY BABY CRY LESS WHEN OTHER PEOPLE HOLD HER ?

A Babies have a natural preference for their parents, but sometimes someone else is more effective at calming a baby down. The other person may not be under the same pressures as you. If you're worn down by the demands of parenting, and possibly a job as well, you will be less relaxed. Your baby will pick this up. Babies can also sense when a parent is tired, depressed, or sick. Your baby may also cry less when someone else holds her because she is enjoying the novelty.

Q DO BOYS TEND TO CRY MORE THAN GIRLS ?

A Babies vary a great deal, so it is difficult to give a definitive answer. In my opinion, male babies cry more than female ones in the first six months. This is why boys have earned the reputation of being more difficult to rear. Boys also sleep less and take up more of a parent's time. It isn't obvious why; the same is reported from different parts of the the world, so the difference may be due to more than just cultural expectation. There are some developmental differences between the sexes (see p. 142) but the discrepancy in crying may be due to other factors. For instance, mothers tend to talk to girl babies more than boy babies, and are more likely to pick them up when they cry.

Q SHOULD I START USING A PACIFIER TO COMFORT MY BABY ?

A New recommendations advise using a pacifier during the first year to reduce the risk of SIDS. Wait until she is a month old to introduce it to avoid interfering with breast-feeding. If she does have one now, bear in mind the usual hygiene and safety precautions. Never use a ribbon to attach a pacifier, or dip it in anything sugary.

Q IF SHE HAS A PACIFIER NOW, WILL SHE ALWAYS NEED ONE ?

A Your baby will give up her pacifier when she no longer needs it—there aren't many children who are still using pacifiers when they go to school. In fact, she will probably give it up long before this. It is best if a baby depends on a pacifier as little as possible. It will not prevent her from crying if she is hungry or has some other need, but using it could affect her speech development. Avoid relying on a pacifier as a cure-all when she is distressed, and don't be tempted to put a pacifier into her mouth when she's not crying.

Q WHAT OTHER COMFORT OBJECTS CAN HELP MY BABY ?

A Young babies can find comfort with a variety of things, such as a favorite blanket, soft toy, or a piece of cloth—anything familiar, as long as it's soft, safe, and clean. It is amazing what babies will become attached to. Sometimes a baby will appreciate being close to something you've worn. In these cases it's undoubtedly the smell she finds reassuring. Some parents try to pacify their baby with a bottle of milk, but this isn't useful unless your baby is actually hungry. Don't be tempted to prop her up with a bottle or leave one in her crib—there is a possibility that she could choke. Also, your baby won't drink the milk if she isn't hungry, which might make you even more frustrated.

Q HOW CAN I COMFORT MY TWINS WHEN THEY'RE BOTH CRYING ?

A Twins can cry simultaneously, creating a stereo effect. This also creates a dilemma about which one you should comfort first. If you are alone with them, you have to make a decision. When they are very small, it may be possible to pick them both up at the same time, but as they get older, this becomes more difficult for you and more dangerous for them. One of them has to wait. Go to the one you think is in greater need, or whichever baby you didn't pick up first last time they both cried. Meanwhile, give a pacifier to the other twin or stroke the back of her neck. The alternative scenario, when each twin cries at different times, may sound easier to cope with, but this gives a parent no peace at all. The solution here is to get them into a synchronized routine as soon as possible, and to enlist any help you can.

COMFORTING AN OLDER BABY

Q WHY DOES MY BABY STILL CRY EVEN NOW THAT SHE'S OLDER ?

A Older babies can cry for a variety of reasons, as shown in the chart below. These include the same basic needs as younger babies, like hunger and thirst. Older babies get bored or frustrated more often than younger babies, especially if they cannot reach something they want. They can also become anxious when separated from a parent.

WHY OLDER BABIES CRY

CAUSES	WHAT YOU CAN DO
Hunger	Try giving a feeding if your baby hasn't had one for three hours or more. If she's not hungry, she'll refuse it.
Thirst	Offer plain water. She may be thirsty, especially if she is having a lot of solids but few drinks.
Dirty diaper	Change her promptly, especially if she has diaper rash.
Boredom	Your baby is interested in doing things, but she may not be able to find what she wants. Talk to your baby, and make a variety of different playthings available to her.
Frustration or helplessness	She may be able to crawl, but she can't walk and she's still too short to reach things. If this is the reason for her crying, she may point to what she wants.
Pain	Teething is a common cause of pain in older babies. They can also cry from earaches and other illnesses— this is usually a more persistent cry, and your baby may be miserable or inconsolable.
Separation or fear	From six months of age, babies can get very upset at being separated from a parent. A sudden noise, a new experience, or a stranger getting too close can make your baby cry. Offer her plenty of reassurance, especially when you have to leave her.
Fatigue	Many babies (and children) cry when they're tired but too excited to sleep.

Q WHY HAS SHE STARTED TO CRY WHEN SOMEONE ELSE HOLDS HER ?

A This is a normal phase of development. Soon after the age of six months, babies become more clingy and wary of strangers. Your baby may also sleep badly, want her favorite cuddly toy more often, suck her thumb more, and generally become more whiny. Whenever you disappear from view, she may behave as if she'll never see you again. This behavior is sometimes called separation anxiety, and it can be stressful for a parent, so you may become anxious, too. However, this will stop in time. Meanwhile, remember her shyness and handle her gently. Never "dump" her on someone's lap. Always hand her over smoothly and slowly and tell her what you're doing and who she's going to. Six months is also an age when most babies stop smiling at strangers and will only smile for a parent. This, too, stops eventually.

Q SHOULD I STOP LEAVING HER WITH OTHER PEOPLE IF SHE ALWAYS CRIES ?

A Not necessarily. She may be expressing anxiety at being separated from you. This is a normal reaction at this age, and unfortunately her crying can make you more anxious, and your child will pick this up. A vicious circle can result, and you could get to the point where you don't dare to leave her, even with your partner or a trusted grandparent. To help your baby get over this stage, never leave her with anyone without telling her, and always let her know that you'll be back.

Q SHE CRIES WHEN MY PARTNER HOLDS HER. WHAT CAN I DO ?

A Perhaps she hasn't yet learned that your partner can be loving, gentle, and fun. Or maybe she has, but it's you she wants at the moment. Sometimes a baby clings to only one parent, which becomes very trying for both parents. Your partner should not take this personally, or give up trying to hold her. If you are within sight when your baby cries for something, you should deal with her yourself. Arrange for your partner to hold her, talk to her, and watch her more often without your being present. You can try this when your baby is already in a good mood, but do not attempt it when she is grumpy or in need of something.

Q DO BABIES CRY BECAUSE OF A WET DIAPER ?

A Yes, they can, especially after they are six months old. A wet diaper is more likely to make her cry if she has a diaper rash because her skin will be raw and sensitive. The solution is to change her diaper more often.

Q HOW CAN I COMFORT MY BABY WHEN SHE CRIES ?

A First attend to any needs she may have. These will be more obvious than when she was younger. Although your baby can't use words yet, she may point to what she wants or strain her whole body in the direction of the desired object, accompanied by urgent noises that convey her wishes. Sometimes you can bring an object to her; at other times she will want to get it for herself. To some extent you can anticipate what she wants— for example, she may enjoy a bus ride more if you lift her so that she can see out of the window. At other times she may need a hug, or to know you are there—you may have to take her with you from room to room to stop her from crying.

Q WHY CAN'T I PREDICT WHEN MY BABY IS GOING TO CRY ?

A Her world has a different focus from yours and it is hard to know what will make her cry from fear or panic. Her responses may seem irrational because they're not the same all the time. Often it's a question of timing and expectations. One day she may be unafraid of the neighbor's dog, the next day she may be terrified. Babies of this age do like surprises, like playing peek-a-boo, but to some extent they have to expect the surprise.

Q CAN I KEEP HER FROM CRYING WHEN SHE FACES NEW EXPERIENCES ?

A With sensitive handling, you may be able to prevent her from crying. Do not force her to confront new things if she is not ready. When introducing her to something new, reassure her with your voice and a gentle touch, and stay close to her. Sit her on your lap for her first ride on a swing, for example, or the first time she pets a dog.

Q OTHER BABIES CRY LESS THAN MINE. WHAT AM I DOING WRONG ?

A You are not doing anything wrong. She may look big and strong compared to when she was younger, but she is still a vulnerable baby. Avoid using other babies as a guide to yours—they are all different. Stay in tune with her moods so that your timing matches her expectations and she grows up secure. If she cries during a certain activity, such as swimming, stop. It may be that she doesn't feel safe or that she isn't enjoying it.

Q DOES A CRYING TWIN SET THE OTHER ONE OFF ?

A They can provoke each other to cry, but it is unusual, and it gets less common as they get older. However, taking turns crying is common. This is actually more wearing for a parent, as you may not get any respite from crying at all. You may notice a seesaw effect—one twin has a miserable day whatever you do, while the other one is no trouble. A day or two later, the happy baby is miserable while the grumpier one is in a great mood. Someone who doesn't know them well may get them confused. There is no real solution to seesawing, but it does help to be aware of it.

PARENT'S SURVIVAL GUIDE

MY BABY CRIES WHEN I GO TO WORK

If your baby cries when you leave her with her caregiver, try to spend time with both of them before leaving. Some parents also arrange to see the caregiver socially at weekends, which helps if you can manage it. Always hand your baby over gently, and explain that you will be back later. When you leave, use the same words—never sneak out for work without saying goodbye. It also helps to greet her in a similar way every time you return. In time, your baby will learn that you always come back, and she will not mind your leaving her. Older babies sometimes cry when the parent returns. This can be distressing, although the baby may only be crying from relief. Finally, make sure that you are happy with your caregiver (see pp. 185–7). It is normal for a baby or young child to cry when a parent leaves, but this soon stops. If your baby persists in crying when you leave her, even after several weeks with the same caregiver, you should investigate because there may be something amiss.

What can I do if my baby has teething pain?

"Teething produces nothing but teeth," according to some doctors, but as a parent I know that this isn't quite true. Teething does not cause fever, seizures, coughs, or other serious symptoms—if your baby has any of these, it has nothing to do with her new teeth. However, teething can result in sore gums and pain.

Symptoms to look for:
- irritability ■ red cheeks
- a lot of drooling
- possible diaper rash
- white patches on gums and, occasionally, a drop of blood when the tooth appears
- chewing on everything.

Types of pain relief

There are a variety of methods of alleviating teething pain and comforting your baby. First rub her gums gently with your little finger. Try other methods of pain relief for your baby before you rely too heavily on gels or medicines.

Pain-relieving gels
A number of teething gels are available from pharmacies. Check the sugar content and age recommendation on the package.

Chamomilla granules
Available from healthfood stores and some pharmacies, these are a homeopathic alternative to gels.

Chilled finger foods are very soothing for sore gums

Medicines
Acetaminophen syrup is useful if other methods don't work, so keep some at home. Follow the dosage instructions and never exceed the recommended dose.

Finger foods
Teething babies enjoy chewing finger foods (see p. 76) and chewing will help your baby to strengthen her jaw muscles. The fibers in pieces of vegetable will also help clean any teeth she already has.

Teething rings

Teething rings are a good alternative to medicinal methods of pain relief. Cooled, water-filled rings are soothing for inflamed gums. Textured rings may encourage the appearance of teeth.

Chill rings in the refrigerator, not the freezer

Water-filled rings
These can be chilled for extra relief. Keep two or more so there is always a cold ring available.

Rattle teethers
The bright colors and the rattle sound are appealing to babies.

Textured teethers
These have a variety of shapes and hard and soft surfaces for your baby to chew, according to her needs.

CRYING AND COMFORTING

OLDER BABIES 6 MONTHS–1 YEAR

COMFORTING YOUR TODDLER

Q WHY DOES MY TODDLER CRY ?

A Although toddlers cry less than babies, many things can still make them cry (see below). They may cry when they're in pain or upset, or when they can't get what they want. The period around two years of age is a time of growing negativity, when your toddler is showing her independence and expressing her needs more, but is unable to wait long for gratification. Crying can also be a means of getting attention, especially if there's a new baby in the house. Toddlers also cry sometimes as a way of getting an older child blamed for something.

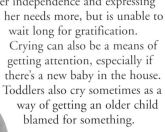

CALMING YOUR TODDLER
Your toddler's new range of emotions can be difficult for her to deal with. Be as sympathetic and supportive as you can.

Q SHE CRIES IN THE BATHTUB AND ON THE POTTY. WHAT SHOULD I DO ?

A Her awkwardness may be a matter of timing as well as her will-power. A toddler can be happy to do what you want her to do if it suits her. You should never have to force her to sit on the potty because she can become so uncooperative that she may decide not to sit on it again for a very, very long time. There is no easy answer, but sometimes you can take advantage of the fact that toddlers are still highly distractable. You could earn her cooperation by subterfuge. Instead of marching her into the bathroom and pulling her clothes off, put a floating toy into the water and try to interest her in that. If you have trouble persuading her to get out of the bathtub afterward, you might have to tempt her with her favorite story.

Q MY TODDLER CRIES WHEN SHE CAN'T DO SOMETHING. WHAT CAN I DO ?

A This is due to frustration, and unfortunately, it is very common. She knows what she wants to do, but is still too young to achieve it. Try to help her help herself. It may be maddening to watch while your toddler takes ages putting her boots on the wrong feet, but she has to learn, so let her try. This is usually more successful than taking over and doing it for her.

WHY TODDLERS CRY

CAUSES	WHY IT MAKES HER CRY
Hunger	Your toddler may cry for food if she's still too young to say she's hungry.
Pain	At any age, your toddler may cry if she hurts herself, or someone else injures her.
Frustration	Your toddler may want a particular toy (or an object that is definitely not a toy). Realizing she can't reach it, or she's not allowed to have it, can bring on tears.
Temper	Your toddler will almost certainly cry if you and she have a clash of wills.
Fear or anxiety	The world is still a strange place to a toddler—she is likely to become frightened and cry if it is dark or if she's left with strangers.
Loneliness or boredom	Some toddlers cry because they're bored and want to do something different. It's worth having an outing every day, even in bad weather, to prevent boredom.
Fatigue	No matter how eager she is to stay up late, fatigue can make her grumpy and tearful.

Q WHY DOES SHE CRY WHEN I TRY TO HELP HER?

A Toddlers can become upset if you do something that they would prefer to do for themselves. Be patient and let her try. If you must help, try to be diplomatic. You will be rewarded later as she becomes more independent.

Q WHEN SHE KICKS AND SCREAMS, HOW SHOULD I REACT?

A This is a temper tantrum, and the less you react, the better. You can't reason with a toddler during a tantrum (see p. 171). Turn your back on her and start to do something else. Once she starts to calm down, ask if she'd like to join you. Don't mention the tantrum—there's no point at this age.

BREATH-HOLDING ATTACKS

Sometimes a toddler will hold her breath, usually after two or three long cries. She may turn blue and pass out for a few seconds. This cures the attack, the breathing restarts, and the toddler becomes conscious again.

Why do they happen?
Breath-holding attacks come on when a toddler is thwarted in some way. They can occur once every few weeks, or even several times a day.

Will my toddler come to any harm?
No. Breath-holding is harmless even when, as sometimes happens, the toddler has a convulsion. It is understandably terrifying for the parent, however.

What can I do during an attack?
If you're sure it's a breath-holding attack, all you need to do is watch over her when she passes out. Otherwise ignore it. Don't give in to her demands. This is a kind of tantrum, and it should not affect your handling of her.

When will breath-holding attacks stop?
These are unusual after the age of three, but some experts say that they can continue until a child is five. Some toddlers have so-called "pallid" breath-holding attacks, but these are caused by pain or fear and are more like a faint.

USING COMFORT OBJECTS

Q MY TODDLER TAKES A SOFT TOY EVERYWHERE. WHAT CAN I DO?

A Don't do anything—it won't do her any harm at this stage. If she is using a comfort object, it is because she feels that she needs it. If you try to stop her from clinging to it, or make fun of her, there is bound to be trouble. When she no longer needs the security the toy provides, she'll stop carrying it everywhere with her. Meanwhile, you must make sure the favorite toy does not get lost. It is worth having a spare one as backup if you can. In my opinion, it is important that you, as a parent, avoid getting involved in any rituals related to the object—once you start hugging and kissing the toy yourself, there is a danger that the situation can become ridiculous.

Q HOW CAN I KEEP MY TODDLER FROM USING A PACIFIER?

A If she uses a pacifier now, try to reserve it for limited situations, such as going to sleep at night or situations that are very stressful. If she's not yet walking, you could stop letting her have the pacifier once she begins to walk. At the very least, do not take it out of the house with you. A toddler shouldn't need a pacifier very much at all, and eventually her need will decrease further. Never give a pacifier when she's not actually clamoring for it. The children you see walking around in the street with pacifiers are usually those who've been given the pacifier even when they weren't miserable. This is a habit that I find deplorable as well as pointless.

Q SHE CRIES WHEN SHE DOESN'T HAVE HER PACIFIER. WHAT CAN I DO?

A If your toddler is asking for the pacifier, try to give her something that will distract her, so that by the time she is 18 months old she gives up the pacifier altogether. If she still cries, you may have to consider letting her have it in certain situations. However, make sure that these are as limited as possible. Try not to forbid the pacifier absolutely and then relent when she has an outburst or a tantrum—this will give your toddler mixed messages that are confusing, and she will think that you don't really mean it when you say "No." As an alternative to a pacifier, many parents suggest sucking a thumb, but this is no better for her and is even harder to give up.

COMFORTING YOUR CHILD

Q MY CHILD STILL CRIES SOMETIMES. IS THIS NORMAL ?

A Yes. Crying is natural and normal. Crying for basic needs such as hunger and thirst is much less common, but anxieties and other complex emotions are sometimes hard for a child to handle (see below). Some of the time you'll be able to predict the situations that upset your child. At other times you'll sense when a major clash of wills is on the way. While your child is growing up, there will be many instances when she'll find it hard to accept that she can't have what she wants when she wants it.

WHY CHILDREN CRY

CAUSES	WHY IT MAKES HER CRY
Hunger	Many young children whine or cry from hunger, especially if they're tired. They may not realize they're hungry. Having a snack handy can prevent this.
Fatigue	Your child may insist she's not tired, but it can still make her irritable and close to tears. If she's tired, give her a relaxing bath, then put her to bed.
Pain	Illness or major or minor injuries can make a child cry.
Fear or anxiety	Common fears and phobias include darkness, thunderstorms, lightning and windy weather, going to the doctor, anticipation of being punished or slapped, going to playgroup, preschool, or school, worry about being abandoned, change of any kind.
Nightmare or night terror	These can cause crying or even screaming at night (see p. 95).
Temper or clash of wills	Outbursts can occur beyond toddlerhood, depending on the child's individual maturity, personality, and temperament.
Sibling rivalry	Sometimes a child of this age may cry in an attempt to attract the attention that a younger sibling is receiving from a parent.

Q WHAT IS THE BEST WAY TO COMFORT MY CHILD ?

A It depends on why she is crying. Fortunately you can begin to use logic when talking to a preschool child. Also use touch to give her reassurance. It is easy to think that a child of this age is quite grown-up, especially if there is a younger brother or sister, but she may still need a good hug from you now and then.

Q SHE ALWAYS CRIES AT THE END OF THE DAY FOR NO REASON. WHY ?

A There is a reason for her crying—she's tired. When you're worn out at the end of the day, your ability to cope is greatly reduced, and it is the same for your child. At such times, try to avoid confrontation or you'll both feel worse. Make bedtime simple and pleasant, and wind up the day as soon as you can with a minimum of fuss.

Q SHOULD I LET MY CHILD CRY OR GO TO HER ?

A It depends on why she's crying. There comes a time when you can't scoop your child up into your arms whenever she falls and scrapes her knee. For one thing, she's getting heavier. More importantly, learning self-reliance is an important part of growing up. So when she cries, wait a few moments to assess what's wrong and what the problem actually is. You can still go to her and offer comfort if necessary. It would be cruel to ignore real distress or a serious scream, but the older she is the more you can afford to wait instead of rushing immediately to her rescue.

Q SHE DOESN'T CRY, BUT SHE'S UNHAPPY OR ANGRY AT TIMES. WHAT'S WRONG ?

A She may be afraid or worried but unable to find the words to explain why. Gently explore what may be troubling her. When she's angry, she may also need to talk it over with you. Don't expect a complex explanation from her. If she's angry it may be difficult for her to calm down sufficiently to give a clear account of the problem. Young children often complain that something is "not fair." You may need to counter this with why it is in fact fair, or alternatively put your arms around her and simply agree.

Q HOW CAN I REASSURE HER WHEN I'M UNSURE MYSELF ?

A The world is an uncertain place and you won't always know how things will turn out. What she needs from you depends on the circumstances. For instance, if you are taking her to a hospital appointment be as confident as possible. However, try not to lie. It is pointless to pretend, for example, that Grandpa won't die when he is very ill. There are times when it is better to admit to uncertainty than to lie to your child.

Q WHAT CAN I DO IF MY CHILD IS SCARED OF SOMETHING ?

A Comfort her and avoid making fun of her. Do not force your child to confront the feared object because this may flood her with fear. The fear will diminish if you're gentle. When your child approaches the object, be there to calm her. Let her take her time, and stop if it becomes too much. If you can, let her have control—fear of the dark can be fought with a night-light or a lamp by the bed, or you can let her turn the light on and off. However if the fear interferes with daily life, ask your pediatrician for advice.

Q SHE CRIES EVERY TIME SHE GOES TO PLAYGROUP. WHAT SHOULD I DO ?

A If she cries purely on being separated from you, this will improve as she gets used to it. Whenever you leave her, handle her gently and don't disappear suddenly or without saying goodbye and telling her you'll be back later. Ensure that you're never late to pick her up, and avoid telling her about all the wonderful things that you did that day. Even if she is the only one who cries at playgroup, try not to make her feel silly. You must, of course, make sure that it is not the playgroup itself that is the cause of her tears. Your child may be unable to tell you about a problem, so come back to playgroup early and unannounced every so often to see what's going on. Talk to other parents—those who have helped at the playgroup may be able to tell you if your child was happy or miserable, and they can also tell you whether their child likes it there. Speak to the staff and find out how they get along with your child.

OFFERING REASSURANCE
Remember that your child is still very young and he will still need a hug and reassurance, even if the reason seems irrational to you.

Q CAN I PREVENT MY CHILD FROM BEING AFRAID OF THINGS ?

A Not always. Young children's fears are often completely irrational. You may be able to prevent some fears from developing by concealing your own phobias if you have any. Fears aren't inherited, but the suggestion that spiders are scary, for instance, can be influential on a child.

Q WILL SHE CRY BECAUSE OF TENSION BETWEEN MY PARTNER AND ME ?

A Yes. Young children are brilliant at picking up tension even when there are no arguments for them to overhear. A child may have tantrums or cry, may act out the conflict between her parents, may sleep or eat badly, or become detached. Every child needs love and security, but a child of warring parents needs even more reassurance that she is loved. There are no easy answers, but both you and your partner should make the security of your child your top priority. If you are going to separate, avoid passing on to her all the uncertainties you and your partner are going through. Give her information rather than hiding the situation from her (see p. 192). One or both parents may be upset, which is normal at this time. However, for the sake of your child you need to be adults, and avoid showing her your own grief or fears.

A hug and a few kind words will help reassure your child

131

GROWTH AND DEVELOPMENT

Your child's physical growth and his social, emotional, and **intellectual development** are inextricably linked. The focus in this chapter is on all aspects of **growth** and development, including vision, hearing, and speech. Developmental **milestones** for each age are discussed alongside suggestions for **toys and activities** that can help your child learn through play. There's also a section on **bringing out the best** in your child—one of the most rewarding aspects of being a parent. This chapter guides you through your child's **all-important early years**, providing reassurance and advice about his progress from birth to his first day at school.

CHILD DEVELOPMENT

Q WHY DO SOME BABIES DEVELOP FASTER THAN OTHERS ?

A It's not always clear why some babies progress more quickly. The trend may run in the family; a toddler who is late learning to walk may have a parent who was also a late walker. The timing is much less important than many parents think.

Q DOES IT MATTER IF MY CHILD IS LATE IN REACHING DEVELOPMENT MILESTONES ?

A Probably not. The ages given below are only average, so many babies will be later and many earlier in reaching certain stages. Also, assessing your baby's progress depends not only on what he is doing, but on how well he is doing it.

Q WHAT IS HAPPENING PHYSIOLOGICALLY AS MY BABY DEVELOPS ?

A Development depends on the maturity of your baby's nervous system—his brain and his nerves. A sheath of myelin around each nerve makes it conduct impulses faster, but at birth many nerves don't yet have myelin, so a newborn's nervous system isn't fully formed. Nerves outside the brain can take up to two years to develop a complete myelin sheath, which is one reason why toddlers lack coordination and why you can't toilet train your child until he is around two years old, when his neural development will enable him to control bladder and bowels. The nerves within the brain are not fully myelinated until he reaches adolescence.

MAJOR DEVELOPMENTAL MILESTONES

Although there are more major developmental milestones to conquer in the earliest stages of childhood than at any other time, developmental progress continues well beyond then—we all continue to learn and mature throughout our life.

By six weeks
- Your baby can smile.
- He can focus.
- He can hold his head in line with his body momentarily if you hold him on his front.

By three months
- Your baby will hold an object placed in his hand.
- He recognizes people and things.
- He giggles when he is happy.

By six months
- Your baby can roll from his front onto his back.
- He can sit propped up.
- He can hold a cup or bottle, usually with both hands.

By nine months
- Your baby can sit unaided.
- He uses a pincerlike grasp.
- He responds to his name.
- He may crawl.
- He may wave bye-bye.

HEAD AND NECK CONTROL
By three months, your baby can hold up his head and shoulders.

BETTER BALANCE
Between the ages of 6–9 months, your baby will learn to sit up unaided.

GETTING AROUND
By nine months, many babies are able to crawl or shuffle around.

Q WHY IS MY BABY SLOWER IN GETTING CONTROL OF HIS LEGS THAN HIS ARMS ?

A This pattern of development is due to the downward direction in which your baby's nerves develop and mature—from the head down to the feet. Thanks to the strength of his neck muscles, your baby has head control before his arm and hand coordination develops. And he can do a lot with his hands before he begins to put his legs to good use. If you watch a nine-month-old playing, you'll notice that he can sit up and manipulate his head and arms in a purposeful way, while his legs do little more than provide a sturdy base to support him. Also, all children learn skills in the same sequence—every baby has to stand before he can walk. However, it is sometimes the case that a child will skip a stage—not all babies crawl, for example. Even so, the skills your baby masters are learned in a predetermined order—it is just a question of when he will reach each stage.

Q DOES MY CHILD'S PERSONALITY AFFECT HIS DEVELOPMENT ?

A Yes. Personality is one variable that makes it hard to predict a child's progress, but it does have an important bearing on it. A child who is more determined and independent may acquire and keep practicing new skills faster than a more placid child. Your child's future may depend more on his personality than intelligence.

Q MY BABY WAS BORN PREMATURELY. WILL THIS AFFECT HIS DEVELOPMENT ?

A Prematurity will not slow down his rate of development, but you must make allowances for the fact your baby has started life at a different point. If, for example, he was born six weeks early, this means at three months his development may be more like that of a six-week-old. By the age of two years, there should be no difference between children who were born prematurely and those who weren't.

By one year
- Your baby may walk if you hold one of his hands.
- He may say his first real word.
- He can hold a pencil in his fist.

By two years
- Your toddler can run, climb, and tackle the stairs.
- He can use two-word sentences.
- He can obey complex orders.

By three years
- Your toddler uses sentences.
- He can dress himself with help.
- He can use the toilet on his own.

By four years
- Your child can explain what a picture is about.
- He is beginning to count.
- He can catch a ball.

By five years
- He is able to speak clearly and usually logically.
- He can read some simple words.
- He can draw and copy.

ON THE MOVE
By three, your child has the coordination to ride a tricycle.

WALKING TALL
Between 12–18 months, most babies will learn to walk.

Bringing Out the Best in Your Child

Q HOW CAN I BRING OUT THE BEST IN MY CHILD AS HE DEVELOPS ?

A The key is to attend to your child's emotional needs as well as his physical ones. All children thrive best in a secure environment that offers them plenty of love. There will be testing times, but try not to lose your patience, criticize unduly, or be sarcastic. It's far better to praise him so that he grows up in an atmosphere where he feels at ease with himself. Whenever you can, reward your child with attention, not candy or presents. This is better than punishing him when he does go wrong. He will often get things wrong, but he has to know that it's all right to learn from his mistakes.

Q HOW CAN I ENCOURAGE MY CHILD'S DEVELOPMENTAL PROGRESS ?

A Spend time doing things with your child rather than ignoring him to concentrate on things you want to do. Have conversations with him all the time about anything, and take his questions seriously. When he's about three years old, he'll probably ask endless questions, most of them beginning with "Why?" Always answer as best you can. Curiosity is the sign of an active mind, and you may find that soon he asks you things you need to look up in order to answer. Find the explanation together in a book or on the Internet, even when your child can't yet read. A love of learning is vital and you're his first and most natural teacher. Give him an interest in books and read to him from early on. If you and your partner read for pleasure, your child will see the satisfaction it brings, and he'll be happy to copy you.

Q ARE SOME PERIODS MORE IMPORTANT FOR DEVELOPMENT THAN OTHERS ?

A Yes. There may not be well-defined periods with sharp cut-off points, but there are windows of opportunity or times when your baby or child is most ready to acquire a certain skill. For instance, there's a window of opportunity at around eight months when a baby is ready to chew. So, if you continue to feed him only milk and sloppy mixtures, he'll take much longer to learn to deal with chunks of food. However, it is rather misleading to think of certain critical periods because all of childhood is critical to your child's development. You only pass this way once with your child, so be sure to make the most of it.

Q IS THERE ANYTHING I CAN DO TO SPEED UP MY CHILD'S DEVELOPMENT ?

A No, and you shouldn't try. You can't teach him to walk sooner than nature intended, or to do anything else until he is ready. With the use of flash cards and other fast learning methods, your child may pick up one or two skills that by repeating he will learn to do automatically. You may even be able to teach him to write in this way. However, until he's old enough for real understanding, these are little more than party tricks. There isn't a useful way of accelerating his progress—by putting pressure on a child, you can do more harm than good and may even discourage him from learning in the long run.

Q WILL THE SPEED OF HIS DEVELOPMENT DEPEND ON HIS INTELLIGENCE ?

A Partly, but not entirely. The link between development and intelligence is not a simple one and it's made more complicated by being a sensitive issue among educators. Babies and children who are intellectually disadvantaged are often slower in several spheres of development because some skills demand some degree of intelligence in their acquisition. But the arrow doesn't go both ways—you can't pinpoint a superior intellect simply from the age at which a baby passes certain developmental milestones. There is a definite link between speech development and intelligence in the sense that a low IQ (intelligence quotient) can delay speech acquisition, but late speech does not necessarily mean that a child is intellectually backward.

Q WHAT FACTORS MAY AFFECT MY CHILD'S INTELLIGENCE ?

A Intelligence is hard to predict as well as difficult to define. We can all think of people, both adults and children, who are academically able but lack emotional maturity. If you measure intelligence simply with an IQ test, statistically, the first-born child is likely to be slightly more intelligent than his younger siblings. In larger families, especially those in which there are only short gaps between successive children, the average intelligence tends to decrease by a few points with each child. Children tend to inherit the intellect of one or both parents, but it's wrong to expect a child to be just like you.

Q HOW CAN I MAXIMIZE MY CHILD'S OPPORTUNITIES FOR LEARNING?

A Let him play—it is vital to his learning. All toys are educationally useful, but some—such as play mats and play gyms incorporating an array of textures, sorting and pairing toys and games, puzzles, jigsaw puzzles, and books—are more valuable than others. Babies and young children get bored easily, so try to vary the selection of playthings available. As soon as your child is interested, teach him colors as well as the similarities and differences between everyday things.

Q WILL PRACTICE HELP MY CHILD DEVELOP HIS SKILLS?

A Yes. Young children enjoy practicing what they have just learned and it is useful for them to do so, since repetition establishes the new skill more firmly. Let your child scribble and paint as much as he wants, dress himself, or help you make lunch, but never force your child to practice.

Q I WORK FULL TIME, SO HOW CAN I HELP MY CHILD'S DEVELOPMENT?

A Establish a daily routine with your child's caregiver. The environment she provides has to be acceptable to you, but not identical to that which you would provide. Variety of experience enriches a child's emotional and social development. When you're not working, spend time with your child. As a working parent your contribution to your child's development will be slightly different from that of a parent who is at home full time, but if you get the balance right, your contribution can be as valuable.

Q COULD CONFLICT AT HOME SLOW MY CHILD'S DEVELOPMENT?

A Yes. Any threat to a child's sense of security will affect him. Emotional stability is vital to development in all areas, so if you and your partner disagree, it is extremely important that you make the effort to shield your child from the conflict.

Q COULD POOR LIVING CONDITIONS AFFECT MY CHILD'S DEVELOPMENT?

A They may. Children from less affluent or more crowded homes tend to do less well in terms of development. It's not the money that counts but the food, housing, heating, playthings, and time that it buys. If you are struggling to provide for your family, you may be short of time and energy to give to your children. Many parents manage to overcome this with dedication and ingenuity.

KEY DEVELOPMENT CHECKS

These checks assess how your child is growing and developing, and screen for a variety of medical conditions, including heart disease, congenital hip dysplasia, and strabismus, so that they can be treated at an early stage before symptoms affect your child's progress. Use these checkups to ask your doctor or pediatrician about any concerns you may have.

What checkups will my child have?
Your child will be examined soon after birth and then at regular intervals throughout childhood. He may be asked to do particular tasks or to talk about something as well as having a medical examination.

Does missing a checkup matter if I think my child is generally developing well?
Yes. There are conditions, such as heart disease, hip dysplasia, and undescended testicles, which are almost impossible for a parent to pick up at a time when treatment would help most.

What if my child is unwell or won't cooperate on the day?
It doesn't matter if your child has a minor illness, such as a cold. However, reschedule the checkup if he has a feverish illness, or has an infection (such as rubella) that could affect others at the doctor's office. Sometimes babies and toddlers are uncooperative because they are hungry or tired. Feed your baby before the checkup, but don't worry if he's a little grumpy. Your doctor may be able to do some of the checks and leave the rest for another day.

How accurate are screening examinations?
You can't rely 100 percent on any screening procedure, but having them done maximizes the chances of any medical condition being picked up at the earliest possible stage. However, a doctor can miss a problem such as congenital hip dysplasia even if your baby has all his checkups at the right time. Talk to your doctor or pediatrician about any concerns that arise between checkups.

TEETH, HEARING, AND VISION

Most babies get their first tooth at around six months, but occasionally a baby is born with a tooth. Other babies are 12 months or older before their first tooth appears. Your child should have all his primary teeth by the time he is 2½ years old.

HOW TEETH DEVELOP

When teething, your baby will probably chew everything within reach and drool copiously and continually. He may also be in pain, which will make him irritable, and one cheek may become flushed. However, he shouldn't be running a fever, have a cough or any other serious symptoms; if he does, consult your doctor.

Your child's primary teeth will probably appear in the following order:
- lower central incisors (6 months)
- upper central incisors (6½ months)
- lower lateral incisors (7 months)
- upper lateral incisors (8 months)
- lower anterior molars (10 months)
- upper anterior molars (14 months)
- lower canines (16 months)
- upper canines (18 months)
- lower second molars (2 years)
- upper second molars (2½ years).

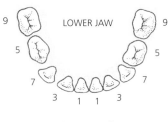

Top teeth

UPPER JAW

LOWER JAW

Bottom teeth

MILK TEETH
Your child will have 20 primary teeth; the numerals indicate the order in which they should appear. He will start losing them when he's about six years old.

Caring for primary teeth

How can I help my child have healthy teeth?
Start brushing your baby's teeth in the morning and evening as soon as they appear. Initially you can hold him on your lap and brush from behind. When he's old enough to sit or stand unaided, brush from the front. Even when he can brush by himself, you should supervise his technique. Only give fruit juice at mealtimes and avoid bedtime drinks unless he brushes afterward. If your child has sweet food, get him to eat it all at once rather than lingering over it. Encourage him to choose healthy snacks and make sure his diet is rich in calcium, minerals, and vitamins. Begin dental checkups at an early age (see p. 212).

Are carbonated diet drinks better for teeth?
No. Carbonated diet drinks don't contain sugar, so you might think they're tooth-friendly, but their acidity makes them harmful—when dissolved, carbon dioxide makes carbonic acid. Put a coin into a diet drink and watch it being eaten away.

Does my child need fluoride drops?
It depends on where you live. Sometimes fluoride is already in the water, either occurring naturally or because it has been added by the water provider. If your area doesn't have fluoride in the water, your child may need drops from babyhood onward. Too much fluoride may discolor the teeth permanently, so don't give fluoride drops without first seeking advice from your doctor or pediatrician.

Can medicines affect my child's teeth?
All medicines containing sugar can have an adverse effect on a child's teeth. Many are now available in sugar-free formulations that still taste good to children. Ask your doctor or pharmacist for sugar-free alternatives whenever possible. Some antibiotics can also be detrimental to dental enamel, especially tetracycline. This is why they shouldn't be given to children under 12 years old (or to women who are pregnant or breast-feeding).

HOW HEARING DEVELOPS

Babies can hear in the womb, but their hearing increases in sophistication once they are born. This development usually follows a set pattern.

■ A newborn is acutely aware of sound. Sudden noises can startle him or make his eyes open wide.

■ By three months, your baby listens to your voice with pleasure and may look toward you. He coos "ah" or "oh" in response to the sound of your voice.

■ By seven months, he can start to localize sound and knows the significance of certain sounds, such as laughter or the doorbell ringing.

■ By nine months, he notices sounds made in other rooms, even when these aren't loud.

■ By 12 months, he understands a number of words and phrases. He is now able to shut out noise when he wants to concentrate on a book or toy.

Will my child have hearing tests?

Yes, at regular intervals. Some hospitals check all babies soon after birth using special equipment. Your child will also have his hearing assessed at some of his development checks, especially those between the ages of 6–9 months. Always talk to your doctor if you have concerns about your child's ability to hear, because impaired hearing will have an add-on effect when it comes to his speech development. Talk to your doctor promptly but don't panic—most hearing loss is temporary and may be the result of blocked tubes caused by a cold or some other ear–nose infection. Chronic secretory otitis media (see p. 219) is another common and treatable ear complaint, resulting in impaired hearing, that occurs in babies and toddlers.

HOW VISION DEVELOPS

A newborn's vision develops as his brain matures and the six muscles around the eyeball become increasingly strong. But visual development is not just a matter of seeing things—your baby also has to understand the significance of what he sees.

■ At birth your baby can turn toward the source of light and blink his eyelids.

■ At eight weeks he begins to focus on things.

■ At 12 weeks he follows a moving toy, but he'll fail to spot small objects.

■ At six months he moves his body into position in order to see things that intrigue him.

■ At 12 months his tear ducts are fully formed, so he gets pink-eye less often (see p. 217).

■ At two years he can see very small objects.

■ At three years his color vision has matured, and the development of the visual nerves is complete.

When should my child's eyesight first be checked?

Your doctor or pediatrician will ask you about your child's vision at his routine development checks. Most pediatric offices perform annual vision screens starting at four years of age. You can start younger if you wish—your child doesn't have to read or know the alphabet, so he can have an eye test at any age. There's no harm in starting checks from the age of 12 months, especially if there's a family history of nearsightedness, farsightedness, or astigmatism (irregular eyeball shape).

What is strabismus?

Strabismus is when a person's eyes look in different directions. Strabismus can be serious if left untreated, but most babies have symptoms from time to time in their first two months because their eyes can't yet work together efficiently. If your baby has symptoms often, or his eyes go in different directions after the age of three or four months, you should see your doctor (if there is a history of strabismus in your family or your partner's, mention this). Your baby may need referral to an opthamologist. However, not all cases need a corrective operation—some can be treated with a patch over the eye, others with glasses or even eyedrops.

What if my child needs glasses?

Most children don't, although some need glasses for a while to correct a temporary eye problem. There are of course other cases when a child will need glasses throughout life and there are many social and educational drawbacks to not wearing glasses if they are needed. If your child needs corrective glasses, it's best not to make a fuss. Many children don't mind glasses, but a parent's negative attitude can put them off. Glasses frames are more attractively designed these days, and plastic lenses are lightweight and virtually unbreakable. So think of glasses as a great benefit to your child, not a handicap, and tell him how great he looks in them.

SPEECH AND LANGUAGE DEVELOPMENT

Q HOW DO CHILDREN LEARN TO SPEAK ?

A Since children usually learn to speak before they can read or write, language acquisition generally means learning to speak and to understand others. The three main factors that determine how quickly a child learns to speak are his inborn ability to use language, his basic level of intelligence and understanding of the world, plus his ability to imitate others, especially his parents and other influential adults.

Q WHAT CAN I DO TO ENCOURAGE MY CHILD TO SPEAK ?

A Give your child lots of time, attention, and eye contact while you are talking to him. Talk to him about what you are doing and keep your speech clear and simple. During conversations, make sure there are as few distractions around as possible, and leave gaps for your child's response. Tell him stories and read books to him; teach him nursery rhymes and silly songs. All of these elements play an important part in a child's acquisition of language. As your child will copy what he hears, be careful to avoid baby talk. He may say "Da-da," but he needs to hear you say "Daddy." When he uses a word, repeat it and put it into a sentence for him, such as: "Yes, Daddy is washing the dishes."

Q WHEN WILL MY CHILD BE ABLE TO PRONOUNCE WORDS PROPERLY ?

A Your child's pronunciation matures as he develops, and consonants are much more difficult to pronounce than vowels. At around five years, he will learn to make "ch," "j," and "l" sounds, but he may not be able to manage some sounds, such as "th" and "r," for another two years or so. Help his pronunciation by always speaking clearly. Do not be tempted to correct your child's pronunciation—if he gets a word wrong just say "Yes, that's right," and then repeat it correctly. Mimicry is fundamental to the acquisition of speech, and it's the reason why twins may pronounce badly for longer than single children.

Q COULD MY CHILD'S SPEECH BE DELAYED BECAUSE WE'RE A BILINGUAL FAMILY ?

A No. Young children exposed to more than one language are as fluent as other children. They do tend to slip from one language into another when speaking, often within the same sentence, a talent that is usually effortless and involuntary. Parents of a bilingual child often worry that he will be so confused that he won't want to talk, but in practice this isn't the case— these children do not speak less or later. If your bilingual child is late speaking, there will be another cause (see opposite).

HOW DOES MY CHILD LEARN TO USE LANGUAGE ?

The pattern of language acquisition

■ In his first eight weeks, a baby makes a limited range of basic burbling noises.

■ From 2 to 6 months, he coos and chuckles, especially when you show him attention.

■ From 6 to 12 months, your baby enjoys a period of vocal play, when he babbles and experiments with a range of sounds but mostly vowels.

■ From 12 to 18 months, he produces a range of one-syllable words. He uses each word alone, but may use the same sound or word to name different things. Babies with different mother tongues begin to make different sounds.

■ From 18 to 24 months, your baby repeats things, and is able to ask for food and drink. He begins to link words into short sentences.

■ From 2 to 2½ years, your child talks a lot, mostly in sentences. He uses the personal pronouns "I", "me," and "you." "He" and "she" soon follow.

■ From 2½ to 3 years, he talks in sentences of at least three words and is able to understand complex requests. He knows 500–1,000 words, including prepositions.

■ From 3 to 4 years, he is perfecting his mastery of his native tongue, including basic grammar, but his pronunciation is still immature.

■ From 4 to 5 years, his vocabulary continues to grow. Both his understanding and articulation increase in sophistication. He knows the letters of the alphabet and may be able to write some of them. His voice still sounds childish, but by now he should have given up baby talk.

Q HOW CAN I STOP MY CHILD FROM USING SWEAR WORDS ?

A Telling him off is of little benefit—young children don't understand the concept of context, so he won't understand why you are angry. The best policy is to ignore him. He will have learned the words somewhere, however, so be sure the adults and other children he comes into contact with don't use bad language in front of him.

Q MY CHILD STUTTERS. WHAT CAN I DO TO HELP HIS SPEECH ?

A All young children hesitate at times, but true stuttering is persistent. The longer a child stutters, the harder it is for him to lose the habit. Even before he is three years old, he may need to see a speech therapist for an assessment. In the first instance, take him to your doctor and, if he is reluctant to refer him to a specialist, stand your ground. Meanwhile, do not speed up your speech to compensate for your child's hesitation, and try not to anticipate what your child will say—give him the chance and he may get the words out.

Q DOES TELEVISION HELP OR HINDER LANGUAGE DEVELOPMENT ?

A For two-year-olds and up, well-made programs can enhance a child's language development and his understanding of the world. Judicious viewing is educational, especially if you watch with him to share the experience and to talk about what is happening on the screen. But make sure the pace of a program is right for his level of development and that the content is suitable. Random viewing is a bad influence, so monitor what your child watches (see p. 158).

Q WHEN SHOULD MY CHILD BE ABLE TO READ ?

A Children can often recognize letters by the age of four, but don't read (or write) until they are five or six years old. If your child starts reading, don't stop him—let him enjoy books, both with you and on his own. Don't pressure him to learn to read, or force him through a reading program. You may confuse him if the program used later at school is different from the one he's familiar with. Even if the same program is used at his school, there is no long-term benefit in pushing your child to read before he is ready.

PARENT'S SURVIVAL GUIDE

MY CHILD STILL DOESN'T SPEAK

A delay in speaking sometimes goes unnoticed because of parental expectations—"a child should be seen and not heard"—while in other families, parents are horrified that their child isn't discussing the meaning of life by the age of two. There's actually a wide variation in normal rates of learning to speak, and if a toddler shows good understanding and has normal hearing, then he will speak eventually. All the same, a child who is 18 months old and isn't saying recognizable words needs assessment.

What could be wrong?
The first thing to check is your child's hearing. He needs to hear to learn to speak, so impaired hearing is an important cause of speech delay. Your doctor or pediatrician can arrange for your child to have a hearing test (see p. 139). Other causes of late speech may include:
- lack of adult verbal stimulation—this can occur in large families and with twins
- emotional deprivation—a child needs affection and security to thrive developmentally
- learning disabilities—this is usually linked to a delay in other areas of development, too
- isolated speech delay—also known as specific language delay. The cause is unknown, but it is often treatable or sometimes resolves itself
- autism—this is linked with lack of social skills or other signs of emotional disturbance.

Sharing his toys teaches your child to communicate

COMMUNICATION
Your child will "talk" to his friends, but it's his chats with you that are most vital to his language development.

GENDER DIFFERENCES

Q IN WHAT FUNDAMENTAL WAYS DO BOYS DIFFER FROM GIRLS ?

A There are the obvious anatomical differences, as well as some discrepancies in height, weight, and strength that are usually seen with the onset of puberty. There are also more subtle social and behavioral differences between the sexes that you may notice from a surprisingly young age. Parents often find marked differences between sons and daughters in terms of emotional and physical development. Those who have only girls find the young sons of friends to be very different creatures.

Q WHAT CAUSES THE DEVELOPMENTAL DIFFERENCES BETWEEN THEM ?

A It's hard to know for sure how much is due to innate characteristics and how much has to do with cultural or societal influences in the child's environment. It isn't just parents who mold a child's behavior—there are grandparents, other relatives, friends, and caregivers, as well as the influence of television, books, billboards, and so on. Your child is exposed to a whole spectrum of experience, whether you approve of it or not. Even so, if you look at very young babies you may spot some early differences at a stage when outside influences are still minimal. It has been suggested that boys differ from girls in the increased amount of emotional security they need; the greater noise they make; the fact that they walk, talk, and become toilet-trained later than girls; and the more boisterous nature of the games they choose to play.

Q ARE BOYS GENERALLY MUCH MORE ADVENTUROUS THAN GIRLS ?

A As young children, boys tend to get up and around more often to explore. In the process, they can make a lot of noise. You'll often know from the hubbub where your little boy is, and so will everyone else. But then, of course, there are plenty of bold girls and timid boys.

Q DO BOYS AND GIRLS LEARN TO CRAWL AND WALK AT THE SAME AGE ?

A There's a wide variation in the age at which babies crawl and take their first steps, so many girls and boys do start at the same age. However, a girl often takes her first steps sooner than a boy.

PARENT'S SURVIVAL GUIDE

I WANT TO HELP MY CHILD AVOID SEXUAL STEREOTYPING

To raise a child entirely free of the constraints of gender stereotyping is practically impossible, since you cannot block out the influences and attitudes of the society in which we all live. However, there are certain positive strategies you can make sure you adopt.

How to challenge stereotyping
■ Choose what your child is exposed to from early on. Select books that show girls and women succeeding, for instance.
■ Gently challenge those who expound more traditional views on gender. There is no reason why your son shouldn't cry when he is hurt, why your daughter shouldn't be a scientist, or why the rolling pin shouldn't belong to Dad.
■ Nurture your son's emotional, softer side and your daughter's bolder impulses.
■ Help children of both sexes acquire a positive "can-do" attitude that will give them more confidence and self-assurance, so opening them up to greater opportunities all their lives.

Q IS IT TRUE THAT BABY BOYS CRY MORE THAN BABY GIRLS ?

A Before the age of three, it seems that boys do tend to cry more, but after this age they tend to cry less. This may be because they grow up with the notion that boys aren't supposed to cry, even when they are injured or feeling upset.

Q DOES THE SPEECH OF GIRLS DIFFER FROM THAT OF BOYS ?

A On average, girls learn to speak sooner than boys, and they have larger vocabularies. Even as babies, girls babble more than boys. However, research shows that mothers talk more to baby girls. Interestingly, baby boys cry more than girls and the noisy streak seems to persist well into childhood and adolescence. Girls speak more and find it easier to talk about feelings than boys.

Q IS IT TRUE THAT BOYS BECOME TOILET-TRAINED LATER THAN GIRLS ?

A On average, practical experience does suggest this to be the case. The reasons are unknown but may include the slower rate at which a boy's nervous system matures compared to that of a girl's; a boy's tendency to be less cooperative; and his tendency to be more impatient and adventurous—sitting on a potty slows a boy down, so he can't be bothered to take the time to learn. Whatever the reasons, among parents it's a matter of common experience that little boys continue to use diapers long after the girls are happily asking for and using the potty.

Q WHY IS MY SON BETTER AT BALL GAMES THAN GIRLS OF THE SAME AGE ?

A The reason for this could be that often spatial awareness is more developed in boys—the difference could be either inborn or acquired. When they are older, on average boys undoubtedly have greater muscular strength than girls, so this may influence their penchant for team ball games and other very physical sports. However, what girls lack in strength, they often make up for in agility and grace.

Q HOW CAN I STOP MY SON FROM PLAYING WAR AND OTHER VIOLENT GAMES ?

A It may be impossible, but you can try your best. Avoid giving your child toy guns and swords, and prevent him from being exposed to books, television programs, videos, and computer games that glorify or portray violence. However, many parents find that their sons still play war games using weapons made of sticks and stones, regardless of the fact that they have been shielded from external influences. This could come down to the effect of the male hormone testosterone, which research shows has a marked influence on masculine behavior.

Q WILL DRESSING UP IN GIRLS' CLOTHES AFFECT MY SON'S SEXUAL PREFERENCE ?

A It's unlikely. Children of both sexes dress up for fun using whatever is available. The current thinking is that homosexuality may be genetic, to some extent at least. In choosing to put on girls' clothes your son may possibly be making a subconscious statement about his future sexual preference. I don't think you should try to mold your child's fantasy behavior; if you wish, tell him what boys are generally expected to wear.

SHOULD I TEACH MY CHILD ABOUT SEX ?

Both boys and girls are generally aware of differences in their genitals when they're around two years old, which is not surprising, since this is the age at which toilet training often starts. A three-year-old knows what sex he is and may go through a phase of announcing he is a boy to everyone he meets.

When should I tell my child about sex?

When he asks. Some children have a knack for asking how babies are born in the most awkward circumstances—while you're sitting on a crowded bus, for instance. Some of the other passengers may be shocked, but the rest may well have been through the same experience themselves. In this situation, it's probably best to reply blandly that the baby comes out of Mommy's tummy. However, each family is different and you must be at ease with your reply. Prepare an answer to "What's a condom?"—this is becoming a common query.

What should I tell my child about sex?

Always answer your child's questions. If he asks where he came from, find out exactly what he means. "From Mommy's tummy" is probably the most straightforward answer to give a very young child. Similarly, you have to gauge what he means when he asks what sex means—he may, for instance, need the answer: "It's what you put on a form when it asks you if you are M or F."
When he hints at wanting to know about the mechanics of reproduction, you can initially tell him that Daddy puts a seed inside Mommy without specifying how this actually happens. He'll ask when he wants to know more.
The ideal is not to be evasive, but to be straightforward and honest without overloading him with too much information all at once.
It's important to avoid giving the impression that sex is dirty or smutty. He should regard it as just another bodily function. Don't tell him that one day he will have sex, because he won't be ready to hear this for many years yet.

LEARNING THROUGH PLAY

Q HOW DOES PLAYING HELP MY CHILD LEARN ?

A Play is not just fun. It stimulates a child's senses, especially vision, touch, and hearing. It hones his powers of observation and helps him develop and practice coordination and other skills. Some toys encourage a child to use his imagination more than others, but all toys can be experimented with. Other toys are designed to provide an outlet for his abundant energy or even aggression. If a child is deprived of play opportunities he may experience learning difficulties later.

Q DOES MY CHILD NEED LOTS OF EXPENSIVE TOYS TO PLAY WITH ?

A No. He needs a variety of toys and they must be appropriate for his age, but there is no reason why they need to be expensive. You can get some good second-hand toys from garage sales or by borrowing toys from libraries, but check that they are safe. Put them in some sterilizing solution or wash them thoroughly. You should also help your child play, especially when he is a young baby. You don't have to play with him all the time, but give him attention when needed and help him to do more complicated things when required.

PARENT'S SURVIVAL GUIDE

I CAN'T COPE WITH MESSY PLAY

Some forms of play can get very messy. You can protect your carpet and your sense of calm if you take a few sensible practical steps.

What can I do to manage messy play?
■ Protect clothes and belongings before you start. For painting, spread out a plastic cloth or old newspapers. Or let your child paint outside.
■ Schedule messy play for just before bath time, or before you were going to wash the kitchen floor. That way cleaning up isn't an extra chore.
■ Supervise your child for his own safety and so that he doesn't create excessive mess.
■ You won't be able to prevent accidents and spills entirely. You just have to accept this.

Q FROM WHAT AGE ARE BOOKS USEFUL FOR MY CHILD ?

A Right from the very start. You can read to your baby even before he's six months. He'll enjoy the closeness of sitting on your lap, listening to the rhythm of your voice, and looking at the pictures.

Q WHAT KIND OF BOOKS ARE MOST SUITABLE AT WHAT AGES ?

A Board books are best for your child to look at by himself at any age, especially if the pictures are clear and the book can withstand drooling and some enthusiastic treatment. It's a good idea to keep some special books that you can read together and put "away" after the reading session.

Q WHAT IS THE BEST WAY OF HELPING MY CHILD TRY NEW THINGS ?

A Provide him with opportunity – let him have a variety of toys and objects of different shapes, sizes, and textures. He'll have fun building towers out of blocks and putting things in boxes. He can play with saucepans, empty spools, and cardboard boxes, and he can water plants from a watering can. He'll probably want to test out everything in sight, so supervise him closely.

Q DO I HAVE TO PROVIDE MY CHILD WITH STRUCTURED PLAY ?

A Given enough opportunities, a child will play by himself, but a little structure to the day helps prevent boredom, especially in toddlers. As well as letting him have his own time to immerse himself in his toys, you should also try to have an outing every day to let off steam and see new things. A period of quiet play with a puzzle or enjoying some time together with a book is also a good idea.

Q IS IT IMPORTANT FOR MY CHILD TO PLAY WITH OTHER CHILDREN ?

A Yes. It teaches a child to socialize, cooperate, to accept the existence of rules, to take turns, and to share. However, a child under three years of age is rarely ready for friendships and sharing doesn't come naturally. So until then, playing alongside another child (sometimes called "parallel play") is more realistic. Invite other children to play, visit friends with babies, and go to playgroups.

Q WHAT KIND OF ROLE PLAY IS MOST EDUCATIONAL ?

A Any kind of role play will help your child develop, but delving into old clothes in a dressing-up box or suitcase will keep him busy for ages. If he wants to dress up, costumes needn't be lavish or complicated—he doesn't need your imagination, he needs to use his own. A few special odds and ends, such as a pirate's eye-patch, a beret, or a toy stethoscope will give an air of authenticity to his make-believe world. Sometimes he'll want to involve you, while at other times you'll need to stay firmly in the shadows. Avoid taking over, however much fun it looks.

Q ARE COMPUTER GAMES A GOOD OR BAD THING FOR MY CHILD ?

A Computer games can improve a child's visual discrimination, his coordination, and his reactions, and can pave the way for learning information-technology skills. However, sitting at a computer teaches a child nothing about interpersonal relationships. Some games are violent, and of those that aren't not all are suitable for children under five. Your child can also get hooked on computer games—even some very young children have been known to give up all other activities, including eating, in favor of not having to leave the screen. They are also time-consuming, so consider the effect they could have, if left unchecked, on your child's other play experiences and on his physical fitness and posture. For the young child, learning to socialize is more important than learning how to use a computer.

Q HOW CAN I ENCOURAGE MY CHILD TO BE CREATIVE ?

A Provide your child with paper, pencils, paints, dry pasta shapes, modeling clay, or dough as soon as he is ready—which will probably be at around 18 months—and he will provide the imagination and enthusiasm, although he won't concentrate for long. Don't spend a long time setting up painting or modeling, or you'll be disappointed when he only spends a short time on the activity. When your child has scribbled you a picture or made something out of cardboard and cotton balls, be appreciative and suspend your critical faculties. He may not be creating representational art just yet, but there is sure to be something praiseworthy about it—"That's a nice shape" or "What lovely colors" are positive comments to have ready on the tip of your tongue.

Q WE LIVE IN AN APARTMENT—HOW CAN I MAXIMIZE MY CHILD'S PHYSICAL PLAY ?

A Make an effort to take your child out. As soon as he can sit up unaided, he'll enjoy swings in the park—even earlier if held on your lap. Later, he can try other playground equipment, run on the grass, or play with a ball. Appropriate clothing makes it possible to go out even in bad weather. Jumping in and out of puddles is a good activity, as is kicking up the fallen leaves in the autumn. Supervise your child—parks are not without the hazards of dog feces, garbage cans, and nearby roads. Look for toddler exercise or gymnastics classes, and don't forget the local swimming pool where you can both go for a splash about as soon as you feel your baby is ready. Many sports centers have baby pools that are heated to a higher temperature than the adult pool and many run organized infant swimming lessons.

Q WHERE IS IT BEST FOR ME TO KEEP MY CHILD'S TOYS ?

A Toys should go into a box or closet when your child isn't playing with them. Having all the toys out at once isn't helpful to his pattern of play and can be physically dangerous for you both in terms of tripping and falling. Many parents also find that mess creates stress, while learning to put away toys helps foster a sense of ownership and responsibility in your toddler. This doesn't happen overnight, so help put his toys away to begin with. Try to have different boxes or places for storing different kinds of toys—it will help teach him the concept of sets and groups.

CREATIVE PLAY
Not only is creative play fun, but it also boosts confidence and your child's sense of self worth.

DEVELOPMENT

6 WEEKS–3 MONTHS

Q HOW IS MY BABY DEVELOPING DURING THIS PERIOD?

A Your baby is developing rapidly during this time, and you'll notice that he has matured considerably over the last few weeks. However, it's not always easy to judge how well he is doing. There will be days when your baby is easy-going and happy and others when he is less relaxed and harder to play with and to please. Moreover, babies differ in their character and in their rate of development. You can get some idea of your baby's general progress by observing what he can do when he is in a good mood, recently fed and content— the checklist opposite is a useful starting point. If he doesn't do all these things, don't worry—he may just be having an off-day. However, always speak to your doctor or pediatrician if you are concerned about any aspect of your baby's progress.

■ **Does he follow things with his eyes?** He may get excited when he sees you or a favorite toy, but he won't start noticing small objects for some time.

■ **Does he follow sounds?** By the time your baby is approaching three months, he should be able to turn his head in response to sounds, but his ability to locate them precisely still has some way to go.

■ **If he is awake in his crib, is he surprised to see your face peering over the side?** He should usually be able to hear you as you approach, so he shouldn't be taken aback to see you appear, just delighted you're there.

■ **Does he make any sounds?** Your baby will probably be making cooing sounds by the time he is three months. If he isn't, tell your doctor.

■ **Do his hands lie open most of the time?** By the age of three months, babies no longer keep their fists tightly closed all the time. The opening of your baby's hands is an essential prelude to his learning how to use them.

■ **What is his posture like?** If, after six weeks, your baby's neck is floppy or his head lolls when he is awake, take him to your doctor for a checkup.

■ **Is your baby alert and mostly good tempered?** It is normal for a three-month-old baby to have some fussy periods, but constant irritability may mean that something is wrong.

A fabric mobile will stimulate and entertain your baby

SAFE TOYS
Hang a colorful mobile over your baby's crib or changing area to create a fascinating diversion, but make sure it is well out of his reach if you leave him alone with it.

Q WHICH TOYS ARE SUITABLE FOR MY BABY AT THIS AGE?

A Provide a variety of different toys for your baby to see and handle, and make sure you spend time playing with him every day. Toys can be fairly simple at this stage, and you can gradually build up a collection that will maintain your baby's interest and build his skills as he develops. Toys aren't just for touching—babies appreciate mobiles to look at and music boxes to listen to. Don't put noisy toys too close to your baby, since there's a possibility that prolonged noise may damage his hearing. Babies also like soft toys, such as teddy bears and dolls—their faces interest them, as do their textures. Brightly colored toys, such as rattles and squeaky animals, are ideal in the early months. Toys your baby can hold, grab, and put in his mouth are good choices, too, but make sure that every toy is safe and suitable. Small parts and ribbons on soft toys can easily choke a baby.

Q WHICH ACTIVITIES WILL MY BABY ENJOY AT THIS AGE?

A He will enjoy your talking to him and smiling at him because this reassures him that you care and teaches him a valuable lesson in how to relate to you. Get close so he can explore your face with his hands (if you wear glasses, you may prefer to take them off first). Nuzzle your baby—he will appreciate the feel and the smell, and so will you, especially just after his bath, when he smells his sweetest. Your baby is never too young for nursery rhymes and songs, and he will enjoy being bounced gently up and down on your lap.

Q **AT WHAT AGE WILL MY BABY START USING HIS HANDS ?**

A By about 12 weeks of age, your baby will discover his hands, and for a while they will be his favorite playthings—a source of endless fun and experimentation. During this stage, which is known as "hand regard," he watches his hands move, puts them together, brings them in and out of his field of vision, and puts them in his mouth and sucks them. If your baby uses a pacifier, try to leave it out of his mouth as much as possible—hands and mouths are designed for each other at this age, and a pacifier will stop experimentation.

Q **WHEN WILL MY BABY START TO REACH FOR TOYS ?**

A Your baby can't reach out for things yet. He may strike out at toys, such as a rattle suspended above him, and he may bat an object tentatively, but hitting it is still a matter of luck before three months. When he does begin to reach for toys, he'll misjudge the distance. His hand–eye coordination will develop in due course.

LOOKING AT TOYS
Even though your baby is not yet old enough to reach out, he may get excited when he sees a toy and will try to follow it with his eyes when it is held suspended above him.

WHAT MIGHT MY BABY BE DOING AT THREE MONTHS ?

SKILL	WHAT MIGHT HE BE DOING ?
Sight	■ He may smile in response to your smile. ■ He may focus and follow a dangling toy, especially if it's brightly colored.
Hearing	■ He may smile when spoken to. ■ He may follow sounds.
Speech	■ He may coo with pleasure. ■ He may make vowel sounds, often in response to a parent's voice.
Coordination	■ He may hold an object placed in his hand but can't yet reach out and grasp, and he can't move his hand with a toy held in it.
Posture control	■ He may move his arms and legs a lot when awake. ■ He may hold his head and shoulders off the floor if placed on his front. ■ His head may lag behind him only slightly if you pull him up from lying on his back to an upright sitting position.
General understanding	■ He may recognize people and objects he knows.
Emotional and social behavior	■ He may respond to parents and adults, including strangers, if they are pleasant to him. ■ He shows pleasure by smiling and making noises.

Note that all of these skills will become increasingly interrelated as your baby develops.

3-6 Months

Q HOW IS MY BABY DEVELOPING DURING THIS PERIOD?

A From the age of three months, your baby is becoming more sociable and his coordination is improving all the time. As you have more to go on it becomes easier to assess how your baby is developing. Remember, though, that his temperment will vary from day to day and this will affect what he does and how he behaves. Relax and enjoy watching what he can do—your pediatrician can always advise and reassure you if you have any concerns about your baby's rate of progress or general health.

■ **Does he study things closely?** Once he is over three months, your baby should be focusing well, especially at close range.

■ **Can he grab things?** His grasp at six months will still be primitive but effective nonetheless. He will use two hands to grapple with larger objects, such as his bottle of milk.

■ **Can he hold things and suck them?** He should be putting things in his mouth to explore their shape, texture, and taste. His mouth will remain a primary means of exploring the world around him for some while yet.

■ **Can he roll from his front onto his back during play or while having his diaper changed?** As his muscle tone and coordination develop, he should have increasing control over his movement and may also anticipate your lifting him up.

■ **Does he pay attention when you speak to him?** He should turn toward you when you talk to him and respond with pleasure and recognition.

Seeing your beaming face as he turns to look at you is sure to make your baby smile

Q WHICH ACTIVITIES WILL MY BABY ENJOY AT THIS AGE?

A He isn't too young to look at simple board books, so take time out every day to sit together and enjoy looking at the pictures. He will also love silly songs and nursery rhymes—he won't mind if you have to make up the odd word here and there. Play on the floor with him as much as you can to improve his muscle tone and general cordination. He may respond to peek-a-boo, but playing hide and seek with toys is still too difficult at this stage—he may look for you behind the sofa or curtains, but he won't know where to look for a toy that has disappeared.

Q WHICH TOYS ARE SUITABLE FOR MY BABY AT THIS AGE?

A Your baby will still have fun with rattles, squeaky toys, and soft toys. But since he is using his hands more, he will also appreciate objects of different weights, shapes, and textures, so the toys you get him now can be more complex. All should still be clean and safe enough to go into his mouth and very noisy toys should be played with only sparingly as the adverse effect of noise on hearing is cumulative. Now that he is at the grabbing and handling stage, activity centers and baby gyms are becoming more interesting to him. You can also give your baby larger toys, such as a teddy bear or a big, soft ball to play with. As babies soon tire of things, it's a good tip to rotate his toys so that he plays with different toys from day to day – this way you'll more easily be able to keep him occupied.

HEARING AND LISTENING
During this period of his development, your baby will learn to localize sounds – for example, he will turn to listen to you as you speak.

Q IS IT NORMAL FOR MY BABY TO SPEND TIME EXAMINING THINGS ?

A Your baby is becoming increasingly attentive and his powers of observation are growing. He grabs things, then looks at them, often inspecting them in minute detail. Pictures in books will be closely scrutinized and textures become very important, not just to feel but to dissect visually. Your baby may spend some time merely contemplating a woven pot holder sitting on the windowsill. His detailed study of objects is something of a physics course, teaching him the fundamentals of cause and effect as he fits one thing inside another and tries to take others apart. He will also lift blankets to look under them and if you give him a ball he may push it away and watch it roll back. A chime ball is appealing at this age, as are toys that right themselves when knocked over.

EXPLORING THROUGH PLAY

By six months, your baby should be able to turn from his front onto his back, which will give him another perspective on the world as well as greater mobility in his play. He will be into everything and learning fast.

Your baby will be intrigued to discover he can make a ball roll at will

WHAT MIGHT MY BABY BE DOING AT SIX MONTHS ?

SKILL	WHAT MIGHT HE BE DOING ?
Sight	■ He may look at things very carefully. ■ He may notice himself in a mirror, but not know he is looking at himself. ■ He may imitate you and may stick his tongue out if you do it first. ■ He may play peek-a-boo with you if you hold up a towel or sheet.
Hearing	■ His localization of sounds is improving, and he turns toward the person who is speaking.
Speech	■ He may laugh, coo, chuckle, and "talk" to you and to his mirror image. ■ He may respond to you with a noise, especially if you use his name. ■ He may say "Ba" or "Da."
Coordination	■ He may put everything in his mouth. ■ He may grasp his feet and put them in his mouth, too. ■ He may reach and touch objects. He may grab things with the palm of his hand and three fingers, but he won't use his index finger and thumb just yet. ■ He may hold toys and his bottle, usually with both hands. ■ He may bang things on the floor or table. ■ He may drop his toys accidentally, especially if you offer him another one, but is not yet able to hold something in each hand at the same time.
Posture control	■ When lying on his back, he may lift his head off the floor first when you're about to pull him up into a sitting position. He may hold out his hands, too. ■ He may roll from his front onto his back. ■ He may support his weight momentarily if you hold him in a standing position.
General understanding	■ He may be beginning to understand the kind of effect he can have on the world around him by grasping, handling, or hitting things.
Emotional and social behavior	■ He may enjoy company and may show it by chuckling, laughing, and making cooing noises.

Note that your baby's skills are becoming more interrelated than they were before—his cooing and chuckling, for example, will improve as his powers of mimicry and general understanding develop.

6-9 MONTHS

Q HOW IS MY BABY DEVELOPING DURING THIS PERIOD?

A This is a very interesting time when you'll notice your baby becoming much more of a real person—with a real personality to match. For this reason, he may not act or react in exactly the same way as other babies you know. His development won't be exactly the same either, but you should speak to your doctor if there is anything specific that is worrying you. Your baby is unique, but you can assess how he is progressing generally from some simple observations.

■ **Can he focus properly?** If you present him with an object, he should be able to focus on it without becoming cross-eyed. See your doctor if you suspect your baby may have a problem focusing.

■ **Does he turn around when you speak to him?** By six months, your baby will be aware of most of your words and actions and should respond.

■ **Can he make sounds that vaguely resemble real words?** Don't worry if the sounds he makes are not recognizable yet—he is experimenting all the time in preparation for saying his first word.

■ **Can he point to objects that interest him?** By nine months, he should be pointing with his index finger and should also be able to grasp small objects between his thumb and index finger.

■ **Can he let go of objects when he wants to?** Between six and nine months his grasping instinct will become more sophisticated so that he becomes able to release whatever he is holding onto at will.

■ **Can he chew finger foods?** He should be able to pick up small snacks to eat and be able to hold a cup or bottle to feed himself, too.

■ **Can he sit up unsupported for several minutes at a time?** By nine months, not only should he be able to sit unsupported, but he should also be able to get himself into a seated position without help.

Q AT WHAT AGE WILL MY BABY BE ABLE TO SIT UNSUPPORTED?

A At six months old, your baby has yet to perfect his sense of balance. He sits only if you put him in a seated position. He has good control in a forward direction, but must be supported with pillows to stop him from falling sideways or backward. He often uses his hands to stabilize his seated position, which means he can't sit and play, so he'll usually only sit for a short while. By eight months, he can sit unsupported for a moment, and by nine months will be able to sit for several minutes.

SITTING ALONE
Your baby will become increasingly stable when sitting, and before long he'll be able to sit and play with toys without tipping over.

Q HOW CAN I ENCOURAGE MY BABY TO LEARN TO SIT UP?

A Although you can't make him sit before he is ready, you can help him. Rather than holding him, try putting cushions or pillows loosely around him to protect him if he tips over. Supervise him, too, but you're unlikely to be quick enough to reach out to stop him from bumping his head. Within a few more weeks, he'll be able to sit most of the time without falling over to either side. If you tilt him gently to one side or remove one of his hands from the floor, he will now automatically put out his other hand in order to keep his balance.

Q WHICH TOYS ARE SUITABLE FOR MY BABY AT THIS AGE?

A He will continue to have fun with many of the same toys as before, but you can also give him strings of big beads to thread, as well as board and fabric books to look at. Wheeled toys, such as simple cars and trucks, are good for babies of this age, since they enjoy pushing them around the floor. Make sure they are safe first—small model cars may not be suitable because of the risk of choking. Your baby will also begin to appreciate bath toys, including waterproof bath books. You can also make improvised toys from empty yogurt cartons and cardboard food packages.

With his pincerlike grasp your baby can enjoy playing with a drumstick

Q WHICH ACTIVITIES WILL MY BABY ENJOY AT THIS AGE ?

A Play on the floor with your baby to encourage the development of his crawling and general coordination. As his posture and balance become increasingly stable, he will enjoy activities that involve sitting, such as banging a drum, tearing up paper, playing with building blocks, or rolling a ball back and forth with you. Provide safe things for him to crawl in and out of, such as a play tunnel or a large cardboard box open at each end. By now he may also be old enough to begin to play hide and seek with toys—try him and see.

DEVELOPING POSTURE THROUGH PLAY
A drum makes a good toy—it offers an incentive for your child to sit and concentrate, while strengthening his back muscles and developing his balance.

WHAT MIGHT MY BABY BE DOING AT NINE MONTHS ?

SKILL	WHAT MIGHT HE BE DOING ?
Sight	■ He may look around the room with interest. ■ He may recognize people and notice their coming and going—from six months he may object strongly if you leave the room. ■ He may see and poke at small objects, such as cake decorations, with his index finger.
Hearing	■ He may notice sounds that are not in the same room, such as a dog barking outside, a car passing the house, or the doorbell ringing. ■ He may turn toward voices and can localize sounds to most places, although not directly behind him or above his head.
Speech	■ He may be able to say a word or two, such as "Mam-ma" or "Dad-da," but doesn't necessarily say them appropriately or with meaning. ■ He may make singing noises.
Coordination	■ He should use a pincerlike grasp, with thumb and index finger. ■ He may poke, prod, and point at objects with his index finger. ■ He may release objects from his grasp at will. ■ He may transfer things from one hand to another.
Posture control	■ He should sit for a minute or maybe longer, and be able to get himself into a sitting position. ■ He may be able to balance sufficiently to be able to move and reach out while sitting. ■ He may be able to pull himself up to stand, but have trouble sitting down again and go down with a resounding thump. ■ He may crawl or move along the floor commando-style, on his tummy and elbows.
General understanding	■ He may respond to his name. ■ He may go after a ball if it rolls out of sight.
Emotional and social behavior	■ He may show attachment to one or both parents and may get very clingy. He may become anxious when his parent or caregiver is not with him. ■ He may wave bye-bye. ■ His attention span may be increasing.

Note that your baby's skills are more interrelated than they were before—his pincer grasp, for example, depends on accurate focusing as much as on fine motor coordination of his hand, finger, and thumb.

GROWTH AND DEVELOPMENT

BABIES 6–9 MONTHS

9 MONTHS–1 YEAR

Q HOW IS MY BABY DEVELOPING DURING THIS PERIOD?

A From the age of nine months, your baby will be on the move, either crawling, shuffling, or, very rarely, even walking. Many parents become very competitive about developmental milestones at this stage, but there is no need to worry if your baby crawls or walks much later (or earlier) than others. He will be progressing in many other spheres too, but, as always, speak to your doctor or pediatrician if you're concerned about any particular aspect of your baby's progress.

■ **Does he babble and make fluent sounds?** As well as babbling, he may also say one word with meaning—maybe "Mam-ma" or "Dad-da."

■ **Has he stopped putting things in his mouth?** By nine months, your baby has other ways of exploring the world, so his mouth is no longer a primary means of investigating shapes and textures.

■ **Can he understand simple requests?** At 12 months, he may be able to give you a toy, give you a kiss, or clap his hands when you ask him to.

■ **Does he understand "Where is…?"** If you hide a toy under a blanket while he is watching, he may show an interest in looking for it there.

■ **Can he remember what happened?** If you open the refrigerator, he may anticipate your offering him his favorite yogurt, or if you get the vacuum cleaner out he will know the carpet is about to be cleaned.

■ **Does he crawl, creep, or walk on all fours?** He may also be able to stand and cruise around the furniture, but some babies leave this until later.

■ **Does he want to feed himself?** At 12 months he should be interested in wanting to hold a spoon and direct it into his bowl—ignore the mess!

■ **Does he limp?** If he is already walking, be alert to any possible physical problems. See your doctor if you suspect your baby may have a limp.

WHEN WILL MY BABY STAND AND START WALKING?

At around 11 months, your baby will probably be able to stand with help and to shuffle sideways while he clings onto furniture. This is often known as "cruising" and is a natural prelude to his learning to walk unsupported.

Cruising

As your baby starts to cruise, the stability of the furniture he uses to cling to is vital. When there's nothing at the right height, he'll sit down and crawl along, but if he finds something else to use as a handrail, he may stand and begin cruising again. By 12–14 months, now and again he will abandon the use of furniture and stand alone for several seconds at a time. By 15 months or so you'll proudly watch him take his first few steps alone— 13 months is the average age at which a baby walks, although some don't do so until 18 months.

STANDING UP
Your baby will pull himself up by holding onto things. To avoid tumbles, remove unstable items of furniture from his path.

Initially, your baby will pull himself up using both hands

As confidence grows, he will reach out and grasp toys

Q WHICH ACTIVITIES ARE SUITABLE FOR MY BABY AT THIS AGE ?

A Your baby will probably spend lots of time pushing around walker-type toys as he experiments with finding his feet. You can improvise with activities much more at this stage, too. Filling and emptying plastic food containers with building blocks, bashing together kitchen utensils to make "music," climbing in and out of large cardboard boxes, and scrunching sheets of old wrapping paper are all simple but amusing activities that will keep your baby occupied in safe, imaginative play. For a period of quieter time, sit together and look at books, enjoying the pictures together—books are becoming increasingly interesting to your baby during this time. Going for a walk in the park and feeding the ducks will get you out in the fresh air and is great fun for both of you. At home, even mundane chores, such as dusting, can be enjoyable for your baby if you give him a clean cloth so he can help you with your housework.

Q WHICH TOYS ARE SUITABLE FOR MY BABY AT THIS AGE ?

A Build on the set of toys your baby has enjoyed for the past few months by introducing things that are more elaborate and require more sophisticated skills to master—boxes to "mail" things into, shape-sorters, cups that fit together, toy cars to push along the floor, toys with knobs or buttons, simple tray puzzles, things that make a noise when banged together, simple musical toys, and toys on strings (string is also useful to secure toys to his stroller or baby carriage, but make sure the string is short so your baby can't get tangled up in it). Make sure that no toy is so small that your baby can choke on it or that any one toy can be taken apart into pieces that are small enough for him to swallow. It is more difficult to be sure that toys are safe for him to fall onto—even toys appropriate for his age group can injure him if he stumbles heavily. More positively, toys that roll, such as a chiming ball, will intrigue and fascinate your baby at this very inquisitive age.

WHAT MIGHT MY BABY BE DOING AT ONE YEAR ?

SKILL	WHAT MIGHT HE BE DOING ?
Sight	■ He may now follow objects that are farther away. He probably "saw" them when he was younger, but more distant objects increase in significance as his world expands.
Hearing	■ He may understand many words, simple statements, and questions. ■ He may obey simple requests.
Speech	■ He may make many different sounds and may enjoy babbling to himself. Most are still vowels, but he may say consonants too, especially "b," "d," and "m." Later he'll master "p," "h," and "w," although the exact order will depend on the characteristics of your native language.
Coordination	■ He may hold out toys for you (often accompanied by a grunt!) if you ask him for them. He may have also learned that he can throw them. ■ He may often wave bye-bye, when asked. ■ He may hold a pencil or crayon in his fist and may make rudimentary marks with it. He may make stabbing movements at the paper. He may also want to use his feeding spoon at mealtimes.
Posture control	■ He should be adept at sitting and may try standing, and even cruise along sideways while holding onto furniture (or you). He may also get around by crawling or creeping, but don't expect him to start walking just yet. ■ He may maneuver from standing to sitting without any trouble.
General understanding	■ He may understand the purpose of many objects, as well as their permanence. When you hide something that he knows exists, he may look for it.
Emotional and social behavior	■ He may anticipate pleasure and may show it. He may delight in seeing people he likes, but remain diffident with most of those he doesn't know.

Note that your baby's skills are more interrelated than they were before—for example, waving bye-bye depends on general understanding and motor skills as well as both vision and hearing.

1–1½ YEARS

Q HOW IS MY TODDLER DEVELOPING DURING THIS PERIOD?

A Between the ages of 12 and 18 months, some areas of a child's development may seem to slow down, which can cause concern for parents. Be reassured that he will still be making vital progress on many fronts—there's also quite a lot of normal variation between one toddler and another, so yours may not be doing exactly the same things at the same time as a friend's child. Ask your doctor for advice if anything is really worrying you, and keep an eye on your toddler's progress by watching what he does and how he does it.

■ **Is he into everything, but still responsive to what you say?** This usually means that his hearing and his social skills are developing nicely. Don't worry if he doesn't always respond—sometimes he'll be far too busy exploring or playing.

■ **Does he understand simple familiar words and phrases, and name a few common objects?** By 18 months he will know the names of several everyday things, such as a spoon and fork, as well as be able to understand what they're for.

■ **Can he copy some of your activities?** Your toddler should have the know-how and the enthusiasm to imitate you—he'll probably love to help you dust and sweep.

■ **Can he walk?** Nearly all toddlers walk by the age of 18 months, but one or two choose to shuffle on their bottom instead, using their hands to help propel themselves along. Consult your doctor if your toddler isn't trying to walk by 18 months.

■ **Is he walking on tiptoe?** This is usually harmless and the foot flattens out within a month or two to enable him to walk on the whole foot. He could also be knock-kneed or pigeon-toed at this stage. See your doctor if toe-walking persists.

■ **Can he get up and down from a low chair?** His movements may be clumsy, but he should be able to coordinate his body to do this fairly easily.

■ **Can he focus properly?** Talk to your doctor if you suspect that there is a problem with his vision.

Q WHICH ACTIVITIES ARE SUITABLE FOR MY CHILD AT THIS AGE?

A Because your toddler is now a good imitator of grown-up behavior, he will appreciate all kinds of things used in fantasy play and will enjoy copying you. Talk to him about day-to-day activities and make gentle suggestions for pretend play, such as having a conversation on a toy telephone or delving into an old suitcase full of dress-up clothes. He may also enjoy "baking" with make-believe dough. Teach him simple songs and nursery rhymes—he will love burbling along or repeating easy words after you. And let him get wet playing with water—he will get lots of fun from pouring water in and out of plastic containers and through funnels—but be careful to supervise him closely at all times. Ball games are fun, and useful for his coordination, strength, and fitness, but make sure the ball is robust enough to withstand boisterous play.

Q WHICH NEW TOYS DO I NEED TO GIVE MY TODDLER AT THIS STAGE?

A As your toddler's walking progresses, he will make the most of wheeled toys, such as a wagon loaded with blocks or a pull-along animal to drag behind him. He will now be ready to enjoy many more different types of picture books, although he may treat the pages roughly. At this stage get him some simple jigsaw puzzles—a floor puzzle makes a good buy and is fun to do together. He will enjoy the challenge of trying to figure out how to fit the pieces together, but he will need your help.

PULL TOYS
Encourage your toddler to walk by making sure he has one or two pull-toys. He will feel very independent taking his favorite duck or doggy for a spin.

Q IS MY CHILD OLD ENOUGH TO ENJOY PLAYING IN THE PARK ?

A Once your child can toddle, he will enjoy going to the park, exploring things, and playing ball. He'll probably like the swings and using the slide—as long as it's not too steep and you hold on to him. If it's raining, dress him up in waterproof clothes and put on boots—he'll love jumping in the puddles. Let him do what he wants at his own pace, but don't let him out of your sight.

Q IS MY TODDLER READY YET FOR PENS AND PAINTS ?

A Yes. Let him have paper, crayons, and pencils, and buy a set of child-safe paints. His attempts at drawing and painting may be crude and lacking in realism, but he needs to learn. At first he may enjoy painting with water rather than paints—just as much fun and a lot less messy for you.

Q WILL I SEE SIGNS OF HIS GROWING INDEPENDENCE AT THIS AGE ?

A By 18 months, your toddler may still complain if you leave the room, although on other occasions he may be perfectly happy to be left alone. And in the park, if you walk on ahead, he may burst into tears. It often surprises parents to find that the situation is quite different if you stay stationary and he leaves your side of his own free will. That's probably because he knows where you are, and he himself makes the decision to leave your side and go off exploring. This is a mark of his growing curiosity and independence. Alternatively, he may show no sign of being interested in where you are, but be in no doubt that it still matters to him. You are his base— keep watch over him discreetly and try not to restrict him too much, since he may become uncooperative and assert himself by running off.

WHAT MIGHT MY TODDLER BE DOING AT EIGHTEEN MONTHS ?

SKILL	WHAT MIGHT HE BE DOING ?
Sight and hearing	■ His vision should be fully developed—he may now make complex use of what he sees and hears. ■ He may localize sounds accurately.
Speech	■ He may use at least four words (perhaps many more) clearly and in a meaningful way. He may call all men "Dad-da," which you may find either amusing or embarrassing. Mostly your toddler indulges in long babbling conversations that mean nothing much to anyone, including you— educators call this talk "jargon." From time to time he may link two recognizable words together appropriately, but this is fairly unusual, so don't worry if he doesn't yet.
Coordination	■ He may copy you doing things such as reading, writing, talking on the telephone, or doing housework, which makes this a great age for pretend play. ■ He may turn the pages of a book, although he may tear them in the process. ■ He may point to pictures. He may "draw" a bit—or scribble a lot! ■ He may build a tower out of three or more blocks. ■ He may use a spoon confidently.
Posture control	■ He may walk well. This may now be his favorite method of getting around, although he may crawl when it suits him. He may be able to stoop down and then be able to stand back up again. ■ He may be able to throw a ball without losing his balance. ■ He may be able to climb stairs on his hands and knees and get on and off a low chair. ■ He may walk backward in imitation of you—not a particularly useful skill, but one that your doctor may test for.
General understanding	■ He may know several parts of his body. He may hold out his arm or leg for you to dress him, and he may be able to take off his shoes and socks (not always at the best moment!).
Emotional and social behavior	■ He is still attached to you, but may be beginning to grow in independence. ■ He may understand what things are meant for. ■ His attention span may have increased. ■ He may now be able to keep playing and still listen to what you are saying.

Note that your child's skills are more interrelated than they were before—climbing on and off a low chair, for example, requires not only physical coordination, but also balance and strength.

1½–2 YEARS

Q HOW IS MY TODDLER DEVELOPING DURING THIS PERIOD?

A Your toddler is still making rapid progress, with his speech, powers of understanding, and level of coordination becoming increasingly sophisticated. As this is a period of refinement and experimentation, you may not feel that his developmental progress is as noticeable as it was, but try to remain relaxed about it. You can, however, observe his everyday actions and skills to assess his overall ability, raising any queries you may have with your doctor or pediatrician.

■ **Can he hear properly?** Occasionally a toddler can have undetected hearing loss. He will still play well both on his own and with you, but you should suspect a problem if he has trouble understanding you or if he is slow to speak.

■ **Is he talking?** He should be acquiring many more words during this period of his development, and his level of understanding should be such that he can communicate with you, even if he doesn't speak in full sentences yet.

■ **Can he identify a range of objects and toys?** From 18 months he should know the names of a variety of everyday things, even if he can't yet say them. He'll probably also be able to name some parts of the body.

■ **Does he know the purpose of certain objects?** During this stage he will come to understand what objects are for and what you are supposed to do with them—for example, that his food goes in his bowl or that you use a pencil with paper. Don't worry if he is not always purposeful in the way he uses things or if he puts objects to other uses than their intended one.

■ **Is he mischievous or naughty?** By the time he is 18 months, you can expect your child to be becoming less cooperative as his confidence and sense of independence grow.

■ **Does he play well both on his own and with other children around?** It would be unusual for a toddler to play cooperatively with other children, but by now he should be able to play alongside them without becoming upset or aggressive.

■ **Are his movements awkward?** Some clumsiness is normal at this age, as is a slight shaking of the hands when playing or carrying things—keep anything fragile or precious that you don't want him to get hold of well out of his way. If the shaking gets worse, speak to your doctor.

PAINTING FUN
A child's easel is a good buy—toddlers love getting messy with paint.

Plastic spill-proof containers are a must

Q WHICH ACTIVITIES WILL MY CHILD ENJOY AT THIS AGE?

A Continue looking at books together. He can own less robust books by this stage, but will need gentle supervision to stop him from becoming rough with the pages or scribbling on them. Encourage your child to be gentle with books. At this age he is very imaginative, so provide plenty of interesting things for him to use in pretend play. Painting is an excellent way for your toddler to express himself, so get him some chunky paint brushes, a selection of child-safe paints, and a waterproof toddler's apron and let him have fun— but put down plenty of sheets of newspaper first.

Q WHICH NEW TOYS DO I NEED TO GET FOR MY TODDLER AT THIS STAGE?

A Popular toys at this age include things that require your toddler's physical input, such as ride-on or climb-on vehicles. You could also get him larger toys, such as a sandbox, a children's pool, or a playhouse. You can also improvise with large cardboard boxes and plastic crates—your toddler will love to use them for pretend play. On a smaller scale, empty spools and string are good for threading games that will encourage hand–eye coordination.

DOES IT MATTER IF MY CHILD IS LEFT-HANDED?

Left-handedness should never be made into an issue for your child. Any old-fashioned ideas suggesting that right-handedness is preferable should be ignored—dexterity and coordination are the skills to be encouraged, not the use of one hand over the other.

When will I be able to tell if my toddler is right- or left-handed?

It should become obvious by the time your child is two. Until then, he will probably alternate the use of his hands. A preference is often not fixed until the age of four, and even then a few left-handers prefer to do some things with their right hand.

How will I be able to tell?

Observe which hand your child chooses when you give him a pencil. Also notice which he prefers for putting things into a box. Watch which foot he uses to kick a ball and which ear he holds a clock up to when you ask him if it's ticking. Give him an empty paper-towel roll and ask him to look through it. By noting which eye he favors, you will get an idea of his preference, but he may not show the same laterality, as it's called, for every activity.

Should I discourage his left-handedness?

No. You should let him choose whichever hand he likes for whatever he is doing. When he can use a knife, fork, and spoon, you can teach him which hand it is usual to use for each piece of cutlery. Trying to change a natural left-hander into a right-hander only leads to trouble. Some research even suggests it can lead to problems with reading and writing, so you are much better off letting your toddler use whichever hand he wants.

Will my child be left-handed because I am?

Not necessarily. Left-handed parents are more likely than right-handed parents to have a child who's left-handed, but even so most left-handers are born to two right-handed parents. Twins are more likely to be left-handed than single children, although it isn't fully understood why.

WHAT MIGHT MY TODDLER BE DOING AT TWO YEARS?

SKILL	WHAT MIGHT HE BE DOING?
Speech	■ Your child may talk a lot, using 30 or so words with clear intonation and expression, but his pronunciation won't be perfect. He may be beginning to use personal pronouns, though not necessarily the right ones. He may use verbs and make plurals out of singular words. ■ He may put words together in simple two-word sentences.
Coordination	■ Your child may be able to build a tower out of six or more blocks. ■ He is possibly able to open a door by turning the handle. ■ He may take off or tug at his diaper and begin to indicate his toilet needs. ■ He may be able to draw simple things on his own, and may be able to copy a straight line. ■ He may be able to wash his hands (when he wants to).
Posture control	■ He may be able to run and climb. ■ He may be getting good at tackling stairs on his own, but use both feet on each step.
General understanding	■ He may be able to name a variety of objects when asked, "What is this?" ■ He may be beginning to understand longer sentences. ■ His understanding may enable him to comprehend subtleties such as "now," "more," "here." ■ He may obey orders, including slightly more complex requests that link two or more ideas together, such as "Bring your socks to me and take your shoes to Daddy."
Emotional and social behavior	■ He may be able to comprehend cause and effect, associating hot water with pain, for example. ■ He may understand that things have a purpose and can use this to generalize. He can therefore make groups of things—such as animals, vehicles and food—in his mind.

Note that many skills are obviously interrelated—for example, your toddler can only obey requests if he can hear you, and he can only copy a straight line if he knows what a pencil is for.

2–3 YEARS

Q HOW IS MY CHILD DEVELOPING DURING THIS PERIOD?

A Children of this age vary a great deal in their development as well as their personality and interests. Watch him play, talk to him about everyday events and the things you do together, and give him simple tasks to do (when he's being cooperative, that is!). You'll be surprised how much he can accomplish by this age. But if any particular area of his development seems to be slower than the rest, talk to your doctor or pediatrician to put your mind at rest.

■ **Can he talk in short sentences of three words or more?** Between the ages of two and two-and-a-half, although his pronunciation of many sounds will still be immature, your child's speech should be clear enough for you to understand.

■ **Does he know what things are for?** He should be able to explain or demonstrate what does what.

■ **Can he use a pencil or crayon?** He may now be able to hold a pencil in his hand, not his fist. If you draw a circle, he may be able to copy it. At this age he'll also scribble spontaneously.

■ **Can he match related objects?** He should be able to pair up a sock with a shoe, a cup with a saucer, a brush with a comb, or a toothbrush with toothpaste. Also, even if he can't name that many colors or letters, he should be able to recognize them and match like with like.

■ **Does he play well?** At this age, imaginative and pretend play take up a lot of his time. He should now be able to concentrate on some activities rather than flitting from one thing to another.

■ **Can he dress and undress himself with help?** Don't worry if he can't do this by the time he is three—it's enough to know that he wants to try.

■ **Is he potty-trained by day?** For many children, nighttime bowel and bladder control is yet to come.

WATCHING TELEVISION

The key to healthy television viewing is to keep it as only a small part of a variety of activities your child enjoys.

How much television should my child watch?
At this age, about half an hour of television or videos a day is plenty, and your child shouldn't watch more than an hour at a stretch. Even high-quality programs appropriate to your child's age can be a bad thing. Watching a lot of television can make him restless, affect his physical fitness, worsen his posture, make him gain excess weight, and impair his social skills by reducing the opportunity to do other things, such as talking and playing.

How can I limit his television watching?
The usual advice is to select with your child in advance one or two programs that day that he wants to watch—and that you are prepared to let him view. This isn't always easy to stick to if he sees that another favorite program is about to come on at the end of his agreed viewing time. However, if you watch with your child, you can distract him with some other activity when it is time to turn the television off.

Q WHICH ACTIVITIES WILL MY CHILD ENJOY AT THIS AGE?

A This is a time for extended periods of pretend play, so provide your child with simple props, such as a plastic tea set, so that he can have teddy bear tea parties. You can also start baking with him—he will love helping you with mixing, shaping, and cutting, as well as decorating cakes and cookies. He can even "assist" you with family meals, helping you set the table, for example—be very patient and appreciative of his efforts, as well as aware of the safety issues. In the backyard, you can enjoy smelling flowers, planting seeds, or collecting leaves and petals.

Q WHICH TOYS ARE SUITABLE FOR MY CHILD AT THIS AGE?

A Your child will find puzzles and books absorbing and they will help him learn, while construction toys and building blocks will help improve his manual dexterity and keep him entertained for long periods of time. Pencils, paints, and modeling dough will continue to provide outlets for his creativity, and by this stage you will probably find he is starting to produce more sophisticated drawings and paintings. Bigger toys, such as a play tent, tricycle, or swing set, will really come into their own now.

Q HOW WILL I KNOW IF MY CHILD IS READY FOR DAYCARE OR NURSERY SCHOOL?

A Ideally, he should be willing to be away from you for a short while, able to communicate with other children and adults, and independent at toileting. This is usually at around the age of two-and-a-half or three years. Some children are more self-reliant than others and will be independent much sooner as a result—it may also be that girls are happier to be separated from their mothers than boys, since they may be more emotionally mature by this age. Only you can judge whether your child is ready for nursery school—if you feel he is still too clingy, don't push him. You could always put your child into a daycare or nursery school for a few trial mornings to see how he copes before deciding whether to send him every day.

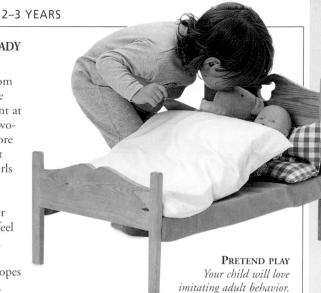

PRETEND PLAY
Your child will love imitating adult behavior.

WHAT MIGHT MY CHILD BE DOING AT THREE YEARS ?

SKILL	WHAT MIGHT HE BE DOING ?
Speech	■ Your child may talk in short sentences. ■ He may be able to remember and recite nursery rhymes. ■ He may tell you what he is going to do—he may give adults a rundown of his activities, even if nobody has asked him to do so.
Coordination	■ He may be able to construct a tower nine blocks high. He may also build a bridge out of blocks if you show him how to do it first. ■ He may hold a pencil in his hand instead of his fist. ■ He is probably able to copy a circle and can draw basic shapes and figures. ■ He may be able to feed himself quite skillfully by now. ■ He may be able to take his clothes off, but not be able to put them on.
Posture control	■ He may run, jump, and climb. ■ He may be able to stand on one foot for a few seconds. ■ He is probably able to manage the stairs, using one foot on each step for going up, but two feet on each step when coming back down. ■ He should be able to ride a tricycle.
General understanding	■ He should know some colors. ■ He may be able to count to five. ■ He is probably beginning to make more complex links, so you can tell him to put his teddy bear on the table in the kitchen, for example, and he will understand. ■ He may understand pairs and groups of things, such as animals, clothes, or vehicles. ■ You may be able to reason with him on occasion.
Emotional and social behavior	■ He may ask questions all the time. ■ He may still be very self-centered, but nonetheless have begun to make friends with children outside the family, and he may also talk happily to other adults. ■ He is probably beginning to gain the confidence and independence to function outside the home away from you; for example, going to daycare or nursery school. ■ He may know his full name and sex, and perhaps his age. ■ He may be interested in his genitals. ■ He may be toilet-trained by day—some children are also dry by night at this age.

Note that many skills are increasingly interrelated—for example, for your child to be able to tell you what activities he plans to do that day depends on both competent speech and good understanding.

3–4 YEARS

Q HOW IS MY CHILD DEVELOPING DURING THIS PERIOD ?

A Try not to be tempted into analyzing what your child can and can't do at this stage. Be confident that he is progressing well and enjoy this period of his growing up – his personality will be coming through more strongly by now. If anything specific concerns you, don't hesitate to seek professional advice from your pediatrician. Observe your child as he plays and you will get a very good idea of where he is on his own unique development path.

■ **Does he hold things close to his eyes?** If your child has to sit very near the television to watch it, he may have a problem with his vision. It's perfectly normal to look closely at fine detail, but he shouldn't need to view everything at close range. It's at around this age that you should take your child to have his first routine eye test, even if you don't suspect that there is anything wrong.

■ **Can he hear you call his name without you raising your voice?** If you have to shout or face him when you speak or he says "What?" a lot, his hearing may be impaired. Bear in mind he may also be being stubborn—if in doubt, ask your pediatrician about getting his hearing checked.

■ **Does he play well by himself?** He should be more imaginative by now and be able to concentrate on things that interest him. Don't worry if his attention span is markedly shorter than an adult's (twins often have particular trouble concentrating, usually because they interrupt each other so much).

■ **Can he run, catch a ball, and ride a tricycle?** He may still be clumsy, but if he can do all these things most of the time there's usually nothing wrong with his coordination.

■ **Does he try to get his ideas across?** Don't worry if your four-year-old can't always find the right words to express himself—he should at least be trying to communicate his thoughts and feelings to those around him.

■ **Has he begun to use prepositions when speaking?** When he needs to, he should be using words such as "on," "behind," and "under." He'll almost certainly use "and" and "but" a great deal.

■ **Does he know his name, age, and sex?** Unless they're very shy, most children of this age take great pride in relating these personal details.

■ **Can he understand the concept of time yet?** Your child is unlikely to be able to tell the time using a clock at this age, but he should have some idea of the concepts of "tomorrow," "later," and "yesterday." Using the term "not now" is also a useful way of getting across the idea of later, according to many parents.

■ **Does your child still have outbursts of temper?** He may well explode with frustration from time to time, but the temper tantrums of early toddlerhood should be on the way out.

■ **Is your child toilet trained?** You should consult your pediatrician if your child still soils the bed—after the age of about four this is usually regarded as abnormal—but don't worry unduly if he still has trouble staying dry right through the night.

Q WILL MY CHILD'S PERSONALITY AND TEMPERAMENT BE MATURING BY NOW ?

A By the time your child is between the ages of three and four years old, you will have quite a good idea of what his personality is like. Some children are confident and bold, whereas others are more reticent. Your child may be restless and adventurous or he may be placid and relaxed. There are advantages and also drawbacks to each of these characteristics. He may resemble you in temperament or he may not—his personality is partly inherited and partly shaped by his environment. If you are calm and unruffled, he may be too, but it doesn't always follow. Whatever he is like, try to accept him without typecasting him—he's still got plenty of time to change and mature. Some of his likes and dislikes, however strong, can still alter, and everyone keeps changing well past the age of four (or even 40!). You can't deliberately change your child's character even if you want to, but you can influence the way in which he responds to his emotions—that is really a behavior issue. You can also help him to integrate into the world by offering reassurance whenever he needs it and by introducing him gradually to new situations and experiences. If your child is still shy or clingy, accept him as he is—there's nothing to be gained by pryng his hands off you, as you'll end up with more trouble if you upset him and do nothing for his sense of security.

Q WHICH ACTIVITIES ARE SUITABLE FOR MY CHILD AT THIS AGE ?

A Improved accuracy and coordination make tracing books fun for your child at this age. For cutting and gluing, let him use felt and other fabrics, as well as paper and cardboard. If he has toy cars, he might like a garage, perhaps made out of a cardboard box. He will enjoy pretend play outside. An old sheet slung over some chairs makes a wonderful tent—supply a snack and a drink and invite a friend or two for your child to play with. By this age there may well be daily demands made to visit the playground in the park.

Q WHICH TOYS ARE SUITABLE FOR MY CHILD AT THIS AGE ?

A Construction toys are special favorites—the more sophisticated types will continue to be so for a few years yet. Toys that make a noise can still give your child pleasure, but he may now be ready for a real musical instrument, too (see p. 164). Looking at books remains a fascinating activity for him and he is now old enough to have books with pages made out of paper rather than board.

DEVELOPING MANUAL DEXTERITY
Between three and four years of age your child's fine motor skills are now sufficiently sophisticated for him to enjoy painting, drawing, modeling, and gluing. You may be surprised by the level of detail he can achieve.

WHAT MIGHT MY CHILD BE DOING AT FOUR YEARS ?

SKILL	WHAT MIGHT HE BE DOING ?
Speech	■ He may speak in sentences and initiate conversations. He may have a huge vocabulary, but shyness may prevent him from using all of it all the time. He may have begun to use prepositions. ■ He may be able to sing.
Coordination	■ He may copy the letter X if you show him what it looks like. ■ He may be able to do jigsaw puzzles, but he may get some pieces the wrong way around. ■ He is probably able to catch a ball. ■ He may be able to climb.
Posture control	■ He may run and skip well. ■ He may be able to play some ball games if the rules are simple. ■ He is probably adept at riding a tricycle.
General understanding	■ He may be able to draw a face and a stick figure. ■ He may be able to explain what a picture is about. ■ He probably asks questions and usually understands the answers. ■ He may be able to follow the thread of many television programs.
Emotional and social behavior	■ He is able to play with other children. ■ He may have far fewer temper tantrums than before. ■ He may be a little less self-centered than he was, but may show off a lot. ■ He is probably very imaginative. ■ He may be becoming more independent in his day-to-day needs, such as using the toilet, dressing himself, using a knife and fork, and helping himself to a drink of water.

Note that many skills are clearly interrelated—for example, he wouldn't be able to play ball games unless he could see the ball and he wouldn't possess a large vocabulary without the understanding to match it.

4–5 YEARS

Q HOW IS MY CHILD DEVELOPING DURING THIS PERIOD?

A Because children, families, and cultures differ, there is a wide range of normal behavior and development within the different age ranges. The main issue at this age is not what your child is doing relative to the child next door, but how far he has progressed in the last year or so. If you feel his progress has been slow, seek the reassurance and advice of your doctor.

■ **Can adults outside the family understand what he says?** Your child's speech should be clear by this age, and, although you won't encourage him to strike up conversations with strangers, adults who don't know him should be able to understand him.

■ **Is he fairly well coordinated on a jungle gym and other playground equipment?** His movements may not be elegant, but they should be effective in getting him to where he wants to be.

■ **Is his drawing or writing developing?** He is far too young for you to expect perfection, but his pencil control will be becoming more accurate, so his drawing and letters will be neater.

■ **Do you have to be careful about what you say in his presence?** Most children of this age have acute hearing and repeat things their parents would much rather they didn't.

■ **Is he beginning to be interested in time?** He may want to know what five minutes are like, especially if he has been told he has to wait five minutes for something he wants.

■ **Is he learning the rules to any games?** They must, of course, be simple, but it's an important step to acknowledge the existence of rules—even if he does later bend them to suit himself.

■ **Can he take turns when playing with others?** He may be very competitive, but he should be learning the art of waiting when he has to.

■ **Does he appear confident?** Of course, your child won't be confident all the time because he will have uncertain moments, but he should be fairly at ease about new experiences that are meant to be pleasant.

■ **Is he aware of traffic?** Being fearful of cars and other vehicles is essential, although he won't have real street sense yet.

■ **Is he dry at night?** Approximately 10 percent of children still wet the bed at the age of five. If your child does, be patient; he will improve.

Q WHICH INDOOR ACTIVITIES ARE SUITABLE FOR MY CHILD AT THIS AGE?

A From the age of four, the construction toys you give him can be more complex, and you will notice that he can make more intricate models—he will love the elements of fantasy play and experimentation they provide. Drawing, painting, and modeling continue to be popular, as does helping in the kitchen—your child will enjoy mixing dough, preparing vegetables, making cupcakes with you, and trying to wash dishes. Give him a chair to stand on and a plastic apron to wear. Offer him more grown-up books, but don't pressure him to read yet. Puzzles can be more challenging than they were, but similarly, don't be too ambitious on your child's behalf—he'll get discouraged if a jigsaw puzzle defeats him completely. You can play board games with him, and he should be mature enough to play some of these with other children, as long as there is an adult within earshot to act as referee. A competitive child may argue over games such as chutes and ladders, so be ready to intervene.

Your child uses fine finger skills to construct toys

CONSTRUCTION TOYS
Encourage your child to use his fertile imagination and increasing dexterity to build a variety of objects using construction blocks

Q WHICH OUTDOOR ACTIVITIES ARE SUITABLE FOR THIS AGE GROUP ?

A Your child will enjoy playing ball games outdoors or splashing in a pool in warm weather. At the park, he is now ready to tackle the jungle gym and may want to learn how to swing himself on the swings—be careful to supervise him. Swimming is a vital skill to learn and this is a good age at which to start taking him to organized lessons at your local pool. If he's interested in a sport, such as baseball, you could find out if there are any fun, junior teams in your area he could join. As with all things, let him have the chance to try but don't pressure him.

Q WHICH TOYS ARE SUITABLE FOR MY CHILD AT THIS AGE ?

A Toys for fantasy play, such as a toy kitchen, playhouse, dollhouse, puppets, and construction toys will give your child's imagination free rein. Also ensure that he has an abundant supply of materials for drawing, cutting (make sure he always uses child-safe scissors with blunt, rounded ends), and gluing. Puzzles and board games will keep him occupied, and if he can learn to play them with friends, so much the better.

Q WHAT KIND OF OUTINGS WILL MY CHILD ENJOY AT THIS AGE ?

A Many parents feel under pressure to take even the youngest of children to the latest amusement park or novelty attraction when in fact it may not be suitable at all. Amusement parks are expensive, the rides are not always suitable for very young children, and there are often long lines. The answer is not to feel guilty—you can all have a lot of fun together as a family at swimming pools and the seaside. Zoos and working farms are also fascinating destinations for young children. Even museums can be worthwhile for the preschooler, as many have interactive exhibits designed with child-appeal in mind. You may not have considered taking your child to an art gallery, but different experiences are vital to his development. Not every place you visit has to be child-oriented—your enthusiasm is important to your child and is part of his learning, so why not let him join in with the enjoyment of your experience? Obviously his attention span won't come close to matching yours, so keep the visit short to maintain his interest. Leave while your child is still fresh and interested, and take a break in the cafeteria or somewhere he can run around.

WHAT MIGHT MY CHILD BE DOING AT FIVE YEARS ?

SKILL	WHAT MIGHT HE BE DOING ?
Speech	■ He may still sound childish in intonation, but he shouldn't use baby talk and should only use a few mispronunciations, except for obviously difficult words. ■ He may be able to sing songs and recite nursery rhymes.
Coordination	■ He may be able to hold a pencil correctly and be able to use scissors. ■ He probably has the aptitude and enthusiasm to learn many new skills, which could include swimming, baseball, tennis, or playing a musical instrument.
Posture control	■ He may hop, skip, run, play with a ball, use a jungle gym, and climb trees. However, some children are more agile than others.
General understanding	■ He may be able to count to 10 (or possibly even higher). He knows many letters of the alphabet by now, perhaps even all of them. ■ He may be able to write his own name, but note that children vary greatly and that some names are much harder to write than others. ■ He may read simple words.
Emotional and social behavior	■ He is usually happy to play alone without a parent around. ■ He may be beginning to make friends outside the family and can also play well with other children, although the occasional fight may occur. ■ He may still be self-centered but less so than he was, so he shows off less than he did.

Note Many skills are obviously interrelated—for example, your child needs both coordination and understanding to write his name. At this age, children differ very much in terms of developmental progress.

THE WIDER WORLD

Q HOW CAN I MAKE SURE I CHOOSE A GOOD PRESCHOOL?

A Start your search well ahead of time, and visit several preschools. Check out all the facilities; assess the space the children have available and whether the equipment provided is both safe and interesting. Apart from the availability of spaces, the hours provided, and the cost, you need to ask:

- What level of supervision is provided?
- Are parents expected to help?
- Are the activities structured?
- Are the children split up into groups for activities?
- Do the children have a choice of activities?
- Are there organized outings?
- Are boys and girls treated equally?
- How is misbehavior handled?

Just as important, decide whether the atmosphere is welcoming. Do you like the leader and the group? Are the children happy? Gut feelings are very important, and you need to listen to them.

LEARNING AN INSTRUMENT

Some people say that no child is too young to learn an instrument, but, as with much of parenting, only you can judge when your child might be ready.

What are the practicalities?

Learning to play an instrument has many benefits and may even stimulate parts of the brain that other forms of communication do not. Also, learning it may give a child the chance to shine at something. Consider these points before letting your child start music lessons:

- the size of the child relative to the size of the particular instrument he is interested in learning—very small children may have trouble reaching notes, for example
- the frequency of music lessons and distance your child will have to travel to get to them
- the time and effort needed to practice
- your child's enthusiasm—there is nothing to be lost in waiting until your child is seven before discussing the possibility of learning an instrument. There's no point in forcing him.

Q HOW CAN I PREPARE MY CHILD FOR PRESCHOOL?

A Tell him about it, but don't give him a long speech. He doesn't need to be overloaded with details or intimidated by the prospect of the new experience. To boost his confidence, take the time to make sure he is able to take his shoes, pants, and underpants on and off, since he may well be required to do this by himself at preschool.

Q DOES HE NEED TO BE TOILET-TRAINED BEFORE HE GOES TO PRESCHOOL?

A On the whole, yes, but he doesn't have to be completely independent because staff generally expect to offer some assistance—talk to the leader or teacher in charge. Even if totally clean and dry, a child may regress when he starts preschool, but don't worry. Provide a bag with a complete set of spare clothing in case of an accident, and hand this over without fuss to the teacher.

Q HOW CAN I KEEP MY CHILD FROM MISSING ME WHILE HE'S AT PRESCHOOL?

A Your child could start by going to preschool part time, about twice a week, to begin with. The first few times he attends, you'll probably be allowed to stay for the whole session. Keep a discreet distance and then gradually fade into the background. However, don't leave without telling him, because it can be very alarming for a child to look up from play to find his parent nowhere in sight. Say good-bye and tell him when you'll be back. Tears may follow, so make a quick exit.

Q ARE THERE ANY PRACTICAL RULES I SHOULD STICK TO?

A Be realistic about what you can achieve during the time your child is at preschool—don't try to cram in a trip to the supermarket *and* getting the car repaired, since there is nothing worse than rushing back to a crying child who thinks you've forgotten him. Another tip is not to tell your child what a splendid time you had while you were away from him. Your activities without him should sound as dull as possible; otherwise, he may resent missing the excitement. Always be available in the event of an emergency—if you can't be reached by phone, give the preschool the number of someone who can be.

HOW SHOULD WE CHOOSE A SCHOOL ?

The school you choose should be appropriate for your child—what suits the child across the street may not be right for yours, so try not to be influenced unduly by other parents' opinions. We are all impressed by good results, but the style of teaching and the atmosphere of a school are as important as academic excellence.

In making your selection of school, think about:
- whether you want a coeducational school.
- the number of children in each class.
- where your child's friends will be going.
- the distance of the school from your home and how you will get your child there.
- which secondary schools the children from each primary school move on to.

Q HOW CAN I TELL WHETHER MY CHILD IS HAPPY AT PRESCHOOL ?

A You can never be sure what your child does when you're not with him, but the things he draws, paints, and makes at preschool can be some indication of how much fun he has had. If you're really not sure how preschool is suiting him, you can always arrive before pickup time and watch your child from a distance, without his knowing you are there. You may find he is happily absorbed in his activities. A child can go on to have a happy day even if he cried when you left him—the occasional tear when you depart is nothing to worry about as long as he is settling in generally.

Q MY CHILD WANTS TO WRITE, BUT HE'S NOT IN SCHOOL—WHAT SHOULD I DO ?

A Teach your child how to hold a pencil and how to form letters correctly. If you're unsure about the best way to do this, talk to the preschool leader. Teaching methods vary and your child could be disadvantaged if he learns the wrong way. He should learn to form letters in lower case, not block capitals, since this is how he will be taught at school.

Q HOW CAN I PREPARE MY CHILD FOR STARTING SCHOOL ?

A Tour the school—some schools arrange for the next year's class to spend a morning with the new teacher, so find out if this will happen. Be positive in your attitude to the school; if you hated your own schooldays, keep quiet. In practical terms, help your child to become independent in using the toilet, and in dressing and undressing. Provide shoes without laces and clothes with elasticized waistbands to make it easier, and teach him to cut up his food. Make sure he can recognize his name—labeling clothes has more purpose if he knows what his name looks like.

Q WILL MY CHILD BE VERY TIRED WHEN HE STARTS SCHOOL ?

A When your child first starts school he is likely to find the experience quite demanding, both physically and emotionally. You should expect him to feel very tired when he comes home, and he may need a nap. He may not be used to spending most of the day away from home. He will also have to adjust to paying greater attention in class than he may have done in preschool. He may be hungry or fussy by the time he gets home, so have a snack and a drink ready to calm him down and boost his flagging energy.

PARENT'S SURVIVAL GUIDE

I'M GOING TO MISS MY CHILD WHEN HE STARTS SCHOOL

Going to school is an exciting time for your child and a time of great change for you. It may be the first time ever you have been without your child's company on a regular basis.

How can I stop myself from missing him?
Organizing yourself as well as your child will give you less opportunity to miss him. Before your child starts school, think how you want to use this freedom, whether in paid work or a new pastime, and investigate new opportunities accordingly. Many parents miss their child, and you may be surprised to find that it's not always the ones without jobs who miss their schoolchild most. Sometimes it is the parents who've worked throughout their child's earliest years who feel especially bereft, maybe because starting school signifies the end of babyhood.

DISCIPLINE AND BEHAVIOR

No matter how adorable and **easy-going** your child is, there will inevitably be times when her behavior falls short of your **expectations**. While it is unreasonable to expect constant **good behavior** from a young child, it is equally damaging to impose no discipline at all. Deciding how to **discipline your child** can be problematic for you and confusing for your child, especially if you and your partner have **conflicting opinions**. By understanding why your child behaves in a certain way, you can help her to distinguish **right from wrong** and, by setting an example, help her acquire good manners and healthy patterns of behavior.

7

BABY BEHAVIOR

Q WHAT IS DISCIPLINE AND WHEN SHOULD IT START ?

A Discipline is an unappealing word that can evoke images of military-like obedience. What it means is learning to behave properly according to an accepted code of conduct. All children have to learn this. If your baby does not begin to learn discipline, she will find it much more difficult to abide by any rules later in life, with serious behavioral and social consequences. Discipline should start in babyhood because this is when you start guiding her, albeit in a gentle way. Don't scold or punish her, but do show her the difference between right and wrong. Be consistent. If you sometimes laugh when your baby drops things on the floor, don't be surprised if she continues to drop things even when you don't want her to.

Q SHOULD I EVER PUNISH MY BABY ?

A No. You should never hit, slap, or shake a baby. No punishment is effective for infants less than a year old because they are too young to understand the significance. If your baby does something dangerous, say a firm "No" as you pull her away. Do not show signs of amusement. If you smile your baby will receive the wrong message.

Q WHAT IS A "GOOD" BABY ?

A People often talk about "good" babies meaning babies who don't cry much, or who sleep through the night. This is illogical because a baby does not choose to behave in this way. Similarly, it's pointless to blame a baby for being "bad" because she cries or fails to sleep.

Q CAN A DIFFICULT BIRTH CAUSE BEHAVIORAL PROBLEMS ?

A Yes. It can make a baby more unsettled and difficult to pacify, but the situation usually improves within one or two weeks. Occasionally, lack of oxygen or some other birth problem produces a more lasting effect on behavior, and can affect other areas of development. A traumatic birth can also make the mother (and often the father) resentful toward the baby, and therefore less able to cope with the demands of parenting.

Q WHAT FACTORS HAVE AN EFFECT ON A BABY'S BEHAVIOR ?

A The behavior of your baby is a result of a combination of nature and nurture. She is born with some characteristics, which you may notice from her very earliest days. However, the way in which you deal with her and your relationship with her is crucial to the way her behavior develops as she grows.

Q WHEN WILL MY BABY BECOME MORE SETTLED ?

A Babies are all different, so this varies, but they usually begin to settle at around three months old, when a daily routine is established. Feeding will be more regular then, even if sleep is still erratic. Of course there will still be times when a baby is more demanding or doesn't understand what is going on, especially if there are changes in her life. Remember not to confuse being unsettled with bad behavior. A baby who feeds and sleeps erratically, or who cries a lot, can be infuriating for a parent to deal with, but babies do not choose to be demanding, so try to be patient.

Q HOW CAN I HELP MY BABY BECOME A WELL-BEHAVED CHILD ?

A The most important thing at this stage is to give your baby love and attention, and a routine that provides her with the security that a young baby requires. Be as consistent as you possibly can in her handling, so that you don't confuse her. Treat her kindly—a loved baby eventually becomes a manageable child. It is essential to set a good example yourself. Even a very young baby will notice if you deal with her roughly, or speak harshly to your partner.

Q WILL SHE BE BETTER BEHAVED IF I STOP PICKING HER UP WHEN SHE CRIES ?

A No. She is crying because she has some need that has not been met—it could be something as simple as food, or maybe she just wants a hug. She will not cry less if you sometimes fail to respond to her, but she may develop the impression that you don't care about her. She will almost certainly persist in crying, which could easily put you in a bad mood in the process.

Q WHAT CAN I DO WHEN MY BABY DOES SOMETHING DANGEROUS OR NAUGHTY ?

A Say "No" and pull her away, whether she is reaching for something dangerous or pulling the cat's tail. She is still too young to understand why what she did was wrong, or to remember it for very long, so explanations are pointless. You will have to keep preventing her from getting into trouble. Fortunately, babies are easily distracted, so you can offer alternative entertainment when she gets into mischief. That will prevent her from crying because she has been thwarted.

Q MY BABY PULLS MY HAIR. WHAT SHOULD I DO ABOUT IT ?

A Say "No," move farther away, and give her something else to grab. If you are holding her, put her down every time she does it. It is a good idea to tie back your hair until she has outgrown the stage of grasping everything, which is usually at around a year old. Do not become angry; it will only upset and confuse her. Your baby cannot help grabbing things—it is her main form of entertainment and experimentation at this stage. She is not trying to annoy you. Avoid laughing sometimes and getting impatient at other times, because the mixed messages will confuse her.

Babies are fascinated by their hands and love grabbing things

ENCOURAGING GOOD BEHAVIOR
As they grow older, babies need clear but gentle guidance. Everyone who deals with your baby should respond to his behavior in the same way.

Q SHE HAS STARTED TO BANG HER HEAD AGAINST THE CRIB. WHAT'S WRONG ?

A Head-banging is a habit that some older babies and toddlers acquire. It is usually a form of attention-seeking, and your baby may do this because she feels insecure for some reason. Sometimes babies bang their heads on the wall or floor. The best remedy for head-banging is simply to ignore it, however dramatic and disturbing it looks, while also making sure your baby has all the love and security that she needs. Occasionally, head-banging is related to an earache, but if this is the case it is a temporary problem and your baby should display other signs of illness, such as a high temperature and a reluctance to feed.

Q I'M SAYING "NO" ALL THE TIME. IS THERE AN ALTERNATIVE ?

A You cannot avoid saying "No" at times, especially when your baby becomes mobile and begins to get into everything. However, try not to say it constantly. Offer your baby something else to do and use a more positive wording. Instead of saying "No. Don't touch that!," try "Let's look at this book now." Fortunately, it is easy to distract a baby. Remove obvious temptations from view—install cabinet safety latches and move fragile or precious objects until she is older (see pp. 198–9). Show pleasure when she does something that you approve of—she will occasionally!

PARENT'S SURVIVAL GUIDE

I KEEP GETTING ANGRY

It is normal to feel exasperated at times, so don't be afraid to confide in someone, especially if you feel you are losing control. The more aggressive you feel, the more urgently you should get someone else involved.

If you are becoming overwrought:
■ put your baby in her crib or playpen and step back from the situation
■ speak to your doctor, partner, or a close friend and ask their advice.

A baby's behavior can be infuriating, but it isn't deliberate, so do not take it out on her. I promise that it will all seem trivial in a year or two—it's just now that things are bad.

BABIES 6 WEEKS–1 YEAR

DISCIPLINE AND BEHAVIOR

TODDLER BEHAVIOR

Q HOW CAN I ENCOURAGE MY TODDLER TO BEHAVE WELL ?

A Children learn by example. To encourage your child to behave well, you need to be considerate, kind, honest, and patient, and give her stability and love. Avoid shouting, aggression, or violence. When you discipline your toddler, be firm but loving. Scold her only when absolutely necessary and be consistent. Learning the boundaries of acceptable behavior is easier when they stay in the same place—if you don't normally let her bounce a ball in the living room, don't let her do so when friends visit. Reward her good behavior with hugs and attention—read her a favorite story or take her on an outing, but don't buy candy as a reward. When your child is older and able to understand more about what she has achieved, you can use formal rewards (see p. 176). For now, all she needs is time with you.

Q WILL I SPOIL MY BABY IF I GIVE HER A LOT OF REWARDS ?

A This depends on the rewards you choose, but in general you won't spoil her by giving her well-merited rewards. A child who lives with approval grows up to be secure, not spoiled.

Q MY TODDLER IS NAUGHTIER THAN OTHERS. AM I TO BLAME ?

A I doubt it. Her personality is not wholly under your control, although she may be responding to your handling of her by being naughty. Make sure that you are as consistent as possible, and as calm as you can be. That does not mean letting her get away with bad behavior—just that your discipline should be loving as well as firm.

Q WHY DOESN'T MY TODDLER PLAY WITH OTHER CHILDREN ?

A Before the age of three, a child rarely plays with other children but can usually play alongside them. Unfortunately, sharing does not come naturally to toddlers, especially with their most prized possessions. If this is a problem, do not stop inviting other children. However, before the next visit, agree with your child which of her toys she is willing to let the other child play with. Put away the things that she won't share.

Q MY TODDLER WILL NOT SIT STILL. IS THIS NORMAL ?

A Toddlers are highly curious and adventurous. Being into everything is their way of exploring the world. They want to know what happens when they swing from the curtain, or open the washing-machine door. It is normal for toddlers to be active all day, especially if they have recently abandoned a daytime nap. This is all part of their normal development. There are, however, some children who are very active and cannot concentrate for long because they are hyperactive (they may have Attention Deficit Hyperactivity Disorder, or ADHD, see p. 225). However, most do not—they are just normal toddlers enjoying life to the fullest. Talk to your doctor if you are concerned.

Q SHE WON'T DO AS I TELL HER. WHAT CAN I DO ?

A Perhaps you are expecting too much too soon from your child. Consider whether your requests are realistic and whether they are phrased in the most appealing way. The truth is that you cannot make a child do something—you can only make her want to do something. It is better to avoid confrontation and use cunning. By the age of two, a toddler may pick up her toys if you do it with her, or if you turn this chore into a game or say, "I bet you can't put those blocks in the box."

Q WHY DOES MY TODDLER SAY "NO" ALL THE TIME AND WHAT SHOULD I DO ?

A Your toddler's emerging ego and independence will inevitably lead to occasional (or not so occasional) conflict with you, especially around two years of age. All toddlers say "No," but some say it more than others. It is extremely annoying but it will pass. Avoid frequent battles of wills by making your requests reasonable. Don't ask her questions to which she can say "No." Instead of saying, "Do you want to go to bed?" give her a choice, such as "Would you like the red or blue pajamas tonight?". Be aware that her saying "No" is also a way of telling you that she actually wants to do things for herself. If, for instance, she says "No" when you run the bathroom faucet, it may be because she wanted to turn the faucet on, not that she doesn't want her hands washed.

Q SHE ALWAYS BEHAVES BADLY IN PUBLIC. WHAT CAN I DO ?

A Many toddlers save their worst behavior for the biggest audiences. However you respond, you can't win everyone's approval. Although there are bound to be some sympathetic parents around who understand what you're going through, other onlookers may blame you for being too soft, while a few will think you're too strict. So just do what you would have done had her outburst been in private: handle her firmly, calmly, and with love.

Q MY TODDLER SAYS "WHY" ALL THE TIME. HOW CAN I STOP HER ?

A You shouldn't. From the age of three, or sometimes earlier, most children ask "Why" a lot. In time, your child will understand that "Why" tacked onto a word or sentence doesn't always make sense. Answer questions like "Why is it hot?" but ignore "Why door?" unless you can figure out what she means.

Q WHAT SHOULD I DO IF MY TODDLER MASTURBATES ?

A Toddlers of both sexes masturbate and you should ignore it. If you are at home, do nothing. If you are in public, stop her by distracting her with something more interesting. This tends to work because children seem to masturbate more when they're bored. There's no need to say that it's dirty or disgusting or to punish your child.

Q IF I GO BACK TO WORK NOW, WILL IT AFFECT MY TODDLER'S BEHAVIOR ?

A It could, and her behavior may regress for a while. Don't be surprised if she is fussier about food, or wets herself if she has recently become toilet-trained. However, it will pass. If you have given her love and security, she will be resilient enough for your work not to have any long-term impact. Make sure your childcare arrangements are as good as they can be (see p. 186) and try to make the transition as simple as possible for both of you.

WHAT ARE TODDLER TANTRUMS ?

A tantrum is an uncontrolled outburst—an expression of rage and temper that usually lasts several minutes. Some children scream, kick, stamp their feet, or even throw themselves dramatically to the ground. Tantrums are often called toddler tantrums because they are so common in this age group.

Is this the same as the terrible twos?
Yes, it is. The peak age for tantrums is 15 to 36 months. Most two-year-olds have at least one tantrum per week, but they grow out of them.

Why do only some children have tantrums?
Placid toddlers may have fewer tantrums, or start having them later, or grow out of the habit sooner than a child who is more high-strung. However, to some extent tantrums are a part of every child's journey to greater independence.

Can I prevent tantrums?
Tantrums are more likely to be triggered when the child has been thwarted in some way. When a toddler wants something, she wants it now and can't understand why she has to wait. Stay firm on important issues, but don't confront your child over trivial matters. A little patience on your part can work wonders in reducing the number of tantrums you have to endure.

How can I help my child?
When she has a tantrum, make sure she comes to no harm. No other restraint is necessary (or effective). Some parents slap, but it's usually unhelpful. The child is not in a frame of mind to learn from it, and she won't be amenable to logic. She is beside herself and doesn't know what she's doing. Hug and reassure her when she calms down.

What can I do to stay calm?
Try not to get flustered by a tantrum, wherever you are. You are more intelligent and more mature than your toddler—and she needs you to stay that way. Just keep her safe. If you're at home, try turning your back on her, or even leaving the room for a short while. The tantrum will stop because there's no point in putting on a play when there's no audience. Above all, don't give in. Ultimately, her tantrum must make no difference whatsoever to your handling of her. She has to learn that losing her temper is pointless.

DISCIPLINING TODDLERS

Q HOW CAN I DISCIPLINE MY TODDLER WITHOUT DAMAGING HER CONFIDENCE?

A Praise her for what she has achieved instead of telling her off when she gets things slightly wrong. Instead of saying "No" or "Don't" all the time, be positive whenever you can, and give her simple reasons for your suggestions. It is far better to say, "Walking on the sidewalk is safer" than to say, "Don't walk in the road."

Q WOULDN'T IT BE EASIER TO LET HER DO WHAT SHE WANTS?

A No. It may be easier in the very short term, but society has rules, even if you don't, so there will be trouble later on. In the long term, a lax attitude is as damaging as discipline that is too harsh. A child needs boundaries that do not change. Letting her do as she pleases is a recipe for anarchy and a spoiled child.

Q HOW CAN I TEACH MY TODDLER THAT SOME THINGS ARE WRONG?

A From the age of about two, you can try telling her why when you tell her not to do something. If she doesn't stop, tell her "No" and remove her swiftly. She has to know when you mean it.

Q HOW SHOULD I PUNISH HER WHEN SHE HAS BEHAVED VERY BADLY?

A It depends on what she has done, but usually a stern and quiet telling off is more effective at this age than a punishment. Punish as rarely as possible—frequent punishments can damage your relationship with your child. The action you take should be appropriate to the misdeed and follow it immediately. Before the age of two, children aren't naughty on purpose. Her apparent misbehavior may be because she is too young to think ahead. She needs time to learn right from wrong.

Q WILL AN OCCASIONAL SLAP HARM MY TODDLER?

A Slapping gives the child the idea that it is acceptable to use violence to solve a problem, making her more likely to hit other children or you. Slapping can also get out of control. Therefore, if used at all, a slap should only be for truly dangerous acts, such as running into the road. A slap should never be hard or aimed at the head, and only ever use the flat of your hand. Don't torment yourself—children with loving parents will not be damaged by one gentle slap.

Q DO THREATS WORK?

A The threat only works if you would actually carry it out. If you tell your toddler that you will abandon her if she doesn't stop screaming, she'll discover sooner or later than you didn't mean it. On the other hand, depriving her of being read a favorite story is a realistic threat. As with all discipline, threats should refer to something immediate. At this age, she's desperate for attention from you, so anything that withdraws this attention for a short while can be an effective threat.

Speak to your toddler firmly but in a calm manner

BEING FIRM
Toddlers need to know when they have done something wrong. Be firm on major issues, but do not worry about trivial matters.

Q IS IT A GOOD IDEA TO SEND HER TO HER ROOM AS A PUNISHMENT?

A No. Banishing her to her room may make her associate her room with being punished. When your child has done something wrong, send her to stand in the hall where you can keep an eye on her. This "time out" takes her away from the scene of her crime and deprives her of your attention. This needn't be for long—two minutes is sufficient time for a two-year-old.

Q HOW CAN WE STOP SHOUTING AND TELLING HER OFF ALL THE TIME?

A Shouting can be effective, but eventually its potency wears off and it only raises the emotional temperature. So keep it for emergencies and try to say the same thing in a quieter voice. Be positive whenever possible. Instead of saying "Don't leave the door open," encourage your child with "Shut the door," or distract her with "Look at this puzzle with me" instead of saying "Don't swing on the curtains." Concentrate on praising her when she puts her shoes away or when she helps you to do something. Decide which issues are important to you as a family and ignore any minor problems. Keep temptations to a minimum. Until she is older, keep vases of flowers or treasured presents safely out of your toddler's grasp.

Q MY PARTNER AND I DO NOT AGREE ON DISCIPLINE. WHAT'S THE ANSWER?

A Differences in the style of discipline you and other caregivers use are common. You, your partner, parents, or caregiver may all handle the same situation differently. Discuss this with the other adults when your child is not present, so that there is some consistency, and to ensure that your authority won't be undermined. However, minor disagreements and discrepancies are normal, so don't give up trying to impose some discipline because of minor conflicts between adults.

Q HOW CAN I TELL IF MY TODDLER HAS A REAL BEHAVIORAL PROBLEM?

A Most toddlers misbehave, some more often than others, and most parents worry at some stage that they have a problem child. There is usually nothing wrong, except perhaps a need for more attention or security. However, your child may have a behavioral problem if she does not relate well to you, dislikes being hugged, fails to engage in eye contact, shows a lack of interest in people, or repeats certain actions in a ritual way, such as rocking or touching all the doorknobs in the home in a certain order. These could be symptoms of autism (see p. 225). If you are concerned, ask your doctor for advice.

PARENT'S SURVIVAL GUIDE

MY TODDLER IS AGGRESSIVE

A child may hit another child as an experiment. She will continue doing this if everyone comes running to see what the matter is. Negative attention is more exciting than no attention at all. Unfortunately, if the other child screams or cries, it provides even better entertainment.

What should I do when my toddler hits another child?
Withdraw attention from your toddler and give it to the other child for a few minutes. If your child demands your attention during this time, say you cannot deal with her because the other child was hurt and upset. You can explain to her later that what she did was wrong. However, at this stage of development children are unable to understand how the other child feels, so don't give too much by way of explanation—to her it is all attention.

My toddler hits and kicks me sometimes. What can I do?
Ignore her by removing yourself from the room or doing something else instead. This will deprive her of your valuable attention and her audience. On no account should you ever allow yourself to become angry or aggressive with your child.

My toddler bit another child. Is it a good idea for me to bite back?
No. You should not bite back because a toddler will not associate you biting her with her biting another child. All it does is give your toddler the idea that biting is acceptable. Biting is painful and dramatic (and can cause infection), so it is almost guaranteed to get parental attention. It is especially common with twin toddlers, but otherwise it's just like any other aggressive act.

PRESCHOOL CHILD BEHAVIOR

Q **HOW CAN I IMPROVE MY CHILD'S BEHAVIOR ?**

A Remember that all children are naughty at times, so you will not eliminate bad behavior. However, there are things that you can do to help a child of this age. Always praise her when she gets things right—this will boost her confidence and encourage her to behave well in the future. Consider using reward charts (see p. 176). These are especially suitable for children of 4–5 years or older. When your child has been naughty, make it very clear to her that it's her behavior that's bad, not her. At some point most parents come close to telling their child that they hate her for doing a particular thing. As well as being a pointless thing to say, this could seriously dent her self esteem.

Q **HOW CAN I HELP MY CHILD GROW IN CONFIDENCE ?**

A The most important thing is to be positive. Praise your child when she does something right, especially if it is a new achievement for her. The world can be a daunting place when you are very young. A small event, such as going to nursery school and painting some pieces of macaroni, may not seem like a challenge to you, but it can be to your child, so be supportive.

Q **HOW CAN I ENCOURAGE MY CHILD TO BE MORE CONSIDERATE ?**

A Young children are naturally self-centered so this can be difficult. It takes time for a child to learn to treat other people as she would like to be treated herself. This is a moral issue as well as a behavioral one. However, persevere with your encouragement and eventually your child will learn.

Q **CAN I TEACH MY CHILD TO BE MORE HELPFUL AROUND THE HOME ?**

A Try to do some things together, such as setting the table for dinner or unpacking the groceries. Only give her chores that she is capable of doing. She'll be discouraged if she can't manage to peel the potatoes by herself. Encourage her by praising her efforts when she tries. Above all, be patient—she will be slower and clumsier than you for many years to come. If you tell her off now, she may give up trying to help altogether.

Q **HOW CAN I TEACH HER TO SHARE THINGS WITH OTHER CHILDREN ?**

A Emphasize that sharing is a temporary thing— even though someone else is playing with her toy, it is still hers, and she will get it back. Decide in advance what she is prepared to let the other child play with. Make sure the shared toys are fairly robust, since she may cry if another child breaks something of hers. Before the friend arrives, put away items that she won't share—but don't be surprised if, when the other child is there, she drops hints about a favorite toy that is in the closet. Set your child a good example by sharing some things of yours with her. You may find that she soon gets pleasure from offering to share her belongings (although she will still prefer to share with a parent rather than with a friend her own age).

Q **MY CHILD IS MOODY AND BAD-TEMPERED. WHAT CAN I DO ABOUT IT ?**

A Some people are naturally moody, and you may simply have to put up with your child's moods and aggression. Let your child know that it is perfectly all right for her to show her feelings, whether they are positive or negative, but that it is not acceptable to act out negative emotions or to hit people or damage their belongings. It may be better for her to have something on which to take out her aggression rather than letting her show aggression toward you or her siblings.

Q **MY CHILD IS RUDE TO PEOPLE. HOW CAN I STOP HER ?**

A Most children can be very outspoken and uninhibited. They may think nothing of saying "You're fat" or "You're stupid." You should tell your child gently that it's not helpful or kind to say such things, even if they may be true, but try not to dwell on the subject. Some children behave rudely simply to attract attention or to show off. Sometimes other people, such as grandparents, inadvertently encourage rude behavior by smiling at the child. If your child continues to behave like this, withdraw your attention from her. Fortunately, most adults expect children to be tactless at times and are usually understanding. Unfortunately, some children use bad language as a way of seeking attention.

HOW CAN I RECOGNIZE PROBLEM BEHAVIOR ?

Many parents think, at least fleetingly, that they have a problem child. Happily, the reality is that most do not. However, if your child has a real problem you should seek professional help. Do not be afraid to ask for advice if you need it.

Speak to your doctor or pediatrician if there are signs of the following:
- poor interaction with parents or others
- repeated violence or disruptive behavior
- marked restlessness or fidgeting
- arson or other serious destructive acts
- soiling pants or the bed after the age of four
- extreme clumsiness.

Q MY CHILD DOESN'T SEEM TO HAVE MANY FRIENDS. HOW CAN I HELP ?

A I don't think this matters very much as long as she gets the chance to see other children. Ask her if she would like a friend to come to your home to play, or you could invite friends of yours with children of similar age. Beyond that, there isn't much you can do. But don't worry—many shy children become outgoing when they grow up. Don't force your child to be sociable—this can make her shyness even worse.

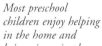
Sweeping the floor is an ideal task for a preschool child

HELPING AT HOME
Most preschool children enjoy helping in the home and being given simple household tasks to perform. Make sure that your child is capable of achieving the task set.

Q MY CHILD'S MOUTH SEEMS TO TWITCH A LOT. IS THIS DUE TO STRESS ?

A Mouth-twitching, excessive blinking, forehead-wrinkling, sniffing, and other repetitive actions can be nervous habits. Also called tics, these habits often begin during periods of stress or conflict in a child's life, such as starting school, a change of caregiver, or parental separation. Although these movements are beyond the child's control, they will stop when she is sleeping. If your child has developed a tic, try to resolve any underlying lack of stability or security that she may be experiencing. Apart from that, as a parent, you should try your best to ignore the tic completely. Scolding, shouting, or punishing her will only make things worse. Seeing the doctor doesn't usually help either, unless your child has other symptoms that you are worried about.

Q WHY DOES MY CHILD MISBEHAVE SO MUCH ?

A There are many reasons for bad behavior, and it's not always the same reason each time for any one child. For example, a child may misbehave because of boredom, tiredness, hunger or thirst, insecurity, a need to show off, jealousy (a special form of insecurity), or family stress, such as separation, divorce, or a bereavement. Some parents have been known to blame their child's bad behavior on medication or food additives. These can occasionally make a child more excitable, but in my experience this is very unusual.

Q DOES FAMILY POSITION AFFECT A CHILD'S BEHAVIOR ?

A The child's position in the hierarchy of the family seems to have some bearing on behavior (see p. 190). Some youngest children, especially the youngest of three children, have a tendency to behave in a very immature way.

DISCIPLINING YOUR PRESCHOOL CHILD

Q IS IT APPROPRIATE TO PUNISH MY CHILD FOR BAD BEHAVIOR?

A Yes, a punishment can be appropriate if it fits the crime and is suitable for her age and her level of understanding. The punishment should swiftly follow the misdemeanor. It is useless to ban a favorite television program the day after tomorrow for what your child did wrong today. There is no point in punishing her for something she can't help doing, like wetting the bed or vomiting. Never respond with force or aggression, or lose control—apart from anything else, it sets a poor example for your child. Do not threaten your child with what will happen when your partner returns. The child will think that the parent at home does not know what to do and may begin to dread the absent one. Also, the time delay will render any punishment meaningless. Discipline, if appropriate, should be immediate.

Q SHOULD I SEND HER TO HER BEDROOM?

A Time without attention from you gives you both a chance to calm down. It need not be long. The idea of this is not to let her find alternative entertainment, but to be deprived of you and of what she was doing. Three minutes is sufficient for a three year old, four for a four year old, and so on. If you send your child to her bedroom a lot she may grow to dislike her room, with serious consequences for her sleeping habits. Keeping your child in the same room as you, but turning your back on her can work as well, and has the added benefit that she is less likely to damage things than if left on her own.

Q SHOULD I SLAP MY CHILD?

A Striking a child is generally opposed. It is most often done out of anger or frustration, and slapping or hitting a child if you're angry with her will make her think that this is a good way of expressing herself. This will lead her to lash out when she is angry. In my opinion, though, a controlled tap on the back of the hand or on the bottom can be acceptable if a child is doing something dangerous. Be very sure that you do not hurt your child. It is the shock value that works, not the degree of pain. Only ever use the flat of your hand, and never hit your child's face or head.

REWARD CHARTS

Every child needs to be praised. Formal rewards are appropriate for children aged 4–5 years or more.

What is a reward chart?
A reward chart involves keeping a chart or record for a limited time, usually between a week and a month. Depending on what you want your child to achieve, the chart could be in daily panels (for example, for staying in her own bed) or divided into more manageable periods—morning, afternoon, and evening—if you're trying to achieve overall good behavior.

How does it work?
For each period of time your child behaves well, she gets a tick or a sticker. You could buy special stickers together—your child has to be interested in the reward process. Keep the chart somewhere central so that everyone in the family can see how well she is doing.

What rewards should I offer?
A row of about six stars should result in a privilege or treat, perhaps playing a game with you, some time alone with you or your partner without her siblings, or even some pocket money. You have to decide what will work best for your child. Don't make each check or star worth too much—you may find it hard to keep your side of the bargain.

How quickly will my child respond?
Your child's progress will depend on your particular goal. Not hitting her baby brother could take two weeks if she currently does so on a regular basis; staying in her own bed all night could take less time. Reward charts will not work on their own unless you deal with the underlying cause—in the case of sibling rivalry, you may need to give the older child more attention and security in addition to using the reward chart. You must choose something that your child is able to achieve in the time allotted. For instance, you cannot teach a child to read using reward charts.

Q I GET SO ANGRY AND END UP SHOUTING. HOW CAN I STOP?

A It is very difficult, but you must try to stop, because eventually shouting loses its effectiveness. Try speaking in a very quiet voice the next time you are angry. Your child may be so surprised that she will listen to you intently. Another method is to say nothing at all if you are upset. Simply continue what you are doing in a completely matter-of-fact way.

Q SHOULD MY PARTNER AND I HAVE THE SAME ATTITUDE TO DISCIPLINE?

A If you don't share the same attitude, your child will receive confusing mixed messages about what is acceptable behavior. She may also learn very quickly to play one parent off against the other. Of course, your parenting style will not be identical to your partner's, but it should be sufficiently similar so that you do not undermine each other. Discuss your attitudes without your child being present and agree on a compromise if necessary. This will avoid heated, destructive arguments in front of her. Make sure that any other caregivers understand your attitudes also.

DEALING WITH BAD BEHAVIOR

Share responsibility for discipline with your partner, so that your child receives a consistent message about what is acceptable.

Crouch down to your child's level when speaking to her

I CAN'T STAY CALM

There are times when a child's behavior can be very difficult to deal with, but it is essential not to lose control. You are less likely to lose your temper if you have realistic expectations that are appropriate to your child's age.

Explain what is right and wrong

Your child may not realize the significance of her actions. Tell her explicitly what is right and what is wrong, and explain the reasons whenever you can, otherwise she will commit the same offence again without knowing it.

Set a good example

It is vital to set a good example. Your child needs to be shown how to behave. She will learn a valuable lesson from the way that you deal with frustration. Seeing you stay in control of your emotions is the only way your child will learn to do the same.

Don't lose your temper

Keeping a cool head is essential, but it is hard because it's difficult not to lose your temper when you are upset. Instead of becoming angry with your child, show sadness to convey disapproval of her behavior. Remember that losing your temper is equivalent to giving her attention, albeit of a negative kind. Parents sometimes find it difficult to believe that children deliberately seek negative attention, but research shows that this does happen. If you find that the situation is becoming heated, try to take a step back. Leave the room and make yourself a cup of tea, or turn your back on your child and at least pretend to read a newspaper or magazine for a while.

Ask for advice

Talk to your pediatrician or a friend. This is particularly helpful if you think the bad behavior is continuous, or if you are finding it impossible to deal with your child. Many parents become exasperated with their children at some time, so it can be reassuring to talk to someone who has had similar experiences and knows how you feel. All children are naughty at times, so don't take it personally.

PRESCHOOL CHILDREN 2½ YEARS ONWARD

DISCIPLINE AND BEHAVIOR

FAMILY
LIFE

Children enrich your life and bring enormous rewards—family life is something to **cherish and enjoy**. However, starting a family will bring major lifestyle changes and is inevitably accompanied by various concerns about your child's well-being. This chapter looks at your family's **emotional and physical well-being**. It explores issues such as handling the well-meaning, but conflicting, advice from family and friends, and the impact on your child of life changes, such as separation, or a new baby in the family. It also helps you deal with **day-to-day practicalities**, such as finding the right childcare and keeping your child safe.

8

BECOMING A FAMILY

Q HOW WILL OUR LIVES CHANGE WHEN WE BECOME PARENTS ?

A Your life will change on physical, social, and emotional planes. For the next few years, you'll have to be physically with your child and care for him, so you will not have the same carefree lifestyle as before. Socially, you'll mix more with other parents of young children rather than with childless people. But perhaps the biggest change is emotional. As a new parent, you may be overwhelmed by the love you feel for your baby. You may also empathize more readily with suffering and cry when you see disasters on the television news. Don't worry—this is normal. Your feelings toward your partner and your own parents may shift as you become a caregiver rather than the one who is cared for. Your child will become the focus of your emotional life. This seems to happen whether or not you have a career or other interests, and it may be nature's way of ensuring survival of the species. Accept that your life has changed, and be flexible in meeting the new demands placed on you.

Q WHAT ARE THE MOST IMPORTANT ASPECTS OF PARENTING ?

A Being caring and consistent. Your relationship with your child creates a pattern that will shape all his future relationships. This is why a child needs love, security, approval, and acceptance from the start. A lack of these can affect his self-esteem, his achievements, and his capacity to be happy. This does not mean that you have to let him do everything he wants; he must learn discipline as well as other skills, but you have to teach it in a loving way. Your child needs boundaries that are constant. Children learn by imitation, so setting a good example is vital. Finally, you must learn to trust your instincts. You will soon know your child better than anyone else.

Q EVERYONE GIVES ME ADVICE, BUT WHY IS IT SO CONFLICTING ?

A There's no doubt that there are many people (not least your own parents) who are only too happy to pass on the benefits of their wisdom. You may find that many people are very free with their advice, but do not offer much practical help. The advice can be welcome and appropriate, but sometimes it isn't, if only because it's out of date. Don't follow advice slavishly—even your doctor's recommendations should come with some explanation—and try to keep an open mind. You may not put it all into practice, but it's polite to make a noncommittal statement along the lines of "I'll bear that in mind."

Q HOW IMPORTANT IS IT TO GET THE FAMILY INTO A ROUTINE ?

A It depends on your lifestyle and personality. Some parents have a relaxed attitude and are content to coast along without a routine, while others, notably working parents, may not be able to afford that luxury. Order and routine help to maintain discipline and reinforce any boundaries you set. A routine is invaluable for those things that must be done every day, like feeding and dressing your baby and preparing your own meals. You can give yourself more leeway on other things. Most of the housework can wait, for instance, although you still need to maintain hygiene. It's wise not to be too rigid in your daily scheduling; the unexpected can crop up with babies and young children around, and you need to be flexible enough to take it in stride.

A NEW BABY
Being a growing family can bring you lots of satisfaction and joy. Older siblings will soon come to accept the new baby in your midst.

I'M FINDING PARENTING QUITE DIFFICULT

Being a parent isn't as easy or as natural as some people assume, and it isn't the same for everyone, either. There may well be times when you feel negative.

Why do I feel so negative?

There are bound to be times when you relate less well to your child or to your partner. You can't expect to have the same feelings for someone all the time. Occasionally, you may have had a difficult day and even seriously doubt your ability to parent. Everyone feels like this from time to time. Your expectations of parenthood may not match the reality, and it can help to discuss this with other new parents and with health professionals. Parenting can be tough, but the rewards far outweigh the difficult times.

My personal life is unstable and uncertain. Can I still raise a happy child?

Yes. It is more difficult to provide a stable and secure home if your life is in a state of flux, but you can still provide what your child needs—love and approval from you, and from your partner if you have one. On a positive note, seeing you deal successfully with problems can be a useful thing for your child, although you do have to shield him from many of the uncertainties you face.

Do you have to have had a happy childhood yourself to be a good parent?

No. Happy children become secure adults who in turn usually become loving parents, so it certainly helps, but it's not essential. If good parents had to have an idyllic past, then most of us would never rear children successfully. It's true that history can repeat itself if you had an unhappy childhood, but only if you failed to learn from it. It may be that

you will be better able to see what a child needs than someone who has never had to deal with trauma. I think that a positive attitude is the most important requisite for parenting.

My partner and I disagree on so many things. How can we raise a well-balanced child?

Children thrive on consistency, so it would be wise for you and your partner to discuss and agree on major issues, such as discipline and finances. However, few parents see eye to eye on everything, and there will be times when you disagree. Don't argue in front of your child and try not to assume you're always right. Each of you brings your own qualities and values to the family. When your child is older, he may benefit from seeing you both resolve your differences. If you handle discord tactfully without aggression, your discussions can teach him useful lessons in negotiation and compromise. What I think you should avoid is any situation in which your youngster can make use of your different stances to parenting and play you off against each other.

What can I do about feeling negative?

Be less hard on yourself. You're probably doing a lot better than you imagine. Try to be less hard on others, too. When the behavior of your partner or your child is difficult, remember that it's the behavior you don't like—not the person. If you feel aggressive toward your child or anyone else, ask for help—speak to your doctor, a friend, or someone from your place of worship.

Q IS PARENTING MORE DIFFICULT THESE DAYS THAN IT USED TO BE?

A In many ways, it is. Although household chores have been made easier by technology and many families are materially better off, the expectations of parenting have increased. However, there are fewer people around to guide you. In many parts of the world, extended families are now the exception, not the norm, and raising children can be a lonely job, especially if you're a single parent.

Q SO CAN I TRAIN TO BE A BETTER PARENT?

A In many areas, hospitals run postpartum groups for first-time parents, and parenting groups to help those with older children deal with particular problems. However, you will probably find that many skills come naturally or are bred from common sense. Parenting is fundamentally a skill that is acquired on the job, so you may wait a long time for positive feedback!

Q WHERE CAN I MEET OTHER PARENTS WITH YOUNG CHILDREN ?

A Other new parents are a good source of moral support. You should try to keep in touch with prospective parents you met at childbirth classes. Your pediatrician may have a list of parent and baby groups in your area as well as postpartum groups and toddler groups. However, you will undoubtedly find that you meet other parents without having to make much effort at all. Now that you're pushing a baby carriage or stroller, other parents will probably strike up conversations with you wherever you are, whether you're in a line at the supermarket, or out for a walk.

Q HOW CAN I KEEP IN TOUCH WITH PEOPLE NOW THAT I'M SO BUSY ?

A It does become more difficult to sustain all your other relationships now that you're a parent. However, it is still possible. Invite friends over in the evening after you have put your baby to bed. To save yourself time and effort, perhaps each friend could contribute something to eat, or you can just order in. Meet up in places that are more family-friendly; you will soon find out where these are. When you are too busy to meet up, phone your friends for a talk now and then. Your phone bills may rise, but you will maintain valuable contact. Make the most of technology such as e-mail, text messages, and fax to keep in touch. Don't forget the humble postcard—stock up on these when you get a chance.

Q HOW CAN I MAKE GOING OUT LESS OF AN EFFORT ?

A Get yourself organized. Going out with a baby or young child demands forward planning and a lot of practice if you want to get out of the house on time. To some extent you need to anticipate the unexpected—dirty diaper, hungry baby, bad weather—so keep a bag packed with items such as diapers and spare clothes (see p. 205). If you drive, keep your car filled with gas—it's stressful to visit a gas station with a howling baby in tow. If going out seems too much of an effort to begin with, limit your outings to a friend's home or a short walk, but don't give up and stay in. It's easy to become isolated, especially as a new parent, so try to go out every day—you'll soon get used to it.

Q WHEN CAN I FIRST LEAVE MY BABY WITH A BABY-SITTER ?

A It depends on the baby-sitter, the baby, and how long you plan to be out. It also depends on when you, as a parent, feel confident about going out without your child, although there has to be a first time. Leaving a baby under three months old is always hard, although an experienced nanny or caregiver, or a good friend who is also a parent, would be able to manage. This is why baby-sitting circles, where parents take turns looking after other people's children, can work. Always leave a phone number where you can be contacted. I would also phone home at least once to ask the sitter how everything is.

HOW WILL I COPE WITH TWINS ?

Having twins usually inspires mixed emotions—delight and dread! You will undoubtedly have to work very hard, so be prepared to accept every bit of support that is offered to you.

How can I adjust to being a parent of twins?
Accept that it's going to be harder. There are no magic answers, but here are some suggestions:
■ put yourself and your babies first. Spend time with them rather than on chores
■ take care of yourself. You'll be better able to care for them if you're healthy and well
■ work as a team with your partner—you'll need each other even more with two babies to care for
■ take each day as it comes. It's impossible to be a perfect parent of one baby, let alone two, so don't feel guilty about it
■ meet up with other parents of twins. They can offer you useful tips as well as friendly support
■ if you're feeling low or in need of professional help, contact your pediatrician, or a support group (see p. 235).

Where can I meet other parents of twins?
Try your local twins club. There, you will meet plenty of people who may have initially felt stunned by having twins, but can now inspire you to rise to the challenge and enjoy your children to the fullest.

THE IMPORTANCE OF GRANDPARENTS

Grandparents are very important to a child. In some parts of the world, it is normal for an extended family to take an active part in child-rearing. Even when grandparents aren't this closely involved, they are an important source of love and security for a child and provide a link with his past. Your own relationship with your child's grandparents may also serve as a model for the way that he relates to you and your partner in years to come.

How can grandparents help?

The most precious thing grandparents can give is time to spend with your child. Even if they still work, grandparents are not under the same pressures as you are and can provide a different perspective. As a result, a child's bond with a grandparent is often strong, special, and enduring. In addition, grandparents can contribute in a practical way—for example, they may have a talent for telling stories, playing table-tennis, or doing magic tricks. Or they may simply provide love, comfort, and unconditional acceptance.

How can I encourage my child to have a good relationship with his grandparents?

From a young age, and certainly by 18 months, you can encourage your child to carry out little tasks, like taking a spoon to grandpa, or showing grandma a treasured teddy bear or a new book. Later he can tell them about new experiences, such as his first day at playgroup. Talk to him often about his grandparents and about the way things were a long time ago. If ever your parents or your partner's parents annoy you, try not to express negative thoughts in front of your child.

We cannot see the grandparents often. How can I involve them more?

Sometimes grandparents are unable to participate as much as they would like because they are in poor health or live too far away. Children grow up fast, so keep grandparents up to date with news by phoning or writing often and sending regular photos. Soon your child will be able to use the phone for himself and write letters. Record your child's voice on tape, or make a video to send. If a grandparent has sent a present, be sure to say thank you properly. To begin with, your child may only be able to scrawl on a card but grandparents tend to be extraordinarily appreciative of such simple gestures.

What's a good way of dealing with interfering grandparents?

This can be difficult. Sometimes your becoming a parent is like an instant replay of your parents' own early parenting days, and their well-meaning advice can be a way of reliving their past. You have to draw the line if they try to become involved in matters that don't concern them. I think the best way is to tell them how much you appreciate them and their kindness, but that you really want to do things your own way. Make it clear that you are not rejecting them, and at the same time try to involve them in more neutral issues.

There is a lot of rivalry between the different grandparents. How can I handle this?

Both you and your partner should try to stay strictly neutral, however hard it is at times. Stay out of discussions about how much, or how little, time or money another doting grandparent lavishes on the child. Sometimes even adults have to be reminded that everyone does things differently and that there is no harm in this.

A SPECIAL RELATIONSHIP
Grandparents have a great deal of value to offer your children, most importantly love, a wealth of experience, and lots of time.

GOING BACK TO WORK

Q WHEN IS THE RIGHT TIME TO RETURN TO WORK?

A This is inevitably something of a compromise. Go back too early and you'll miss out on the early months with your baby. Leave it too late and you'll be out of touch at work. Some parents have to return after a few weeks because of financial restraints or career pressures. Give yourself time to investigate your legal rights before taking maternity leave. You may also want to look into more flexible work options in order to spend more time at home with your young baby. Whenever you decide to go back to work, make sure you are as happy as you can be with your childcare arrangements.

Q HOW CAN I GO BACK TO WORK AND STILL SUCCEED AS A PARENT?

A Being at work can make you a more fulfilled person and expand your interests, so that you can return home to your child with renewed enthusiasm. But it can be hard. You may intend to spend "quality time" with your child when you are at home, but you'll both be tired and it will require a lot of effort to do things together. As well as giving your child attention, you'll have to squeeze in the practicalities, such as buying food and clothes (yours and your baby's) and taking your baby to the doctor for his immunizations.

Q WOULD PART-TIME WORK BE BETTER FOR MY CHILD AND ME?

A Yes, probably. Part-time work can be a good and effective way of combining parenting and a career, and your child will certainly benefit from seeing more of you. It is becoming easier and more acceptable for either parent to work part time. But there are drawbacks. The financial rewards tend to be disproportionately low compared with full-time work, and your employer may indirectly put a lot of pressure on you to complete a normal day's achievements in four hours or less. So before you decide whether to take a part-time job, look carefully at all the possible consequences. For instance, the trip to and from your part-time work is usually just as expensive and time-consuming as it is for people who work full time, and the benefits, such as pension plans, may be far less if you work part time.

Q IS IT MORE CONVENIENT TO WORK AT HOME?

A If you do the kind of work that can be done at home, it may be a lot more convenient. You will save on traveling time and gain flexibility when your child is ill, or when you just want to be with him. But working at home is not a completely cost-free option. You will still need childcare, whether it's provided by a relative or is a more formal arrangement. If your child is cared for at home, it can be distracting and you will probably face many interruptions from friends and family. There is also the risk of professional isolation, and the difficulty of switching off mentally when the day's work is done.

Q HOW WILL I COPE WITH WORK WHEN MY CHILD IS ILL?

A It's a challenge. Parents often think that they'll be able to delegate the care of a sick child to someone else. Indeed, there's no reason why a good caregiver can't carry out clear instructions regarding doses of medicine and checking temperatures. However, it's not as simple as that, because if your child is ill, he'll probably want one of his parents to be with him. I believe a sick child is entitled to this so, unless his illness is trivial, you or your partner should take time off from work to be with him even if it creates havoc with your job. You may be able to work at home, and with reliable childcare be able to go back to work once your child starts to recover.

Q HOW CAN I FIND MORE TIME FOR MY CHILD?

A Eliminate unnecessary chores and prioritize the essentials so that you can dedicate more of your time to being with your child. My suggestions include: cooking simpler meals, batch-cooking in larger quantities and using the freezer more, shopping less often and more efficiently, using mail order where possible, and giving up ironing clothes if you can. When you come in, take a relaxing bath with your child (this gets bathtime over for both of you, and you can talk and play) and, if you feel it would not tire him too much, let your child stay up a little later on the days you are at work. Keep your weekends free for your child.

Q WHAT SORT OF CHILDCARE IS BEST FOR MY CHILD ?

A It depends on the age of your child, the hours that you intend to work, and the length of your trip to work. He can be cared for outside your home at daycare or by a caregiver, or in your own home by a nanny or au pair (see chart, overleaf). You should be aware, too, that what's right for you and your baby right now will probably change as he grows up.

Q A RELATIVE HAS OFFERED TO BABYSIT. IS THIS A GOOD IDEA ?

A This is clearly cheaper than many forms of childcare and can work, but relying on a relative has its drawbacks. It can be hard to keep the arrangement on a businesslike footing. Many parents also find it uncomfortable to tell a relative what to do with their child, and when they do, the caregiver can take it personally. You need to know where to draw boundaries, and with a first baby it's not always easy to have the confidence to do so, especially if the relative has raised children herself.

Q HOW CAN I HELP MY CHILD GET USED TO BEING CARED FOR BY SOMEONE ?

A Whatever age your child is, try to get him used to the caregiver gradually. Meet the caregiver several times with your child. If you can afford it, leave him in the other person's care on a part-time basis before you go back to work. When you go back to work, you should make sure that you pick him up promptly. Give your child time at the end of the day. Even though you'll both be tired, he'll need this time with you.

Q HOW WILL A CHANGE OF CAREGIVER AFFECT MY CHILD ?

A Children dislike change, and your child will have to give up attachments he had to the old caregiver and move on to a relationship with the new one. He may be fine, but he may misbehave, cry, have trouble sleeping, refuse his food, or even wet himself. If you have changed the caregiver for a good reason, don't let any of this discourage you. Be there for your child, and take time off from work if necessary. You are his stability and he needs to be able to rely on you when other things are changing.

Q WHAT IF THE CHANGE OF CAREGIVER DOESN'T WORK OUT AS PLANNED ?

A Then you will have to consider changing the caregiver again. Don't continue using unsatisfactory childcare because you fear change. However, the new caregiver may simply need time to adjust to your child and vice versa, and things may settle down after an initial transitional period.

Q IS IT POSSIBLE TO MAKE MORE TIME FOR MYSELF NOW THAT I AM BACK AT WORK ?

A This is the hardest thing of all, but it is possible. Schedule some time for yourself every day. To begin with, this may be only 10 minutes a day listening to some music or reading a magazine, but it's the principle that counts (and that works out as 70 minutes each week). You may be so busy that you're not sure what to do with your snatched moments of freedom, but you must think about it (on your way home, for example). It's not a selfish thing. It's vital to take this time in order to keep you, your family, and your work going.

PARENT'S SURVIVAL GUIDE

I FEEL I'M FAILING AT EVERYTHING

At some time or other, every working parent feels they're failing at both work and parenting. Fatigue and the effort of juggling both home and work can take their toll. However, the following suggestions may help you cope:

■ accept the situation—your commitment to work, even if it is not total, is invaluable

■ don't feel guilty—you are almost certainly doing better than you think

■ change what needs changing—if part-time work would suit you, see if it would be possible

■ don't allow people to undermine your confidence; no matter how proficient you are at parenting and working, someone will try to persuade you that you are wrong—they probably don't understand your situation

■ be an adult—by all means share concerns with your partner, a trusted friend, your doctor, or a counselor at work, but don't take out your problems or frustrations on your child

■ take care of yourself—you need to be healthy to be able to do your best at home and at work.

WHAT KINDS OF CHILDCARE ARE THERE ?

TYPE OF CHILDCARE	WHAT ARE THE BENEFITS ?	WHAT ARE THE DRAWBACKS ?
DAYCARE CENTER/ NURSERY SCHOOL The quality of daycare and nursery schools varies widely, so be sure to investigate as many options as possible before enrolling your child. Some large companies provide on-site childcare, which can be a huge convenience, but standards and availability may vary.	■ The staff may be highly trained and work to a high standard. ■ Children learn to get along with other children from an early age. ■ Your child may experience things he might not at home. ■ If the daycare is where you work, breast-feeding is easier. ■ You don't have to make a special trip on your way to work to take your child to the caregiver.	■ There is less one-to-one interaction. ■ It cannot cater to a sick child, and you or your partner will usually have to take time off from work. ■ The hours are fixed and may not be flexible enough for you to do overtime. ■ Your child may be exposed to infections from an earlier age. ■ Your child will be in unfamiliar surroundings. ■ Daycare/nursery school can be expensive and there are often long waiting lists.
CAREGIVERS (FAMILY CARE) Childcare is provided in a caregiver's own home, often with her own children. Caregivers are usually untrained but often quite motivated and experienced.	■ Caregivers are convenient since they're often near your home. ■ Because the caregiver will probably have other children to care for, and may also have her own children around, it is more like a family group. ■ Caregivers are often experienced mothers themselves. ■ Caregivers can be the least expensive childcare option.	■ From a young age, your child may be exposed to infections carried by the other children. ■ Caregivers cannot take care of a sick child. ■ Your child will not be in familiar surroundings or have many of his toys with him. ■ There is no formal training for caregivers. ■ Finding a good one is hit-and-miss, and the best ones tend to be oversubscribed.
NANNIES Nannies can either live with you or come to your home on a daily basis. Sometimes you may be able to share a nanny with another family, especially if you work part-time. Often you can use an agency to help you find a nanny.	■ If you have only one child, it is a one-to-one relationship. ■ Nannies can often take care of a very young baby or child. ■ Care in your own home means that it is less difficult when your child is unwell. ■ The hours are usually flexible—you don't have to wake a child early to get him ready or put him to bed late just to fit around your working pattern.	■ Nannies are expensive, with daily (live-out) nannies being the most expensive option of all. There will be additional expenses, such as food and outings. ■ Your privacy may be affected, especially with a live-in nanny. ■ Many qualified nannies will not do housework other than tidying up the child's bedroom and doing his laundry unless you arrange this at the outset. ■ There can be high turnover of nannies.
HOUSEKEEPER These are unqualified but tend to be more versatile than nannies. They do not usually have sole charge of the children, but they may if they are experienced.	■ The benefits are much the same as with a nanny, but they may not have sole charge. ■ In addition, a housekeeper may do significant amounts of housework. ■ An experienced housekeeper can be akin to having a good caregiver but in your own home.	■ Housekeepers vary a lot in experience and training. ■ They are usually more expensive than a caregiver and can cost nearly as much as a qualified nanny.
AU PAIRS Au pairs are usually young people of either sex, age 18–27, who come from abroad to study English for up to two years. Au pairs are not usually expected to work more than five hours a day, nor to have sole charge of children for all of this time.	■ They are often very willing to help with household chores as well as with the children. ■ In addition to her normal hours, an au pair is supposed to be available for babysitting for around two evenings a week (but this may cost you more). ■ They are especially good if you work part-time and have school-age children.	■ You won't be able to work full time without additional help. ■ Au pairs can be inexperienced in caring for very young children. ■ All the arrangements are usually done by phone and letter, so you will not have met the au pair before she arrives. ■ Au pairs can be very homesick. ■ They rarely stay for longer than a year. ■ Your privacy may be affected.

WHAT SHOULD I DO ?	WHAT SHOULD I ASK AT INTERVIEW ?
■ Visit during a session and be prepared to stay an hour or more to assess the place and the staff. Use your instincts to get a feel for the daycare center. ■ Look for signs that the youngsters (and the staff) are happy. There should be plenty of equipment, toys, and artwork, and the equipment should be in good condition. ■ Make sure there are sleep areas and that the kitchen and toilets are clean. ■ Check whether there is an outside play area. ■ Talk to other parents to find out if they're satisfied. ■ Make sure the daycare or childcare center is licensed.	■ Ask about the staff-to-child ratio, the age range cared for, and the experience and training of staff. Inquire about staff turnover. ■ Request any literature that is produced by the daycare center or nursery school. ■ Ask about the daily routine and what meals the children are given. ■ Ask whether your child will have an assigned caregiver, and what happens if that person is ill. ■ Ask how long other children have been there—I'd worry if the longest any child has stayed is a few months.
■ Visit her home and see where the children are cared for, and where they eat or take naps. Find out how she keeps the children busy, or whether she just sits them in front of the television. Look at and ask about safety measures, like smoke alarms, stair gates, and swimming pool covers. ■ Talk to other parents who have used her—you should request and take references. That means contacting them yourself. Don't rely on letters of reference alone. ■ Decide whether you like her or not. If she does not seem capable and reliable, look elsewhere. ■ Find out about hours and rates, and vacation arrangements; she may expect payment when you are away (or she is). ■ A formal contract is a good idea.	■ Ask how long she has been a caregiver, how many children she cares for, and what her attitude to discipline is. ■ Ask about the daily routine and whether she has to pick any children up from school. ■ Ask if there are any health problems in the family, whether she smokes, and if there are any pets. ■ Ask if she leaves the children with other people. Some carers think nothing of leaving their partner or an elder daughter in charge for hours while they go shopping. ■ Ask if she has ever had to deal with an emergency and whether she has a first-aid certificate. ■ Ask what happens if you're late picking up your child or if he is ill during the day.
■ Find out about the candidate's experience, training, and qualifications, including whether she has any children of her own. ■ Make sure that her needs fit in with yours in terms of living in or living out. Agree on pay and conditions, such as sick leave and vacation time. ■ Make sure you are clear about her intended hours and duties, including any housework. ■ Always ask for and take references. Ideally, speak to the referees yourself. Don't rely on letters of reference alone. ■ A formal contract is a good idea.	■ Ask about her last job and why she left it. ■ Talk about how she would fill your child's day, whether indoors or out, what she would do in bad weather, and whether she could cope with a sick child. ■ Let her meet your child and watch how she interacts with him. ■ Ask how she would feel if you were late home from work. ■ Find out her attitude to timekeeping. ■ Find out if she smokes or has health problems. ■ Ask whether she has a first-aid certificate and a driver's license.
■ Find out about the candidate's experience and training, and whether she has any children of her own. ■ Always ask for and take references. Ideally, speak to the referees yourself. Don't rely on letters of reference alone. ■ Discuss pay, hours, and duties. ■ A formal contract is a good idea.	■ Ask about her last job and why she left. ■ Talk about how she would fill your child's day, whether indoors or out, what she would do in bad weather, and whether she could cope with a sick child. ■ Ask if she has a first-aid certificate and a driver's license. ■ Ask how she would feel if you were late home from work. ■ Ask her attitude to timekeeping. ■ Ascertain whether she smokes or has health problems.
■ Find out basic information such as age, education to date, how long she has been studying English, what children she has cared for, any other jobs she has done, and how long she is planning to stay. ■ Always ask for and take references. Ideally, speak to the referees yourself. Don't rely on letters of reference alone. ■ Discuss pay and vacation arrangements. ■ Confirm what you have agreed in a formal letter.	■ You will usually only be able to interview on the telephone. ■ Find out about her skills—for example, whether she can cook or if she has a driver's license. ■ Ask whether she has any health problems, such as allergies, and ask whether she smokes. ■ Ask her about her childcare experience. ■ Ask her why she wants to come to your country and how much time she wants to spend studying while in your home.

FAMILY LIFE

FATHERS AT HOME

Q **IS IT BECOMING MORE ACCEPTABLE FOR A FATHER TO STAY AT HOME ?**

A Yes. Fathers now play a far more active role in parenting and attitudes have come a long way in just a couple of decades. It is now acceptable (and expected) for fathers to take an active part in feeding, changing, and bathing their babies, and generally taking care of their families. In fact, the nurturing role of men has evolved and developed, just as the physical work of many jobs has diminished. It is not surprising therefore that some fathers will choose to be the parent who stays at home while the mother goes out to work, if only because they realize what they are missing out on. However, it could simply be a practical issue of who has the better-paid job. In most societies, it is still more difficult for a father at home. The pressures are less than they once were, but they exist.

BEING A FULL-TIME FATHER
Staying at home with your child can be a very rewarding experience. You are in the privileged position of seeing your child grow and develop from an early age.

Q **WILL BEING A FULL-TIME FATHER AFFECT MY WORK PROSPECTS ?**

A This depends to some extent on your career, but it probably will affect your prospects, as it would for a woman. The harsh fact is that, however much society claims to value child-rearing or promotes flexible working, taking a few years off for parenting sets back a person's progress at work. As a man who chooses to stay at home, you may be viewed with suspicion by employers—or with a grudging respect. Believing that fathers should be more involved in child-rearing is different from making it easier for them to do so!

Q **HOW WILL IT AFFECT MY CHILD IF I'M THE MAIN CAREGIVER ?**

A Your child could potentially benefit. He will grow up with a less stereotyped view of the sexes and a wider vision of what men can achieve. On the minus side, there are a few relatively minor drawbacks. Some children get teased by comments such as "You have a funny Mommy!" Your partner, if you have one, may have to make more of an effort to show that she is a mother as well as the main wage-earner.

Q **WHAT OBSTACLES AM I LIKELY TO FACE AS A FATHER AT HOME ?**

A Any man will face problems if he is the main caregiver, especially since most practical aspects of childcare are geared to women. An obvious one is that baby changing and feeding facilities are usually situated in ladies' restrooms—men's toilets tend to be very poor places to deal with babies and young children. You may also encounter many more subtle pressures. For example, you may find it difficult to fit in with other stay-at-home parents, who are usually mothers. They may be wary of you, or uncertain how to relate to you, so they may not include you socially even if you are a lone parent. It will probably take you longer to build up a support network of other parents, and you may feel socially isolated at first. If you have recently given up work to stay at home, you will probably feel a bit lost, and your self-esteem may suffer slightly. You may also have to put up with a fair amount of teasing from your male friends.

Q WHAT OTHER ISSUES DO I NEED TO CONSIDER ?

A Running a home and keeping a family going means a lot more than simply watching the baby. You will also have to organize the household and find time for the chores (cleaning, shopping, laundry, ironing), or else enlist the help of someone else who can. The brunt of this should not fall on your partner when she gets home from work. In addition, you will not be able to disappear to a softball or hockey game, for example, as soon as your partner gets home—you will both have to plan your leisure activities carefully. The unexpected will crop up from time to time, so be prepared for emergencies.

Q WHERE CAN I MEET OTHER FATHERS WHO ARE ALSO THE MAIN CAREGIVER ?

A Ask your doctor or pediatrician, put an advertisement in a local newspaper, talk to other parents—the word will soon get around. If you are able to, make use of modern technology and search the Internet for useful contacts. If you are a single father, join a single parents' group. You will probably soon find out that you are not automatically excluded from mother-and-baby groups, even though a male presence is unusual. On the contrary, you may well be welcomed with open arms.

PARENT'S SURVIVAL GUIDE

MY FRIENDS MAKE JOKES ABOUT ME BEING THE MAIN CAREGIVER

There is bound to be a certain amount of teasing from your male friends, but just be yourself and be confident. You'll find that your good friends will respect your decision and support what you're doing. Perhaps they would make the same choice if their partner earned more, or if they had your courage.

How can I change my friends' attitudes?
Unfortunately, there is no magical solution. All you can do is let people see that being a full-time father hasn't changed you radically. Your deeds will speak for themselves, and a happy child will be the most powerful testament you could ask for. Your friends will eventually get used to the idea and tire of the jokes.

Q IS IT POSSIBLE TO FIT IN BETTER SOCIALLY ?

A You can try; just be aware that it may take some time. When mixing with other parents—for instance, at your child's daycare—don't be afraid to roll up your sleeves and help. You could also invite other parents and their children to your home, although if it's mostly mothers, you may find it more comfortable to do so when your partner or another female relative is there. You already have things in common with other parents, and in time you will become more accepted socially because people will get to know you. It also becomes less of an issue as more and more fathers elect to stay at home with their child.

Q HOW CAN WE STILL FUNCTION AS A COUPLE ?

A This is more difficult. Parents are good at putting their children first, but have little time or energy left for each other. Make time for each other where you can. Reassure your partner that you still love her. A reassuring touch or kind gesture can go a long way. If there's no time for sex, make sure you have a hug every day—nonsexual touching has benefits too. Do things together that require little energy, like sharing a candlelit dinner at home (it could even be a carry out meal) or watching a movie. Schedule some time together, making an appointment if necessary. Meet when your child is at daycare—some couples do this and pretend to be lovers on an illicit rendezvous. Every so often, try to have a weekend together away from home without your child. You'll find that your own parents or friends are aware of this need and will offer to care for your child while you go away for a night.

Q HOW CAN I FIND TIME TO RELAX ON MY OWN ?

A It is hard. Instead of becoming frantic with all the things you have to do, try to make time for yourself. Exercise is important for your emotional as well as your physical health. If your child goes to daycare or nursery school, you may be able to find an hour or so to work out at the gym; some gyms offer babysitting for younger children. Fathers who stay at home after several years of full-time work often say they find being at home very stressful. One reason is that, when you have a young child, you have to respond to his needs and are not always in control in the same way that you once were in the office.

SIBLINGS

Q IS THERE AN IDEAL WAY TO SPACE SIBLINGS ?

A When to have another baby depends on many factors, such as the temperament and health of the first child, the relationship between you and your partner, and practical considerations such as your age and money. On the whole, I think two to three years is a good interval—long enough for a parent to have emerged from caring for a baby, but still short enough for the children to play together as they grow up. However, people are increasingly choosing to start their families later in life and may therefore decide, on a practical and biological level, to have their children fairly close together. Although this may mean caring for two or more very young children at the same time, older parents may feel that they cannot afford to wait. For many parents, spacing children cannot be planned and depends on how easily you conceive. Although you may conceive quickly if you did so last time, there's no guarantee that history will repeat itself. As a rough guide, anyone under 30 should give themselves at least six months to get pregnant; those over 30 may need slightly longer.

Q WHAT'S THE IDEAL NUMBER OF CHILDREN ?

A There's no one answer that suits every family. You may aspire to the supposed ideal of two children, while other parents want three or more, especially if they grew up in a large household themselves. Many children who are closely spaced can form strong bonds, but may also fight a lot and be very hard work. An only child tends to be lonely, but this isn't always so, and increasingly, parents are opting to have only one baby.

Q DOES POSITION IN A FAMILY HAVE AN EFFECT ON CHILDREN ?

A First-born children tend to be high achievers and perhaps more highly strung than subsequent children, reflecting their parents' anxieties and expectations. Second-born children don't routinely have any particular characteristics, but they may be less conformist. Third-born children are possibly more relaxed but can be naughtier and take more risks. However, these are only rough guides. It's unrealistic to expect your child to have exactly these characteristics.

TELLING YOUR CHILD ABOUT A PREGNANCY

You may be bursting to share the good news, but a youngster who's about to be "replaced" by a baby, as he sees it, may be less than thrilled.

■ DO tell your child about the pregnancy, and definitely break the news before he hears about it from someone else.
■ DO both tell him you love him.
■ DO make him feel special.
■ DO help him become more independent in feeding, using the toilet, and other daily needs.
■ DO organize things for the labor and birth. A trustworthy person he knows will need to take care of him, and he'll have to know what the arrangement is well in advance of that time.

■ DON'T tell him too soon—nine months is an eternity to a young child. The younger your child, the less likely he is to notice your pregnancy, so the longer you can wait.

■ DON'T tell him you're having another baby to please him, for him to play with, or because he's such a good boy. It's not true, and he'll only blame himself if things go wrong.
■ DON'T tell him he needs to be big and help you with the new baby. Being big may be the last thing on his mind—when the baby is born, he will probably prefer to be small again.
■ DON'T plan to toilet-train him, start him in daycare, swap bedrooms, or move him from his crib just before the baby arrives. He will have enough changes to cope with after the birth.
■ DON'T burden him with the side effects of pregnancy or how tired you are. He'll be upset for you, may feel guilty, and could be more likely to resent the new baby.

PARENT'S SURVIVAL GUIDE

I'M NOT SURE HOW TO COPE WITH SIBLING RIVALRY

Some children have no problems accepting another sibling into the family. However, a toddler may throw things, poke the baby's face, take away her rattle, or even tip the carriage over. He may also refuse to eat, have sleep problems, wet the bed, and indulge in tantrums or other forms of attention-seeking behavior. If all is well in the first few days and weeks, don't assume you have escaped sibling rivalry—the symptoms can arise any time in the first six months after the birth. Try the following:

■ give your older child plenty of attention
■ make him feel grown-up—for instance, by letting him stay up late; he needs the privileges rather than the responsibilities of being older

■ don't keep telling him you're too busy now
■ let him visit you and the new baby in the hospital
■ point out how helpless the baby is compared with him—let him help you if he wants to, or watch as you change the baby's diaper or feed her
■ try not to hold the baby all the time—your other child needs you, and putting the baby down for a rest will give you more time as well as encourage the baby to go to sleep
■ encourage him to get to know the baby—he'll feel special once he gets a few smiles from his sister
■ give him a present from the baby
■ don't leave him alone with the baby
■ don't expect him to love the new arrival—he will eventually, but he can't love to order.

Q HOW CAN I GET MY CHILD TO HELP OUT WITH THE NEW BABY?

A You may be able to encourage a four- or five-year-old (especially a girl) to help with baby-related chores, but you should allow your child to help, not expect it or coerce him. If it happens, be suitably impressed and grateful. It's unrealistic to expect your child to grow up suddenly because the baby has arrived. Most children just don't have the maturity. It's also positively dangerous to leave a child to watch over a young baby.

Q WILL MY CHILD BECOME JEALOUS OF THE NEW BABY?

A Probably. Even if you do your best, you will be busier and more tired with a new baby to care for and will have less time for your first child. There'll be times when a young child may want you and he can't have you. Boys tend to show more jealousy than girls at this stage. The change in their routine may involve a little ill-feeling along the way. This is only natural, so expect a bit of an upheaval on and off, but don't let it paralyze family life.

Q CAN A STEPCHILD EVER HAVE A CLOSE BOND WITH THE NEW BABY?

A Yes. It's less a question of blood ties and more a matter of shared experience. If a stepchild lives with you as part of the family, it's entirely possible for him to be close to the new baby. However, to ensure that he feels included, involve him in the fun aspects of caring for a baby. If, on the other hand, your stepchild doesn't live with you, it will be harder and you may find there's little to bind the children. Don't push the sibling connection. The baby is only a half-sibling to your stepchild and he may not think of her as his sister.

A NEW FAMILY MEMBER
Encourage your child to touch the new baby and talk to him. She will soon enjoy being the big sister.

FAMILY LIFE

SEPARATION AND DIVORCE

Q IS IT BETTER TO STAY TOGETHER FOR OUR CHILD'S SAKE ?

A No. Obviously, it would be stupid as well as cruel to separate on a whim, but if there are genuine reasons for the partnership breakup, then I do not believe you can patch things up to avoid hurting the children. It is better to have two happier parents living apart than to live in a home where there is bitter conflict or violence. You will have to balance the costs, both emotional and financial, to every member of the family against the possible benefits of separation. This is hard, since you must do it at a time when you may be feeling vulnerable and unsure. If there are no potential benefits of separation, then stay together!

Q HOW IS SEPARATION LIKELY TO AFFECT MY CHILD ?

A Separation is a form of bereavement and affects children profoundly. Your child is likely to be shocked by the news that you will separate, even if you and your partner have obviously been getting along badly for some time. The separation itself can bring a lot of insecurity. After all, if Mommy and Daddy fell out of love with each other, what's to stop them falling out of love with their child? A child may blame himself for the breakup. He may also worry about practicalities such as where he will live and who will keep the dog. After the separation, you may have worries about money and other material possessions. These additional concerns may be absorbed by your child, who may not be able to understand that suddenly some of life's treats, such as regular vacations, have to be sacrificed.

Q HOW CAN I PROTECT MY CHILD FROM CONFLICT ?

A Have your disagreements well away from your child—even a young child can understand the gist of what you are saying—and keep your discussions nonviolent and low-key. Don't be critical about your partner to your child and don't forbid your partner to see your child. Never lash out at the child, even verbally. Always put your child's welfare first and ask yourself at every step of the separation or divorce if you are doing things in ฟy that is best for him.

Q CAN I MAKE SEPARATION EASIER FOR MY CHILD ?

A Yes. Make sure your child knows you still love him and that you are separating from each other, not from him. The ideal is for both parents to carry on as a parenting team. You should not treat your child as a messenger or go-between. Encouraging children to take sides is one of the worst things you can do. Unfortunately, many separating parents do just that. Tell your child in good time about the impending separation, and reassure him on the practical front. He needs to know he can still see Daddy or Mommy often. You may also need to spell out that everything won't change and he can still go the the same daycare and play with his friends. Continuing with the same routine will comfort you both. Tell the grandparents. They are usually well placed to support your child and give ongoing love. Expect your child to be angry, upset, or confused. Do not try to convince him it will be better. To him, it probably won't be, but it should be survivable. You may find that he is more relaxed after the separation.

Q SHOULD WE HIDE OUR DISTRESS FROM OUR CHILD ?

A It's fine for a child to know that you're both sad, but in my opinion he shouldn't see you cry. It is just too upsetting for young children. You have to be his parent, not the other way around, and he is in no position to comfort you however much you may need it.

Q WHAT CAN I DO TO CONVINCE MY CHILD I LOVE HIM ?

A Reassure him often with words and actions. A child whose parents are separating is often insecure, and with good reason. He may need to be specifically told you will always love him—it may help him to hear that you love him even when he is naughty. Don't try to outdo your ex-partner with gifts for your child; it's not material things that matter most right now. I also think it's unwise to give a child the impression that you and your partner never loved each other (even if it's true). If you didn't care for each other in the past, it puts across confusing messages about his existence and about relationships in general.

TELLING YOUR CHILD ABOUT SEPARATION OR DIVORCE

This is likely to be one of the most difficult things you'll ever have to tell your child, and knowing how to approach it can make all the difference.

When should I tell my child?

Tell your child in good time, well ahead of the separation but soon after you have made some arrangements. He will not benefit from a lot of uncertainties. Choose a time when you're not rushing out or busy in the house—you will need to give him your undivided attention. Don't leave it too late in the evening, either. Your child won't feel like sleeping just after you break the news because he will probably be confused and upset.

Should I speak to my child with my partner?

Yes. It's preferable to tell him together and give the same information. If both of you are there, he is more likely to realize that you both love him and that he is not losing a parent. However, if this isn't possible, make sure your partner finds time to talk to your child soon. With children of different ages, try to see each separately, but with your partner.

What should I tell my child?

Your exact words depend on how old your child is. Decide what to say before you start. In general, you need only say you have not being getting along well, and that you have decided to separate. You can say more later, when your child has gotten over the initial shock.

DOs

- Tell your child you will always love him.
- Give him a big hug.
- Tell your child you will both still be his parents.
- Reassure your child about where he will live.
- Explain the fate of any family pets.

DON'Ts

- Insult each other or argue in front of your child.
- Go into too many details yet.
- Say choosing your partner was a mistake.
- Say anything to prejudice your child against your partner.
- Say that you love him more than his Daddy does (or the other way around).
- Ask him to take sides.

Q THE SEPARATION IS TAKING ITS TOLL ON ME. WHAT CAN I DO?

A Take care of yourself so that you can cope with the stresses you and your child are facing. You're likely to be busier than before and may be trying to manage on a smaller income. Eat well, take time to exercise and, lest you forget, have fun. Keep in touch with friends—you need their support more than ever. If you start to feel that you arc having difficulty coping on your own, it may be a good idea to talk to your doctor.

Q MY EX-PARTNER AND I GIVE OUR CHILD DIFFERENT MESSAGES. WHAT CAN I DO?

A It's all right for you to differ on some things, but you should come to agreements on the big issues. Young children need consistency and security. You can scc why it happens, of course. You and your partner probably have very different points of view, and sometimes trying to win over a child comes into it, too. It's a good idea to meet your ex-partner regularly, without your child present, to find a common approach to matters like discipline, education, and money.

Q SHOULD I KEEP IN TOUCH WITH FORMER IN-LAWS?

A Yes, if you can, if only for your children. Grandparents are important to a child, so try to keep the relationship going. Sadly, grandparents can and do take sides, and if they are your in-laws they will probably sympathize more with your ex-partner. Their disappointment at the separation is understandable because they have lost somcthing too, but this may be unhelpful for your child. You may need to accompany your child when he meets his grandparents to be sure that they're not saying things that could lead to misunderstandings.

Q IS THERE ANYONE ELSE WHO CAN HELP?

A You may find it very helpful to talk to your doctor or someone from your place of worship. Joining a single parent group can also give you support and information. If you are worried that your child is not dealing very well with the situation, you may want to involve his teacher at nursery school or daycare, or a counselor experienced in helping children.

SINGLE PARENTS

Q DOESN'T A CHILD REALLY NEED TWO PARENTS ?

A Parenting is hard work, and so is growing up. That's why the ideal is two parents who can help share the responsibilities, but a child can develop and thrive with just one. It's better to have one loving parent than two less committed ones, so a single parent shouldn't feel guilty. In fact, most single parents give their best despite the odds.

Q MY CHILD ASKS WHY HE DOESN'T HAVE TWO PARENTS. WHAT SHOULD I SAY ?

A It depends on your situation and his level of understanding. You can give an older child more detail than a younger one. One day your child will need to know, but to begin with, it may be enough just to explain that families don't always have two parents. To avoid misunderstandings, it can be helpful to brief relatives and friends about what they should and should not talk about in your child's presence.

Q HOW CAN I HELP MY CHILD FEEL SECURE ?

A Provide as stable and secure a home as you can. Protect your child from any upheavals by being sure of yourself. Make it easy for him to talk about (and see) his absent parent and try not to be judgmental even if the relationship ended badly. The relationship between yourself and your ex-partner will probably be very important to your child, especially if you separated recently. Act confident even if you don't feel that way—you can succeed as a single parent. It is difficult, of course, but your sense of achievement at raising your child on your own will be all the greater.

Q WHERE WILL MY CHILD FIND A ROLE MODEL OF THE OPPOSITE GENDER ?

A Hopefully, your ex-partner will still fulfill the role. In addition, there are bound to be people in your life, whether they are relatives or friends, who can fulfill the role. It's really as a schoolchild and adolescent that a boy most needs a father-figure, and a girl most needs a mother. By this time you will hopefully have built up a network of people who can help. Your child will also have ⋯olteachers to guide him.

Q WHO WILL CARE FOR MY CHILD IF SOMETHING HAPPENS TO ME ?

A You have to make provision with someone you trust. Talk it over with close friends and family, or, if you would rather, approach your doctor or social service agency. Another thing you must do as a single parent is make a will.

Q WHAT'S THE HARDEST THING ABOUT BEING A SINGLE PARENT ?

A Money and time may be in short supply. You will also have to provide your child with love and discipline and face any problems without the benefit of another adult to back you up. However, I think the hardest thing is to allow your child to grow up. All parents have this to deal with, but the closeness and exclusivity of the relationship when you're a single parent makes it specially hard, for example, to give a youngster the freedom to stay with friends or learn to cross the street.

Q I FEEL GUILTY ALL THE TIME. HOW CAN I HANDLE THIS ?

A At one time, single-parent households were the exception, but they are now common in most societies. Your child is much less likely to stand out than he would have, say, 20 years ago, so there is no need to feel guilty, especially if you do your best for your child. In fact, for some single parents the difficulty will be that they do too much for the child at the expense of their own comforts. I suggest you put your child first so that he is as happy and secure as possible, but don't forget that you should come a close second.

Q HOW CAN I COPE FINANCIALLY ON MY OWN ?

A Poverty is something many single parents face. Unfortunately, immediate financial concerns can make it harder to plan for your future by, for example, going back to college. You can control your spending by eliminating any unnecessary expenses, and be sure to claim all the benefits and tax breaks you are allowed. To keep out of debt, you will need to be well organized. Don't enter into any agreement to make regular payments of any kind unless you're absolutely sure that you can meet the payments.

Q HOW WILL MY CHILD REACT WHEN I START DATING AGAIN?

A Your child may not mind, especially if he is used to your going out. However, be prepared for him to be upset, bewildered, or jealous. Always reassure him, and keep your promises about when you'll be back. Handling a social life is bound to be a challenge, but that's no reason to avoid it.

Q IS IT A GOOD IDEA TO FIND ANOTHER PARTNER TO GIVE MY CHILD STABILITY?

A No. Rushing into another relationship too soon can prove disastrous. Only do this when *you* are completely ready. It's difficult for someone to become a substitute father or mother, and it's unfair to have those expectations. If you enter a second relationship for the wrong reasons, it may lead to difficulties later.

Q HOW CAN I GET A BREAK AS A SINGLE PARENT?

A One option is to team up with another single parent and babysit for each other. You could also go on outings with her and all your children, which can make the practicalities easier. If you don't know any other single-parent families, join a single parents' group. Grandparents who live nearby are another obvious source of help.

Q WHAT KIND OF VACATION IS BEST FOR ME AND MY CHILD?

A Camping vacations are more affordable and can work well, especially if you go with friends. Activity vacations can be excellent for single-parent families, since there are things for young children to do, often under the supervision of trained staff, while you unwind.

PARENT'S SURVIVAL GUIDE

I'M WORRIED ABOUT KEEPING IN TOUCH WITH MY EX-PARTNER

Contact with an absent parent is very important to your child as he grows up, even if it doesn't seem so now.

How much contact should my child have with my ex-partner?
No one answer is right for every family. However, the child should usually have regular, frequent contact from the start, and enough of it to ensure that both parents have an influence on his upbringing. This can be difficult to arrange because you and your ex-partner may not agree on timing of contact, and may also find it hard to exchange views. Whatever you do, don't involve the child in making the decision, or involve him in any haggling that may take place.

My ex-partner doesn't want to see our child. What can I do?
Sometimes an ex-partner finds it too painful. Some parents also think that cutting off contact will help a child "forget" and get over the separation more easily. It doesn't. All you can do is impress on your ex-partner how important it is for both parents to show they care for the child, even if they no longer care for each other. Leave avenues of contact open unless there are strong reasons not to (such as violence toward the child).

My child doesn't want to see his other parent. How can I handle this?
Children sometimes find it stressful to see the absent parent and many get nervous beforehand. I think you should still try to arrange meetings, but keep them short and keep the location neutral. You could meet somewhere away from either home, especially if it's somewhere your child likes, such as a playground, and stay during the visit. Although your child may initially be upset at seeing his other parent, I still think it's worth it in the long run and that he may eventually change his mind.

My child says he'd rather live with his other parent. What should I do?
You should normally do nothing in the first instance. A young child who is hurt or angry—not even necessarily with you—may say this as a way of getting attention or to make you feel as hurt as he is. Only act on statements like these if your child is old enough to know what he wants, and if you have explored other possibilities, like changing the pattern of visits. Many children who decide to live with the other parent are doomed to bitter disappointment, especially if, as sometimes happens, the other parent does not agree to the change.

DEATH AND BEREAVEMENT

Q HOW OLD DOES A CHILD HAVE TO BE TO UNDERSTAND DEATH?

A There's no precise age, because it depends on what experiences each family has had, but most people underestimate how much children can understand. Even though young children may not realize that death is permanent, by the age of three they can begin to understand the concept. The important point for you to stress is that death is forever and is therefore different from "going away." Be matter-of-fact when talking to your child about death and avoid euphemisms such as "gone to heaven" and "fallen asleep." Of course you'll be upset, but don't feel you can't let your child see you cry. However, he won't be able to make sense of what you are trying to explain to him if you're too distraught. He may also associate death with pain or suffering.

Q SHOULD YOUNG CHILDREN EVER GO TO FUNERALS?

A Funerals are an opportunity to say goodbye. I think even a young child should attend if he had a close relationship with the person concerned. A useful guide is that the closer the child's bond with the deceased relative, the more closely he should be involved after death, but you must also be guided by your feelings and what's normal in your culture. Also, if your child attends the funeral, he is less likely to wonder what happens after death—reality is often easier to cope with than the imagined. Raw, uncontrolled emotion, however, is unhelpful for children; they should usually be shielded from sights like open caskets and from relatives who are unable to control their grief.

Q IS IT WRONG FOR ME TO SHOW MY EMOTIONS?

A No, it isn't. Death is a momentous event, and if it happens to a close family member, then your child should see it as very serious and important to you. However, there is a difference between being sad or upset and being totally incapacitated by grief. Seeing you cry constantly could be unhelpful for your child. Amid the tears, you should try to find opportunities to talk with pleasure of the good memories you both have of your loved one.

IF A PET DIES

Although the loss of a beloved pet can be an emotional time for a child, it can also help him understand death.

How can I help my child overcome the death of our pet?
Explain to your child that animals don't live as long as people and that their death is normal. You need to mark the animal's life and its death; talk about pleasant memories so you can both go on having something to be happy about. It may be appropriate to have a burial for your pet and mark the spot with a stone or post. Your child can participate in this. I know several young children who pick flowers to place on a dog or cat's grave. Far from being morbid, this simple act seems to bring comfort. If the animal was actually put to sleep by a vet, I think it's best to avoid mentioning it.

Is it best to get another pet immediately?
No. If your child is very young and won't notice the difference, chances are he won't mind if it's no longer there. If he's old enough to care, wait a while. Another pet too soon may fail to live up to expectations. It's hard to judge what the right timing is, but the younger the child, the shorter it can be.

Q HOW CAN OUR CHILD COPE WITH A MISCARRIAGE OR A STILLBIRTH?

A A young child may not need to know anything about a miscarriage, especially if it occurred in the very early stages of pregnancy. If he is older, you could explain that something went wrong before it turned into a baby. A stillbirth is usually more difficult to handle because your child will have anticipated a little brother or sister. In addition, you will be trying to come to terms with your own grief. I think it's best to tell him what happened and agree that the loss of the new baby is very sad. Do not try to minimize what happened, but avoid discussing what might have been had the baby lived.

Q MY PARENT IS VERY ILL AND MIGHT DIE. WHAT SHOULD I TELL MY CHILD ?

A This depends on the age of your child, but most children understand a lot more than adults think. Don't tell him that Grandpa is on a business trip if he's in the hospital. You don't have to mention the diagnosis, but I think it's wise to prepare your child by telling him his grandparent is very ill and that he may not get better. This may lead your child to say something like, "You don't look dead yet, Grandpa," but fortunately these embarrassing remarks are rare. You do have to make time for your child, however hard it is for you. You may well be tired and upset as well as busy with practicalities like hospital visiting, caring for your elderly parent, or supporting your other parent, but your child still has needs. He will cope less well with the situation if you are preoccupied or intolerant of his questions.

HELPING YOUR CHILD DEAL WITH DEATH
Make sure that you choose a quiet time to tell your child about a relative's illness and that you give her your undivided attention. She may not fully understand, but she will be better prepared to deal with the death.

PARENT'S SURVIVAL GUIDE

I DON'T KNOW HOW TO HELP MY CHILD COPE WITH HIS FATHER'S DEATH

Children can and do survive the death of a parent, but it is the most difficult loss for a child, and it can be hard for you to help him because you are grieving yourself. Your child may feel guilty about having been naughty, and may even believe he has caused the death. He may also be anxious about you, the surviving parent. He needs reassurance about your own state of health and that you still love him, however sad you are. Allow him to grieve, too, and to talk about the dead parent.

How can I help my child?
Make sure you spend plenty of time with your child and surround him with as much stability as you can. Now is not the time to move, change school or daycare, employ a new caregiver, or even move your child from a crib to a big bed. Allow your child to continue with his usual activities, like attending school and inviting his friends to your home. Enlist the help of friends and relatives. They too may be grieving, but they may still welcome the chance to help your child. Try to cover up any physical symptoms you might have. Get medical help, of course, but don't worry your child unnecessarily—he may fear losing you, too.

My child doesn't seem to have reacted to the death yet. What's the usual time lapse?
There's no fixed time. It can sometimes take weeks for a child to show obvious signs of grief. This does not mean your child is unaffected. He may initially be in shock, or he may have difficulty in expressing his feelings. The usual stages of grief for both adults and children are first numbness or shock, followed by denial, then yearning, sadness or depression, anger or guilt, and finally acceptance. The time taken to go through each stage varies immensely.

What can I do if my child's behavior becomes difficult?
This is normal. In fact, it would be surprising if your child lost a parent and his behavior did not alter at all. A child's grief may show itself in many different ways, especially since the feelings of loss are unfamiliar and he is not able to cope with them. Your child may regress around this time and start wetting the bed again or sleeping badly, or his behavior may become unreasonable. Most importantly, try to understand what he is going through even if your own grief is intolerable. Get expert help from a bereavement counselor—your doctor can put you in touch with a specialist.

SAFETY IN THE HOME

Q WHAT'S THE BEST WAY TO KEEP MY CHILD SAFE ?

A Be aware of what your baby or child can do at each stage of development and stay at least one step ahead of him. For example, the first time your baby manages to roll over, he could be rolling off your bed.

Q HOW CLOSELY DO I NEED TO SUPERVISE MY CHILD ?

A A baby under a year old needs constant supervision while awake. This means taking him from room to room with you—even to the bathroom. A toddler still needs to be watched closely. If you must leave your toddler on his own for a moment, make sure the room is as safe as it can be, but remember, no room is totally toddler-proof. Your toddler is almost insatiably curious, to the point of being a danger to himself—few toddlers are sedate and sensible.

Q MY PARTNER IS LESS AWARE OF DANGERS THAN I AM. WHAT CAN I DO ?

A You have to talk about this together. Saying nothing may upset your partner less, but your child's well-being is at risk. You should also tell anyone who cares for your child, whether it is a relative or a nanny, about your safety practices.

Q WHAT SAFETY PRECAUTIONS SHOULD I TAKE IN MY HOME ?

A The chart opposite details specific child safety precautions you can take for each room of the house. There are also general principles you should follow that apply to all rooms. For example, make sure that furniture has no sharp edges; keep all electric outlets covered when not in use and make sure there are no electric cords hanging down from surfaces; as soon as your child is old enough, teach him about potential dangers, such as open fireplaces and hot irons.

HOW CAN I ENSURE THAT MY CHILD IS SAFE WITH A PET ?

For many people, the family is not complete without a pet. Caring for an animal can give a great deal of pleasure as well as teach your child a lot. If you have a pet, or are planning to get one, follow the advice below to make conditions as safe as possible.

Should my child be a certain age before I get a pet?

I wouldn't advise getting one too soon after the birth of a baby because you won't be able to give the animal the attention it needs. Of course, this depends on the type of pet—for example, a fish is less demanding than a dog!

Can a furry pet cause allergies?

Yes. It is not clear why allergies occur, but many experts believe that if they run in your family you should not get a furry animal like a cat, dog, or rabbit until your child is three years old. Being exposed to fur at a young age may increase the risk of developing allergies such as asthma and eczema.

Is a dog likely to harm a new baby or a young child?

This could happen. The way in which dogs behave toward young children varies. Some established pets (either dogs or cats) can show behavior akin to sibling rivalry when a new baby arrives in the household. Be sensitive and introduce your pet and the baby to each other gently. Don't leave your child alone in a room with the dog (even when your child is much older)—the most placid dog can snap at a child who pulls his tail or teases him.

Is it safe for a cat to be in the same room with a baby?

If your cat has a nice disposition, it is probably safe, as long as the cat is not able to get into your baby's crib while he is asleep. Unless you are sure this won't happen, keep an eye on the situation. It is doubtful whether cats can really suck the breath from babies as they are rumored to do, but they can lie in the crib or carriage and cause overheating and allergies, as well as pass on fleas or infections.

SAFETY TIPS

LOCATION	WHAT TO DO
THROUGHOUT YOUR HOME	■ Fit child-proof latches onto drawers and cabinets before your child is active. ■ Put covers over any electric outlets that are not in use. ■ Have a smoke alarm installed on every floor of your home. ■ Avoid long dangling cords, especially on lamps and on the iron. ■ Put matches and plastic bags out of your child's reach. ■ Household chemicals should always be locked up out of your child's reach and should be stored in their original containers, ideally with child-resistant tops. ■ Install window safety devices such as window guards to protect against falls. ■ Place any breakable items out of your child's reach. ■ Avoid sharp-edged furniture.
KITCHEN	■ Always stay with your child while he is eating in case he chokes. ■ Keep knives and other sharp objects in a drawer with a child lock or out of his reach. ■ Avoid tablecloths and mats—by pulling on the tablecloth, your child could bring hot food or sharp objects down on top of himself. ■ Keep mugs of hot drinks or hot pans out of your child's reach and make sure saucepan handles don't stick out over the side of the stove. Use the back burners if possible. ■ Put a guard, if available, over the knobs on the stove. ■ Keep the kitchen floor clean and mop up any spills right away. ■ Turn off electrical items, including the dishwasher and washing machine. ■ Keep the iron and ironing board out of your child's reach. ■ Keep any pet food bowls out of your child's reach. ■ Get a fire extinguisher for the kitchen.
HALL AND STAIRS	■ Never leave anything lying on the stairs. ■ Before your child is mobile, fit safety gates at the top and the bottom of the stairs. ■ If the stairs are carpeted, make sure that the carpet is well fitted and that there are no loose or frayed pieces of carpet that you or your child could trip over. ■ Make sure that the banisters are secure. ■ The spaces between the banister rails should be no more than 4 in (10 cm) to keep your child from falling through them or getting his head or a limb stuck. ■ Ensure that the front door is childproof so that your child cannot run into the street.
BATHROOM	■ Never leave your child alone in the bathtub. ■ When running a bath for your child, pour cold water in first, then add hot water. ■ Put a nonslip mat in the bathtub. ■ Keep medicines locked up or out of your child's reach. ■ Keep the toilet lid closed. ■ Cover the hot faucet with a washcloth or towel while your child is in the bathtub.
BEDROOM	■ Never leave your baby unattended on a changing table. ■ A crib should comply with federal safety regulations. ■ Don't put toys with strings that are longer than 1 ft (30 cm) in his crib. ■ Always make sure the crib sides are up when your baby is in his crib. ■ Once your child can sit up, put the mattress height down to its lowest level.
LIVING ROOM	■ If you have a fireplace, use a sturdy fire screen that cannot be tipped over or easily moved. ■ Don't put anything that is hot or heavy on a low table or shelf. ■ Make sure that shelves are secure. ■ Keep any alcohol, cigarettes, lighters, or matches out of your child's reach. ■ Patio doors should be made of shatterproof glass. ■ Remove any poisonous houseplants.
PLAY AREAS	■ Separate toys for older children and toys for younger children. ■ Don't leave toys lying around on the floor, and throw away any that are broken. ■ Don't leave favorite toys out of your child's reach where he may be tempted to climb up and get them. ■ If you buy a playpen, make sure it complies with federal safety regulations.

BABY SAFETY

Q **HOW CAN I MAKE SURE MY BABY IS SAFE WHILE HE IS ASLEEP?**

A For the first few months, your baby should sleep on his back in the same room with you, and up to six months old, follow the guidelines for reducing the risk of SIDS (see p. 46). Make sure his crib is safe. To prevent overheating, do not make the bed too tightly. During the first year, avoid fluffy bedding such as comforters and pillows. Do not use crib bumpers, place the crib next to a radiator or fireplace, or let your baby lie in direct sunlight. If painting the crib, use nontoxic paints and varnish.

Q **IS IT A GOOD IDEA TO BUY A PLAYPEN FOR MY CHILD?**

A A playpen can be a good place for him to enjoy himself safely from when he's about three months until he's able to climb out! Make sure the playpen conforms to recognized safety standards. Even though the playpen is relatively safe, do not leave him unsupervised in it for any length of time.

Q **HOW CAN I MAKE SURE THAT HE IS SAFE ONCE HE STARTS TO CRAWL?**

A Think ahead—your baby will be on the move before he is a year old, so now is the time to try to see things from his perspective. Put covers over electrical outlets, and make sure that low-level glass panes are made of shatterproof glass or covered with safety film. Remove dangerous or breakable objects and lock up chemicals and medicines. Watch out for houseplants, some of which are toxic. Reduce the chances of your child being burned or scalded—watch where you put down your hot drink, and do not iron near your baby; either wait until he falls asleep, or put him in a playpen.

Q **HOW CAN I MAKE THE STAIRS SAFE FOR MY CHILD?**

A Until he is competent at going up and down the stairs on his own, use safety gates at both top and bottom. Once he is crawling, teach him to come down the stairs backward. Make sure the banisters are safe—the spaces between bars should be no more than 4 in (10 cm); otherwise, a youngster may poke his head between them and get stuck. If your banisters have horizontal bars instead of vertical posts, consider changing these or boarding them in. Don't put loose rugs near stairs.

CHOOSING SAFE TOYS

Although seemingly harmless, there are potential hazards in the simplest of toys. Follow the guidelines below to ensure that your child plays safely.

What should I look for when choosing toys and equipment for my child?
Always choose toys and equipment that meet safety standards—if the label or package does not state this, then don't buy the toy. Toys are also allocated age ranges, so check that a toy is suitable—if in doubt, don't buy it. Avoid second-hand toys that may have loose parts. If buying a large item, such as a playpen, look for good design and sturdy construction. Remove or securely sew on any loose tags or ribbons on teddy bears or soft toys that he might choke on. Avoid giving your child cheap toys, especially if the toy was bought in a country where toy-safety standards are lower. Once a toy is broken or worn out, throw it away.

Check toys for the approved safety mark

SAFE PLAY
Make sure that soft toys are safe for your child to play with by removing any ribbons or labels that he may choke on.

Q MY BABY CAN STAND. HOW CAN I PREVENT HIM FROM HURTING HIMSELF ?

A Make sure he can't reach anything dangerous. You may not be able to redecorate and refurnish all of your home to make it completely safe, but you can move certain items to avoid accidents. For example, place heavy table lamps out of his reach and remove tablecloths rather than run the risk of him pulling them onto himself. Everything that could be used as a support probably will be, so all your furnishings must be robust and safe—small, wobbly tables are dangerous and so are slim, elegant bookshelves that can easily topple over under a baby's weight.

Q I'VE HEARD BABY-WALKERS CAN BE DANGEROUS. IS THIS TRUE ?

A Yes. Although a baby-walker can be fun for your baby for a short period of time, they can also be extremely dangerous—more accidents occur with these than with any other single item of baby equipment. Sitting in one, your baby will move faster than he can cope with, which can be lethal near stairs because your youngster may fall headfirst down them. Baby-walkers can also topple over on flat surfaces. Many parents think a baby-walker will help teach a baby to walk, but this is not the case. In a walker, your baby's hips are at the wrong angle for walking, and one leg may dip down lower than the other. Furthermore, a walker does not teach the crucial art of standing, since your baby sits in it. If anything, using a walker delays walking independently. If you do have one, limit the amount of time he spends in it and never let your child use it unsupervised.

Q HOW CAN I ENSURE THAT THE KITCHEN IS A SAFE PLACE FOR MY BABY ?

A Lock up household cleaning products and other chemicals, and any sharp or dangerous implements, and keep plastic bags out of his reach. Turn pan handles to the back of the stove when in use, and use the back burners if possible. Keep your baby away from the oven—even the outside of the door can become dangerously hot. Avoid trailing electrical cords—coiled cords are safer than straight ones because your baby is less likely to grab them. The best way to keep your baby safe in the kitchen is never to leave him unsupervised. Ideally, while you are cooking, your baby should be in his highchair eating or playing—or put a gate across the kitchen doorway so that you can talk to each other and still keep him safe.

PARENT'S SURVIVAL GUIDE

I WORRY THAT OTHER PEOPLE'S HOUSES ARE UNSAFE

Keeping your concern in perspective
Although it's natural to feel anxious about your baby's safety when you are visiting someone else's home, try not to let anxiety ruin your visit. Do keep a close eye on proceedings, but don't ruin your own and everyone else's enjoyment by being overly protective.

Keeping an eye on your baby
When you are visiting someone else's home, you shouldn't worry unnecessarily, but you do need to watch over your baby more closely than usual. For example, Grandma may have left hot coffee on the edge of the table, or she may have left medication within your child's reach—even iron tablets can make a baby seriously ill. Even if a container has a child-resistant top, this doesn't mean that it is totally childproof, so beware of any hazards.

Other people's safety awareness
If you leave your baby with a relative or friend, bear in mind that they may have slower reflexes or be out of practice at childcare. If you are not happy that they are sufficiently safety-aware, don't leave your child alone with them.

Q WHAT SAFETY PRECAUTIONS SHOULD I TAKE IN THE BATHROOM ?

A Never leave your baby unattended in the bath, even when he is can sit up on his own; ignore the doorbell and turn on the telephone answering machine. Until your baby can sit up on his own, constantly support his head and back while he is in the bath. Make sure you have everything you need before he gets into the bath so that you do not have to leave him alone or unsupported for a moment. Run all the bathwater before your baby gets into the bath—approximately 3 in (8 cm) of water—and make sure that the water is sufficiently warm, but not hot. If the hot faucet becomes very hot to the touch, place a wet washcloth over it so that he can't burn himself if he grabs hold of it. Always use a nonslip mat in the bath so that he can sit up safely to play. Do not rely on bath seats, rings, or other aids. Cover or turn off radiators.

TODDLER SAFETY

Q WHICH DANGERS SHOULD I BE AWARE OF AT THIS STAGE ?

A Be aware that your toddler is extremely active and curious, so don't leave any objects lying around with which he may be able to harm himself or others. Your toddler is constantly on the go, but has no perception of danger. He will be exploring and deliberately pushing his world to the limit, and objects will be used and misused. To him, an electric outlet may seem like the perfect place to insert a nail file that's been left lying around. One of the main concerns is that he may be able to open the front door on his own now, so it might be wise to fit a bolt high up on the inside.

Q HOW CAN I MAKE SURE MY TODDLER'S BEDROOM IS SAFE ?

A Make sure the windows are securely fitted with safety devices such as window guards to keep your child from falling out. Your toddler may have started trying to climb out of his crib, which is hazardous—if this is the case, then he is ready to make the transition to a big bed. If there is a radiator in his room, turn down the thermostat so he doesn't burn himself. Any toys kept in his room should be safe for him to play with on his own (see p. 200). If he has toys that should only be played with under supervision, don't leave them where he can find them if he wakes up early.

HOW CAN I MAKE SURE SHE IS SAFE WHEN SHE PLAYS OUTSIDE ?

Toddlers benefit from fresh air and playing outside. To ensure that she can play happily and without any harm, look out for potential hazards.

Keeping her safe in the playground
Most playgrounds have soft, bouncy surfaces to cushion your child should she fall off a slide or swing. However, she could still hurt herself, so always supervise her on playground equipment, especially if she is trying it out for the first time.

Parasites in the soil
Keep your child away from dog and cat feces. Toxocara is excreted by dogs and causes blindness. Toxoplasma can be found in cat feces and causes a range of symptoms; this parasite doesn't become infectious for a few days, but in a backyard or park, you can't tell how old feces are.

OUTSIDE PLAY
A sandbox offers your toddler hours of fun and games. When it is not in use, cover it to keep it from being used as a toilet by animals.

Water
If you have a pool in your backyard, make sure that it is fenced off. The fence should be high enough to prevent a child from climbing over it, and the gate should be kept locked. In some states a fence is legally required for an in-ground pool.

Plants in the park or backyard
Teach your child to avoid touching plants and flowers and tell her that she should never eat a berry from a bush or tree—even if it does look very attractive. In your own backyard, avoid or eliminate the following: laburnum, foxglove, lily of the valley and yew berries, toadstools, fungi, and poison ivy.

Chemicals
Keep all pesticides and other chemicals safely locked up. There can also be chemical residue on plants, which is another reason why your child shouldn't pick and eat plants.

Traffic
Your child may tire of the park or backyard and want to venture farther. Keep an eye on her so she doesn't wander into the street.

Q HOW CAN I KEEP MY TODDLER SAFE IN THE BATHROOM ?

A It is vital that you always supervise your toddler's bathtime. Don't be tempted to answer the telephone or go to the door. Your toddler is not safe in or near water when he is on his own. He will also wander in and out of the bathroom when it isn't bathtime, so turn down the hot water thermostat to prevent him from burning himself if he turns on the faucet. Keep toiletries, cleaners, bleach, razors, and even shampoo well out of his reach. To prevent your toddler from locking himself in the bathroom, you should either remove the bolt or key, or move the bolt higher up on the door where he can't reach it.

Q HOW CAN I PREVENT ACCIDENTS FROM HAPPENING ON THE STAIRS ?

A Teach your toddler to climb up and down the stairs safely, but until you are happy that he is competent going up and down on his own, use stair gates at both the top and the bottom so that he is not able to make any unsupervised attempts. Make sure that stair carpets are securely fitted and that there are no loose or frayed ends, and avoid leaving things on the stairs that he could trip over.

Q WHICH SAFETY MEASURES SHOULD I TAKE IN THE KITCHEN ?

A Keep appliance cords short, and store matches and all dangerous utensils out of reach. Ideally, knives should be locked up, but this may not always be possible. Your toddler should be out of the way when you are cooking, especially if you are frying food or making an elaborate meal that requires a little more concentration than usual. If this is not feasible, then you could ask him to help you with the preparations and talk to him about how to do things safely. Always stay with your toddler while he is eating in case he chokes— besides, it is lonely and boring for your toddler to eat on his own. If anything gets spilled, mop it up promptly to avoid slips and falls.

Q SHOULD I KEEP HIM OUT OF THE LIVING ROOM FOR SAFETY'S SAKE ?

A I don't think so. There is no reason to exclude your toddler from a particular room. Instead, make sure it is safe by moving any fragile objects and supervising him so that he doesn't run riot. Allowing him access to the "best room" also has its benefits, since you can teach your toddler the importance of behaving well in certain places.

Q HOW CAN I MAKE SURE HIS PLAYTHINGS ARE SAFE FOR HIM TO USE ?

A Buy only good-quality toys that meet safety standards—if this is not stated on the packaging or label, then don't buy the toy. Discard worn-out toys. However, you can't always guard against injuries caused by your toddler using something in a way never intended by the manufacturer. One example is that of a child running while holding a pencil—it can go up his nose, or into his eye or mouth. You shouldn't stop him from having pencils, but teach him to use them and carry them correctly.

Toddlers are naturally curious about stairs

SAFETY
Stair gates are the perfect solution to keep active toddlers from climbing the stairs. Be sure to keep the gate shut at all times.

PARENT'S SURVIVAL GUIDE

I KEEP SAYING "NO" ALL THE TIME

I'm always telling him not to do things. What can I do?
Whenever possible, avoid saying "No" by distracting him with something else. In time, he will stop doing dangerous things, but in the meantime you have to prevent accidents.

Keep repeating your safety message
If he persists in a certain activity, repeat your safety message. He is not being stubborn—he can't understand danger and has a short memory.

Set a good example
Always set a good example. If you want him to learn about road safety, make sure you never cross the street against the light.

PRESCHOOL SAFETY

Q WHICH DANGERS ARE IMPORTANT NOW THAT MY CHILD IS GETTING OLDER?

A You need to be aware that your child is becoming more independent and capable, but still has a limited sense of danger. He may even think he is immortal and invincible, like a cartoon character. Make sure windows and doors are safe, keep poisonous substances locked up, and start teaching him basic street-safety awareness.

Q HOW CAN I TEACH MY CHILD ABOUT SAFETY?

A When you're doing things with him in the kitchen or the backyard, give him a running commentary. For example, if you are in the kitchen making a cake, you can tell him in a positive way about the importance of being careful with kitchen utensils and hot ovens, and show him that you are putting these precautions into practice. Conversely, if he sees you put a knife into your mouth to lick it, don't be surprised if he copies you.

Q HOW CAN I KEEP MY CHILD SAFE AND STILL LET HIM BE INDEPENDENT?

A You can't protect your child all the time but you can reduce risks and avoid exposing him to unnecessary hazards. Let him become more independent in controlled circumstances. For instance, a child can learn to handle small tools such as a screwdriver or hammer under close supervision. Teach him good safety habits and try to explain why the safety rules are important, so that he can apply the guidelines in other situations.

Q WHAT SHOULD I TELL MY CHILD ABOUT TALKING TO STRANGERS?

A Avoid scare tactics—your child must learn safety without fear. Explain to him that not all strangers are bad, but that he should not talk to strangers or accept anything from a stranger. If someone is simply returning something that belongs to the child, he should get no closer than an arm's length away. Tell your child that he must never go anywhere with a stranger (there are exceptions, like a police officer in a uniform). This is especially important if your child always does as you say, since he may accept a ride from a stranger who claims that he or she is acting on a parent's behalf. On the whole, it is perfectly safe for him to talk to grownups he knows well.

IS HE READY FOR A BIKE?

From the age of about 18 months, a toddler can use a tricycle, although he may not pedal effectively until he is three. Around the age of five, many children are ready to graduate from a tricycle to a bicycle. Use training wheels to help give him confidence. When he is ready, encourage him to try to cycle on two wheels.

How can I make sure he is safe?
Get a bike that is the right size for your child now—you can sell it when he outgrows it. Although it may seem more economical to invest in one that will last him longer, a bike that is too high could put him off cycling and could also cause him to fall off more. He should be gently challenged by cycling, not totally defeated. Fit the bike with a bell or horn so he can warn others, and make sure he always wears a helmet. Don't let him cycle on roads, or sidewalks by himself where he could wobble and fall into the road. Once he has mastered the basics of using pedals and brakes, you may want to consider cycle safety lessons.

Q HOW CAN I PROTECT MY CHILD AGAINST SEXUAL ABUSE?

A In addition to never going anywhere with a stranger, tell your child not to keep a secret, especially if someone asks him to. If someone says or does something in a way he doesn't like, he should tell the person to stop, and then tell you. No stranger should touch his body, especially not his private parts (if he asks, these are the parts covered by a swimsuit)—with obvious exceptions, like visiting the doctor.

Q MY SON PLAYS ROUGH GAMES WITH HIS FRIENDS. HOW CAN I KEEP HIM SAFE?

A Little boys enjoy very physical forms of play but don't always have much common sense. Make sure they don't play with dangerous objects, such as pieces of metal or sharp sticks, and supervise their play, for your child's sake and that of his friends. If it gets too rough, break it up at intervals for a snack or a drink before the situation gets totally out of hand.

OUTINGS WITH CHILDREN

Q SHOULD I TAKE ANYTHING WITH ME WHEN I'M OUT WITH MY CHILD?

A Yes, but how much depends on how long you will be out. You may even need food and drink (snacks or a meal, or both) and something to entertain him with. Tie a toy, using a short ribbon no longer than 8 in (20 cm), onto his stroller or his car seat, so that he can't lose it—or throw it at you when you are driving. A potty (or change of diaper) is also a good idea. Take his changing bag, filled with the essentials (see below). If he suffers from motion sickness, you'll need a plastic bag, some paper towels, and a change of clothes.

Q WHERE CAN I CHANGE MY BABY'S DIAPER WHEN WE ARE OUT ON A TRIP?

A Most department stores, supermarkets, and highway service areas provide diaper-changing facilities. Unfortunately, these are usually in the ladies' room, although some places have a family room, which is more convenient for fathers. Otherwise, use the luggage shelf of the car or the car seats if out in the car. If you are desperate, find a quiet spot in a park.

Q HOW CAN I FEED MY BABY WHEN WE ARE OUT AND ABOUT?

A You can stop and feed your baby almost anywhere as long as it is hygienic. Depending on the weather, you can breast-feed, bottle-feed, or give solid food on a park bench. All you need is his food, a spoon, a bib, and paper towels to mop up spills. Take a couple of plastic bags with you for used items. Most restaurants will happily heat up baby food for you, and many have highchairs. Alternatively, you can restrain your baby by securing a harness to an ordinary chair—add a booster seat and you have a highchair.

Q HOW CAN I KEEP MY BABY CONTENTED ON LONG TRIPS?

A Make sure your baby is fed and changed before you start the trip. With luck he will fall asleep in the car, and soothing music may help. Failing that, provide a toy or two in case he doesn't sleep. Most babies are happy with a string of beads stretched out across the baby seat, a small soft toy, or a board book. If the toy is attached to the car seat, you won't have to keep picking it up.

WHAT SHOULD I TAKE WITH ME WHEN I GO OUT WITH MY BABY?

Take more diapers than you need

Toys will occupy your baby

CHANGING BAG
A lightweight baby changing bag holds all you need when out on a trip with your baby.

Carrying a few essential items when you are out with your baby will help you have a more enjoyable trip. Take a spare bottle of milk or formula, some clean diapers, diaper-changing equipment, and a change of clothes in case he spits up or his diaper leaks. If it is warm, take sunblock and a sunhat. Taking a few toys to keep him occupied is a good idea, too. You may also want to include the following:

- his bowl, spoon, and a bib
- a box of baby wipes and some paper towels
- a bottle of water
- a bag for dirty diapers
- a cell phone if you have one.

FAMILY LIFE

How can I make the car comfortable and safe for my child?

Whether you have a tiny baby or an older child, you need appropriate restraints to cushion him from car movements and to prevent him from being thrown out of his seat in the case of a sudden stop or an accident. A car seat (see below) provides the necessary restraint. Make sure your child is occupied and, if you need to attend to him, stop the car rather than take your eyes off the road. For your child's comfort during summer, put a sunshade over his seat and/or on the side or rear window. Finally, it's a good idea to fill up with gas before you set off—visits to a gas station are more stressful with a crying baby or restless child.

What is the best type of car for a young family?
The ideal car is one that is safe, reliable, and convenient. Four doors are more convenient than two as you can get your child (and his equipment) in and out of the back more easily. Ideally, you should have central locking so that you can drive secure in the knowledge that all the doors are locked shut. In addition, always engage the child safety locks on the back doors so your child cannot open a door by accident. Never put your child in a seat that has an airbag in front of it—an inflated airbag can kill a child. Your car also needs the right anchorage points for child safety seats or harnesses, although most child car seats can be secured using an adult three-point or lap safety belt.

Does my child need a special car seat?
Yes. Holding a small child on your lap or in your arms is not safe, even if you are both strapped together. If there was an accident, your weight could crush a child. Without a restraint, your child could be thrown out of the car. Buy a seat that meets the current safety standards. Choose a seat that is suitable for your car and for your child's weight.

■ Rear-facing baby seats are designed for babies from newborn up to 22–28 lb /10–13 kg (about 12 months)—weight is more important than age.
■ Forward-facing car seats are suitable for the weight range 22–40 lb/10–18 kg, from about 12 months up to the age of three or four. Weight is more important than age, but there is variation between models. Some child seats have an integral harness, others use adult three-point belts.
■ From about four years of age up to at least eight years of age and 80 lbs (36 kg) children can use adult three-point seat belts with a booster seat to prevent the seat belt rubbing their neck. Use a booster seat for older children up to 5 ft (1.5 m) tall.

Car safety
Make sure the seat is the right size for your baby.

Can I install a child's car seat myself?
Yes, you can, but make sure you install it properly; this is as important as buying the right model. If you're not sure how to install the seat yourself, get professional help. In addition, always make sure the buckles are fastened securely. Any car restraint is useless if your child is not securely strapped in.

What should I do when my child unbuckles his car seat belt?
This is a discipline issue. Stop the car and fasten the belt again. Explain to your child that the journey cannot continue unless he leaves the buckle alone. If he unbuckles it again, stop the car again. Don't lose your temper, even though it's hard not to, especially when this happens on a highway.

Q MY BABY HOWLS IN THE CAR. IS THERE ANYTHING I CAN DO ?

A A screaming baby can be distracting and stressful, so stop the car as soon as it is safe to do so. If you are on a highway, drive on to the next exit rather than stop in the breakdown lane. Your baby may need a rest stop and you probably do too. Talk to him, feed him, change him, and then reinstall him in his car seat. A change of toy can be useful, as can some soothing music.

Q HOW CAN I KEEP MY CHILD ENTERTAINED ON A LONG TRIP ?

A Try to make the trip interesting for him. Talk to him about what he can see out of the window (this has the added benefit of reducing motion sickness, see below) and play word games with him. If he can count, he is old enough to keep a tally of all the red cars he sees, or all the gas stations. Listen to suitable cassettes together— either stories or songs you can both sing along to—and provide unbreakable toys that have no small pieces that he could swallow. Soft toys and hand-held puzzles (without loose pieces) are good. Don't allow any pens or pencils, as he could poke his eye if there is a sudden stop. For your own sanity, avoid noisy toys. Many children sleep well in the car. If this is the case, try setting off when he is very tired, not when he has just had a long nap.

ENCOURAGING ROAD SAFETY

Drill into your child's mind that he must stay on the sidewalk when walking and, when crossing, you must cross together and hold hands. Do not run.

Explain that you are:
- finding a safe place to cross
- looking and listening before you cross
- continuing to look and listen as you cross. Eventually he will get the message.

When can he cross the road by himself?
This depends on the road, but I don't think he can cross on his own until he is six or seven years old. However, he won't have proper traffic sense until around the age of 10 or 11. This often surprises parents, but visit any primary school when it's time to go home and you will see how little traffic awareness children have.

Q SHOULD I LET MY CHILD EAT AND DRINK IN THE CAR ON LONG TRIPS ?

A Yes, but not too much. Take some food such as sandwiches or fruit, small boxes of fruit juice, and some paper towels to catch the mess. However, someone still needs to supervise your youngster— even an older child can choke, and most children get food all over a car seat. You could also buy food while you're out. It helps if your child is used to eating snacks like crackers, cheese, or fruit because these are readily available. Unfortunately, this isn't a total safeguard—toddlers have been known to refuse what is offered if it is not the same type of cheese/crackers/apple they have at home!

Q WHEN CAN HE USE AN ADULT CAR SEAT BELT ?

A Not until he is at least four years old. Even then he should be in the back of the car and he must only have the three-point seat belt and not the lap belt (see opposite). In addition, he needs a good booster seat to raise him to a better height and prevent the seat belt from digging into his neck.

Q DO ALL BABIES AND YOUNG CHILDREN GET MOTION SICKNESS ?

A Very few young babies suffer from motion sickness so there is no need to worry about this when he is very young. This happy state of affairs lasts for approximately 18 months, after which time many children are, unfortunately, prone to motion sickness.

Q CAN I PREVENT MY CHILD GETTING MOTION SICKNESS ?

A From the age of about 18 months to two years onward, many children suffer from motion sickness. Your child may feel nauseated and look pale and he may vomit without warning. If he is prone to this, keep him occupied, but not by concentrating on a book or toy inside the car, train, or plane. Encourage him to look out of the window, don't let him eat too much, and don't smoke. If it is a long trip, consider a drug for motion sickness. There are syrups and tablets suitable for young children—ask your pharmacist. Some of these drugs can make a child drowsy, but this can benefit both of you on a long journey. Some homeopathic remedies may help, or you can try acupressure bands that fit onto both wrists. Whichever remedy you use, it is still wise to have a plastic bag, paper towels, and a change of clothes ready just in case.

GOING ON VACATION

WITH A BABY

Q WHAT'S THE BEST CHOICE OF VACATION WITH A BABY ?

A The main things to consider are safety and hygiene for your baby, and relaxation for you. This means you may have to rule out exotic locations and long trips. Ideally, your destination will have facilities for babies as well as stores that stock baby essentials. All the same, it's wise to take the diapers you normally use, and anything else that could be hard to obtain on vacation. Your baby's skin needs protection from the sun—sunny places are fine as long as you're prepared for the inevitable restrictions they present. Babies are also more likely to be bitten by mosquitoes and other insects.

Q IS A PASSPORT NECESSARY FOR A BABY ?

A Yes, if you want to take a vacation abroad. All babies, no matter how young, are required by law to have their own passport if they are taken outside their country.

Q DOES MY BABY NEED IMMUNIZATIONS FOR TRAVELING ABROAD ?

A Your baby's basic immunizations must be up to date. Depending on your destination, your baby may need other vaccinations, too— ask your doctor. You cannot always rely on advice from a travel agent.

Q WILL AIR TRAVEL BE DIFFICULT WITH A BABY ?

A Not if you are organized and buy tickets ahead of time. On some airlines you must purchase a seat for your child after age two. Prior to that age, you will have to hold your baby on your lap, unless you buy an airplane seat for him and strap his infant seat into it. Some airlines provide sky-cribs; it's worth checking when you book your tickets. Take milk with you onto the plane—the cabin crew should be able to heat it up for you. Also remember to take diapers. Give your baby a breast- or bottle-feeding (or a pacifier) during ascent and descent to avoid an earache. If the flight is long, your baby may become dehydrated. He may also be jet-lagged on arrival. If he is unsettled for more than a few days after you arrive, talk to a doctor.

SUN PROTECTION

Sun protection is essential. Without it, your baby can quickly become overheated, dehydrated, or painfully burned. Sunburn is also a risk factor for skin cancer.

Protect your baby from harmful rays
The first line of protection is to avoid exposure. Babies under six months should stay out of the sun altogether. All children should ideally stay in the shade when the sun's rays are strongest, from about 11 am to 3 pm. Remember also that sunlight is usually stronger at high altitude or near water.

Keep him well covered
Use a sunshade on your carriage or stroller and dress your baby appropriately. He should wear a cap with a flap at the back or a sunhat with a brim large enough to shade his face and neck. Protection on his arms and legs is also important, even if it's very hot. Bear in mind that flimsy fabrics offer little protection against the sun's ultraviolet rays, so your baby can burn through a thin shirt.

Use sunscreen
The sun protection factor (SPF) your baby requires depends to some degree on the natural pigment of his skin and how long he'll be out in the sun, but all babies need some protection from ultraviolet rays. Use a sunscreen with a sun protection factor (SPF) of at least 15, preferably 30. Apply it evenly half an hour before going outside, and reapply often.

Increase his fluid intake
When it's hot, encourage your baby to drink as much as possible. If you're breast-feeding, offer feedings more often. If you're bottle-feeding, give him plain water or very diluted fruit juice.

WITH A CHILD

Q WHAT'S THE BEST KIND OF VACATION WITH A YOUNG CHILD ?

A You can be a bit more adventurous when babyhood is behind you, so many types of vacations can now fit the bill. Children are often fascinated by foreign travel, but they tend to be impatient on trips. Hygiene and safety are still considerations, so you may prefer to stay in a hotel or apartment that caters to children. However, you could now consider camping and activity vacations, and beach vacations as long you're careful about sun protection. One thing to consider if you're renting a car abroad is whether a car seat will be available.

Q IS THERE ANYTHING SPECIAL I NEED TO TAKE ?

A Make sure that favorite toys are packed in a bag that can be kept with your child for the trip; if your child is bored, the trip will be a struggle. Avoid putting medicine or a favorite teddy bear into luggage checked into the hold.

GETTING READY
Allow your child to get involved in packing her personal belongings into a bag. It will contribute to her sense of excitement and make her feel like a responsible person.

Give your child her own special bag for the vacation

WHAT SHOULD I CONSIDER WHEN TRAVELING BY AIR ?

Children age two and over usually have their own seat on a plane (babies usually travel on a parent's lap), but reserve your seats in advance to get a location that suits you. Your child will almost certainly prefer a window seat so that he can look out.

Travel abroad
Talk to your doctor about whether your child needs any special immunizations. Babies as young as six months can have yellow fever vaccine, for instance, which is a requirement for some destinations. Your child may also need antimalarial tablets for certain areas. Protective clothing and insect repellent are also a must because antimalarial drugs aren't infallible and mosquitoes tend to favor young skins. Make sure that you pack plenty of sun protection and several sunhats.

Before boarding the plane
Try to hang onto your stroller for as long as possible before boarding—managing an excited toddler plus your luggage in an airport can be exhausting. You should be able to keep it until you reach the gate, but it may then go into the hold. Give your child travel sickness medicine well before you board so it has time to work.

Take some food
Take along some snacks for your child in case the airline meal is unsuitable. Also take a drink and some hard candy to suck or gum to chew on during ascent and descent to prevent an earache as the pressure changes. Supervise him so that the candy or gum does not go down the wrong way.

Keep your child amused
Although many airlines provide goody-bags and video programs for young children, you should take enough of his own toys and books to keep him occupied during the flight.

Dealing with jet lag
Establish the new time zone as soon as possible, and organize mealtimes and bedtime around this. If he has trouble sleeping, try a dose of his travel sickness medicine before bedtime to make him drowsy. It is not harmful and may do the trick.

FAMILY LIFE

CHILD HEALTH

We all want our children to be **healthy** – not just free of disease, but in peak condition and able to enjoy life to the full. However, we also have to accept that **minor illnesses** are common in the first few years of any child's life. Being able to distinguish minor ailments from more **serious symptoms** can prevent a great deal of parental anxiety. This chapter provides you with the information you need to care for your sick child and offers guidance on when to seek **medical help**. There is commonsense advice on caring for your child at home and a **first-aid section** that will enable you to handle an emergency should one arise.

KEEPING YOUR CHILD HEALTHY

Q HOW CAN I KEEP MY YOUNGSTER HEALTHY ?

A Give your child the right foods for her to grow and thrive. Fresh air and exercise are important—a sedentary childhood based around home, television, and computer does not make strong bones. Keep your youngster clean and teach her good hygiene habits from an early age such as washing her hands before meals and after using the toilet. Protect but don't overprotect your child and seek appropriate help when she is sick. Take her to all her routine health check-ups and make sure that you get her immunizations done on time (see opposite).

Q WHERE CAN I GET ADVICE ?

A You can speak to your pediatrician if you need advice. Your pediatrician may be available for telephone consultations, and this can be extremely useful if you are unsure whether your child requires medical evaluation.

Q DOES MY CHILD NEED VITAMIN SUPPLEMENTS ?

A It depends. A child who eats a good balanced diet and isn't from a group of people at high risk of vitamin deficiency does not need vitamin supplements. Unfortunately, many children do not eat well, so it's probably a good idea to give supplement drops from about four to six weeks until five years of age (see p. 72). Avoid iron-based supplements.

Q SHOULD I KEEP MY CHILD AWAY FROM PEOPLE WITH COLDS ?

A No. Unless your child has a serious immunity problem, you don't need to keep her away from colds or other everyday viruses. She may get a lot of colds in childhood, but it's all part of building up valuable immunity. Each time your child is exposed to a particular virus or to bacteria, she develops antibodies against it so that next time she comes into contact with it, she should not be so susceptible to illness.

HOW OFTEN SHOULD I TAKE MY CHILD TO THE DENTIST ?

Your child needs to visit the dentist regularly—at least every six months—for check-ups, even if her teeth look perfect. It's important for her to get used to sitting in the chair without fear. Look for a dentist who is good with young children—ask your friends, neighbors, or pediatrician.

When should I start taking her to the dentist?
I think the earlier you start, the better. You can leave it until the age of two. Better still, you can take her as soon as she has teeth, even if it's just to watch you sitting in the chair (if going to the dentist usually worries you, try to hide the fact!). At first your child will probably want to sit on your lap to be "examined"– in reality these visits will be little more than a social call because there aren't many teeth to examine. As she grows older, she'll be able to sit in the chair on her own.

Will my child need a filling?
Most children's primary teeth never need a filling, but it's important to treat any cavity before it enlarges and becomes painful (if it isn't already) and the tooth needs to be taken out. A child shouldn't have to lose a primary tooth prematurely as these teeth affect speech development. Loss of primary teeth too early can also cause poor positioning of the permanent teeth.

What if my child does need treatment?
Try to be calm, but don't pretend it won't hurt. Many new techniques reduce pain and avoid the noise of the drill, but some treatments can hurt. If a cavity is shallow, she may need no injection, but a deeper one may demand an injection of local anesthetic—the gum can be numbed first with a cream. The dentist may recommend a sedative or even a general anesthetic, in which case ask for the treatment to be carried out at a hospital where a fully qualified anesthesiologist can do it.

WHAT IS IMMUNIZATION ?

This is giving a vaccine by mouth or injection to a child to make her resistant to a particular virus or bacterium. Vaccines work by stimulating the immune system to make antibodies to the infection. The diseases your child will be immunized against are all infectious and unpleasant; some are fatal while others may cause permanent disability.

What illnesses can be vaccinated against?

■ **Polio** (poliomyelitis) A virus that affects the nervous system and can cause permanent paralysis or even death if it affects the chest muscles.

■ **Diphtheria** A serious throat infection that can spread to the heart and nervous system.

■ **Tetanus** A potentially fatal bacterial disease that can paralyze the muscles, causing painful spasms.

■ **Pertussis** (whooping cough) A bacterial illness that causes persistent severe coughing, and can result in vomiting, convulsions, and lung damage.

■ **Hib** (Hemophilus influenzae b) A bacterial infection that causes a range of serious illnesses, including meningitis and pneumonia.

■ **Chickenpox** A virus that produces a rash of blisters; may lead to pneumonia and encephalitis.

■ **Measles** A virus that can cause chest infections, convulsions, and permanent brain damage.

■ **Mumps** A virus that can cause painful inflammation of the salivary glands. It can affect the nervous system and cause meningitis.

■ **Rubella** This virus produces a rash and fever, and can cause serious defects in unborn babies.

■ **Hepatitis B** A virus that may damage the liver.

Are vaccines completely safe?

No vaccine (or medicine) is totally risk-free, but the potential benefit of these immunizations vastly outweighs the risk for almost every child. If you are concerned about immunization, talk to your pediatrician who will advise you about possible risks.

Do vaccines have any side effects?

Sometimes. The main side effects are fever and crying or irritability in the first 24–48 hours after the injection. There may also be redness or soreness at the injection site and a lump that can last several weeks. Some vaccines have other effects: for instance MMR (measles, mumps, and rubella) can produce a raised temperature or even a mild rash 10 days later.

When should a child not have immunizations?

A baby shouldn't be immunized during a feverish illness; postpone it until she is completely recovered. Putting it off doesn't mean she has to start the course again. Talk to your pediatrician before the immunization if she has a severe egg allergy; has had a seizure or convulsion; is being treated for cancer; or has a disease that affects her immune system.

IMMUNIZATION TIMETABLE

Your pediatrician will do your child's immunizations. All immunizations are given by injection; in some cases, such as measles, mumps, and rubella, they are combined into a single injection. If your child misses an appointment don't worry, but arrange for her to have the vaccine as soon as possible.

AGE	WHAT IS GIVEN
birth	Hepatitis B
2 months	Diphtheria, tetanus, pertussis, Hib, polio, pneumococcal, hepatitis B
4 months	Diphtheria, tetanus, pertussis, Hib, polio, meningitis C, pneumococcal
6 months	Diphtheria, tetanus, pertussis, Hib, pneumococcal, influenza
6–18 months	Polio, hepatitis B
12 months	MMR (measles, mumps, rubella), meningitis C, varicella (chicken pox)
12–15 months	Diphtheria, tetanus, pertussis, Hib
12–18 months	Pneumococcal
1–2 years	Hepatitis A
4–6 years	Diphtheria, tetanus, pertussis, polio, MMR (measles, mumps, rubella), varicella
Yearly to 5 years	Influenza

CHILD HEALTH

213

WHEN YOUR CHILD IS ILL

CHILD HEALTH

PARENT'S SURVIVAL GUIDE

I'M UNSURE WHETHER TO CALL THE DOCTOR

You don't necessarily need to. If your baby or child has a runny nose but is otherwise well, you may not need the doctor. However, if your baby is very young (under 12 months) you should call your pediatrician for all but the most minor ailments.

When should I call the doctor?
You should always call your pediatrician if you don't know what is wrong with your child. The younger the child is, the sooner you should phone. It's better to have the occasional false alarm than to leave things too late. Always call if your child develops any of the following symptoms:
- a high fever you can't control (see p. 220)
- trouble breathing
- is vomiting and/or has diarrhea and is under 12 months, or there's blood in her stools
- is listless and refuses her food
- pain (especially abdominal pain)
- a swelling in the groin or testicle
- a persistent earache (a baby may cry or pull on her ear)
- an unexplained rash.

When is it an emergency?
Go to the nearest hospital emergency department immediately or call an ambulance if your child:
- has a burn or severe bleeding
- has had or is having a seizure
- is listless or unconscious
- has a possible fractured or broken bone
- has a headache with neck stiffness, dislike of bright light, or a rash that does not disappear when pressed with a glass (see p. 218)
- has severe difficulty breathing or is so short of breath she can't speak.
- has a possible neck injury.

Q WHAT ARE THE KEY SIGNS OF ILLNESS IN A CHILD ?

A A baby or child who is ill won't do what she usually does. She may refuse her feedings and smile or play less than usual. She could be clingy, miserable, and out of sorts. A sick baby can be listless, a sick child drowsy or apathetic. She may also be feverish or show symptoms related to that illness, such as a cough, runny nose, or a rash.

Q MY CHILD'S NOSE IS ALWAYS RUNNY. HOW LONG DO COLDS LAST ?

A Ordinary colds can last longer than parents imagine—up to three weeks or more. Because very young children have not built up an immunity to cold viruses, they get frequent colds, sometimes six or more a year. One cold followed by another can give the impression of a constant infection. Colds aren't usually serious unless there are complications such as an ear or chest infection, or your child has a disease of the immune system.

Q MY CHILD HAS TUMMY ACHE. WHAT COULD THIS BE ?

A Many completely different conditions can cause abdominal pain, including: common viral infections (swollen glands in the abdomen can cause pain); urinary tract infections; strangulated hernia; appendicitis; bowel obstruction; and constipation. The right treatment depends on the cause. Since it's almost impossible for a parent to be sure what's wrong, always consult your pediatrician unless your child has only fleeting pain before passing a stool.

Q MY CHILD HAS DIARRHEA. COULD THIS BE SERIOUS ?

A It can be, because diarrhea causes fluid loss, which can lead to dehydration (see p. 220). Always consult your pediatrician if your child is under 12 months, she is also vomiting, or there is blood in her stools. Diarrhea can be caused by recurrent gut infection at any age. Children under two sometimes have episodes of intermittent diarrhea. Although it's common, the cause is unclear. It could be caused by diet, for example, if she has too much fiber or too little fat, or if she simply is not chewing her food properly. If in doubt, you should talk to your pediatrician.

Q MY CHILD HAS A HEADACHE. SHOULD I BE CONCERNED ?

A Headaches are amazingly common in children, and they strike terror into the minds of most parents. Occasionally a headache is a symptom of a serious illness like meningitis (see p. 218), but the vast majority are minor. The most common reason for headaches in children is fever and they occur because the fever causes the blood vessels inside the skull to dilate. Other causes of headache include: tension or stress; migraine; head injury; encephalitis (inflammation of the brain); brain tumour. If you are concerned, talk to your pediatrician.

Q I FIND IT DIFFICULT TO TALK TO MY PEDIATRICIAN. WHAT'S THE ANSWER ?

A Try to be as clear as possible about your child's symptoms and when they started. Ask for definite advice on what to do if your child doesn't improve, or when to come back for a follow-up appointment. Always mention if you're concerned about a specific illness because, say, someone else at daycare has it or it runs in your family—your pediatrician may be able to put your mind at rest. Many pediatricians are parents too, and will understand your concerns. If you still have problems, then perhaps she is not the right doctor for your family.

HOW CAN I TELL IF MY BABY OR CHILD HAS A FEVER ?

A feverish child may feel hot when you touch her—feel her forehead with the palm of your hand or your lips. She may look flushed and she may tell you that she has a headache or that she feels cold. However, to be sure she has a fever you have to take her temperature.

How should I take my child's temperature?

You can take her temperature in her armpit, mouth, or, using an ear sensor *only*, her ear. Normal body temperature gives a reading of 98.6°F/37°C by mouth, about 1°F/0.5°C lower if measured in the armpit; any reading above this indicates a fever. Armpit readings don't reflect body temperature as accurately, but a child under four may not be able to keep a thermometer under her tongue.

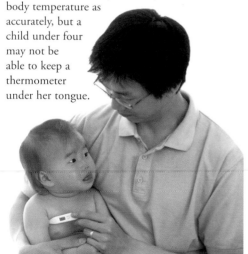

DIGITAL THERMOMETER

Digital thermometers are battery-operated and last for years. Accurate and almost unbreakable, they are ideal for children. Digital thermometers can be used in the mouth or armpit and take only a couple of minutes. For infants, a rectal temperature taken with a digital thermometer is most accurate. Most digital thermometers "beep" to indicate the correct reading.

EAR SENSOR

This measures infra-red  *radiation in the ear canal. It takes only one second, so it is ideal for a sick baby or child. However, the instrument is much bulkier and more expensive than a digital thermometer. In my experience, measurements can also be a bit erratic. To monitor your child's fever over the course of any illness, always use the same ear and take three readings each time.*

LIQUID CRYSTAL STRIP

A small, heat-sensitive strip that is placed on the child's forehead for half a minute or so. The strip is quick and easy to use, but it is inaccurate because it measures skin rather than body temperature. You can probably get the same information by feeling your child's forehead.

TAKING A TEMPERATURE

Sit your child on your lap and put the thermometer in her armpit. Wait for 2–3 minutes before you take a reading.

Childhood Illnesses

WHAT IS IT ?	WHAT ARE THE SYMPTOMS ?	WHAT SHOULD I DO ?
INFECTIOUS DISEASES		
FLU (influenza) Caused by a wide range of viruses.	■ Aches and pains, sore throat, fever, and a headache. ■ Runny nose and cough. ■ Loss of appetite.	■ Relieve pain, treat fever (see p. 220), give fluid. ■ See your doctor if: you are in doubt about the diagnosis; her condition worsens; she is no better after 3 days, is short of breath, or has an earache.
SCARLET FEVER Caused by streptococcus bacteria. ■ Highly infectious.	■ Sore throat (see Tonsillitis). ■ Rapidly spreading spots on trunk; area around mouth unaffected. ■ Red patches on tongue.	■ Inform your doctor—your child needs antibiotics. ■ Relieve pain and treat fever (see p. 220). Give lots of fluids. ■ Keep her away from other children.
CHICKENPOX (*varicella*) Virus that also causes shingles. ■ Incubation 14–21 days; highly infectious day before rash and until spots crust over.	■ Unwell with fever for a day. ■ Red spots start on trunk and turn into small oval blisters, then crust over; blisters continue to appear for a few days—crusts fall off within 1–2 weeks. ■ Possible ulcers in mouth.	■ Keep child cool and lightly clothed and cut nails. ■ Soothe itching with calamine lotion or a lukewarm bath with a tablespoon of bicarbonate of soda. ■ If itching is severe, try antihistamine syrup. ■ If mouth is sore, give soft foods and lots of fluid. ■ See doctor if your child won't drink or is unwell. ■ Keep her away from other children.
PARVOVIRUS INFECTION (slapped cheek disease) ■ Highly infectious during 14–21 day incubation period.	■ Bright red rash with well-defined edge on one or both cheeks. ■ Possible lacy-looking rash on arms, legs or trunk. ■ Mild fever, though child usually well.	■ No specific treatment. ■ See your doctor if: child has a high fever; is generally unwell; symptoms not typical. ■ No need to isolate child, but do keep her away from pregnant women. Parvovirus in early pregnancy can cause miscarriage.
HAND-FOOT-AND-MOUTH DISEASE Caused by coxsackie virus. ■ Incubation 2–10 days.	■ Mild fever day before spots. ■ Small spots or blisters (tender but not itchy) on hands, feet, inside mouth, and often buttocks. ■ Mouth may be very sore.	■ Control any fever (see p. 220). ■ Give soft foods and lots of fluid if mouth is sore. ■ No need to isolate; not very infectious. ■ See your doctor if child is unwell, or illness lasts more than 3–4 days.
ROSEOLA INFANTUM Common virus in children under three. ■ Not very infectious.	■ Sudden high fever for 1–3 days. ■ As fever drops, small pink-red spots appear on trunk, sometimes spreading to limbs.	■ See your doctor to confirm diagnosis. ■ Treat fever to prevent convulsions (see p. 220). ■ Keep her away from other children for a week after rash clears, although not very infectious.
MEASLES Potentially serious virus. ■ Incubation period 8–20 days – infectious.	■ Unwell with high fever for four days before rash appears. ■ Blotchy rash starting at neck. ■ Puffy red eyes and cough.	■ Contact your doctor. Measles can have serious complications. ■ Treat your child's fever (see p. 220). ■ Keep her away from other children.
MUMPS Virus spread in saliva. ■ Incubation period 12–28 days—infectious in early days.	■ Painful swelling on one or both sides of the face. Possible inflammation of testes or ovaries. ■ Difficulty eating. ■ Generally unwell with mild fever.	■ Contact your doctor. There can be serious complications. ■ Give soothing drinks instead of solid meals. Use a straw—it makes drinks easier to swallow. ■ Treat any fever (see p. 220); no need to isolate.
RUBELLA (German measles) Caused by virus; infectious. ■ 14–21 day incubation.	■ Lumpy swellings at back of neck. ■ Reddish rash on face, spreading to trunk and limbs. ■ Mild fever and generally unwell.	■ Contact doctor—rubella resembles other rashes. ■ Treat fever if any (see p. 220). ■ Keep child away from pregnant women because rubella can cause birth defects.
KAWASAKI DISEASE Cause unknown, may be infection. Can have long-term effects.	■ Fever for more than five days. ■ Rash, spots, and swollen glands. ■ Sore gums and red eyes. ■ Red, peeling hands and feet.	■ See doctor at once. Hospital treatment needed to prevent later complications such as heart disease. ■ If you're worried about the possibility of Kawasaki, mention it specifically to doctor.

WHAT IS IT?	WHAT ARE THE SYMPTOMS?	WHAT SHOULD I DO?

RESPIRATORY PROBLEMS

WHAT IS IT?	WHAT ARE THE SYMPTOMS?	WHAT SHOULD I DO?
CHEST INFECTION Can be bacterial or viral. Includes bronchitis and pneumonia.	■ Cough and fever—often high. ■ Child unwell—may vomit or refuse food.	■ See doctor, who will check lungs with stethoscope; antibiotics usually prescribed. ■ Treat fever (see p. 220) and give lots of fluids.
BRONCHIOLITIS An infection of the tiny air passages in the lungs (bronchioles). Usually affects babies under 12 months.	■ Cough and symptoms of a cold. ■ Fever. ■ Rapid breathing or shortness of breath and/or audible wheezing and distress; baby may turn blue. ■ Inability to feed.	■ For mild cases, treat fever (see p. 220) and give fluids. Sit child in steamy room to ease breathing. ■ See your doctor for anything other than mild cases or if your child has difficulty breathing; she may need hospital treatment. ☎ CALL 911 if child turns gray or blue.
CROUP Cough in children under three, caused by laryngotracheo-bronchitis or epiglottitis, or, rarely, by foreign object.	■ Harsh, barking cough. ■ Noisy breathing, especially on inhaling. ■ Hoarseness, often worse in early morning.	■ For a mild attack, treat fever (see p. 220), sit child in steamy room and give lots of fluid. ■ Call your doctor if: you notice rapid breathing or difficulty breathing, or you are in doubt about her condition. Never put your finger down your child's throat—if it's epiglottitis she could choke to death. ☎ CALL 911 if child turns gray or blue.
PERTUSSIS *(whooping cough)* Serious infection caused by bacterium *Bordetella pertussis*. ■ Illness may last six weeks, complications can last longer.	■ Mild fever initially. ■ Mild cough and cold in first week, then cough with "whoop" occurs in uncontrollable bouts. ■ Cough can cause vomiting, convulsions, and suffocation. ■ Babies don't "whoop," but can turn blue and suffer convulsions.	■ Contact your doctor urgently. Your child may need antibiotics and hospital treatment. ■ Can cause long-term complications such as lung damage, which will make child more susceptible to other infections.

EYES, EARS, NOSE, AND THROAT

WHAT IS IT?	WHAT ARE THE SYMPTOMS?	WHAT SHOULD I DO?
COMMON COLD Caused by any of over 200 viruses.	■ Runny or blocked nose. ■ Sneezing. ■ Sore throat (in early stages). ■ Mild cough and/or mild fever. ■ Pink eye.	■ Treat symptoms such as fever (see p. 220) and give lots of fluids. ■ See your doctor if child: has high fever; is short of breath; has a bad cough; has an earache.
CONJUNCTIVITIS Viral or bacterial Inflammation of the covering of the eye. ■ Highly infectious.	■ Pink eye (one eye often pinker than the other). ■ Painful eyes. ■ Swollen eyelids (in severe cases).	■ If eye not red or lid swollen, wipe eyelids with cotton wool and cooled boiled water (see p. 29). See doctor if eyelid swollen or eye red—she needs antibiotic drops or ointment. ■ Keep her away from other children.
EAR INFECTION About half are viral, half bacterial. Commonly an infection of the middle ear— known as otitis media	■ Earache (one or both ears). ■ In a baby, pulling at ear. ■ High fever and loss of appetite. ■ Miserable, crying child. ■ Discharge if ear drum bursts.	■ If mild, can treat at home for 24 hours with pain-relieving drugs such as acetaminophen. ■ See doctor if child is in severe pain or if there is discharge from the ear—she may need antibiotics. ■ If only one ear affected, encourage child to sleep with that ear on pillow to allow discharge to drain.
TONSILLITIS About half are viral and the rest bacterial. Very common in under eights. ■ Highly infectious.	■ Sore throat and/or bad breath. ■ Difficulty swallowing. ■ High fever. ■ Swollen, tender glands in neck. ■ Abdominal pain (especially under age five) and possible earache.	■ Treat pain and fever (see p. 220) and give lots of soothing drinks. ■ See your doctor if: very high fever; illness lasts more than 24 hours; your child has an earache. ■ Bacterial cases of tonsillitis respond to antibiotics. ■ Keep her away from other children.

WHAT IS IT?	WHAT ARE THE SYMPTOMS?	WHAT SHOULD I DO?
SKIN, HAIR AND NAILS		
COLD SORES (*Herpes simplex*) Localized virus linked with colds or flu. ■ Highly infectious.	■ First symptom is tingling or pain on lip or nostril. ■ Blisters surrounded by red area that becomes weepy and crusted.	■ Keep child from touching sore. If noticed early, sore may respond to antiviral cream—ask doctor. ■ See doctor if: this is first attack; there is more than one cold sore; sore is near eye; child won't eat or drink; sore looks infected; child unwell.
IMPETIGO Bacterial skin infection which, rarely, can cause kidney disease. ■ Highly infectious.	■ Sore patch, usually near mouth, that spreads quickly and forms messy, weepy, yellow crusts. ■ Possible fever.	■ Tell child not to touch it. See your doctor. Depending on severity, may need antibiotic cream or antibiotics by mouth. Keep away from other children and adults. ■ Treat fever (see p. 220); give lots of fluid.
HEADLICE Common infestation. Lice are small insects that cannot jump. Not easy to see—there may only be 10 on head.	■ Pale brown lice crawling in hair. ■ Eggs (pinhead size) close to scalp or empty eggs ("nits") on hair, looks like dandruff. ■ Gritty brown powder on sheets (blood digested by lice). ■ Itching is a late symptom.	■ Apply a lotion (or shampoo) formulated for headlice. Or use less effective "bug-busting" method: wash hair, then saturate child's hair with conditioner and comb thoroughly with fine-toothed comb and rinse. Repeat every 3–4 days for at least two weeks. Tea tree oil may also help. ■ No need to isolate child.
BOWEL AND BLADDER PROBLEMS		
PINWORMS Common infestation with white, threadlike worms. Spreads via eggs in stools if hands not washed.	■ May have no symptoms. ■ Itching around anal area, especially at night when the worms are more active. ■ Worms visible in the stools.	■ See doctor if in doubt. Treatment available by prescription. ■ Doctor may treat whole household. Bathe in morning after treatment; wash clothes, sheets, towels in very hot water and iron them; cut nails. Wash hands after using toilet and before food.
GASTROENTERITIS Common infection, which can be viral or bacterial.	■ Loose, runny stools and possible vomiting. ■ Pain just after bowel movement. ■ Dehydration if severe.	■ Replace lost fluid and treat fever (see p. 220). ■ See doctor if child: is under 12 months; is vomiting persistently; has blood in stools; has high fever; or seems unwell.
URINARY TRACT INFECTION (UTI) Infection anywhere in urinary system, usually in bladder or kidneys.	*Baby or child under three* ■ Crying, drowsy, refusing feeds. *Child age 3 or older* ■ Passing urine more often. ■ Burning or stinging on urinating. ■ Abdominal pain and/or fever.	■ Always see doctor for suspected UTI for tests on urine sample. Antibiotics may be needed. ■ Give plenty of fluids to flush through urinary tract. ■ Treat fever (see p. 220).

MENINGITIS

WHAT IS IT?	WHAT SHOULD I DO FIRST?
Inflammation of the membranes around the brain: can be viral or bacterial. Bacterial meningitis needs urgent hospital treatment. Meningococcal meningitis can cause blood poisoning and may be fatal within hours. **How will I recognize it?** *In a baby*: your baby should be seen by a doctor immediately if she has any of these symptoms: high fever, won't eat, nonresponsive, persistent high-pitched cry, dislike of light. A rash that remains if pressed may indicate blood poisoning; **call 911** for an ambulance. *In an older child*: some or all of the above symptoms, severe headache, stiff neck, drowsiness, and confusion.	Trust your instincts. If your child seems really sick, call your doctor immediately or go straight to the hospital, where medical evaluation and tests can confirm the diagnosis and treatment. Be persistent until you feel that you understand any problems she may be having and the care necessary to treat them. **Preventing meningitis** Many people carry bacteria that may cause meningitis in their throats. However, infection is rare and may come from another source. MMR vaccine (see p. 213) protects against some types of viral meningitis and Hib (see p. 213) prevents many bacterial cases.

CHRONIC ILLNESSES

WHAT IS IT?	WHAT ARE THE SYMPTOMS?	WHAT SHOULD I DO?
ASTHMA Respiratory disorder in which air passages become inflamed and tend to tighten up and become narrowed, causing the symptoms. Especially common in children over two. Can be mild or severe. ■ Associated with hay fever and eczema. Attacks can be brought on by "triggers."	■ Coughing, especially at night. ■ Shortness of breath, difficulty breathing in and out, and wheezing. ■ Some children cough up phlegm. ■ Acute attacks can be severe with extreme shortness of breath—child may turn blue from lack of oxygen.	Always see the doctor for suspected asthma. A child needs an inhaler for quick relief from attacks. It's harder to treat babies because their asthma does not always respond. Antibiotics are of little use. **What parents can do** Stay calm. Help your child use inhalers regularly and take asthma in stride. Try to eliminate possible triggers such as dust mites, pets, and cigarette smoke.
ECZEMA Disorder involving inflammation of the skin. Common in babies from age 3–18 months and can resolve eventually, usually by adolescence. Usually occurs in families with asthma, hay fever, and other allergies.	■ Itching and scratching, especially at night (and lack of sleep for you both). ■ Raw or dry-looking patches on face, skin creases such as elbows and back of knees—what many parents think is dry skin is eczema, and vice versa. ■ May have small red spots. ■ Affected skin may get infected, mainly in diaper area—infected areas become weepy.	See your doctor. Creams and emollients help, especially in the bath. Your doctor may prescribe mild steroid cream or ointment—stronger creams are usually unsuitable. Chinese herbal medicine (see p. 227) can help some children. **What parents can do** Avoid soap. Wash clothes in mild non-irritating detergent and rinse well; clothe baby in cotton, not synthetics; keep fingernails short (try scratch mittens on a baby). Ask your doctor about diet; eliminating certain foods may help.
OTITIS MEDIA WITH EFFUSION Occurs when thick sticky fluid collects in the middle ear. Common in 2–5-year-olds because the tube that connects the ear to the back of the throat gets blocked easily. Not every child needs surgery—many cases clear naturally.	■ Symptoms can be in one or both ears. ■ Hearing loss (sound waves travel poorly through fluid). ■ Delayed speech. ■ An earache, especially with repeated acute infections.	See doctor for hearing tests and/or tympanometry (measures how well the eardrum moves). Treatment is to insert tiny tubes in the eardrum under anesthetic to equalize pressure. Child may need adenoids removed, too. **What parents can do** If child has difficulty hearing, speak to her directly with as little background noise as possible. Attend medical check-ups, whether or not child has tubes.
DIABETES MELLITUS Caused by lack of insulin, the hormone that helps glucose enter the body cells. Cause is unknown, but possibly a reaction to infection. Children with diabetes often need insulin.	■ Often sudden onset with thirst and passing large amounts of urine. ■ Weight loss. ■ Abdominal pain and vomiting and possible dehydration. ■ Listlessness or coma. ■ Smell of ketones on breath—resembles nail polish remover. ■ Infection, either chest or urinary.	See your doctor without delay, but do not panic. Your child needs treatment in the hospital, then as an outpatient. **What parents can do** Reassure her and don't panic. Give her injections until she can do it herself. She does not need as strict a diet as adult diabetics because she is still growing. Find out as much information as you can.
EPILEPSY Repeated seizures or convulsions that appear unprovoked. Two main types: generalized (whole body) and partial (e.g., one limb). Many possible causes; may run in families; some children grow out of it.	■ Twitching in partial seizures. ■ In major generalized convulsions (grand mal), whole body stiffens, then jerks uncontrollably. Child may wet or soil herself. No recollection of event afterward. ■ Petit mal is a form of epilepsy with short "blank" periods, as if day-dreaming.	See doctor urgently—child will need expert assessment and hospital tests. Anticonvulsant treatment enables virtually normal life, but tell the preschool and later the school. **What parents can do** Try to help child lead normal life. Provide her with bracelet or medallion engraved with medical information.

CHILD HEALTH

TAKING CARE OF A SICK CHILD

Q HOW CAN I BEST CARE FOR A SICK CHILD AT HOME ?

A You should reduce any fever and pain with acetaminophen, and provide plenty to drink to counteract dehydration. You don't need special training, but watch over your child. Children change quickly when ill—mostly for the better, but occasionally for the worse. Give her lots of love and provide undemanding activities; you can read to her or let her watch television or a video.

PARENT'S SURVIVAL GUIDE

MY CHILD HAS A FEVER

Much of a child's distress when ill is due to the fever, so relieving this can make her feel better. Fever can also lead to dehydration. In children between six months and four years, a high fever may cause seizures, known as febrile convulsions (see p. 231).

What should I do?

■ Take off excess clothing—your child doesn't need more than her underwear (or diaper). If she is in bed, cover her with a cotton sheet (with or without a light blanket). Don't listen to anyone who tells you to wrap your child up—it will raise her temperature.

■ Give her acetaminophen liquid (dose as recommended on the bottle) which should start working after about 20 minutes. Don't give it to a baby under three months without first consulting your doctor. Never give aspirin to a child under 12 unless it has been prescribed as there is a risk of a rare complication, called Reye syndrome, developing.

■ Encourage your child to drink plenty of fluid.

■ Take her temperature every 3-4 hours throughout the illness (see p. 215).

■ If her temperature is over 102°F/39°C by mouth, cool her down by sponging her with lukewarm water (not cold). Take your child's temperature every 10 minutes until it begins to fall and she starts to look better. Call your pediatrician if your child's temperature is not beginning to fall within half an hour.

Q DOES A SICK CHILD NEED TO STAY IN BED ?

A No. If your child is very ill she may prefer her bed, but she may like to lie on the sofa near you; leave it up to her. There are very few reasons for forcing a child to stay in bed. However, you may need to keep her indoors.

Q WHY IS IT IMPORTANT FOR HER TO DRINK AND WHAT SHOULD I GIVE HER ?

A Drinks help replace the body fluid lost through sweating and prevent dehydration. Severe dehydration from fluid loss can cause kidney failure and even death. A good fluid intake will really speed up recovery. You can let her have more or less anything she feels like, but not tea or coffee. Give small quantities at a time. Leave a drink beside her, she may drink more if she has a straw. You can still breast-feed a baby even if she has diarrhea, but children and bottle-fed babies with stomach upsets should avoid milk. Give plain water, diluted fruit juice, or rehydration solutions. Ask your pediatrician or pharmacist.

Q WHAT SHOULD I DO IF MY CHILD WON'T EAT ?

A Many parents worry about a sick child's lack of appetite, but fluids are what matters. Unless your doctor has advised otherwise, your child doesn't need to eat while she's sick. She'll regain her appetite when she feels better.

Q SHOULD MY CHILD BE DROWSY WHEN SHE'S SICK ?

A It's normal for anyone to feel tired and sleep more when sick. However, your child should be able to stay awake, and you should be able to rouse her if needed, for instance to take medicine. If you can't wake her, call your pediatrician.

Q MY PEDIATRICIAN SAYS MY CHILD DOESN'T NEED ANTIBIOTICS. WHY ?

A She probably has a viral infection. Antibiotics only work on bacterial infections. Viruses live inside the body's cells so antibiotics don't reach them. Antibiotics can affect the normal bacteria present in the body and their overuse can make these resistant to infection. It is not always easy to tell whether an illness is viral or bacterial, so your pediatrician may have to make a guess.

WHAT'S THE BEST WAY TO GIVE MEDICATION ?

Choose a time when your child is most likely to be relaxed, and stay calm yourself. Give medicines at regular intervals following the instructions on the label and use the spoon, syringe, or dropper provided. Aim to give the whole dose at once (never exceed the prescribed dose of any medicine) and always finish a course of antibiotics. Remember to keep all medicines out of reach of children.

GIVING MEDICINE BY MOUTH

Measure out the dose *before* you pick up your child. Touch your baby's bottom lip with the spoon, syringe, or plastic dropper provided to encourage her to open her mouth. You may need to have a drink ready if she doesn't like it.

Using a syringe
Fill the syringe from the bottle. Sit your child on your lap and syringe the medicine into her mouth. If necessary, tilt her slightly so the medicine stays in.

Using a dropper
Fill the dropper from the spoon. Pick your baby up and lean her back slightly on your arm. Support her head and hold her free arm so she can't swipe at the dropper. Encourage your baby to open her mouth by touching her lips with the dropper.

She spits out her medicine. What can I do?
Wait until she is calm, then try again. Try using her favorite spoon, or mix the medicine with jam. Don't add medicine to a drink—it tends to cling to the cup. If your child still refuses, talk to your pediatrician, who may try another medicine or, rarely, suppositories or injections.

ADMINISTERING SUPPOSITORIES

Explain to the child what you are doing. Wash your hands. Lie your child on her side with her knees bent up as far as she can. Gently insert the suppository—pointed end first. Ask your child to stay still for a few minutes. Wash your hands.

INSTILLING EYE-, EAR-, OR NOSEDROPS

These usually have to be given, or "instilled," three or four times a day for five days, so you need to develop a good technique that you can both cope with. Fill the dropper before you pick up your child. Reassure your baby or child throughout.

Giving eyedrops
Sit down on a flat surface such as a bed, lay your child across your lap, and hold her head steady with one arm. Get someone else to hold her if necessary. Gently pull the lower eyelid down with your thumb, then instil the drops into the space between the eyeball and the lower lid. If your child resists (she may next time even if the first time went smoothly), hold her arms and head more firmly. It may help to have someone distract her by dangling or holding a small toy or something shiny above her head, which will make her look up.

Giving eardrops
Lay your child on his side. Hold his head gently but firmly as you let the drops fall into the ear canal. Keep him still for a few seconds, so that the drops run completely into the ear canal; if he sits up too soon the drops will leak out.

Giving nosedrops
Lay your child on her back and tilt her head back, holding her arms down if possible (you may need someone to help). Gently hold her head with one hand and drop the nose drops into the nostril. Try to persuade her to "sniff" the drops up her nose.

WHEN YOUR CHILD IS IN THE HOSPITAL

Q **HOW CAN I PREPARE MY CHILD FOR THE HOSPITAL?**

A Tell her ahead of time, and explain that hospitals are places where they make children better. There are many books, videos, toys, and even computer games related to hospitals that can help get your child used to the idea. Some hospitals have a special day when children can visit and play with some of the equipment. When she asks about her forthcoming visit to the hospital, answer simply and honestly but without overloading her with detail. Avoid making promises you can't keep if, for instance, you're not sure you'll stay in with her.

Q **WHAT DOES MY CHILD NEED TO TAKE TO THE HOSPITAL?**

A She will need a suitcase, which she can help you pack, containing: pajamas or nightgowns; a bathrobe; slippers; a toothbrush and toothpaste; soap and a washcloth; a hairbrush or comb; a favorite stuffed animal; a favorite book; and a small game or toy.

Q **SHOULD I STAY IN THE HOSPITAL WITH MY CHILD?**

A Most hospitals expect parents to stay with a child under five, and I think you should do so if you are able to. Ask the nurses what you can do to help them take care of your child. You may be able to assist with changing and bathing her, and with feeding. Your presence can really help your child's recovery, even if the two of you do nothing more demanding than gazing out of the window or watching television. You may be provided with an adult bed or cot next to your child, or you may have to doze in an armchair. If it isn't possible for you to stay in the hospital with your child, try to spend as much time there as you can and be sure to be there for operations or tests.

Q **MY CHILD IS TERRIFIED OF NEEDLES. WHAT CAN I DO?**

A Children fear blood tests and injections more than almost anything else about being a patient. This is normal. You can help her relax by being with your child, holding her hand, and explaining that although it will hurt a bit, it doesn't last.

Q **WILL MY CHILD NEED SPECIAL ATTENTION WHEN SHE COMES HOME?**

A It depends on why she was in the hospital and for how long. Be prepared to spend time helping your child get back to normal. Don't treat her like an invalid, but be patient. Although children bounce back quickly from illness, the routine at home is probably very different from that in the hospital. Indulging your child totally wouldn't be good for her, but you can afford to be relaxed about minor things like what she wears. Attend follow-up appointments and make sure you give her any medicine the doctor has prescribed.

PARENT'S SURVIVAL GUIDE

MY CHILD NEEDS AN OPERATION

Having been involved in operations as a doctor and a mother (and as a child in the more distant past), I believe that surgery can be as hard for the parent as for the child.

Find out as much as possible
Inform yourself, so that you can prepare your child for the practicalities. She needs to know about the strange operating gowns, why she can't eat or drink, the funny machines, and so on. The anesthesiologist will visit you and your child before the operation. Ask how your child will be put under. It could be with a gas, or it might be by injection—this can now be made painless with anesthetic cream. Explain to your child that when it's all over, she will wake up in a special recovery room.

Helping your child
Stay with her. About an hour and a half before the anesthetic, she may be given some medicine to make her sleepy (pre-med). Read your child a familiar story, or just sit by the bed and hold her hand. A smile inspires confidence and can boost her morale. Talk about the fun things you'll do when she gets home, but don't promise anything too rash. One or both parents can usually stay with their child while she is being given anesthesia or until she's under, and then join her in the recovery room afterward.

CHILDREN WITH SPECIAL NEEDS

Q WHAT DOES THE TERM "SPECIAL NEEDS" MEAN ?

A This term applies to children whose development, communication, and learning abilities or behavior are such that they will need special attention in order to realize their full potential. "Special needs" covers a wide range of conditions and is a more positive term that replaces the words "handicapped" and "disabled."

Q WHO DECIDES WHEN A CHILD HAS A LONG-TERM PROBLEM ?

A Your child's doctor may be the first to notice any delays in development. If a long-term problem is suspected, your doctor may then arrange for your child to have a full developmental assessment, including hearing tests and vision tests. A final diagnosis will take into account the results of these tests.

Q MY CHILD HAS SPECIAL NEEDS. WHERE CAN I GET HELP ?

A Whether you need medical, practical, or financial help, talk to your doctor or pediatrician. She can refer you to any of the agencies that may benefit your child, including special education departments, social services, child psychiatrist, or physical therapist, and even relevant support groups. Teamwork will help support you as a family.

Q WHERE CAN I MEET OTHER PARENTS WITH SIMILAR CHILDREN ?

A Volunteer organizations and support groups can put you in touch with other families in a similar situation. Many support groups have local branches and are run by parents whose children have the same needs. Occasionally, a condition is so rare that there will be very few other children who have it. In that case ask your pediatrician or doctor who to approach, or look on the Internet for additional information.

THE REWARDS OF SPECIAL NEEDS
Children with special needs can be very rewarding to care for and often go on to lead fulfilling lives as adolescents and adults.

PARENT'S SURVIVAL GUIDE

MY CHILD HAS A SERIOUS CONDITION

It can be a great blow to learn that your child has a serious illness or special needs. In fact, it's like a bereavement. You may feel you have lost the chance to have a healthy child and the anticipated "normal" parenting. You may go through recognized stages:

- shock on being told the diagnosis and inability to believe it
- anger at health professionals, your partner, or even yourself
- depression, which can be severe
- finally, acceptance and the ability to live family life with the disability.

Get professional help
It can be hard to ask for help and to accept it, especially when there is resentment against doctors or parents of so-called "normal" or healthy children. Sometimes, parents of special needs children find it is easier to talk to other parents who are going through a similar experience. Much the same goes for those whose child has leukemia or another serious illness. With modern treatments, the outlook is immeasurably better these days, but the whole family needs support. Your healthcare providers can help.

CHILD HEALTH

SPECIAL NEEDS

WHAT IS IT?	WHAT ARE THE SYMPTOMS?	WHAT CAN BE DONE TO HELP?
DOWN SYNDROME This is a chromosome (genetic) abnormality present from birth. Down syndrome is the most common special needs problem. **What causes Down syndrome?** Most people are born with 23 pairs of chromosomes. In Down syndrome there is either an an extra chromosome at position 21 or a "rearrangement" (called a translocation) at chromosome 21. Many babies with Down syndrome are born to older mothers. It's not certain what happens, but it is related to the way egg cells divide and grow.	■ Distinctive facial features include a round face, slanting eyes, and a wide nose. ■ Large tongue that may protrude, short fingers and toes. ■ Some learning difficulties. ■ Many children with Down syndrome have gut and heart problems and a tendency to get recurrent coughs and chest infections. Your child should be assessed for heart defects as a baby.	The outlook varies. Many children with Down syndrome are affectionate and sociable; some are able to cope with normal schooling. Those with severe learning difficulties need more specialized help. A child with Down syndrome can learn, but it takes patience and perseverance. Your child will need assessment to find out how she is affected. About half have heart defects, which can limit their life expectancy. **What parents can do** Encourage her to become as independent as possible. Even if she is limited intellectually, she will find pleasure in things like music that you can do together.
CEREBRAL PALSY This is a brain (cerebral) disorder that causes loss of muscle power (palsy). Cerebral palsy is quite common and can be mild or severe, affecting one limb or more. Children with cerebral palsy are often intelligent, but the muscle weakness makes it hard for them to communicate. A child can get very frustrated, both with her inability to do things and with the attitude of people around her. Symptoms may change as a child gets older, but the condition doesn't deteriorate. **What causes cerebral palsy?** Nobody knows. It was thought to be caused by trauma at birth but this doesn't explain every case, and it seems certain that factors before birth are important.	The symptoms vary depending on the severity and type of cerebral palsy. ■ Your baby may be unusually floppy at birth, or later show delay in sitting up. ■ Some children have uncontrollable twisting or writhing movements. ■ The early muscle floppiness may disappear, and limbs become stiff as well as weak.	The challenge in caring for a child with cerebral palsy is bringing out her intelligence and encouraging her to use the senses that she has. She will need assessment by many different experts, from speech therapists and physical therapists to psychologists, especially if she is very physically impaired. **What parents can do** Show her a lot of love and patience and keep a positive outlook. Focus on what your child can do. Continue the physical therapy techniques at home. Try to get her into a mainstream school.
HEARING IMPAIRMENT Many children have some degree of temporary hearing impairment, either partial or total (see p. 219). A few children have more permanent hearing loss. Routine development tests help pick up hearing impairment, but if you are concerned about your child's hearing at any time, talk to your doctor or pediatrician. **What causes the impairment?** In some cases the middle ear fails to conduct sound—so-called "conductive deafness," which can be the result of ear infections. The other main cause of impairment is "sensorineural deafness," in which nerves in the ear don't send impulses to the brain. This can be inherited or follow infections such as rubella in pregnancy, or meningitis in childhood.	Symptoms depend on which part of the sound spectrum is affected and the severity of the deafness. ■ Inability to hear high-pitched sounds. ■ Your baby does not respond to your voice. ■ Your child fails to do as you ask—assuming this is not just bad behavior! If slightly deaf, your child may appear badly behaved and hard to control because she can't communicate easily. ■ Your child may be slow to learn or speak.	Treatment depends on the cause and the extent of impairment. Tubes can relieve deafness from chronic secretory otitis media (see p. 219), while hearing aids may be needed for more permanent loss. Many children with permanent hearing loss do well at normal schools, with some special help. **What parents can do** Speak clearly to your child, avoiding interruptions, minimize background noise, and give her time to express her needs. If your child's hearing is severely affected, learn sign language. This helps you both communicate and won't prevent speech from developing.

WHAT IS IT?	WHAT ARE THE SYMPTOMS?	WHAT CAN BE DONE TO HELP?
CYSTIC FIBROSIS (CF) An inherited (genetic) condition that affects the glands that secrete mucus and certain enzymes in the body. This causes very sticky mucus to collect in the lungs, which leads to recurrent infections. In the gut, the lack of certain enzymes means the body can't absorb fats and nutrients. There is no cure for cystic fibrosis, but treatment can prolong life. **What causes cystic fibrosis?** If both parents carry the cystic fibrosis gene, they can have a child affected by the disease. About one person in 20 has the gene but is healthy and often unaware of being a carrier.	■ Failure to gain weight. ■ Your baby may fail to pass meconium or stools at birth. ■ Frequent chest infections or chronic cough. ■ Constipation or diarrhea with motions that are bulky and smelly because of their high fat content. The abdomen can be swollen and feel uncomfortable. ■ Children with CF will be small for their age.	Physical therapy helps keep the lungs clear, and a special high-energy, high-protein diet with plenty of vitamins helps the digestive system. Children with CF usually need to take pancreatic enzymes before meals to replace what their own body can't make. Affected children need prompt treatment for chest infections. If lung damage is severe, heart failure may develop; some children need a heart–lung transplant. **What parents can do** Learn how to carry out daily chest physical therapy. Teach your child how to cough up the phlegm. Make sure you help your child keep to her diet and take any medication.
AUTISM A disorder of development that impairs a child's ability to interact with people, her communication, and her imagination. It can be mild or severe—there are several variants, often grouped as autism spectrum disorders. Autism affects boys more than girls, and is usually diagnosed between six months and three years of age. **What causes autism?** No one really knows, but it probably reflects some type of brain damage at some point—inflammation of the brain from the measles virus can cause similar symptoms.	■ Babies may dislike hugs and show little eye contact. ■ Children may throw tantrums when anything changes and/or need elaborate rituals for trivia. ■ Repetitive behavior, such as rocking back and forth. ■ May be attached to strange objects, yet detached from people. ■ Speech can be immature and lack expression. ■ Child may repeat whole sentences parrot-style (all children go through this, but in autism it's lasting).	Your child needs to be referred to a specialist for diagnosis. The sooner the diagnosis is made, the better the outlook. There is no cure, but many therapies from reward systems and behavioral modification to massage and physical therapy can help. Autistic children need individual attention to help them relate to others. Severe autism impairs a child's ability to learn, but children with mild autism can be integrated into society with expert help. **What parents can do** Help him develop social skills so that he can become as independent as possible.
ATTENTION DEFICIT HYPERACTIVITY DISORDER (ADHD) This covers a range of behavior problems including hyperactivity and attention deficit disorder. There are no tests for this condition—the diagnosis is based on expert assessment. It is more common in boys, and there is no cure, but consistency, understanding, and loving firmness can help children fulfill their potential. **What causes ADHD?** The exact cause of ADHD is unknown. It may be due to an imbalance of chemical transmitters in the brain. There is sometimes a family history, which shows that ADHD is probably inherited. Some research focuses on small differences in brain scans between average children and those with ADHD.	■ Poor concentration and short attention span. ■ Constant restlessness. ■ Impulsive behavior. ■ Clumsiness. ■ Poor social skills. ■ Disruptive behavior. All young children have these to some extent, but in ADHD the symptoms are not in keeping with the child's age.	See your doctor, who may arrange expert assessment. Every child with ADHD needs an intelligence test, which helps pinpoint strengths and weaknesses. The challenge is to maximize a child's potential and make his behavior acceptable to others. Drugs can increase attention span, but correct handling at home and later at school is important. **What parents can do** Accept your child as he is. Keep calm and positive to help build up his self-esteem. Try to get your child into a routine and always communicate clearly.

CHILD HEALTH

COMPLEMENTARY THERAPIES

Q WHICH COMPLEMENTARY THERAPIES CAN HELP A CHILD?

A There are many therapies used for children. The most common of these include:

■ homeopathy—treatment is based on the theory that a substance that in large doses causes specific symptoms will, in tiny doses, relieve the same symptoms (see opposite)

■ herbal medicine—the use of the active medicinal constituents of plants; Chinese herbal medicine can be effective for childhood eczema

■ aromatherapy—using herbal oils (called essential oils) mixed into a massage oil or inhaled as a vapor using a special burner

■ osteopathy—a system of manipulation. The method most frequently used to treat children is cranial osteopathy.

Despite the rapidly growing popularity of complementary medicine, there is still limited scientific evidence that these treatments work. I am entirely tolerant of complementary medicine and of those who find that it helps them. However, it is odd that in an era when medical practitioners are under pressure to produce more and more scientific evidence for the effectiveness of their treatments, complementary practitioners offer little proof that their methods work. Complementary therapists do, however, give their patients a lot of time and individual attention, so there is something many doctors could learn from them.

Q HOW CAN I FIND A COMPLEMENTARY THERAPIST?

A This depends on the therapy. In the United States and Canada, some complementary therapies have official associations with referral facilities, but others do not. It is therefore important for a parent to be sure that a practitioner is suitably qualified. Be especially wary of anyone who claims to be able to relieve or cure a condition that nobody else can treat. If you are consulting a practitioner who is not medically qualified, it's a good idea to check any unexplained symptoms with your doctor. Your doctor or pediatrician may also be able to provide names of respected complementary practitioners in your area.

Q ARE COMPLEMENTARY THERAPIES COMPLETELY SAFE?

A No. As with any treatment, there are potential risks. Many herbal medicines, for instance, are not manufactured to strict standards or subjected to rigorous testing because legally they are not considered medicines. They can thus be impure and the dose can be inexact. In addition, many herbal remedies contain active ingredients and may be dangerous if used incorrectly or in combination with prescription drugs. Sometimes, treatments such as manipulation can be risky— for example, in a child with brittle bone disease. However, the greatest problem is that parents who choose alternative therapies may abandon medical help, and their child's condition may worsen. I think it's vital to think of complementary medicine as just that—a complement to conventional therapy.

Q WHAT IS CRANIAL OSTEOPATHY AND WHAT CAN IT RELIEVE?

A Cranial osteopathy is very gentle manipulation of the bones of the skull, which is said to encourage the normal flow of fluid around the brain. It is popular with some parents who have found that it helps colic, feeding and sleeping problems, birth trauma, dyslexia, and clumsiness, although not every child responds.

Q HOW CAN AROMATHERAPY HELP CHILDREN?

A Although there is little objective evidence, aromatherapy can sometimes be effective for:

■ minor cuts and grazes (tea tree oil)

■ postnasal drip (lemon and eucalyptus oils)

■ chickenpox (lavender and tea tree oils)

■ headlice (a blend of tea tree, rose, eucalyptus, lemon, lavender, and geranium oils)

■ diaper rash (tea tree oil used as an antiseptic rinse when washing cloth diapers)

■ sleep problems (usually lavender oil).

Essential oils are diluted in a base oil and either applied to the affected area, used in massage, or inhaled as vapor. When using aromatherapy, make sure that the oil is suitable for a child and that she does not taste or swallow it; the oils are all very strong and some of them are toxic.

Q DOES HERBAL MEDICINE HAVE ANY BENEFITS?

A Yes. Chinese herbal medicine can be especially useful for eczema, but the treatment can have powerful side effects. Western herbalism has also claimed to help many conditions, from ear infections to immune deficiencies. Echinacea is a remedy advocated as an anti-infective and immune stimulant, which may help prevent colds. However, because herbs can be very strong drugs and can interact with other medicines, I think it is best to consult a medical herbalist for advice.

Q IS ACUPUNCTURE EVER USEFUL FOR CHILDREN?

A No, hardly ever. Acupuncture can help relieve pain in adults, but there are few conditions in children that qualify. It's important to remember that acupuncture can be an uncomfortable treatment and children are afraid of needles. With this in mind, it's best to avoid acupuncture in children, especially if there's a conventional treatment that works. There can be no justification at all for using acupuncture for behavioral or developmental symptoms like bed-wetting.

WHAT IS HOMEOPATHY SUITABLE FOR?

Some complaints, such as those listed below, respond well to homeopathy. Most of the remedies are available from homeopathic practitioners or health food stores, and are made from lactose or sucrose so they taste good to children.

What can I treat at home?
There are many common complaints that you can treat at home using homeopathy, including:
- **colic** If your baby brings her legs up and screams a lot, try Colocynth (bitter cucumber). If she burps and vomits a lot, a good remedy might be Carbo vegetalis (vegetable charcoal). If she is furious, is not soothed by being carried, and strains to fill her diaper, try Nux vomica (poison nut)
- **teething** Chamomilla (chamomile) might help pain or sleeplessness from teething
- **mild eczema** If your child has a mild form of eczema that is dry, you can try Sulphur. To treat moist eczema, try Petroleum.
- **sleep problems** For a baby over three months who won't sleep through the night or who wakes very early in the morning, you can try Chamomilla (chamomile). It may also help to calm a baby who is restless at bedtime.
- **common cold** For a baby with a stuffy nose, try giving her Kali bichromicum (potassium bichromate). For a toddler with catarrh or a cold, try Pulsatilla (wind anemone) tablets twice a day
- **bumps and bruises** Swelling and bruising can be relieved with Arnica cream. If there is an open cut or graze, don't use the cream but give the Arnica in tablet form
- **night fears** Calcarea carbonica (crushed oyster shells) or Phosphorus could be worth trying
- **bed-wetting** If your child wets the bed early in the night, try Equisetum (scouring rush). If she wets it later, try Lycopodium (club moss).

How do I give the remedies?
Homeopathic remedies come either in tablets or granules. Babies can take homeopathic tablets crushed and mixed in a little cooled boiled water. Give half a teaspoon at a time, and make up a fresh solution daily. A baby on solids will usually take a crushed tablet or granules off a spoon, while a toddler or child can suck the tablet whole.

When should I see a homeopath?
Homeopaths are either practitioners who aren't medically qualified or doctors who practice homeopathy as well as conventional medicine. You should see a medical homeopath if your child has severe eczema or asthma, since these two conditions need expert treatment. A child with hyperactivity also needs to see a homeopath before treatment starts so that the remedy can be matched to the child's symptoms.

How long does treatment last?
Some treatments for minor ailments may only need a single dose, although if your child has long-term problems she may need to continue treatment for months. However, with homeopathy it is normal to stop the treatment as soon as improvement occurs—unlike conventional drugs.

When should I see the doctor?
Always see the doctor if your child's symptoms persist, if symptoms change, or if they could be due to a serious illness.

FIRST AID

Q WHAT SHOULD I DO IN CASE OF AN ACCIDENT ?

A The same principles apply to every accident, whether it's a mishap in the kitchen or a car.
■ Assess the situation quickly. You may have to take steps to prevent further injury and protect yourself. After a car accident, for instance, stopping traffic is as vital as seeing to your child.
■ Reassure your child and keep calm. An air of confidence and competence will help your child.
■ Decide whether you need help. Your child needs urgent hospital treatment if she: is unconscious; has difficulty breathing; has lost a lot of blood; has a burn—unless it is small and superficial (see opposite); has broken a bone.

Q CAN I TAKE MY CHILD TO THE HOSPITAL MYSELF ?

In general, call for an ambulance, unless the injury is minor and you can take your child to the hospital yourself. If you're unsure, call your doctor—if you can't get through, go to the hospital anyway. Never give an injured child anything to eat or drink; she may need a general anesthetic.

Q IS IT A GOOD IDEA TO TAKE A FIRST-AID COURSE ?

A Yes, it is. The information on these pages is no substitute for first-aid training. You are more likely to save a child's life if you have taken an approved course.

FIRST-AID KIT

Every home (and car) should have a first-aid kit. It can help you cope with minor injuries as well as some serious ones. Keep the kit accessible and clearly labeled but out of a child's reach, and check stocks regularly. Write important phone numbers, such as your doctor or local hospital, on a card, and tape it to the lid.

YOUR BASIC KIT

Gauze roller bandages

Assorted gauze dressings with bandages attached

Triangular bandage to make a sling

Tape to secure dressings

Nonstick gauze dressings

Scissors to cut dressings or bandages (or clothing)

At least 6 safety pins

Adhesive bandages

Tweezers for removing splinters

Antiseptic cream, wipes, or liquid

USEFUL EXTRAS
■ Roll of sterile cotton batting
■ Gauze pads
■ Eye pad with bandage
■ Disposable gloves
■ Cotton swabs
■ Two small clear plastic bags and plastic wrap to dress burns or seal chest wounds
■ Clean pillowcase or sheet—for large burns or other wounds
■ Thermometer (see p. 215)
■ Flashlight (at least nearby), in case of a power failure
■ Foil emergency blanket for a car kit
■ Whistle to summon help—especially important for the car kit

In theory, first-aid boxes shouldn't contain medicines, but in practice it's useful to keep acetaminophen liquid and a clean 5ml medicine spoon and calamine lotion in, or near, a home first-aid kit.

IF YOUR CHILD IS BLEEDING

Severe bleeding needs urgent treatment to prevent shock from developing (see p. 231). Your child is likely to be upset, but don't panic or you'll be less able to help her.

What should I do first?

■ Gently remove or cut away clothing.
■ Apply pressure directly onto the wound with your fingers, or over a sterile dressing.
■ Raise the injured limb and support it so that it is higher than her heart (chest).
■ If possible, lay your child down.
■ Once bleeding stops, put another dressing over the original one and bandage firmly in place. If any blood seeps through the dressings, add another one.
■ Take your child to the hospital or
☎ DIAL 911 FOR AN AMBULANCE.

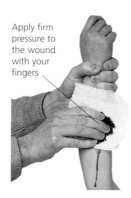

Apply firm pressure to the wound with your fingers

If there is a foreign body

IF there is something such as a piece of glass in the wound, DO NOT try to remove it. Press firmly against either side of the object. Then build up padding on either side of the object, until high enough to bandage over the top without pressing on the object.

For minor cuts and abrasions

Wash abrasion with water and try to remove any gravel, although this may restart bleeding. Apply pressure to stop bleeding and cover with an adhesive bandage or sterile pad. See a doctor if there is any dirt left in the wound.

IF YOUR CHILD HAS A BURN

The effect of a burn is much the same whatever the cause, and your aim is to cool the burn as soon as possible. A burn can be partial thickness, full thickness, or a combination of both. A partial-thickness burn affects only the top layer of skin and is very painful. It looks red and raw, but usually heals well. A full-thickness burn affects all the skin layers and may be painless. The area may look white or waxy, and scarring is usually severe.

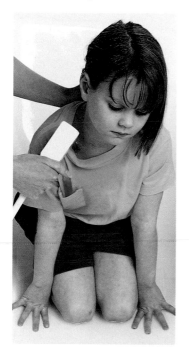

What should I do first?

■ Cool the burn. Run cold water slowly over it for least 10 minutes. If the burns are on her trunk, put her in the bathtub and use a shower, but don't let her get cold. There's no need to remove her clothes before you start.
■ Cover the burn with a nonstick sterile dressing (a hand or foot can be enclosed in a plastic bag).

DO NOT apply butter, fat, ointment, or lotions.
■ Take your child to the hospital if: the burn is larger than the palm of her hand; there is a full-thickness burn, however small; it's a chemical or electrical burn; the burn is in her mouth or on her face— swelling can block the air passage. IF you're not sure, go to the hospital, or call your doctor.

IF CLOTHING IS ON FIRE

DO NOT let her run around. This will only fan the flames. DO lay your child down so the flames can't burn her face. Put out the flames with water.
■ Alternatively, wrap her tightly in a woolen or cotton blanket or coat (NOT nylon), and roll her along the ground to smother the flames.
☎ DIAL 911 FOR AN AMBULANCE Even if she seems well after this ordeal, she will need hospital assessment.

FIRST AID EMERGENCIES

WHAT IS IT?	WHAT ACTION SHOULD I TAKE?
HEAD INJURY All head injuries should be seen by a doctor. Wounds on the scalp may hide underlying damage such as a concussion, skull fracture, or a neck (spinal) injury.	■ Watch your child closely. If she loses consciousness, clear and open the airway and be ready to resuscitate (see p. 232). ■ ☎ CALL 911 FOR AN AMBULANCE or take your child straight to a hospital emergency department. ■ Treat bleeding scalp wounds by applying pressure.
EYE INJURIES Children often get foreign objects in their eyes. Most of these can be easily removed. **What are the symptoms?** ■ Blurred vision and pain in affected eye.	■ Wash out the eye with clean, cool water. ■ Open the eye carefully. If you can see something on the lid and can remove it easily, do so using a cotton swab. ■ If there's something stuck in the eye or on the colored part of the eye, or the eye is bleeding, take your child to the hospital.
NOSEBLEED Nosebleeds can occur as a result of falling over, rough play, and even sneezing, nose-blowing, and nose-picking are relatively common in childhood.	■ Sit your child down with her head over a bowl. ■ Pinch just below the bridge of the nose for up to 10 minutes. ■ After 10 minutes release the pressure; if the nose is still bleeding, reapply pressure. ■ If bleeding continues for more than 20 minutes, call a doctor.
FOREIGN OBJECTS IN EAR OR NOSE Children often try to put small objects in their ears or nose. For objects in the mouth or airway, see Choking (p. 234).	■ If the object is up your child's nose, tell her to breathe slowly through her mouth and take her to a hospital emergency department. ■ If the object is in her ear, take her straight to the hospital.
BONE, JOINT, AND MUSCLE INJURIES Children often break bones, although their bones are soft and may split (greenstick fracture) rather than break. Dislocation occurs if a bone comes out of its socket. Joints may be sprained following a fall and muscles can be strained during exertion. **What are the symptoms?** ■ Pain and tenderness. ■ Swelling and/or deformity.	■ Keep the injured limb immobilized. You can strap it to another (uninjured) part of the body. An injured arm may be more comfortable in a sling, but if she has hurt her elbow, don't attempt to move the arm—support it in the position you found her. Any attempt to move it could damage the blood vessels or nerves at the elbow. ■ Take your child to the hospital if her injury is minor and you can support the injured part; otherwise, call an ambulance. ■ Don't give your child anything to eat or drink until the doctor says you can, because she may need an anesthetic.
FINGER AND TOE INJURIES Babies and young children often crush their fingers or toes in doors or drawers. Although they're acutely painful, most of these injuries are minor. If a finger or toe is severed, it may be possible for doctors to reattach a digit or even a whole hand, but you must act fast.	■ Run cold water onto the injury or apply ice to reduce swelling. ■ If the skin is broken, clean it and apply an adhesive bandage. **If a finger or toe is severed** ■ ☎ CALL 911 FOR AN AMBULANCE immediately. ■ Put the severed part in a plastic bag and wrap it in a cloth. ■ Place this in a container filled with ice (another plastic bag will do), labeled with the time of the accident and your child's name. ■ If necessary, apply pressure to the limb to stop bleeding.
STINGS Young children may be stung by bees and wasps. This can hurt and be frightening. **What are the symptoms?** ■ Pain and swelling at the site of the sting. ■ Rarely, anaphylactic shock may occur.	■ Rinse the stung area in cool water or apply an ice pack. ■ If you can see that the stinger is still there, remove it. ■ Give her acetaminophen liquid and apply antiseptic cream or calamine to the site of the sting. ■ ☎ CALL 911 FOR AN AMBULANCE if the sting is on or near the mouth (it can swell up and stop her from breathing) or if she appears unwell.
ANAPHYLACTIC SHOCK This is a rare, serious allergic reaction. Causes include insect stings, nuts, and drugs. **What are the symptoms?** ■ Blotchy rash all over body. ■ Puffy eyelids and face. ■ Difficulty breathing. ■ Possible unconsciousness.	■ ☎ CALL 911 FOR AN AMBULANCE immediately. ■ If your child carries an epinephrine injection, administer it immediately. ■ Help your child sit up to allow her to breathe more easily. ■ Check her breathing and pulse every few minutes. ■ If she loses consciousness, clear and open the airway and be ready to begin resuscitation (see p. 232).

WHAT IS IT?	WHAT ACTION SHOULD I TAKE?
SHOCK This results from major loss of blood or other body fluids, or from conditions such as anaphylactic shock (see opposite). **What are the symptoms?** ■ Pale, clammy skin. ■ Rapid but shallow breathing. ■ Rapid, weak, or absent pulse. ■ Thirst, confusion, and weakness. ■ Possible unconsciousness.	■ Lay your child down on a blanket and raise her legs so that they are higher than her chest, unless you think that she has broken her leg. ■ Deal with any condition such as bleeding or burns that may have caused the shock. ■ Don't give her anything to eat or drink, because she may need an anesthetic. Moisten her lips with water if she is very thirsty. ■ ☎ CALL 911 FOR AN AMBULANCE. ■ If she loses consciousness, clear and open the airway and be ready to begin resuscitation (see p. 232).
SEIZURE OR CONVULSION Caused by temporary electrical overactivity in the brain. The most common cause of a seizure is high temperature (see p. 220). Other causes include epilepsy (see p. 219) and meningitis (see p. 218). **What are the symptoms?** ■ Sudden loss of consciousness. ■ Noisy breathing or breath-holding. ■ Rigid muscles, then jerking limbs. ■ Child may wet or soil herself. ■ Possible frothing at the mouth.	■ Clear a space around your child, but don't try to restrain her or put anything in her mouth. ■ Note the duration of the seizure. ■ If she has a high temperature, remove her clothing and sponge her with tepid (not cold) water to help the cooling (see p. 220). ■ Place her in the recovery position (see p. 233) once the seizure stops and call your doctor. ■ ☎ CALL 911 FOR AN AMBULANCE if: this is your child's first seizure, she has had a recent head or other injury; the seizure lasts longer than 10 minutes. Call your doctor if you are not sure what to do.
ELECTRIC SHOCK Even safe electrical appliances and sockets become lethal when a child pokes at them with a metal implement or wet fingers. **What are the symptoms?** ■ Deep burns. ■ Muscle spasm. ■ Unconsciousness—breathing may stop.	■ Break the electrical contact BEFORE you touch your child. Turn off the power at the circuit breaker. If you can't do this, stand on a telephone directory or a thick rubber mat and use a wooden broom handle to push your child away from the electricity. ■ If she is unconscious, clear and open the airway and be ready to begin resuscitation (see p. 232). ■ ☎ CALL 911 FOR AN AMBULANCE. ■ If she is conscious, treat any burns (see p. 229).
DROWNING AND NEAR-DROWNING Drowning kills because inhaled water stops air from reaching the lungs. Drowning can cause spasm of the throat that can stop breathing. Very cold water can lead to hypothermia.	■ If possible, pull your child out of the water immediately but don't become a victim yourself. Carry her with her head lower than her body so that water can drain out of her mouth. ■ Keep her warm with blankets. If she loses consciousness, clear and open the airway; be ready to begin resuscitation (see p. 232). ■ ☎ CALL 911 FOR AN AMBULANCE.
HYPOTHERMIA Babies can develop hypothermia if left in a cold room because their temperature control system is underdeveloped. **What are the symptoms?** ■ Skin looks pink and healthy but feels cold. ■ Unusually quiet and limp. ■ Refuses feeding.	■ It's really important to rewarm a baby or child gradually. Take the baby into a warm room, then wrap her in a blanket. ■ For a child brought in from outside, replace any wet clothes with warm, dry ones. Cuddle her and give her high-energy food such as chocolate. ■ Always get medical help: phone your doctor or take your child straight to a hospital emergency department.
HEAT EXHAUSTION AND HEATSTROKE Usually occurs in very hot weather. **What are the symptoms?** ■ Headache and dizziness. ■ Cramplike pains in limbs or abdomen. ■ Pale, clammy skin and rapid, weak pulse. **If heatstroke there will also be** ■ Hot, flushed, dry skin. ■ Body temperature above 104°F/40°C.	■ Lay your child down in a cool place and raise her legs. ■ Give her water to drink. ■ If she is unconscious, it could be heatstroke; cool her down as quickly as possible. Take off her clothes and cover her with a cold, wet sheet. Keep her cool until her temperature falls to about 100°F/38°C. ■ ☎ CALL 911 FOR AN AMBULANCE.

IF YOUR CHILD IS UNCONSCIOUS

If you find your child unconscious or if she collapses, it is important to follow a routine known as the ABC of resuscitation.

A Check the **Airway**
B Check **Breathing**
C Check **Circulation**

IF YOUR BABY STOPS BREATHING IN HER CRIB

Picking her up, or simply touching her, may be enough to restart your baby's breathing. If she does start to breathe, you must still take her to the hospital immediately since she will need to be examined by a doctor. If she does not start breathing, start resuscitation—follow the sequence below.

FOR A BABY

1 Check your baby for some kind of response. Tap the sole of her foot very gently with your finger. Never shake a baby.

2 If your baby does respond, leave her where you found her, make sure she is comfortable, and reassess her regularly.

Tilt her head up

3 If your baby does not respond, shout for help. Open her airway by tilting her head up very gently with one finger under her chin.

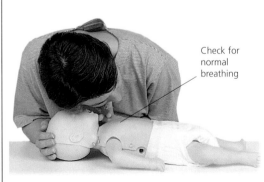

Check for normal breathing

4 Keeping her airway open, check for signs of normal breathing. Put your face close to her face and look along her chest for movement, listen for sounds of breathing and feel for breath on your cheek. Look, listen, and feel for no more than 10 seconds.

5 If your baby is breathing normally, lie her on her side or cradle her in your arms and check for continued breathing.

Seal your lips around her mouth and nose

6 If she is not breathing, carefully remove any obvious obstructions. Put her on her back with her head in a neutral position and her chin lifted. Seal your lips around her mouth and nose. Breathe out until her chest rises, then remove your lips and watch the chest fall. Repeat the sequence 5 times.

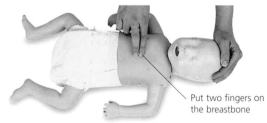

Put two fingers on the breastbone

7 If there's no circulation, combine rescue breathing in step 6 with chest compressions. Place two fingers on the lower third of the breastbone and press down to one third of the depth of her chest. Release the pressure and repeat at a rate of about 100 per minute. Give 30 compressions, then two breaths. After four cycles, call 911 or your local EMS if this has not already been done by someone else. Continue with cycles of 30:2 until help arrives or the baby responds.

BABY AND CHILD HEALTH

FOR A TODDLER OR YOUNG CHILD

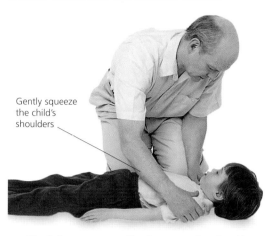

Gently squeeze the child's shoulders

1 Check for a response. Gently squeeze her shoulders or call out her name to see if she responds.

2 If your child responds, leave her where you found her, and reassess regularly.

3 If your child does not respond, shout for help. Open her airway by tilting her head back, and placing your fingertips under her chin to lift it.

4 Keeping the airway open, look, listen, and feel for breathing by putting your face close to your child's face and looking along her chest. Look listen and feel for no more than 10 seconds.

Position limbs to keep her stable

5 If your child is breathing normally, put her in the recovery position. Place her on her side on a firm surface, bend the uppermost arm and leg up and tilt her head slightly back, so that any fluid in her mouth can drain easily.

☎ CALL 911 OR YOUR LOCAL EMS.
Recheck your child's breathing every few minutes until help arrives.

Seal your mouth over hers and blow

6 If she's not breathing normally, carefully remove any obstructions. Tilt her head, lift her chin, and pinch the nostrils closed. Seal your mouth over hers and blow steady for 1–1½ seconds until the chest rises. Keep her head still and let the chest fall. Repeat 5 times.

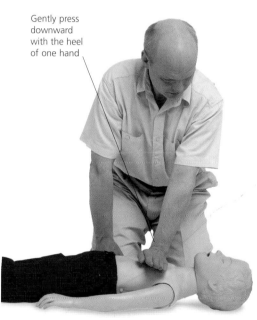

Gently press downward with the heel of one hand

7 If there is no circulation, combine rescue breathing in step 6 with chest compressions. Place the heel of one hand over the lower third of the breastbone. Keep vertically over your child's chest with your arm straight and press down on the chest about one third of the depth of the chest. Lift your fingers to avoid pressure on the ribs. Release the pressure and repeat at a rate of about 100 per minute. Give 30 compressions and then two breaths. After four cycles of compressions and breaths, call 911 or your local EMS. Continue with cycles of 30:2 until help arrives or the child responds.

BABY AND CHILD HEALTH

IF YOUR CHILD IS CHOKING

This is a very common emergency that requires prompt first aid. Babies put everything in their mouths (not just food) and young children run around with food, drink, or toys in their mouths despite their parents' efforts to stop them.

FOR A BABY

1 Lay your baby along your forearm and give her up to five back slaps.

2 If she is still choking, turn her on her back. Place two fingers on her breastbone and give up to five sharp downward thrusts toward the mouth (these are called artificial coughs).

3 Check her mouth to see if the object has been expelled. Remove anything you can see.

4 If obstruction has still not cleared, repeat steps 1–3 three times and ☎ CALL 911 FOR AN AMBULANCE

IF your baby becomes unconscious, see page 232.

FOR A TODDLER OR YOUNG CHILD

1 Encourage your child to cough. Leave her alone unless she becomes distressed.

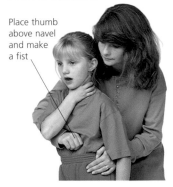

Place thumb above navel and make a fist

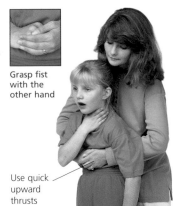

Grasp fist with the other hand

Use quick upward thrusts

2 If she is in distress, stand or kneel behind her and wrap your arms around her waist. Make a fist with one hand. Place the thumb side of your fist against the middle of her abdomen, just above her navel.

3 Grasp your fist with your other hand and press into her abdomen with a quick upward thrust. Check her mouth and remove anything you can see. Repeat until the object is cleared or help arrives. Stop if she becomes unconscious.

IF YOUR CHILD BECOMES UNCONSCIOUS

Use the following techniques if you know your child has choked on an object; otherwise, see p. 233. ☎ CALL 911 FOR AN AMBULANCE.

1 Straddle the child's legs. Place the heel of one hand just above your child's navel and the heel of your other hand on top.

3 Look in her mouth, and if you can see an object, carefully remove it with a hooking motion, using your finger.

2 Perform five abdominal thrusts, pressing inward and upward each time.

4 Attempt to give rescue breaths (see p. 233). If you are successful, keep going. If you cannot get air into the lungs, repeat steps 2–4 until emergency help arrives or the blockage is cleared.

USEFUL ADDRESSES

UNITED STATES

Adoptive Families of America
2309 Como Avenue
St. Paul, MN 55108
(800) 372-3300
www.adoptivefam.org

**Allergy and Asthma Network/
Mothers of Asthmatics, Inc.**
2751 Prosperity Avenue
Fairfax, VA 22031
(800) 878-4403
www.aanma.org

American Academy of Pediatrics
141 Northwest Point Boulevard
P.O. Box 927
Elk Grove Village, IL 60007
(847) 228-5005
www.aap.org

American Red Cross
1621 N. Kent Street
Arlington, VA 22209
(703) 248-4222
www.redcross.org

Autism Society of America
7910 Woodmount Avenue
Bethesda, MD 20814
(800) 3-AUTISM
www.autism-society.org

**Children and Adults with
Attention Deficit Disorders
(CHADD)**
8181 Professional Place
Landover, MD 20785
(800) 233-4050
www.chadd.org

Cystic Fibrosis Foundation
6931 Arlington Road
Bethesda, MD 20814
(800) FIGHT-CF
www.cff.org

Depression After Delivery
P.O. Box 1282
Morrisville, PA 19067
(800) 944-4773

**Epilepsy Foundation of
America**
4351 Garden City Drive
Landover, MD 20785
(800) 332-1000
(800) 332-2070 (TTY)
www.epilepsyfoundation.org

Hydrocephalus Association
870 Market Street
San Francisco, CA 94102
(415) 732-7040
www.hydroassoc.org

**Juvenile Diabetes Research
Foundation International**
120 Wall Street
New York, NY 10005
(800) 533-CURE
www.jdrf.org

La Leche League International
(800) LA LECHE (*US & Canada*)
www.lalecheleague.org

**March of Dimes/Birth Defects
Foundation**
1275 Mamaroneck Avenue
White Plains, NY 10605
(888) 663-4637
(914) 997-4764 (TTY)
www.modimes.org

**National Down Syndrome
Society**
666 Broadway
New York, NY 10012
(800) 221-4602
www.ndss.org

National Kidney Foundation
30 East 33rd Street, Suite 1100
New York, NY 10016
(800) 622-9010
www.kidney.org

**National Information Center
for Children and Youth with
Disabilities**
P.O. Box 1492
Washington, DC 20013
(800) 695-0285
www.nichcy.org

**Office of Rare Diseases
National Institutes of Health**
31 Center Drive
Bethesda, MD 20892
(301) 402-4336
rarediseases.info.nih.gov/ord

Parents Without Partners
Tel: (904) 278-1867
www.parentswithoutpartners.org

**Sickle Cell Disease Association
of America, Inc.**
200 Corporate Pointe
Culver City, CA 90230
(800) 421-8453
www.sicklecelldisease.org

**Spina Bifida Association of
America**
4590 MacArthur Boulevard, NW
Washington, DC 20007
(800) 621-3141
www.sbaa.org

Stepfamily Foundation
333 West End Avenue
New York, NY 10023
(800) SKY STEP
www.stepfamily.org

**Sudden Infant Death Syndrome
(SIDS) Alliance**
1314 Bedford Avenue
Baltimore, MD 21208
(800) 221-7437
www.sidsalliance.org

**United Cerebral Palsy
Association**
1660 L Street, NW
Washington, DC 20036
(800) 872-5827
(202) 973-7197 (TTY)
www.ucpa.org

**US Consumer Product Safety
Commission**
(800) 638-2772
(800) 638-8270 (TTY)
www.cpsc.gov

CANADA

**Canadian Down Syndrome
Society**
811–14th Street N.W.
Calgary, AB T2N 2A4
(800) 883-5608
www.cdss.ca

**Canadian Foundation for the
Study of Infant Death**
586 Eglinton Avenue East
Suite 308
Toronto, ON M4P 1P2
(416) 488-3260
www.sidscanada.org

**Canadian Immunization
Awareness Program**
Canadian Public Health
Association
400–1565 Carling Avenue
Ottawa, ON K1Z 8R1
(613) 725-3769
www.immunize.cpha.ca

**Canadian Institute of Child
Health**
384 Bank Street
Suite 300
Ottawa, ON K2P 1Y4
(613) 230-8838
www.cich.ca

Canadian Paediatric Society
2204 Walkley Road
Suite 100
Ottawa, ON K1G 4GS
(613) 526-9397
www.cps.ca

Canadian Red Cross
170 Metcalfe Street
Ottawa, ON K2P 2P2
(613) 740-1900
www.redcross.ca

**Children and Adults with
Attention Deficit Disorder
(CHADD)**
1376 Bank Street
Ottawa, ON K1H 7Y3
(613) 731-1209
www.chaddcanada.org

Children's Aid Societies
www.childwelfare.ca

**Children's Safety Association
of Canada**
385 The West Mall
Suite 250
Etobicoke, ON M9C 1E7
(416) 620-1584
www.safekid.org

Juvenile Diabetes Foundation
7100 Woodbine Avenue
Suite 311
Markham, ON L3R 5J2
(877) 287-3533
www.jdrf.ca

La Leche League
see under UNITED STATES

**Learning Disabilities
Association of Canada**
323 Chapel Street
Ottawa, ON K1N 7Z2
(613) 238-5721
www.ldac-taac.ca

**Multiple Birth Families
Association**
P.O. Box 5532
Station F
Ottawa, ON K2C 3M1
(613) 860-6565
www.mbfa.ca

**PASS-CAN—Postpartum
Adjustment Support Services
Canada**
3–460 Woody Road
Oakville, ON
(905) 844-9009

INDEX

ACKNOWLEDGMENTS

The author would like to thank:
Dr Janet Gray, Mary Knott and Alison Pottle (Harefield Hospital) for their expert advice in preparing parts of this book. Special thanks to Jemima Dunne and Salima Hirani at DK for their wisdom and encouragement.

Dorling Kindersley would like to thank the following:

DESIGN ASSISTANCE Revised edition: Edward Kinsey; Nathalie Godwin (jacket design). Original edition: Spencer Holbrook, Edward Kinsey, Dawn Young.

EDITORIAL ASSISTANCE Original edition: Corinne Asghar, Claire Cross, Jane de Burgh, Jessica Orbe, MD for medical assistance, Valerie Kitchenham, Julia North, Christine Zografos.

PICTURE CREDITS Collections: Anthea Sieveking 56bl; Tim Woodcock Photolibrary: 223cr.

ADDITIONAL PHOTOGRAPHY Original edition: Ruth Jenkinson, Steve Gorton.

ART DIRECTION FOR NEW PHOTOGRAPHY Revised edition: Izabel de Cordova

MODELS FOR REVISED EDITION Claire Stevens, Cameron Stevens, Fran Oliver, Luke Gullis, Chennell Hinton, Jessica Hinton, Ian Hinton, Michael Langley, Euan Thomson.